Ace Attorney Miles Edgeworth INVESTIGATIONS™

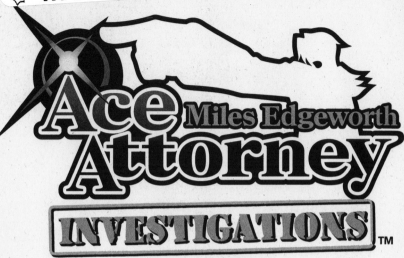

VOLUME 1

Story by Kenji Kuroda
Art by Kazuo Maekawa
Supervised by CAPCOM

Translated by Sheldon Drzka

Lettered by Christy Sawyer

KC KODANSHA COMICS

This book is a faithful translation of the book released in Japan on June 5, 2009.

CONTENTS

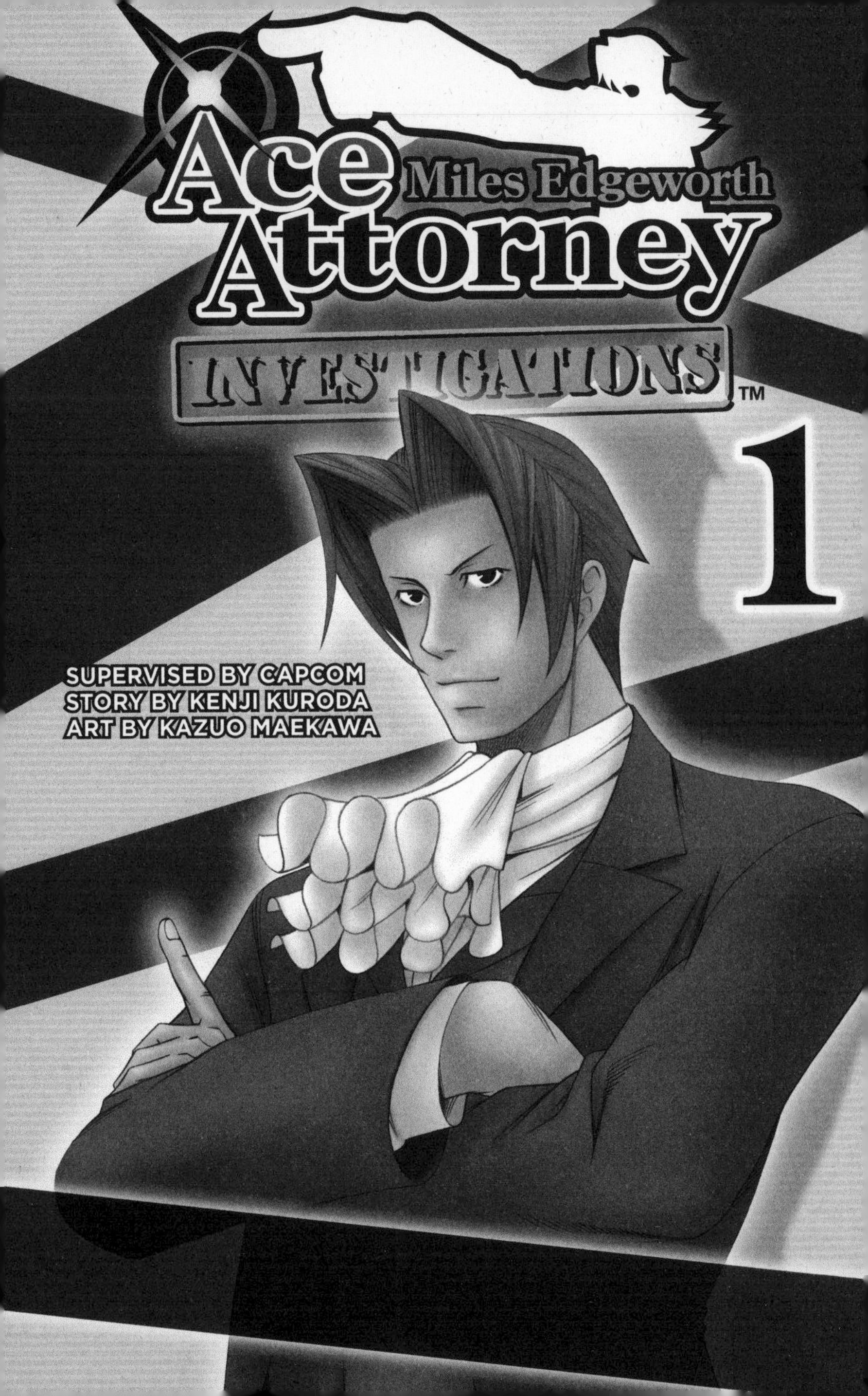
Ace Attorney
Miles Edgeworth
INVESTIGATIONS™
1
SUPERVISED BY CAPCOM
STORY BY KENJI KURODA
ART BY KAZUO MAEKAWA

INTRODUCTION

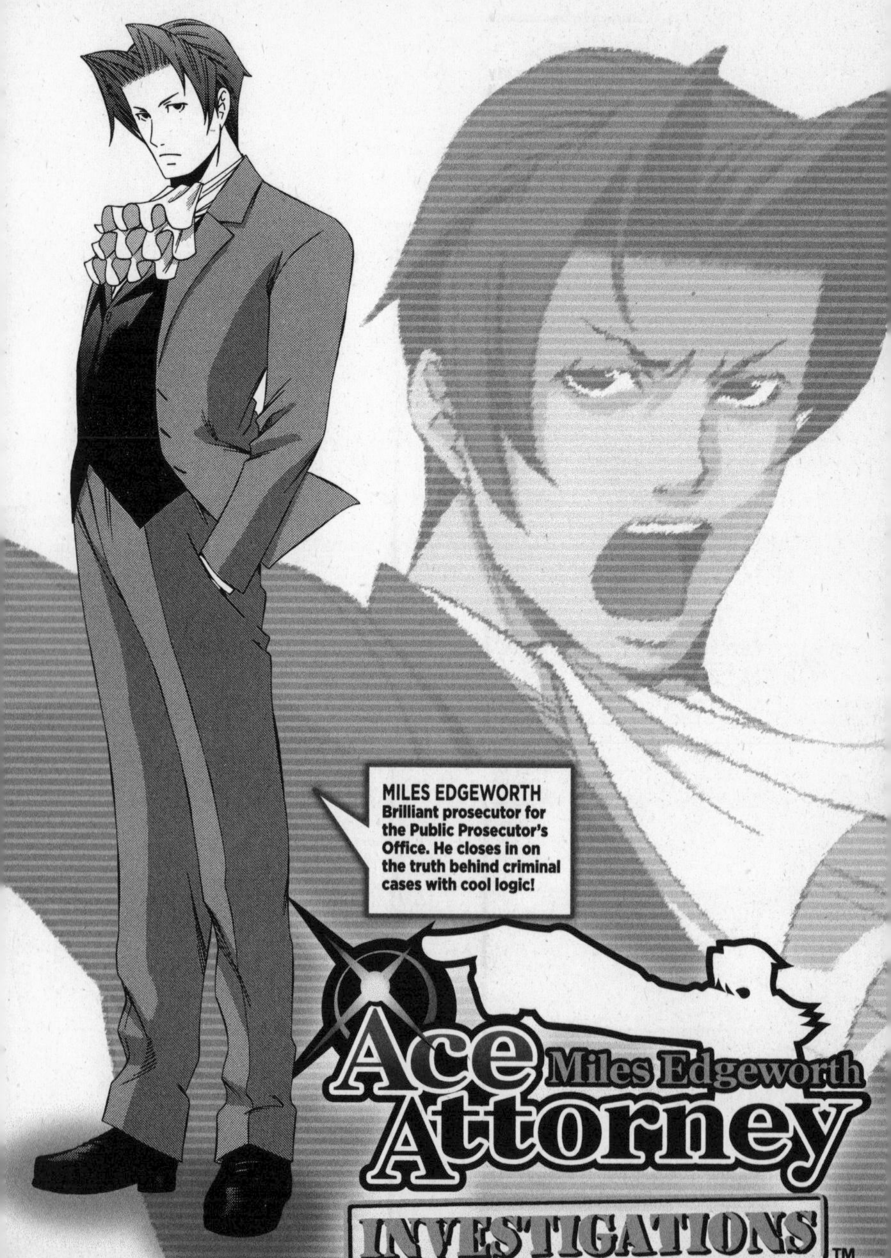
MILES EDGEWORTH
Brilliant prosecutor for the Public Prosecutor's Office. He closes in on the truth behind criminal cases with cool logic!
Ace Attorney Miles Edgeworth
INVESTIGATIONS
TM

The characters, laws, and court procedures in this work are all fiction. Accordingly, the court system of this story is set in the near future,where the demand for expedited trials creates a different system than that of present-day.

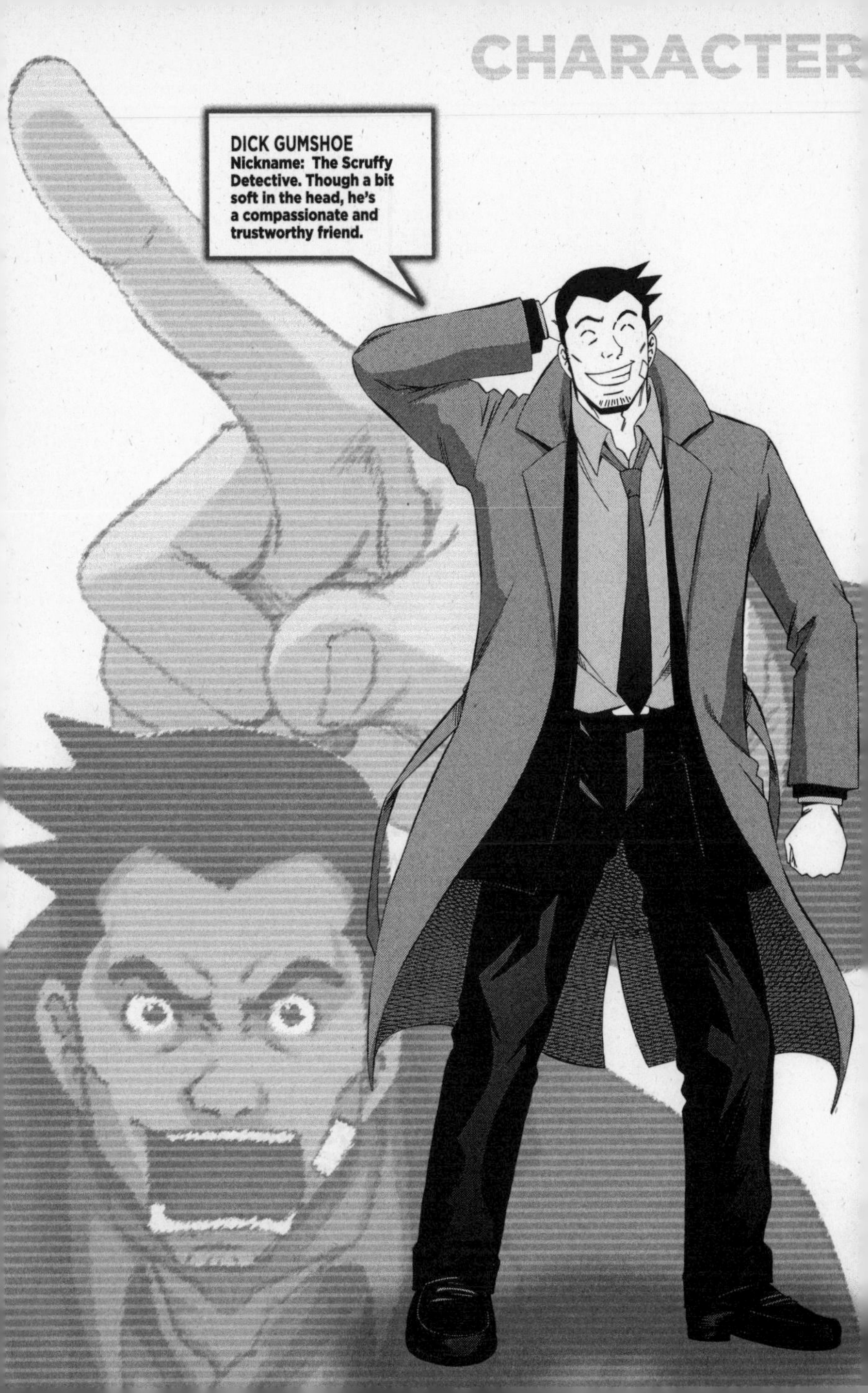
CHARACTER
DICK GUMSHOE
Nickname: The Scruffy Detective. Though a bit soft in the head, he's a compassionate and trustworthy friend.

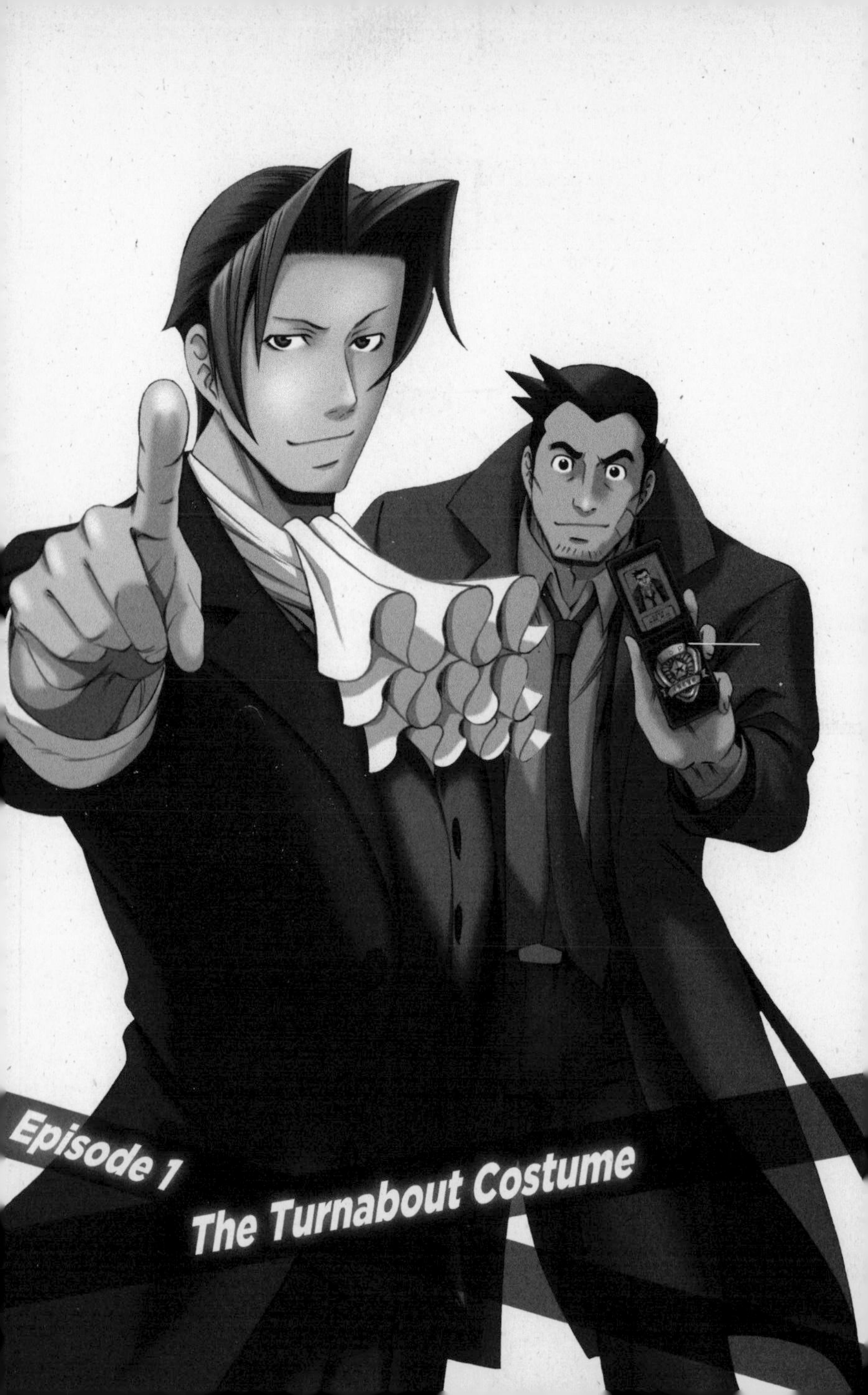
Episode 1
The Turnabout Costume

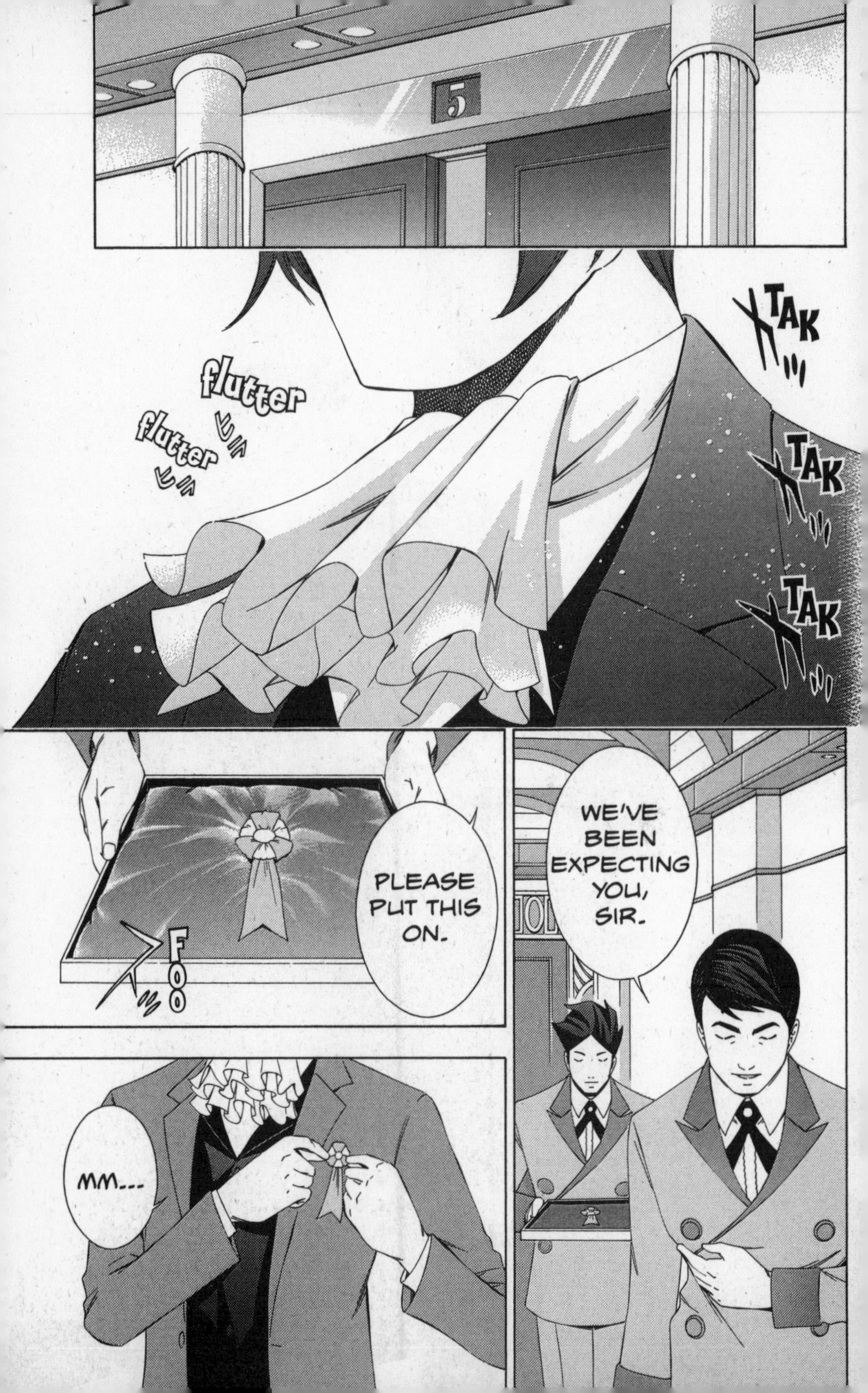
TAK
TAK
TAK
flutter
flutter
WE'VE BEEN EXPECTING YOU, SIR.
PLEASE PUT THIS ON.
FOO
MM...

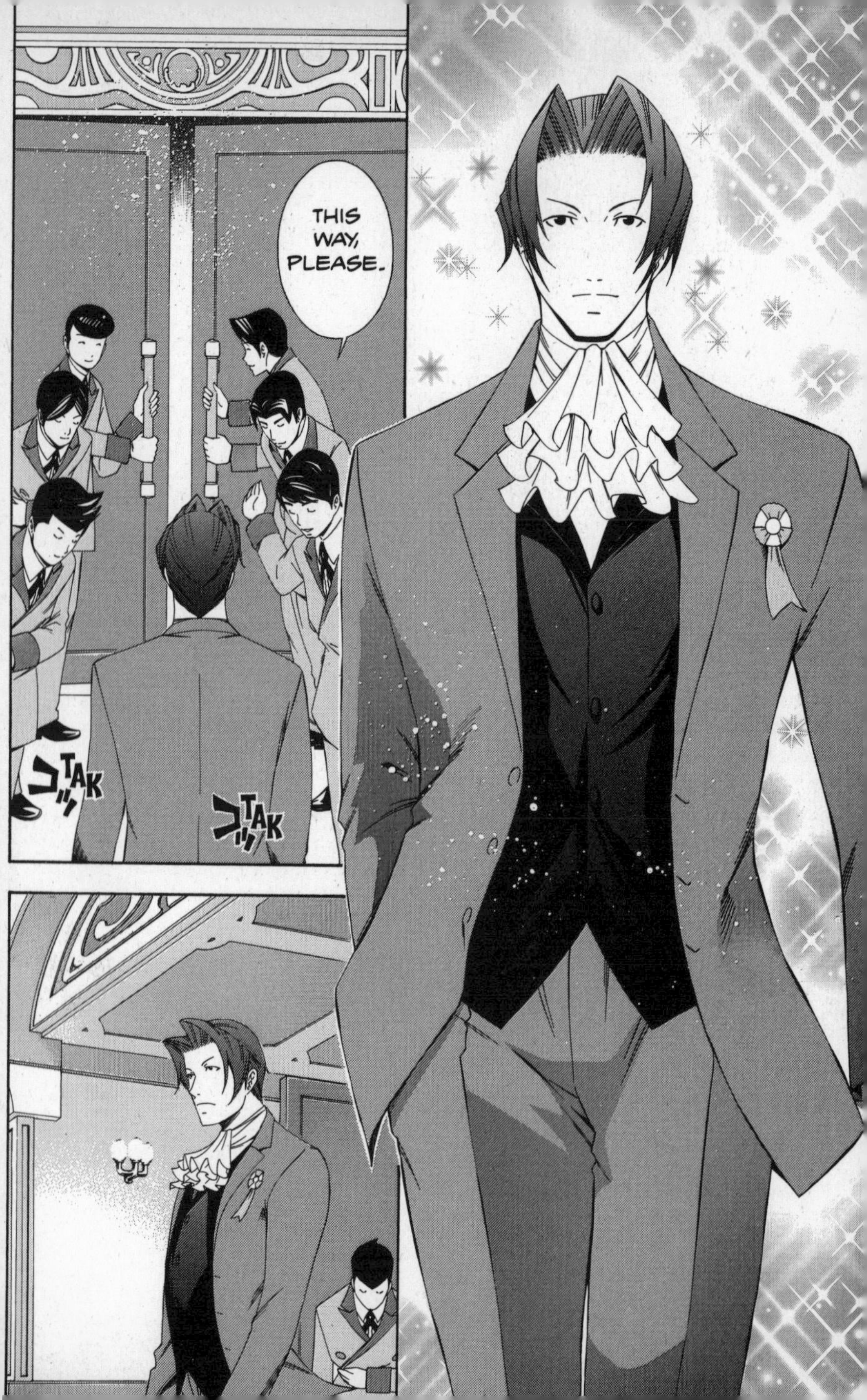
THIS WAY, PLEASE.
コツ TAK
コツ TAK

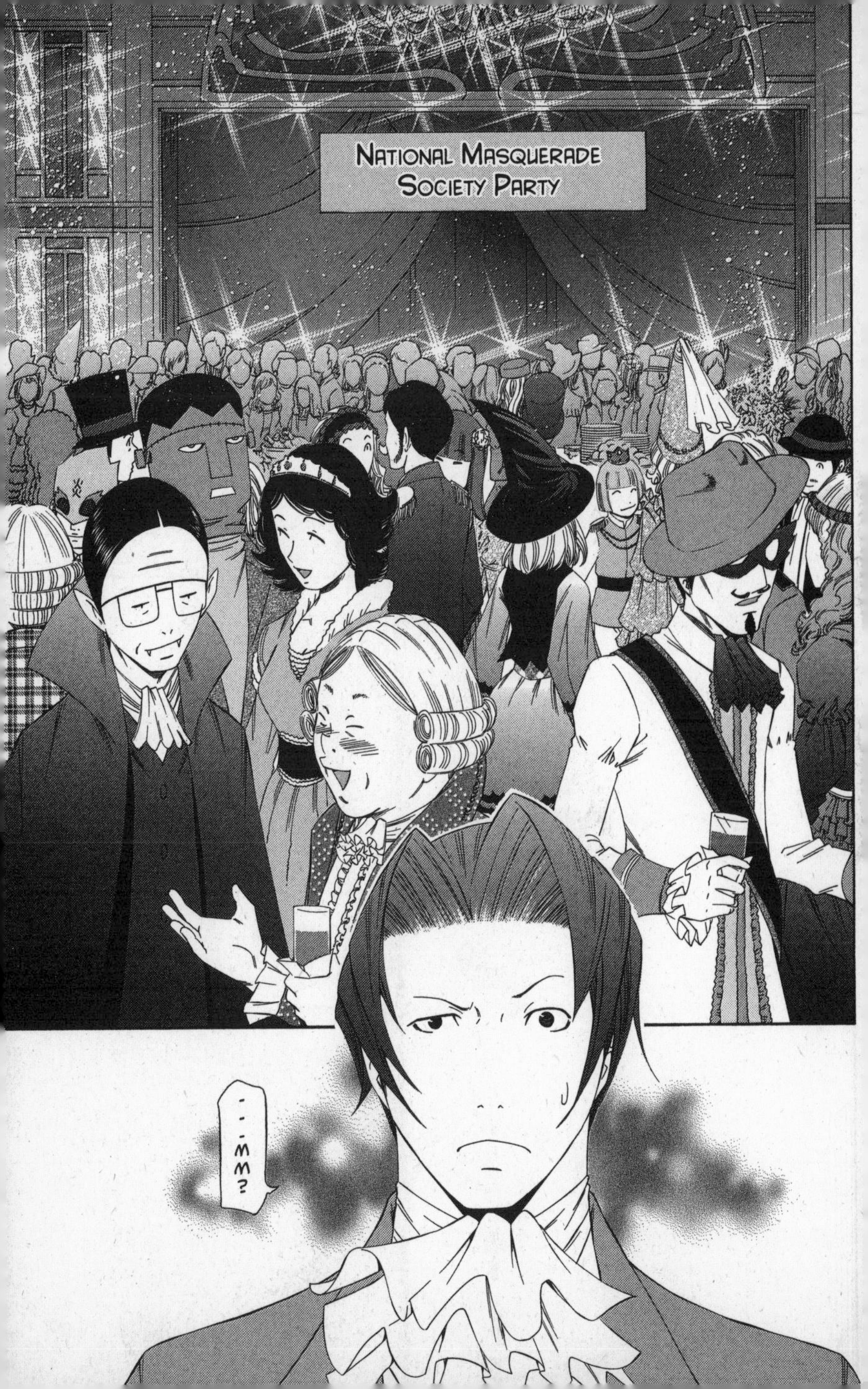
National Masquerade Society Party
...Mm?

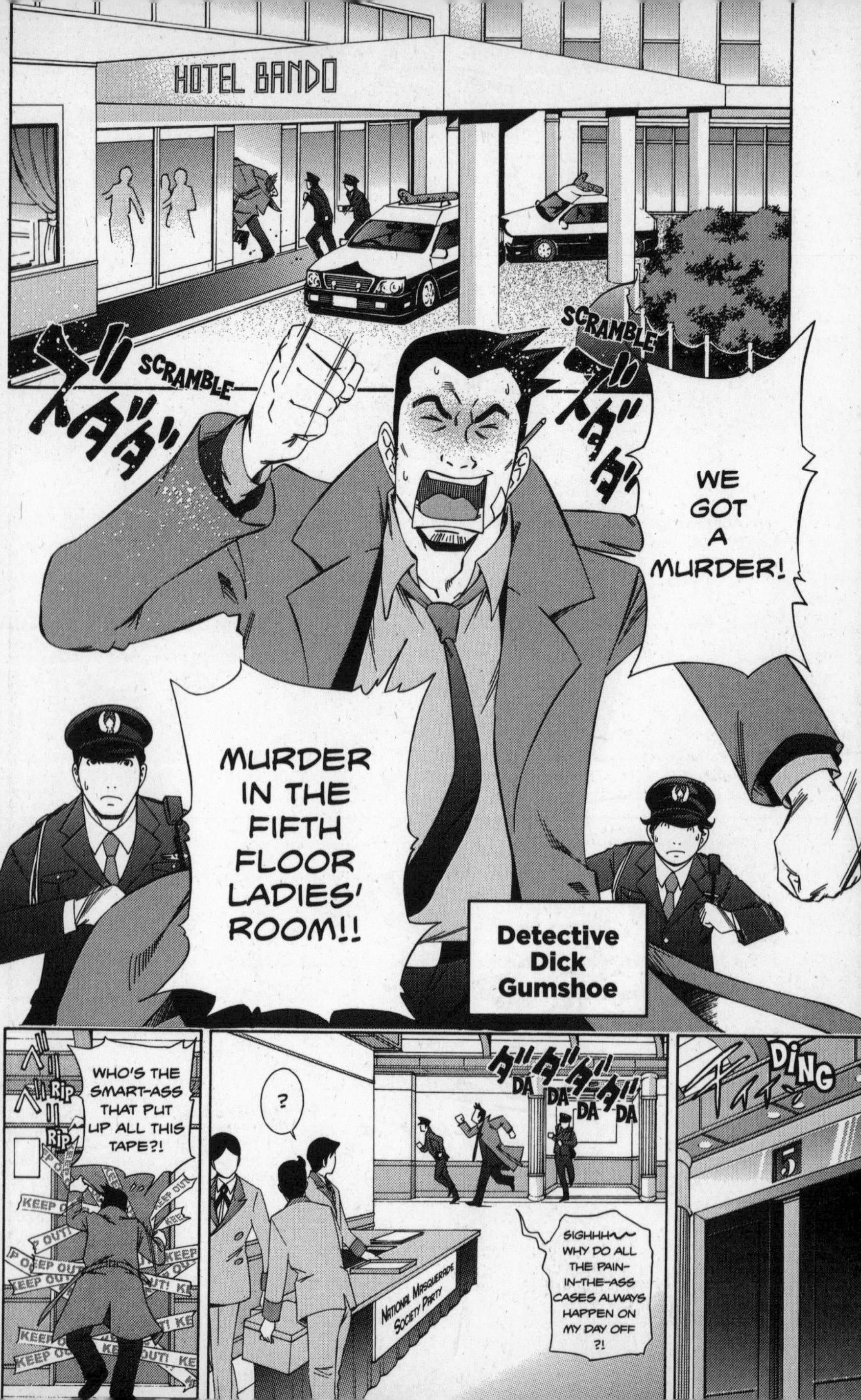

HOTEL BANDO
SCRAMBLE
SCRAMBLE
WE GOT A MURDER!
MURDER IN THE FIFTH FLOOR LADIES' ROOM!!
Detective Dick Gumshoe
DING
5
DA DA DA DA
SIGHHH~ WHY DO ALL THE PAIN-IN-THE-ASS CASES ALWAYS HAPPEN ON MY DAY OFF ?!
?
NATIONAL MASQUERADE SOCIETY PARTY
WHO'S THE SMART-ASS THAT PUT UP ALL THIS TAPE?!
RIP
RIP
KEEP OUT!

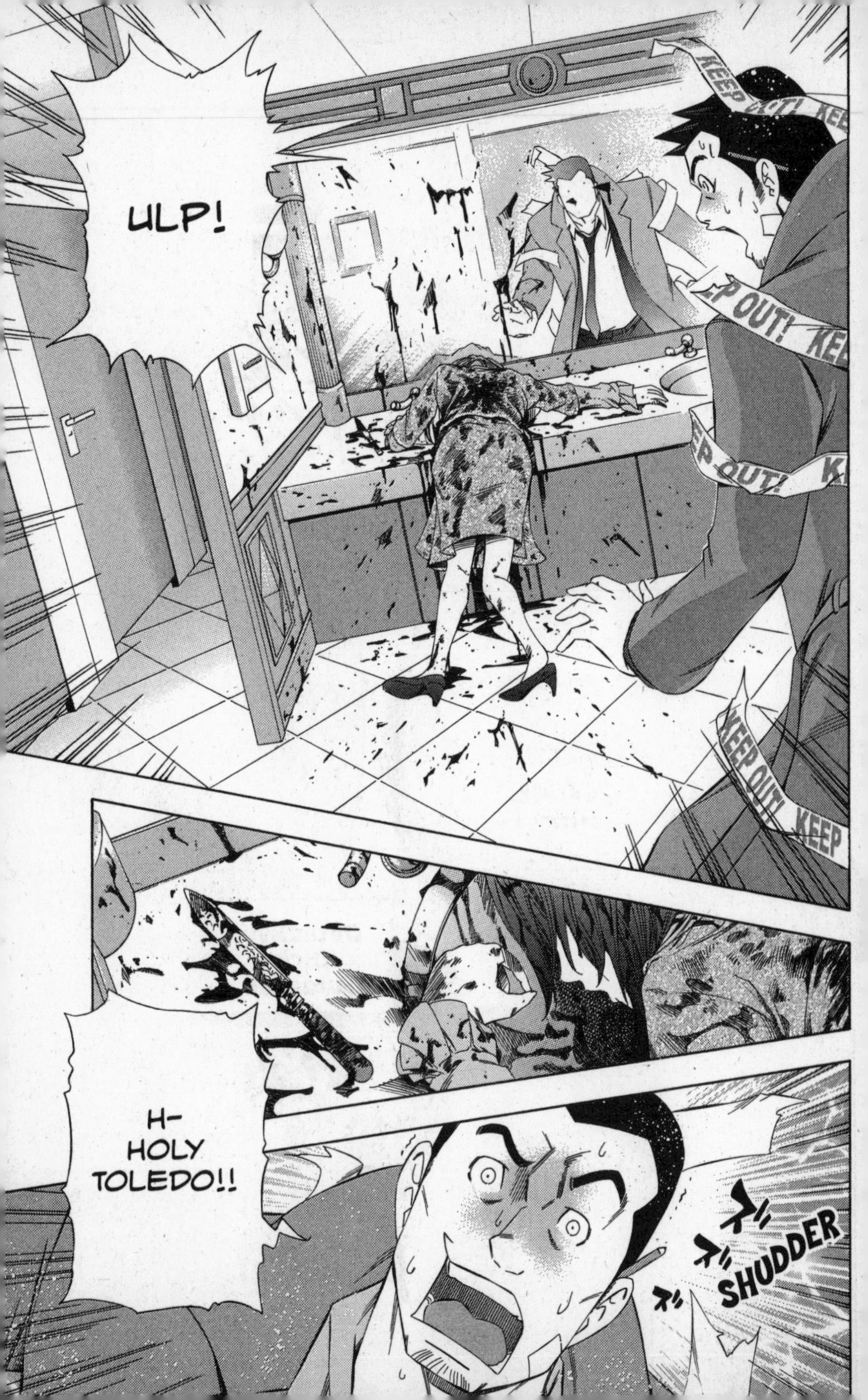
KEEP OUT! KEEP
KEEP OUT! KEEP
KEEP OUT! KE
ULP!
KEEP OUT! KEEP
ズ ズ ズ SHUDDER
H- HOLY TOLEDO!!

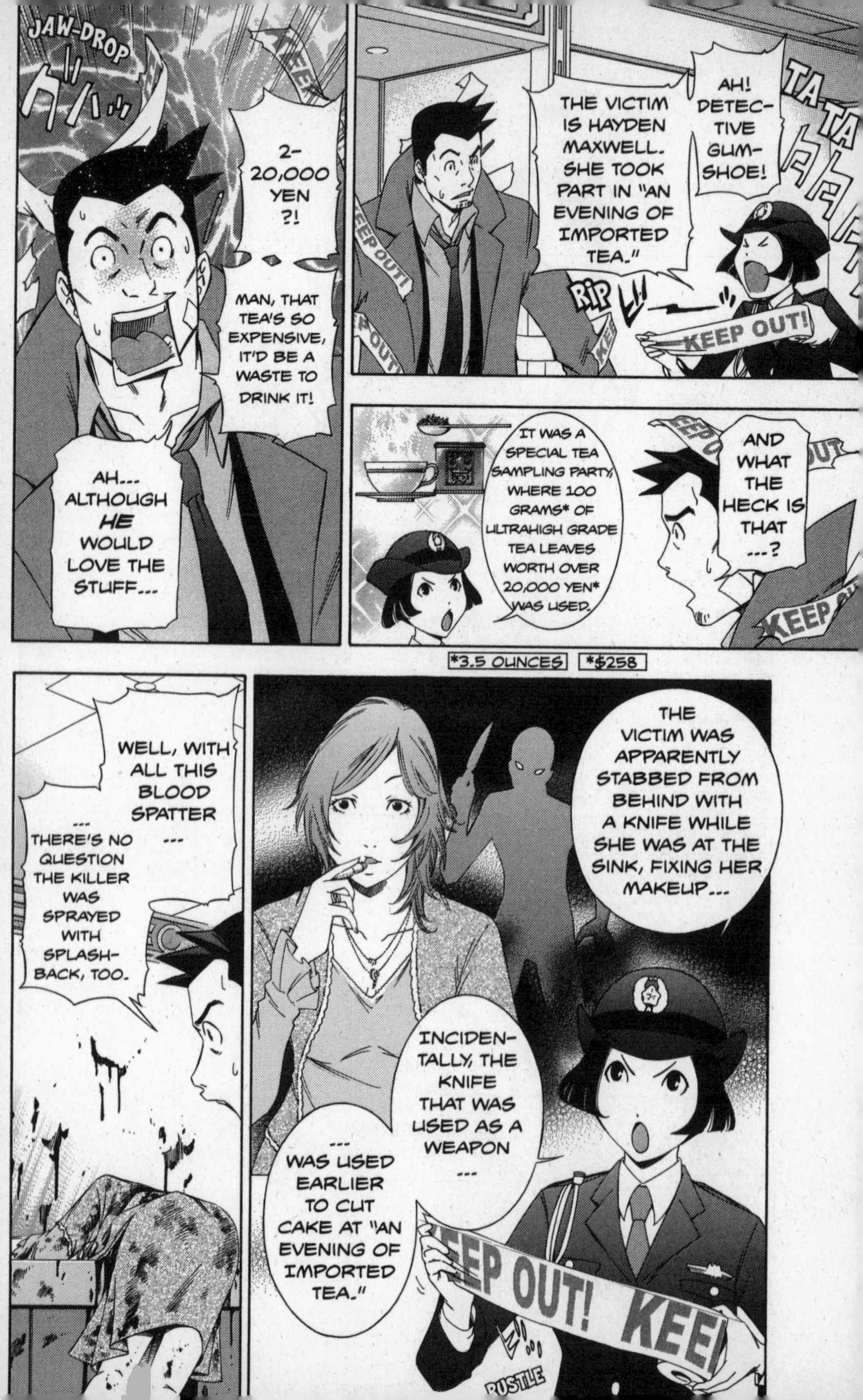
TA TA
AH! DETECTIVE GUMSHOE!
THE VICTIM IS HAYDEN MAXWELL. SHE TOOK PART IN "AN EVENING OF IMPORTED TEA."
RIP
KEEP OUT!
AND WHAT THE HECK IS THAT ...?
IT WAS A SPECIAL TEA SAMPLING PARTY, WHERE 100 GRAMS* OF ULTRAHIGH GRADE TEA LEAVES WORTH OVER 20,000 YEN* WAS USED.
JAW-DROP
2- 20,000 YEN ?!
MAN, THAT TEA'S SO EXPENSIVE, IT'D BE A WASTE TO DRINK IT!
AH... ALTHOUGH HE WOULD LOVE THE STUFF...
*3.5 OUNCES *$258
THE VICTIM WAS APPARENTLY STABBED FROM BEHIND WITH A KNIFE WHILE SHE WAS AT THE SINK, FIXING HER MAKEUP...
INCIDENTALLY, THE KNIFE THAT WAS USED AS A WEAPON ...
... WAS USED EARLIER TO CUT CAKE AT "AN EVENING OF IMPORTED TEA."
KEEP OUT! KEE
RUSTLE
WELL, WITH ALL THIS BLOOD SPATTER ...
... THERE'S NO QUESTION THE KILLER WAS SPRAYED WITH SPLASH-BACK, TOO.

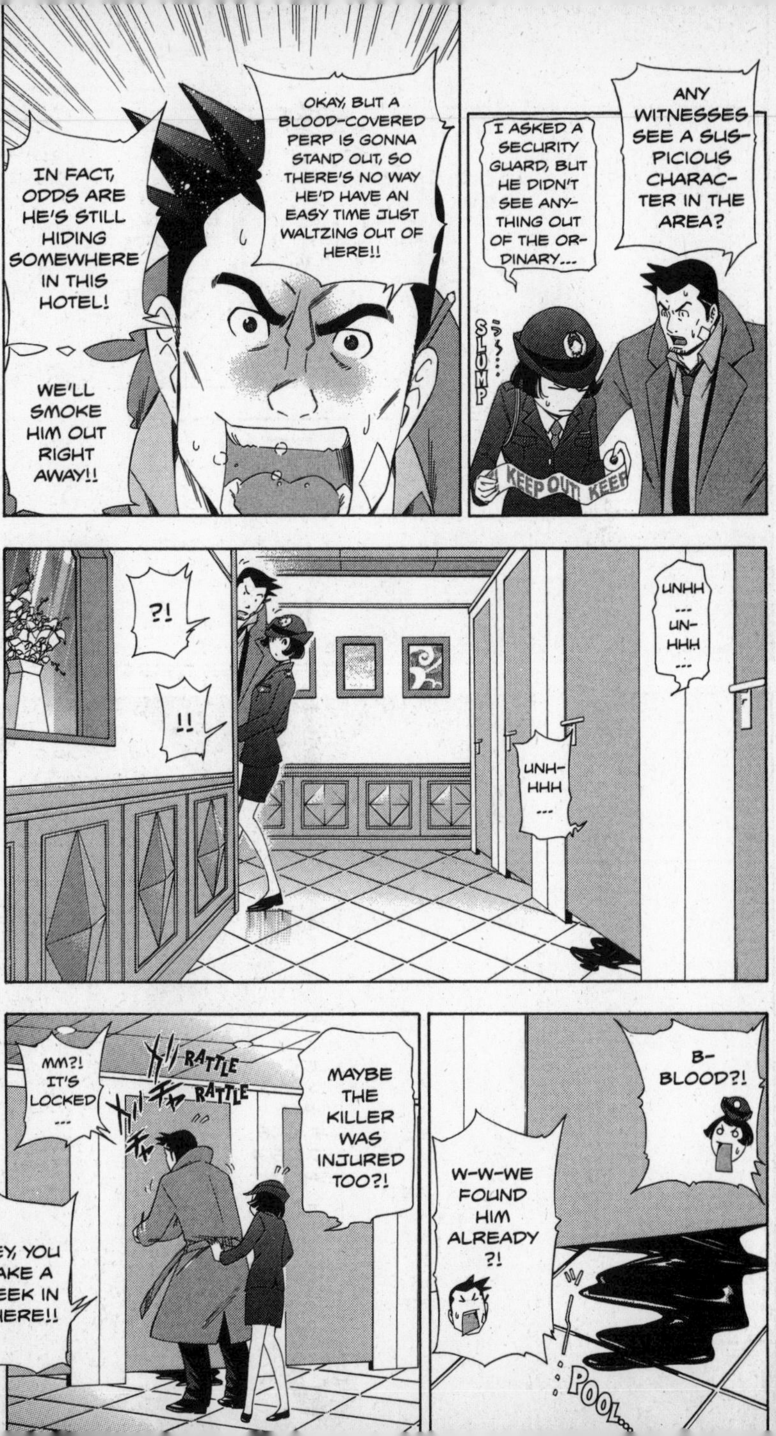
ANY WITNESSES SEE A SUSPICIOUS CHARACTER IN THE AREA?
I ASKED A SECURITY GUARD, BUT HE DIDN'T SEE ANYTHING OUT OF THE ORDINARY...
SLUMP
KEEP OUT! KEEP
OKAY, BUT A BLOOD-COVERED PERP IS GONNA STAND OUT, SO THERE'S NO WAY HE'D HAVE AN EASY TIME JUST WALTZING OUT OF HERE!!
IN FACT, ODDS ARE HE'S STILL HIDING SOMEWHERE IN THIS HOTEL!
WE'LL SMOKE HIM OUT RIGHT AWAY!!
UNHH... UN-HHH...
UNH-HHH...
?!
!!
MAYBE THE KILLER WAS INJURED TOO?!
RATTLE
RATTLE
MM?! IT'S LOCKED...
HEY, YOU TAKE A PEEK IN THERE!!
B-BLOOD?!
W-W-WE FOUND HIM ALREADY?!
POOL...

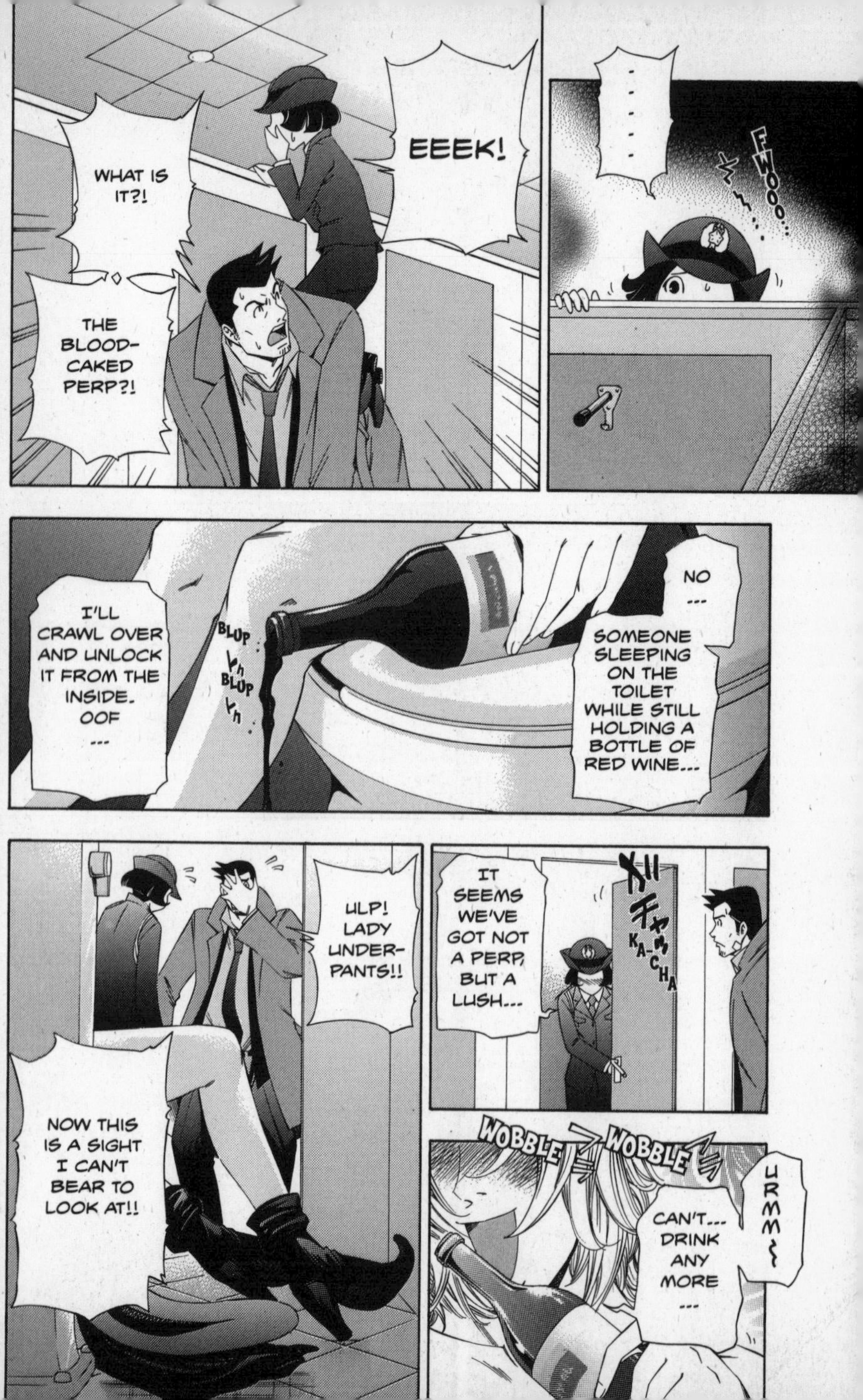
......
FWOOO...
EEEK!
WHAT IS IT?!
THE BLOOD-CAKED PERP?!
NO ... SOMEONE SLEEPING ON THE TOILET WHILE STILL HOLDING A BOTTLE OF RED WINE...
BLUP
BLUP
I'LL CRAWL OVER AND UNLOCK IT FROM THE INSIDE. OOF ...
KA-CHA
IT SEEMS WE'VE GOT NOT A PERP, BUT A LUSH...
WOBBLE
WOBBLE
URMM~
CAN'T... DRINK ANY MORE ...
ULP! LADY UNDER-PANTS!!
NOW THIS IS A SIGHT I CAN'T BEAR TO LOOK AT!!

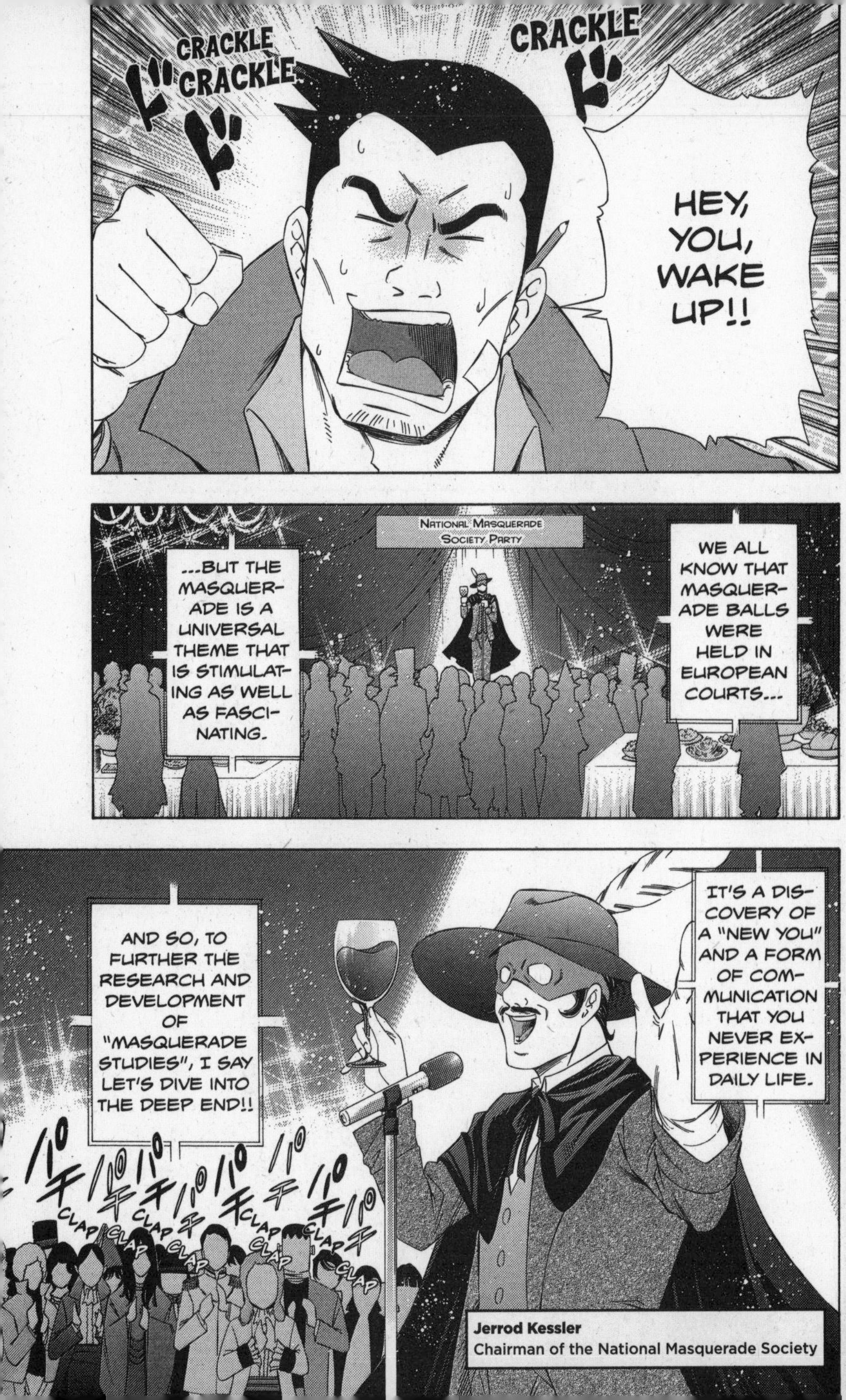
ド
CRACKLE
HEY, YOU, WAKE UP!!
ドドド
CRACKLE CRACKLE
NATIONAL MASQUERADE SOCIETY PARTY
WE ALL KNOW THAT MASQUERADE BALLS WERE HELD IN EUROPEAN COURTS...
...BUT THE MASQUERADE IS A UNIVERSAL THEME THAT IS STIMULATING AS WELL AS FASCINATING.
IT'S A DISCOVERY OF A "NEW YOU" AND A FORM OF COMMUNICATION THAT YOU NEVER EXPERIENCE IN DAILY LIFE.
AND SO, TO FURTHER THE RESEARCH AND DEVELOPMENT OF "MASQUERADE STUDIES", I SAY LET'S DIVE INTO THE DEEP END!!
パチパチパチパチパチパチ
CLAP CLAP CLAP CLAP CLAP CLAP CLAP CLAP CLAP
Jerrod Kessler
Chairman of the National Masquerade Society

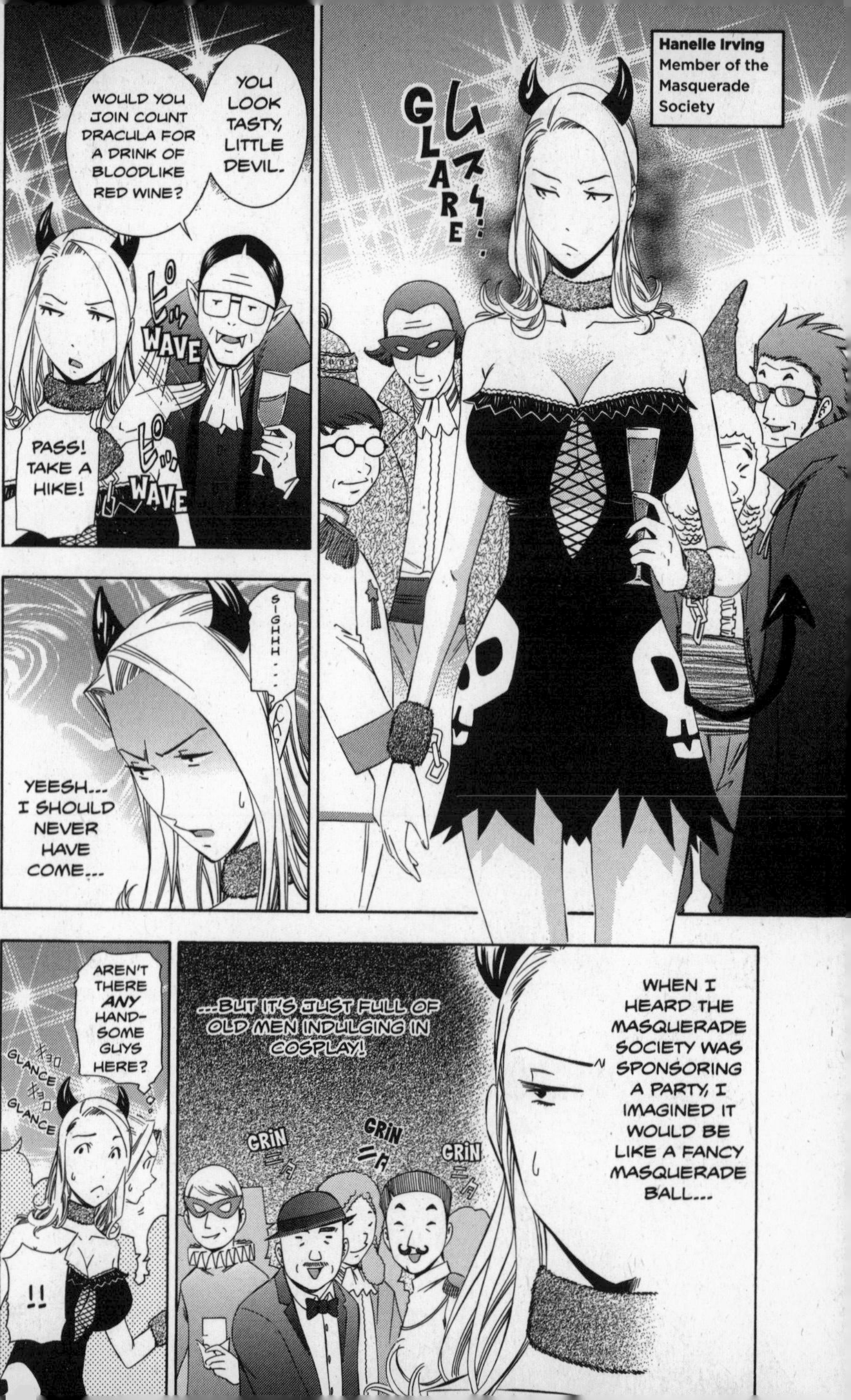
Hanelle Irving
Member of the Masquerade Society
GLARE
YOU LOOK TASTY, LITTLE DEVIL.
WOULD YOU JOIN COUNT DRACULA FOR A DRINK OF BLOODLIKE RED WINE?
WAVE
WAVE
PASS! TAKE A HIKE!
SIGHHH...
YEESH... I SHOULD NEVER HAVE COME...
WHEN I HEARD THE MASQUERADE SOCIETY WAS SPONSORING A PARTY, I IMAGINED IT WOULD BE LIKE A FANCY MASQUERADE BALL...
...BUT IT'S JUST FULL OF OLD MEN INDULGING IN COSPLAY!
GRIN
GRIN
GRIN
AREN'T THERE ANY HANDSOME GUYS HERE?
GLANCE
GLANCE
!!

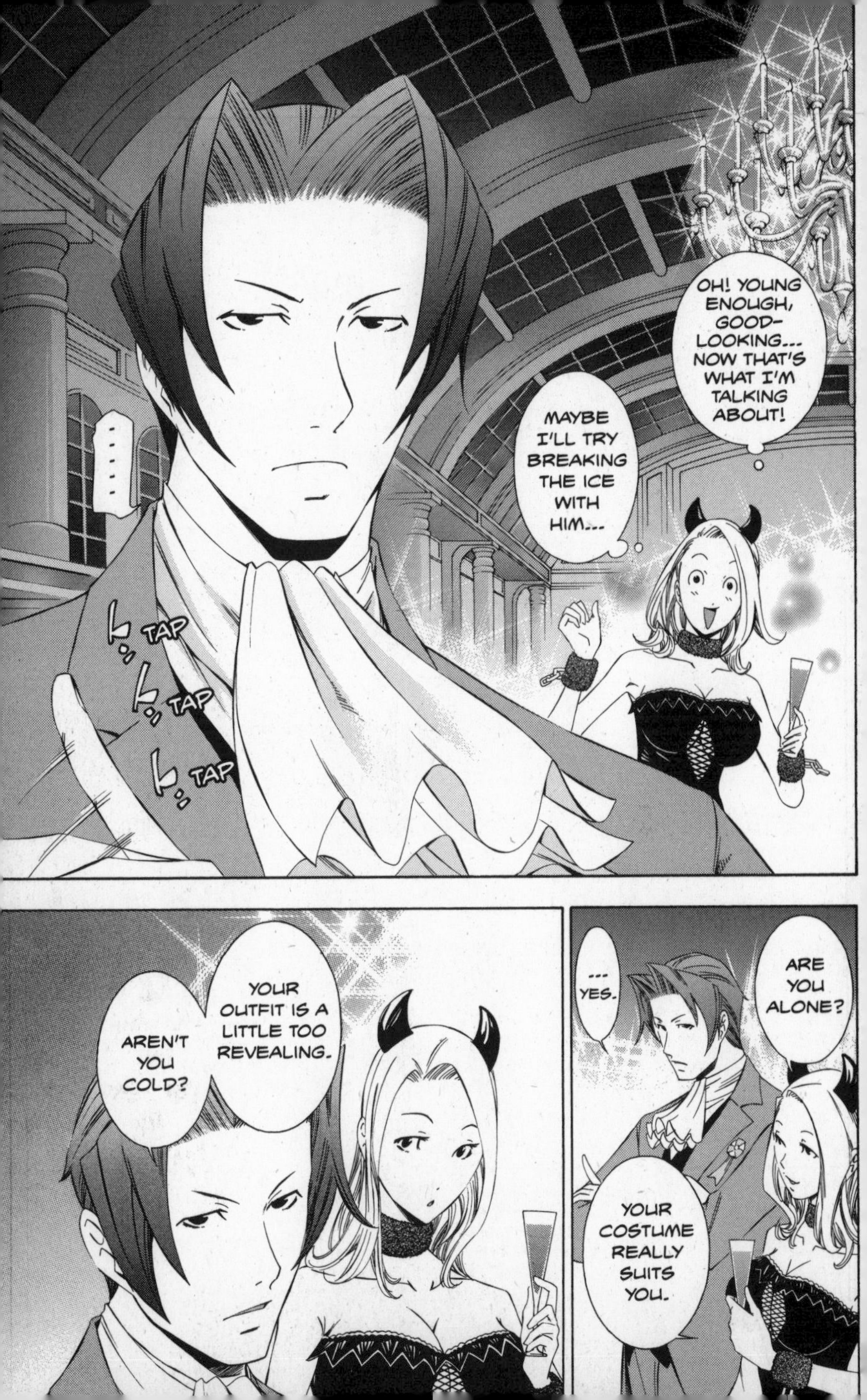
OH! YOUNG ENOUGH, GOOD-LOOKING... NOW THAT'S WHAT I'M TALKING ABOUT!
MAYBE I'LL TRY BREAKING THE ICE WITH HIM...
......
TAP
TAP
TAP
ARE YOU ALONE?
...YES.
YOUR COSTUME REALLY SUITS YOU.
YOUR OUTFIT IS A LITTLE TOO REVEALING.
AREN'T YOU COLD?

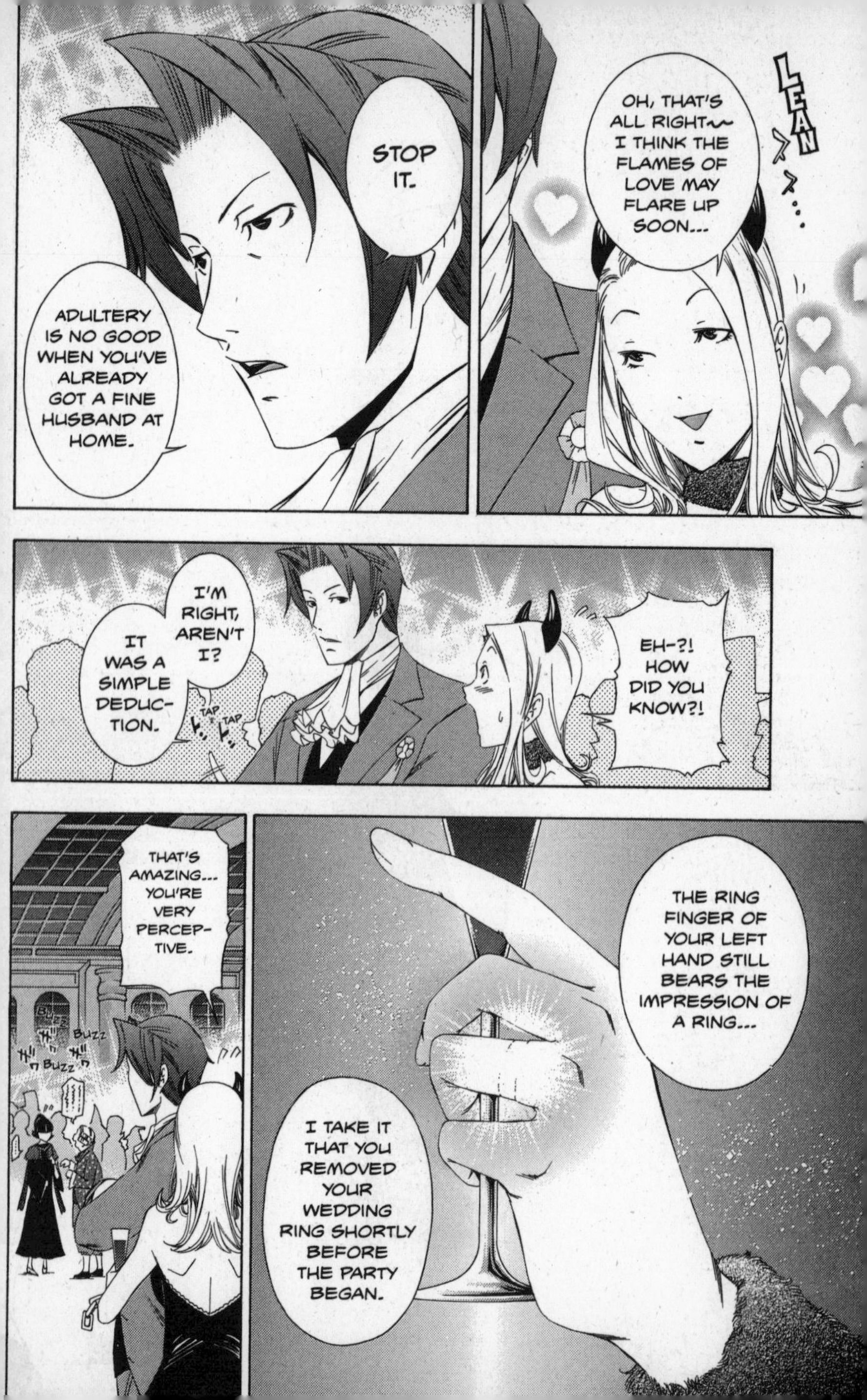
LEAN
OH, THAT'S ALL RIGHT~ I THINK THE FLAMES OF LOVE MAY FLARE UP SOON...
STOP IT.
ADULTERY IS NO GOOD WHEN YOU'VE ALREADY GOT A FINE HUSBAND AT HOME.
EH-?! HOW DID YOU KNOW?!
I'M RIGHT, AREN'T I?
IT WAS A SIMPLE DEDUCTION.
TAP TAP
THE RING FINGER OF YOUR LEFT HAND STILL BEARS THE IMPRESSION OF A RING...
I TAKE IT THAT YOU REMOVED YOUR WEDDING RING SHORTLY BEFORE THE PARTY BEGAN.
THAT'S AMAZING... YOU'RE VERY PERCEPTIVE.
Buzz Buzz Buzz

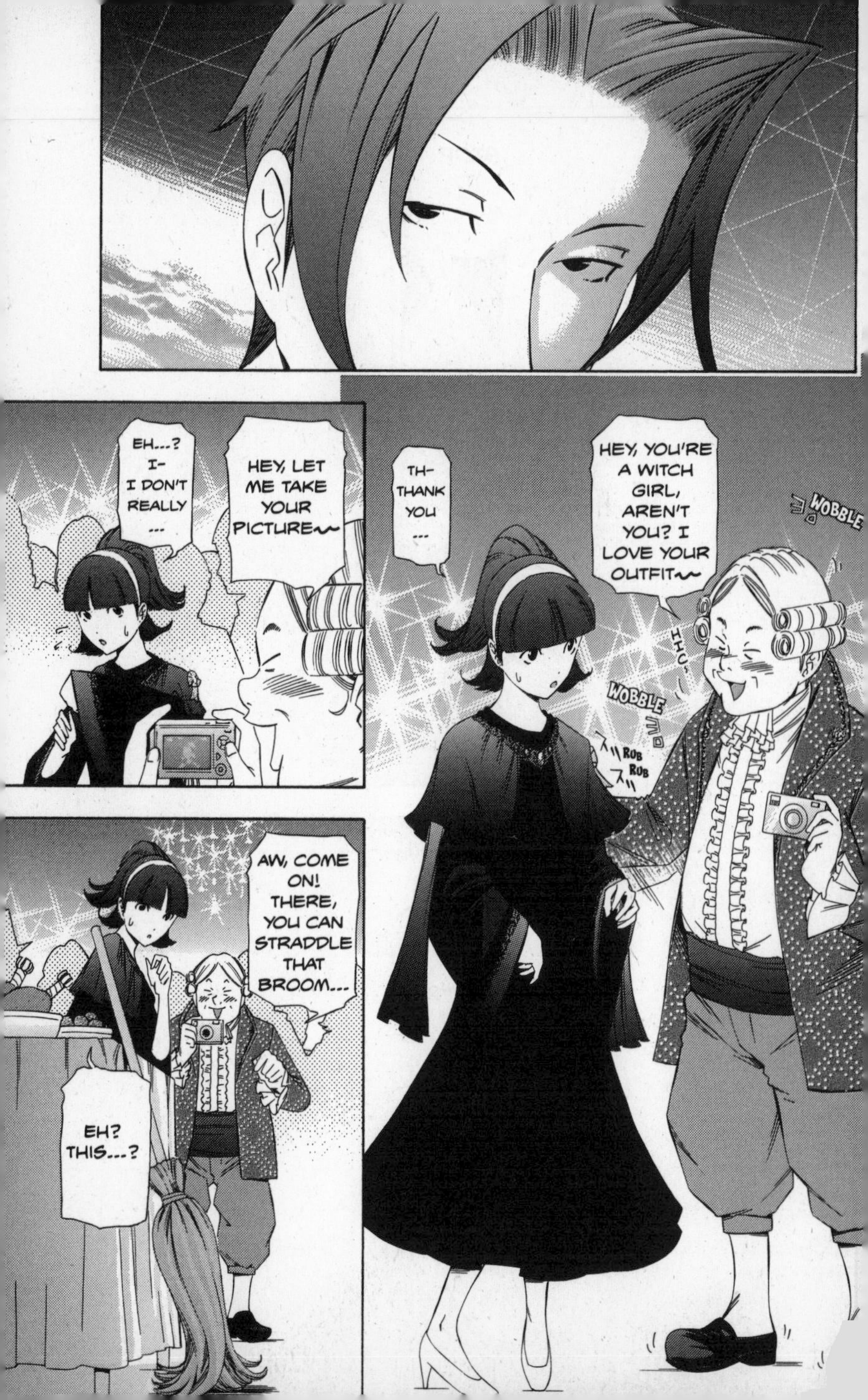
HEY, YOU'RE A WITCH GIRL, AREN'T YOU? I LOVE YOUR OUTFIT~
WOBBLE
TH- THANK YOU ...
HIC
WOBBLE
RUB RUB
HEY, LET ME TAKE YOUR PICTURE~
EH...? I- I DON'T REALLY ...
AW, COME ON! THERE, YOU CAN STRADDLE THAT BROOM...
EH? THIS...?

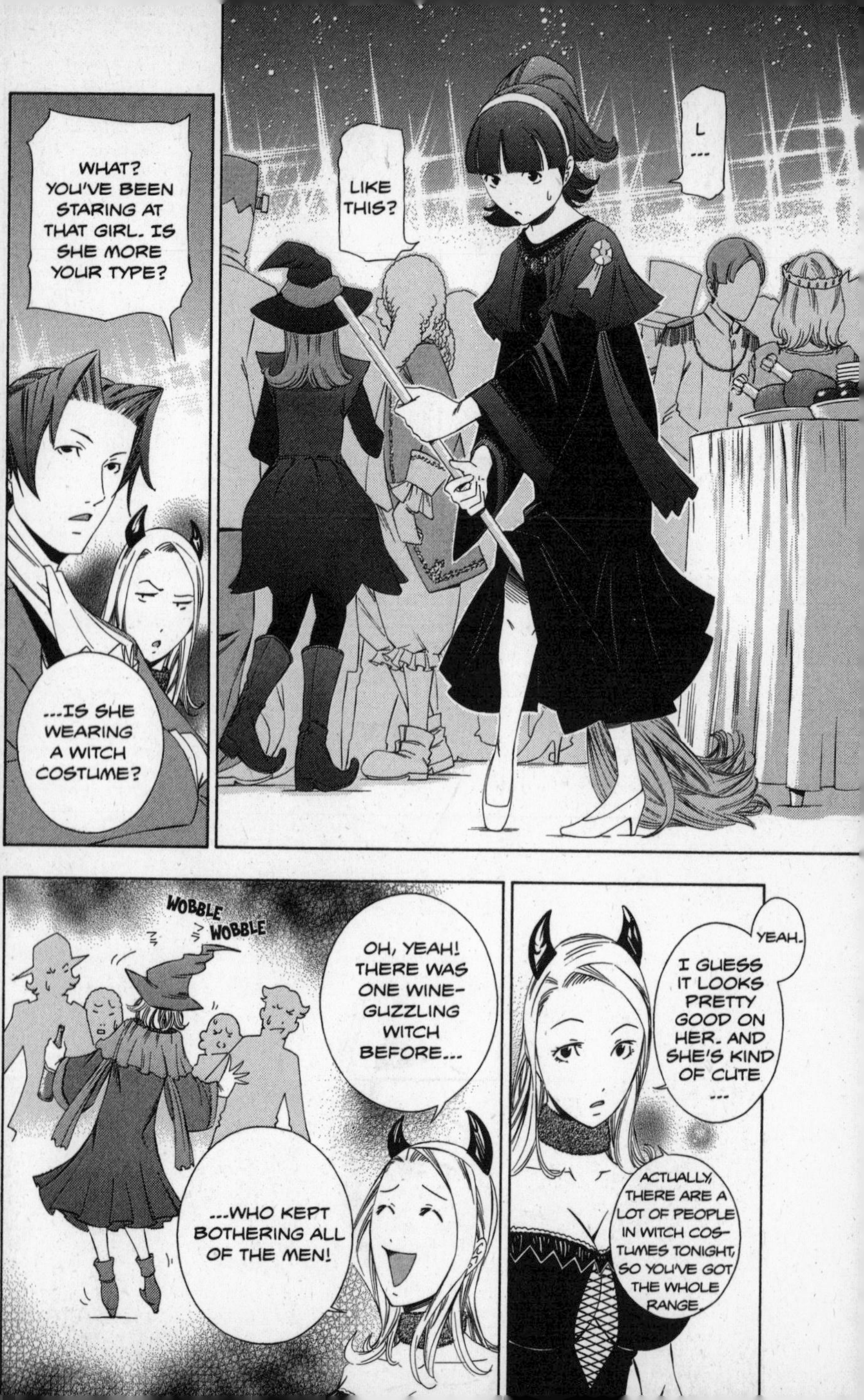
L ...
LIKE THIS?
WHAT? YOU'VE BEEN STARING AT THAT GIRL. IS SHE MORE YOUR TYPE?
...IS SHE WEARING A WITCH COSTUME?
YEAH.
I GUESS IT LOOKS PRETTY GOOD ON HER. AND SHE'S KIND OF CUTE ...
ACTUALLY, THERE ARE A LOT OF PEOPLE IN WITCH COS-TUMES TONIGHT, SO YOU'VE GOT THE WHOLE RANGE.
OH, YEAH! THERE WAS ONE WINE-GUZZLING WITCH BEFORE...
WOBBLE WOBBLE
...WHO KEPT BOTHERING ALL OF THE MEN!

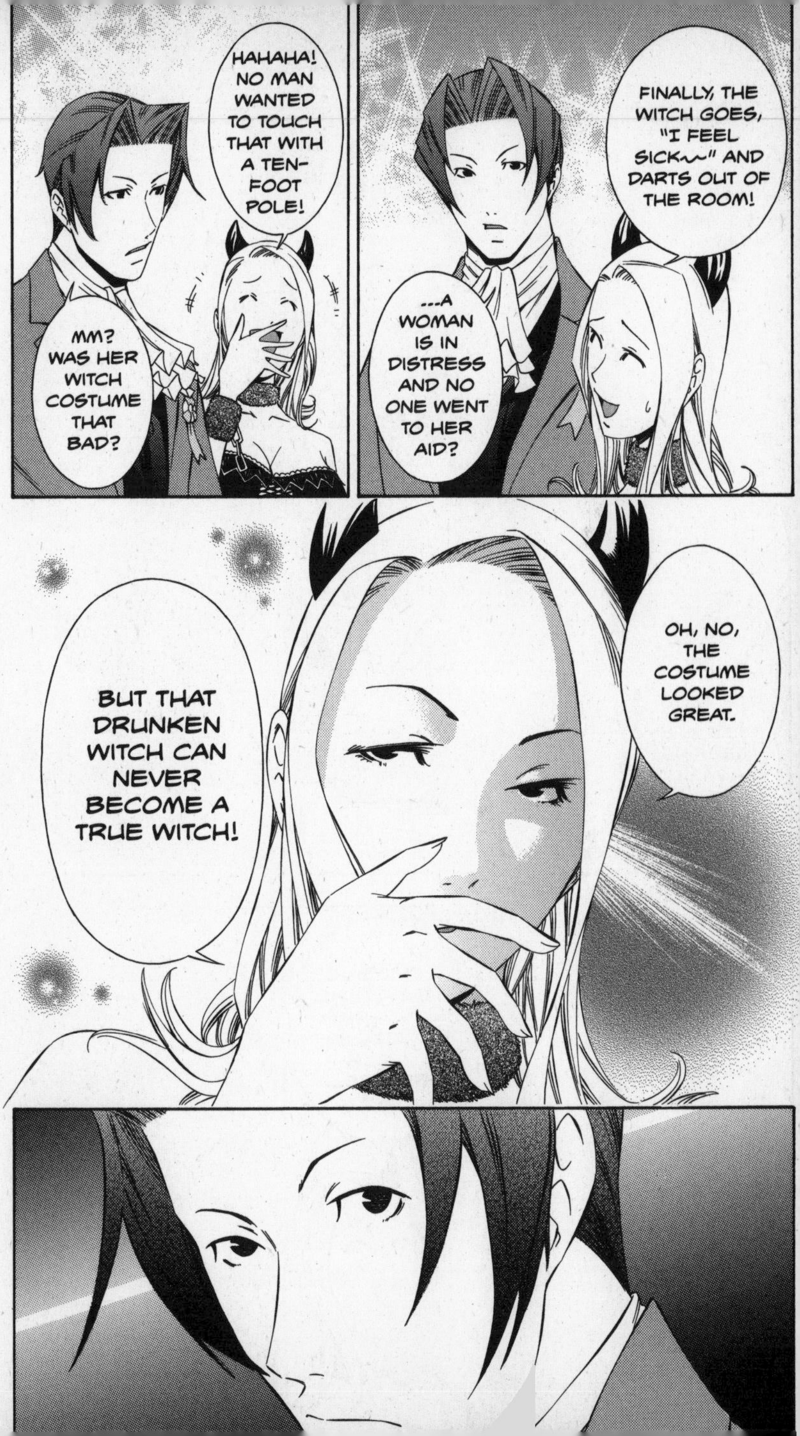
FINALLY, THE WITCH GOES, "I FEEL SICK~~" AND DARTS OUT OF THE ROOM!
...A WOMAN IS IN DISTRESS AND NO ONE WENT TO HER AID?
HAHAHA! NO MAN WANTED TO TOUCH THAT WITH A TEN-FOOT POLE!
MM? WAS HER WITCH COSTUME THAT BAD?
OH, NO, THE COSTUME LOOKED GREAT.
BUT THAT DRUNKEN WITCH CAN NEVER BECOME A TRUE WITCH!

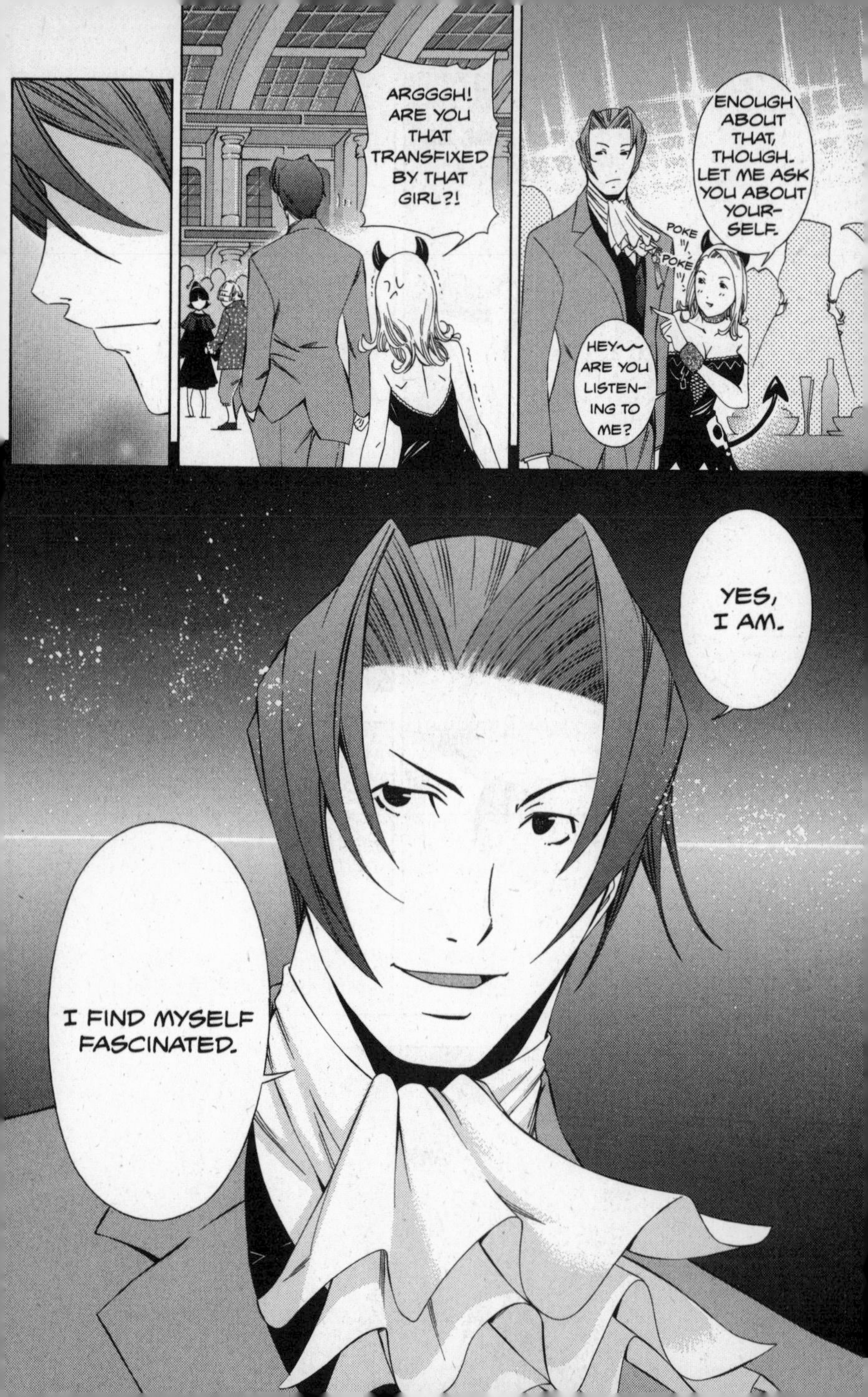
ENOUGH ABOUT THAT, THOUGH. LET ME ASK YOU ABOUT YOURSELF.
POKE POKE
HEY~~ ARE YOU LISTENING TO ME?
ARGGGH! ARE YOU THAT TRANSFIXED BY THAT GIRL?!
YES, I AM.
I FIND MYSELF FASCINATED.

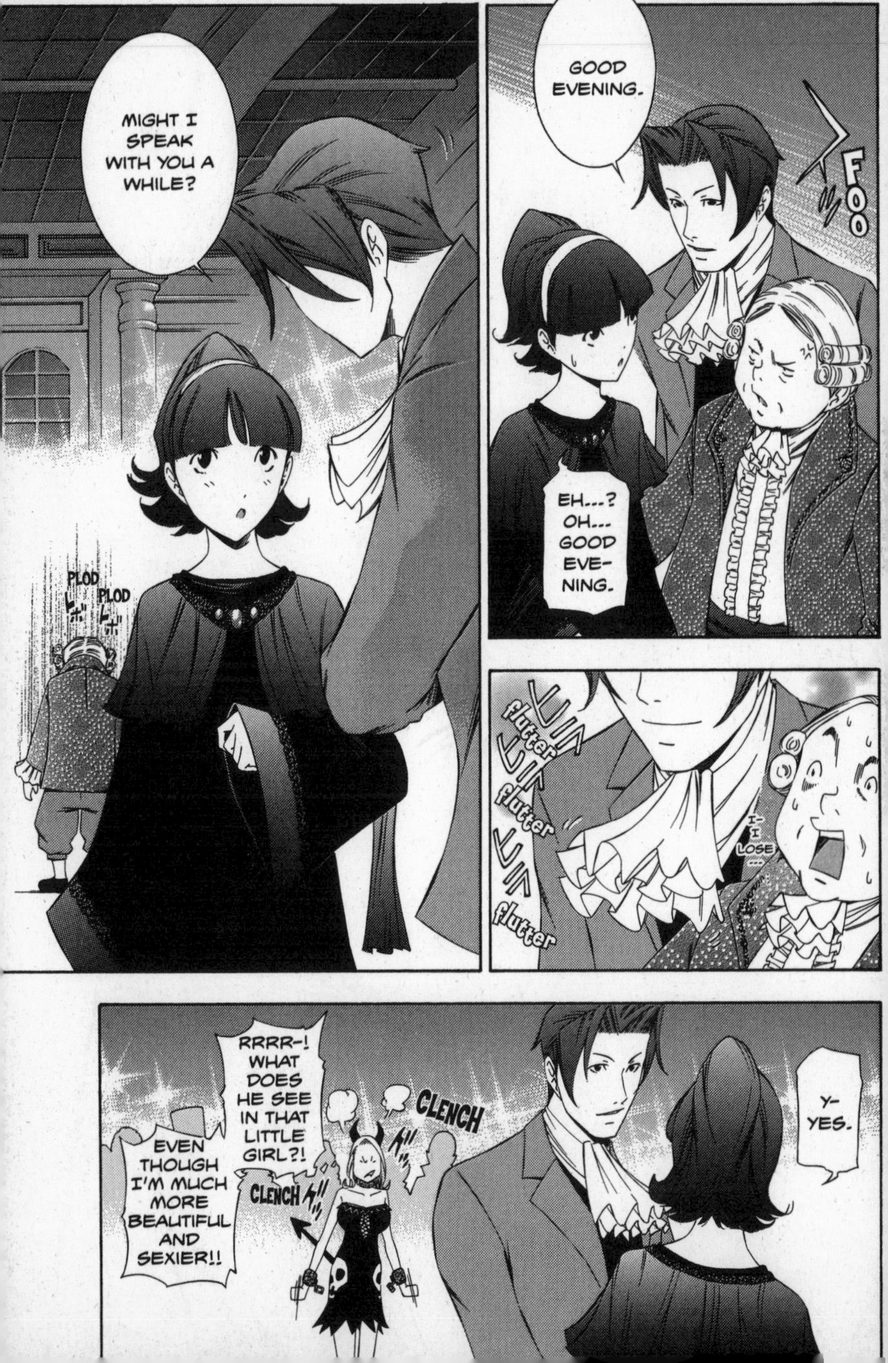
GOOD EVENING.
FOO
EH...? OH... GOOD EVE- NING.
flutter
flutter
flutter
I- I LOSE...
MIGHT I SPEAK WITH YOU A WHILE?
PLOD
PLOD
Y- YES.
CLENCH
RRRR-! WHAT DOES HE SEE IN THAT LITTLE GIRL?!
CLENCH
EVEN THOUGH I'M MUCH MORE BEAUTIFUL AND SEXIER!!

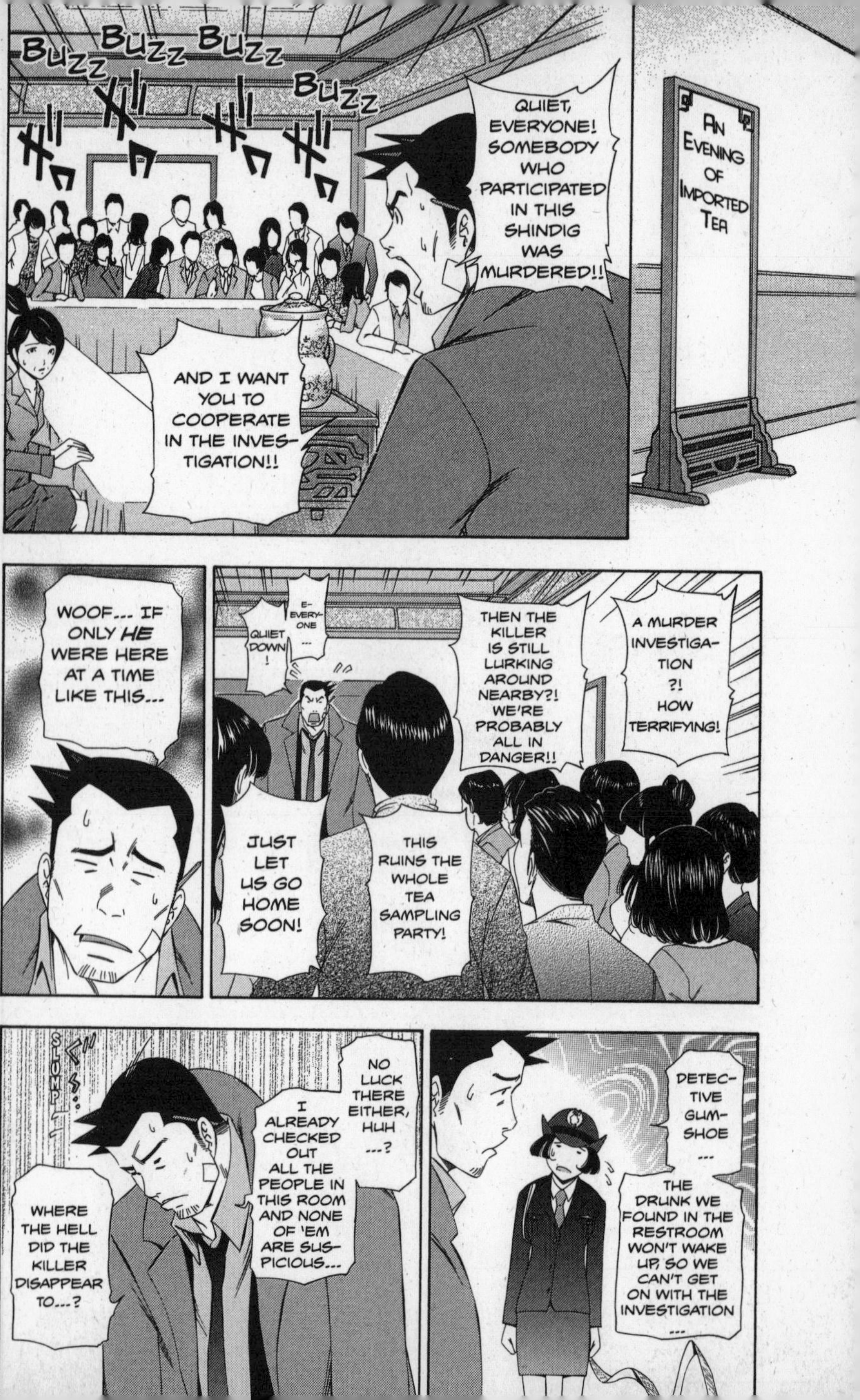
Buzz Buzz Buzz Buzz
An Evening of Imported Tea
QUIET, EVERYONE! SOMEBODY WHO PARTICIPATED IN THIS SHINDIG WAS MURDERED!!
AND I WANT YOU TO COOPERATE IN THE INVESTIGATION!!
A MURDER INVESTIGATION?! HOW TERRIFYING!
THEN THE KILLER IS STILL LURKING AROUND NEARBY?! WE'RE PROBABLY ALL IN DANGER!!
E-EVERYONE ...
QUIET DOWN!
THIS RUINS THE WHOLE TEA SAMPLING PARTY!
JUST LET US GO HOME SOON!
WOOF... IF ONLY HE WERE HERE AT A TIME LIKE THIS...
DETECTIVE GUMSHOE ...
THE DRUNK WE FOUND IN THE RESTROOM WON'T WAKE UP, SO WE CAN'T GET ON WITH THE INVESTIGATION ...
NO LUCK THERE EITHER, HUH ...?
I ALREADY CHECKED OUT ALL THE PEOPLE IN THIS ROOM AND NONE OF 'EM ARE SUSPICIOUS...
SLUMP
WHERE THE HELL DID THE KILLER DISAPPEAR TO...?

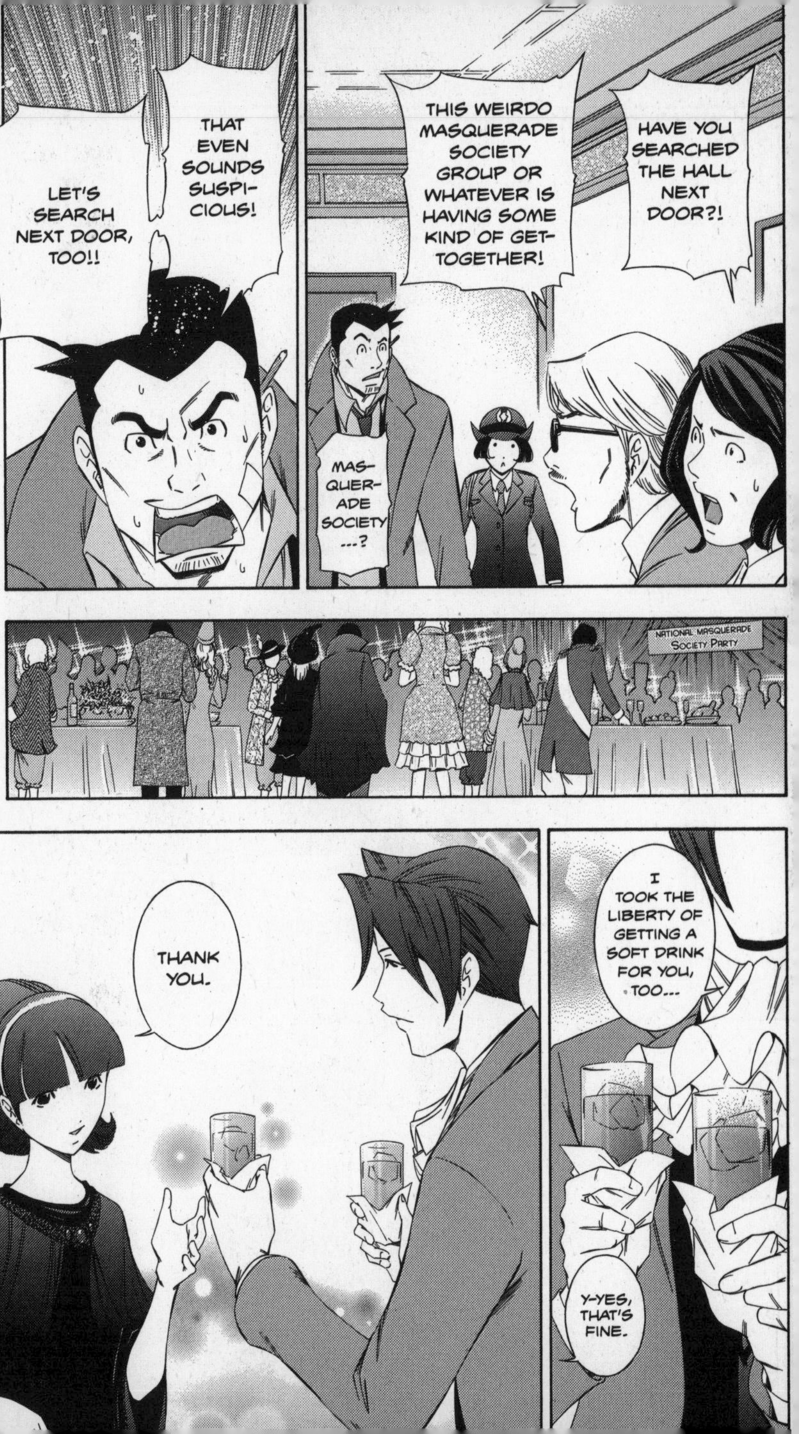
HAVE YOU SEARCHED THE HALL NEXT DOOR?!
THIS WEIRDO MASQUERADE SOCIETY GROUP OR WHATEVER IS HAVING SOME KIND OF GET-TOGETHER!
MASQUERADE SOCIETY...?
THAT EVEN SOUNDS SUSPICIOUS!
LET'S SEARCH NEXT DOOR, TOO!!
NATIONAL MASQUERADE SOCIETY PARTY
I TOOK THE LIBERTY OF GETTING A SOFT DRINK FOR YOU, TOO...
Y-YES, THAT'S FINE.
THANK YOU.

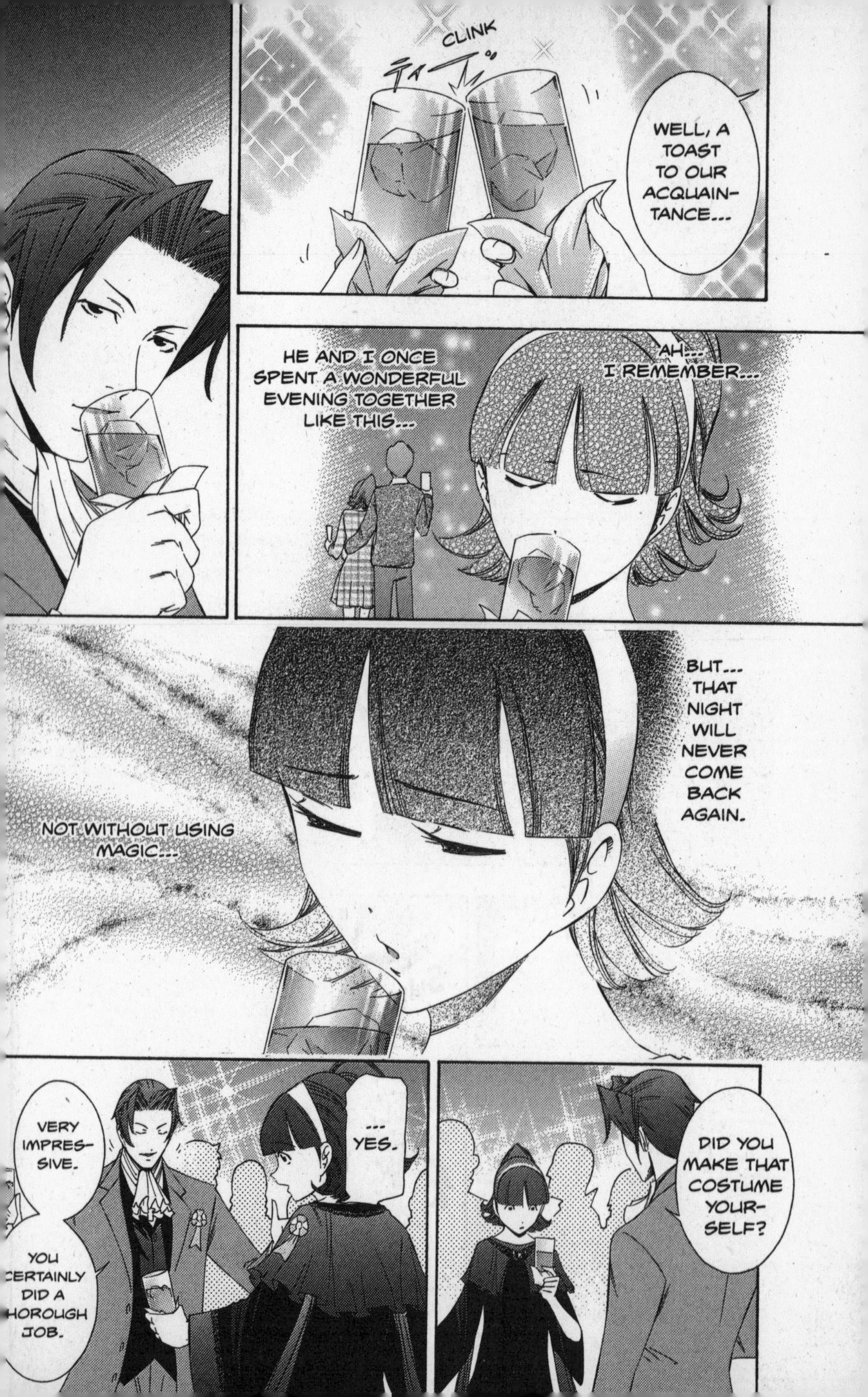
CLINK
ティーン
WELL, A TOAST TO OUR ACQUAINTANCE...
AH... I REMEMBER...
HE AND I ONCE SPENT A WONDERFUL EVENING TOGETHER LIKE THIS...
BUT... THAT NIGHT WILL NEVER COME BACK AGAIN.
NOT WITHOUT USING MAGIC...
DID YOU MAKE THAT COSTUME YOURSELF?
...YES.
VERY IMPRESSIVE.
YOU CERTAINLY DID A HOROUGH JOB.

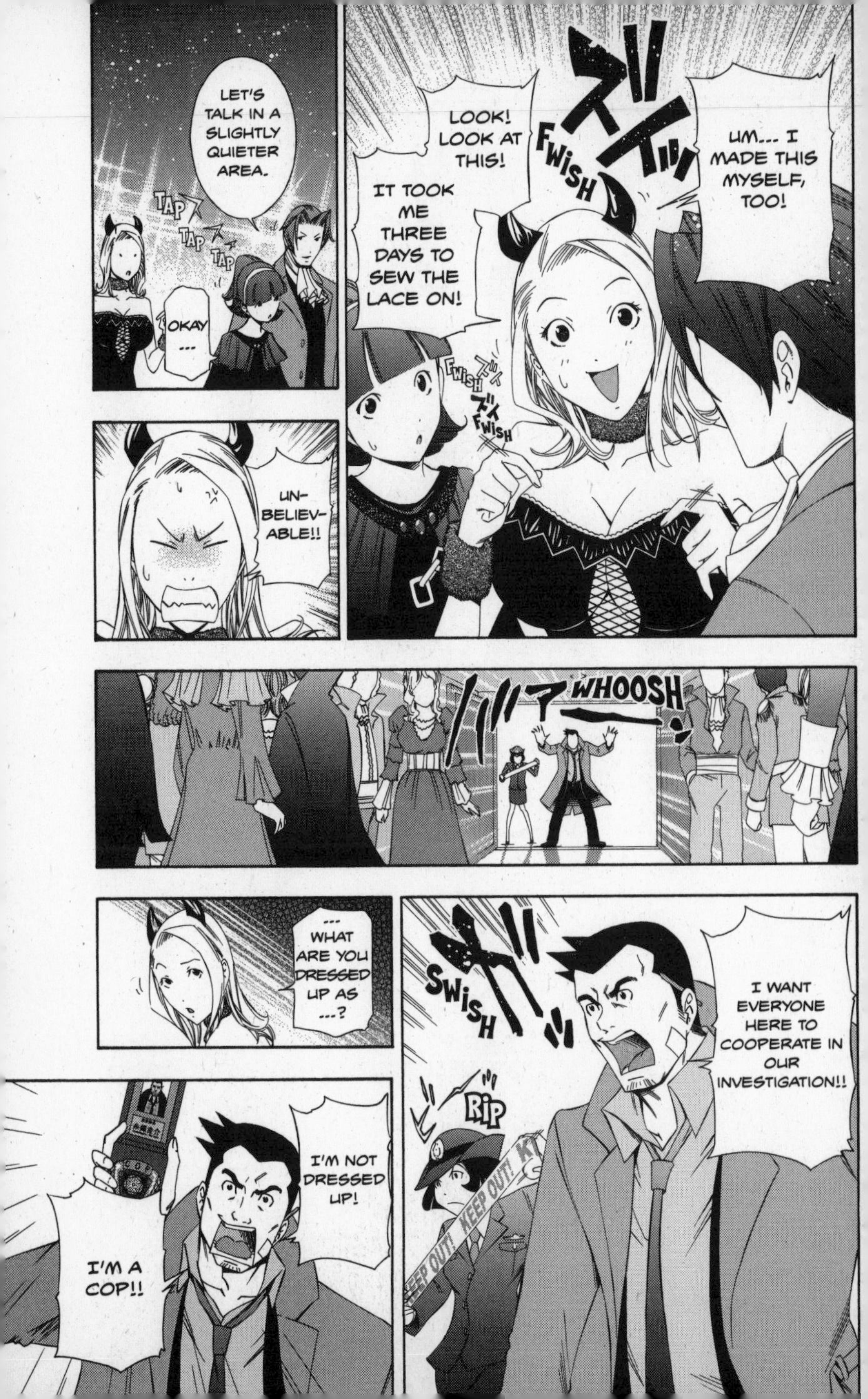
UM... I MADE THIS MYSELF, TOO!
FWISH
LOOK! LOOK AT THIS!
IT TOOK ME THREE DAYS TO SEW THE LACE ON!
FWISH
FWISH
LET'S TALK IN A SLIGHTLY QUIETER AREA.
TAP
TAP
TAP
OKAY ...
UN-BELIEV-ABLE!!
WHOOSH
I WANT EVERYONE HERE TO COOPERATE IN OUR INVESTIGATION!!
SWISH
RIP
KEEP OUT! KEEP OUT! K
... WHAT ARE YOU DRESSED UP AS ...?
I'M NOT DRESSED UP!
I'M A COP!!

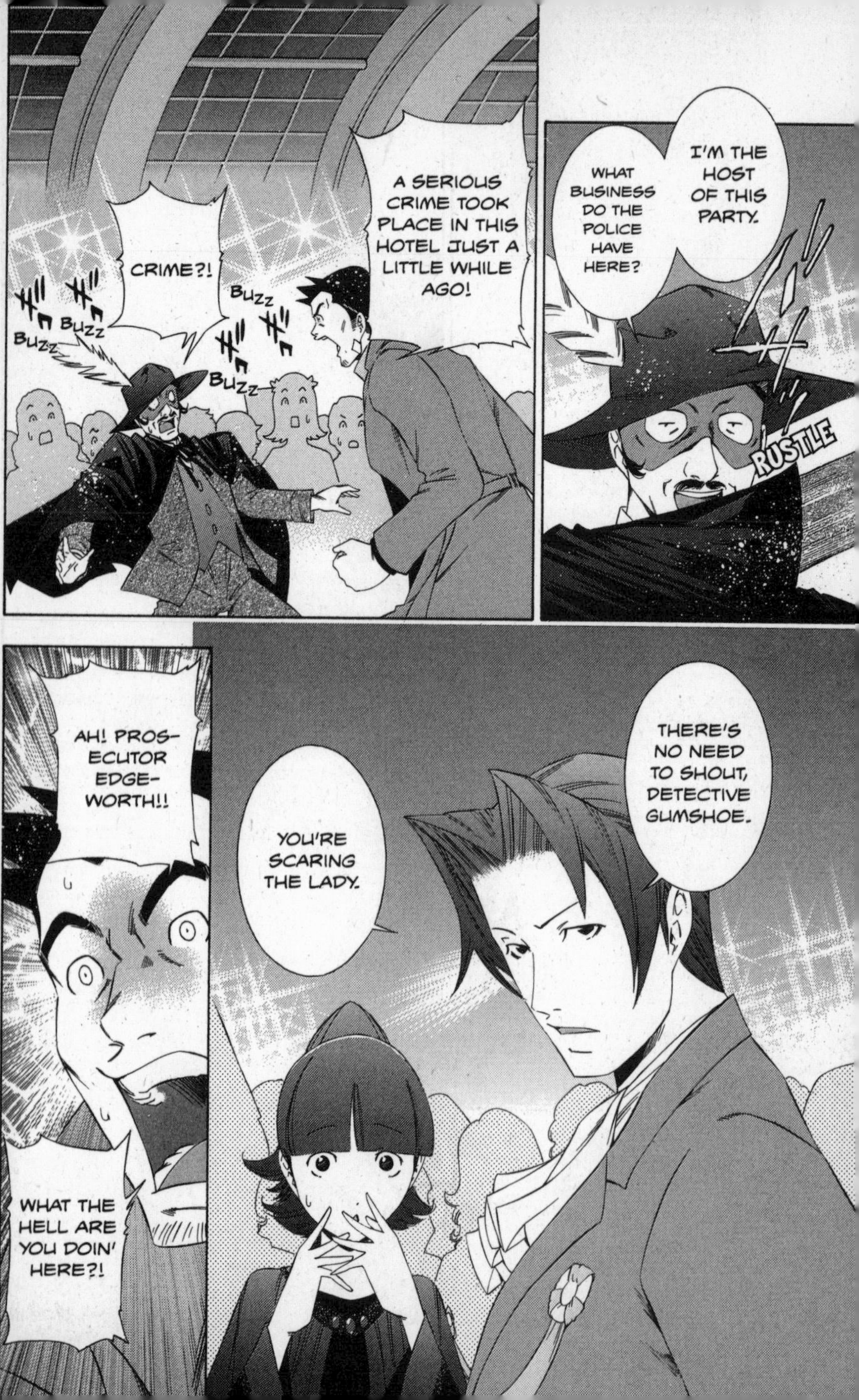

I'M THE HOST OF THIS PARTY.
WHAT BUSINESS DO THE POLICE HAVE HERE?
RUSTLE
A SERIOUS CRIME TOOK PLACE IN THIS HOTEL JUST A LITTLE WHILE AGO!
CRIME?!
Buzz
Buzz
Buzz
Buzz
THERE'S NO NEED TO SHOUT, DETECTIVE GUMSHOE.
YOU'RE SCARING THE LADY.
AH! PROSECUTOR EDGEWORTH!!
WHAT THE HELL ARE YOU DOIN' HERE?!

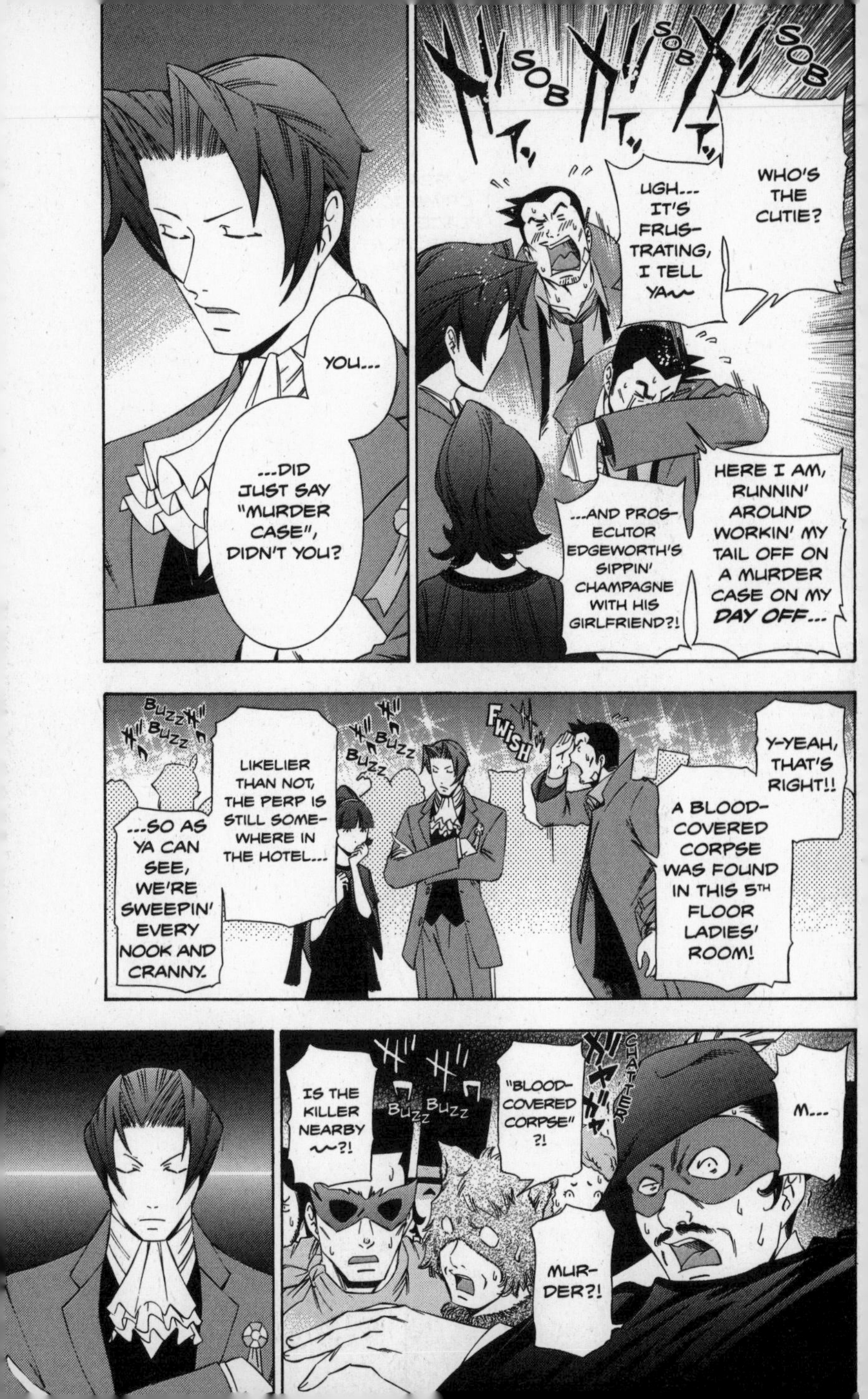
SOB
SOB
SOB
WHO'S THE CUTIE?
UGH... IT'S FRUS-TRATING, I TELL YA~
HERE I AM, RUNNIN' AROUND WORKIN' MY TAIL OFF ON A MURDER CASE ON MY DAY OFF...
...AND PROS-ECUTOR EDGEWORTH'S SIPPIN' CHAMPAGNE WITH HIS GIRLFRIEND?!
YOU...
...DID JUST SAY "MURDER CASE", DIDN'T YOU?
FWISH
Y-YEAH, THAT'S RIGHT!!
A BLOOD-COVERED CORPSE WAS FOUND IN THIS 5TH FLOOR LADIES' ROOM!
BUZZ BUZZ
LIKELIER THAN NOT, THE PERP IS STILL SOME-WHERE IN THE HOTEL...
BUZZ BUZZ
...SO AS YA CAN SEE, WE'RE SWEEPIN' EVERY NOOK AND CRANNY.
CHATTER
M...
"BLOOD-COVERED CORPSE"?!
MUR-DER?!
BUZZ BUZZ
IS THE KILLER NEARBY~?!

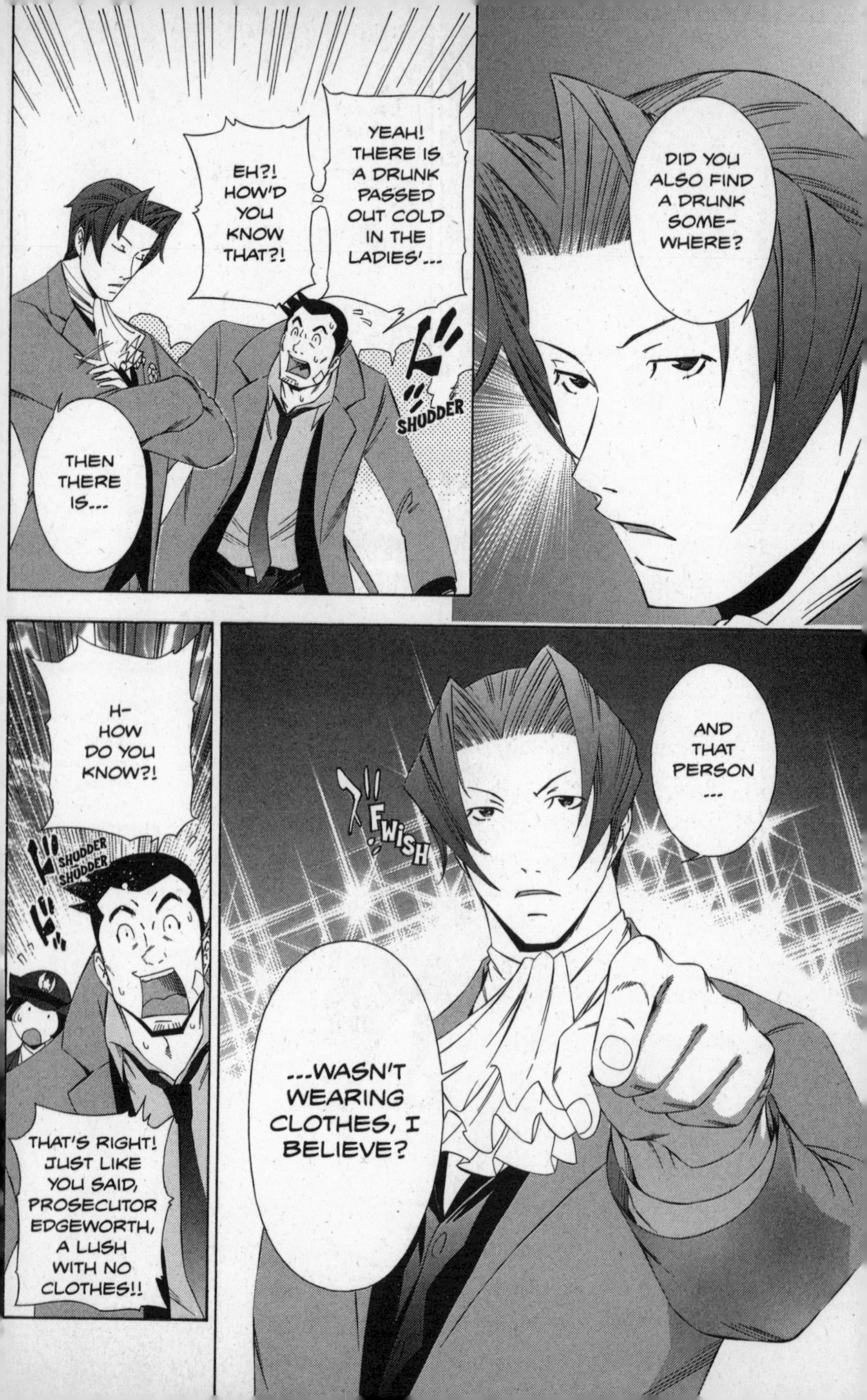
DID YOU ALSO FIND A DRUNK SOME-WHERE?
YEAH! THERE IS A DRUNK PASSED OUT COLD IN THE LADIES'...
EH?! HOW'D YOU KNOW THAT?!
SHUDDER
THEN THERE IS...
AND THAT PERSON ...
FWISH
...WASN'T WEARING CLOTHES, I BELIEVE?
H- HOW DO YOU KNOW?!
SHUDDER SHUDDER
THAT'S RIGHT! JUST LIKE YOU SAID, PROSECUTOR EDGEWORTH, A LUSH WITH NO CLOTHES!!

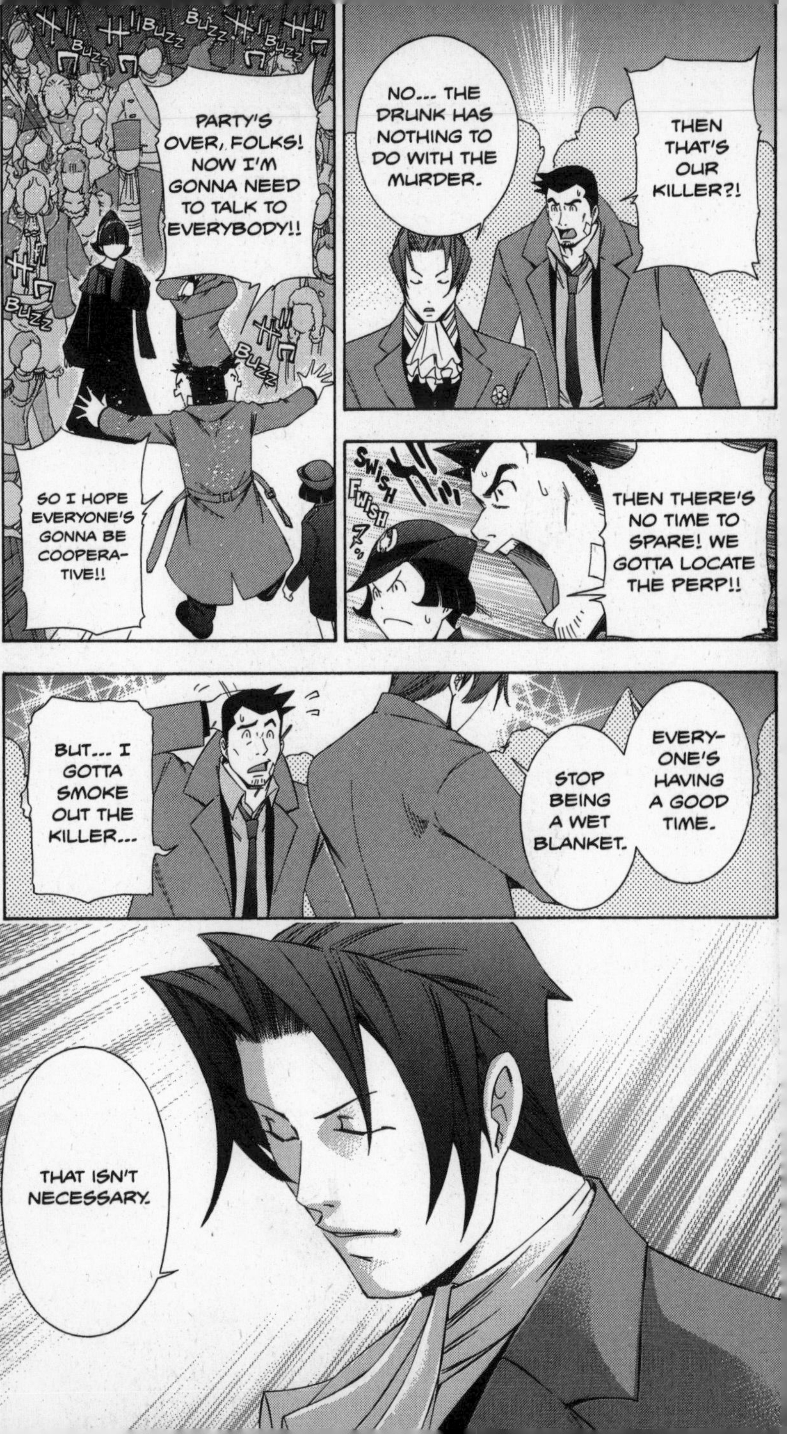
THEN THAT'S OUR KILLER?!
NO... THE DRUNK HAS NOTHING TO DO WITH THE MURDER.
THEN THERE'S NO TIME TO SPARE! WE GOTTA LOCATE THE PERP!!
SWISH
FWISH
BUZZ
BUZZ
BUZZ
BUZZ
PARTY'S OVER, FOLKS! NOW I'M GONNA NEED TO TALK TO EVERYBODY!!
BUZZ
BUZZ
SO I HOPE EVERYONE'S GONNA BE COOPERA-TIVE!!
EVERY-ONE'S HAVING A GOOD TIME.
STOP BEING A WET BLANKET.
BUT... I GOTTA SMOKE OUT THE KILLER...
THAT ISN'T NECESSARY.

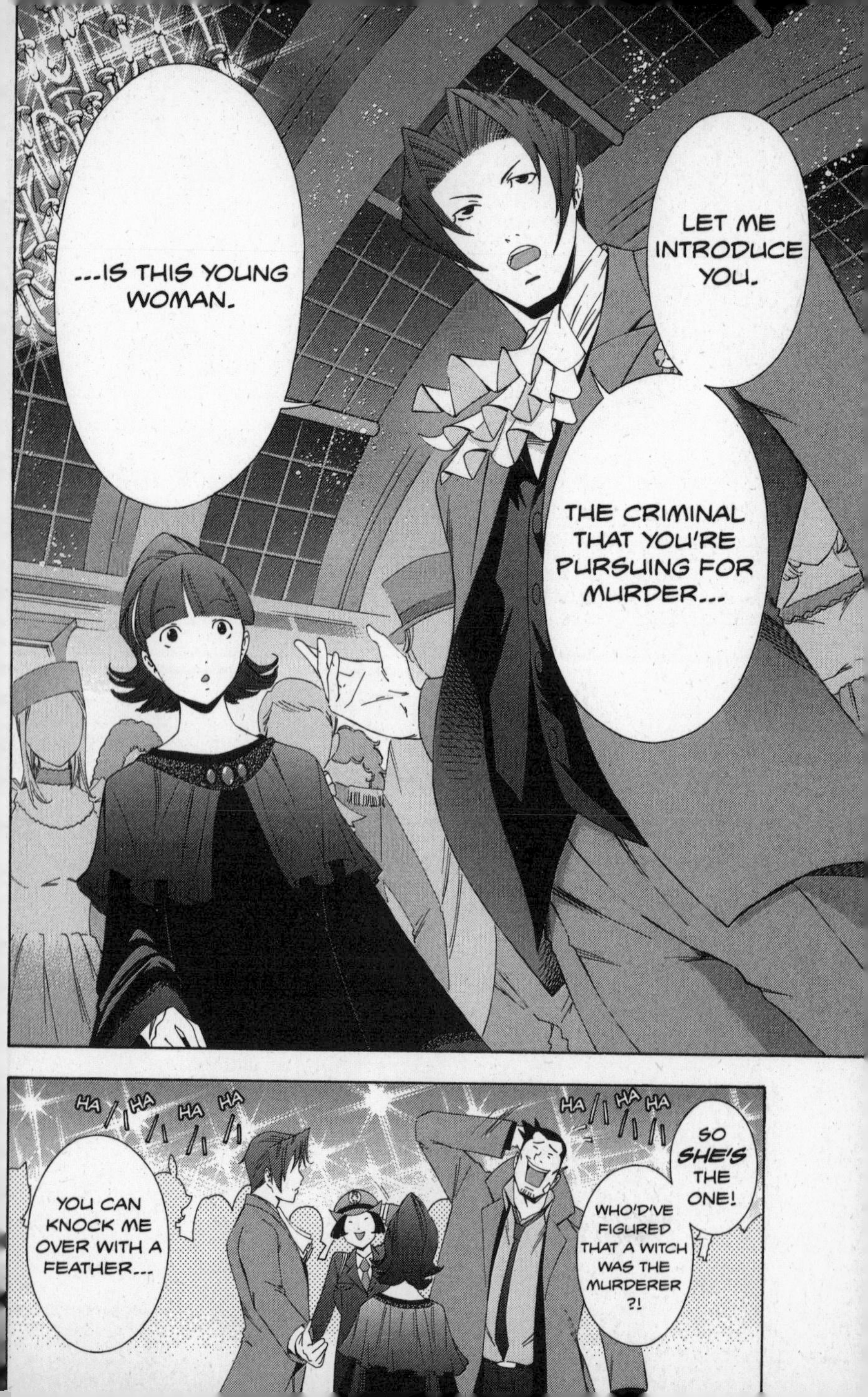
LET ME INTRODUCE YOU.
THE CRIMINAL THAT YOU'RE PURSUING FOR MURDER...
...IS THIS YOUNG WOMAN.
HA HA HA HA
SO *SHE'S* THE ONE!
WHO'D'VE FIGURED THAT A WITCH WAS THE MURDERER?!
HA HA HA HA
YOU CAN KNOCK ME OVER WITH A FEATHER...

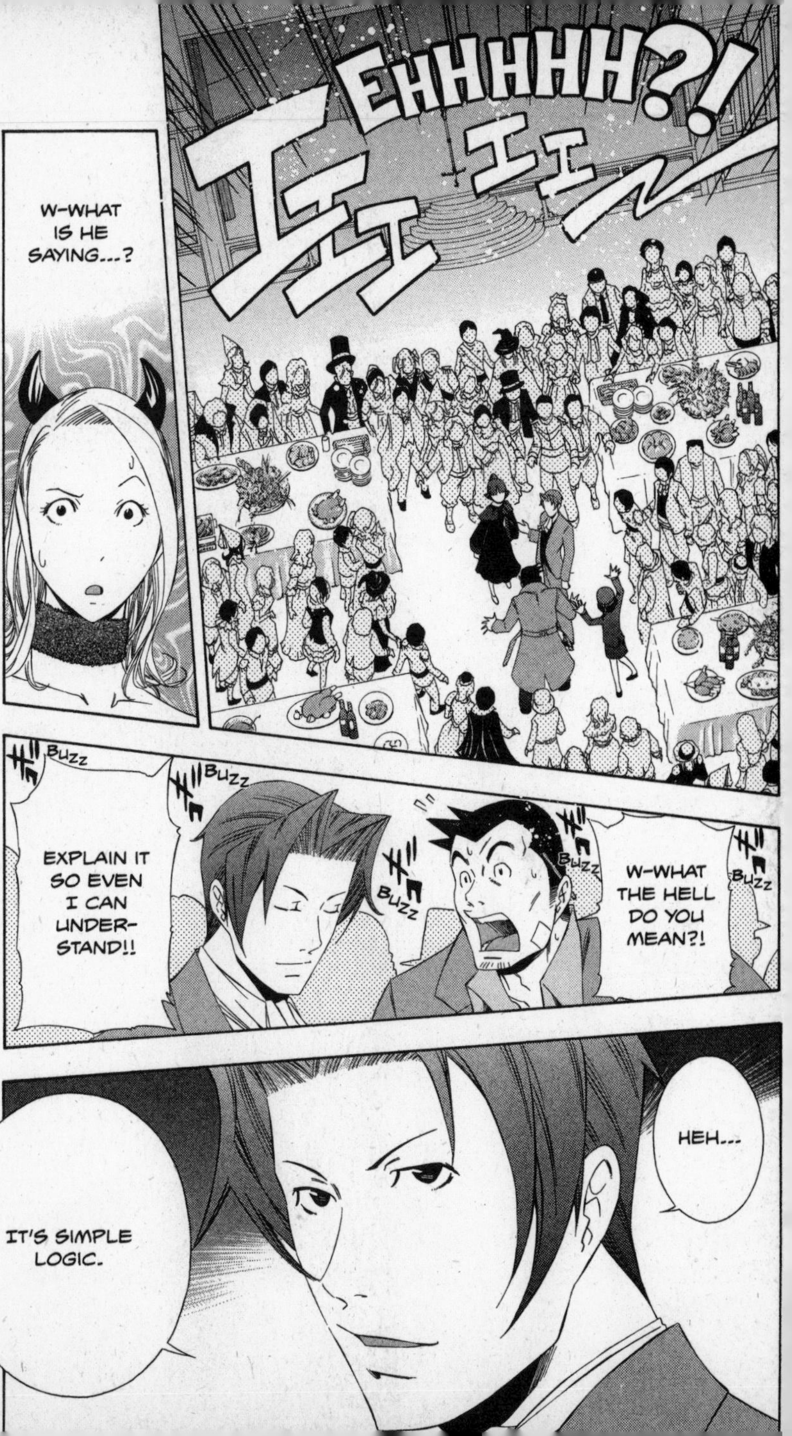
EHHHHH?!
W-WHAT IS HE SAYING...?
Buzz
Buzz
W-WHAT THE HELL DO YOU MEAN?!
Buzz
Buzz
Buzz
EXPLAIN IT SO EVEN I CAN UNDER-STAND!!
HEH...
IT'S SIMPLE LOGIC.

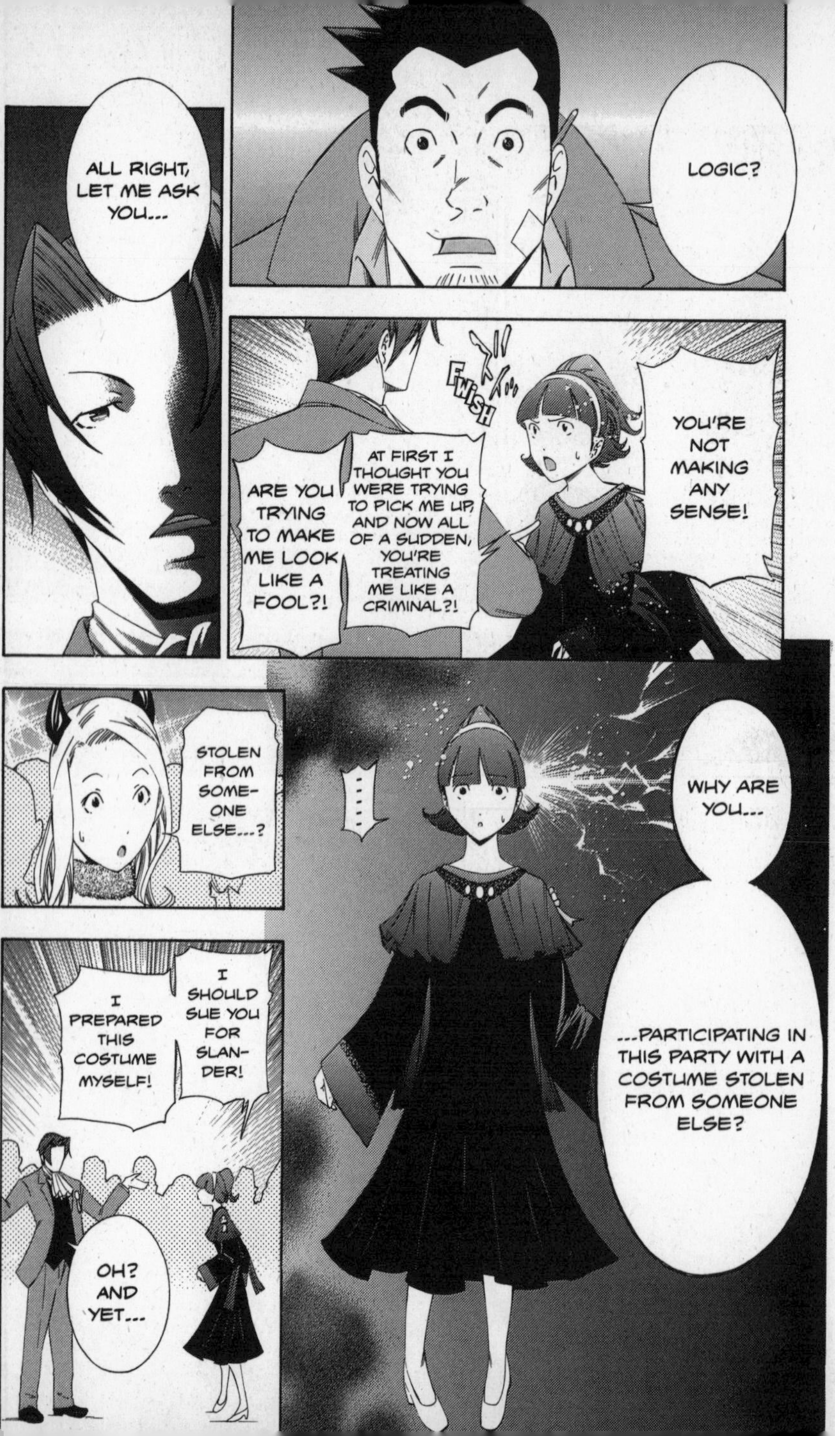
LOGIC?
YOU'RE NOT MAKING ANY SENSE!
FWISH
AT FIRST I THOUGHT YOU WERE TRYING TO PICK ME UP, AND NOW ALL OF A SUDDEN, YOU'RE TREATING ME LIKE A CRIMINAL?!
ARE YOU TRYING TO MAKE ME LOOK LIKE A FOOL?!
ALL RIGHT, LET ME ASK YOU...
WHY ARE YOU...
...PARTICIPATING IN THIS PARTY WITH A COSTUME STOLEN FROM SOMEONE ELSE?
......
STOLEN FROM SOME-ONE ELSE...?
I SHOULD SUE YOU FOR SLAN-DER!
I PREPARED THIS COSTUME MYSELF!
OH? AND YET...

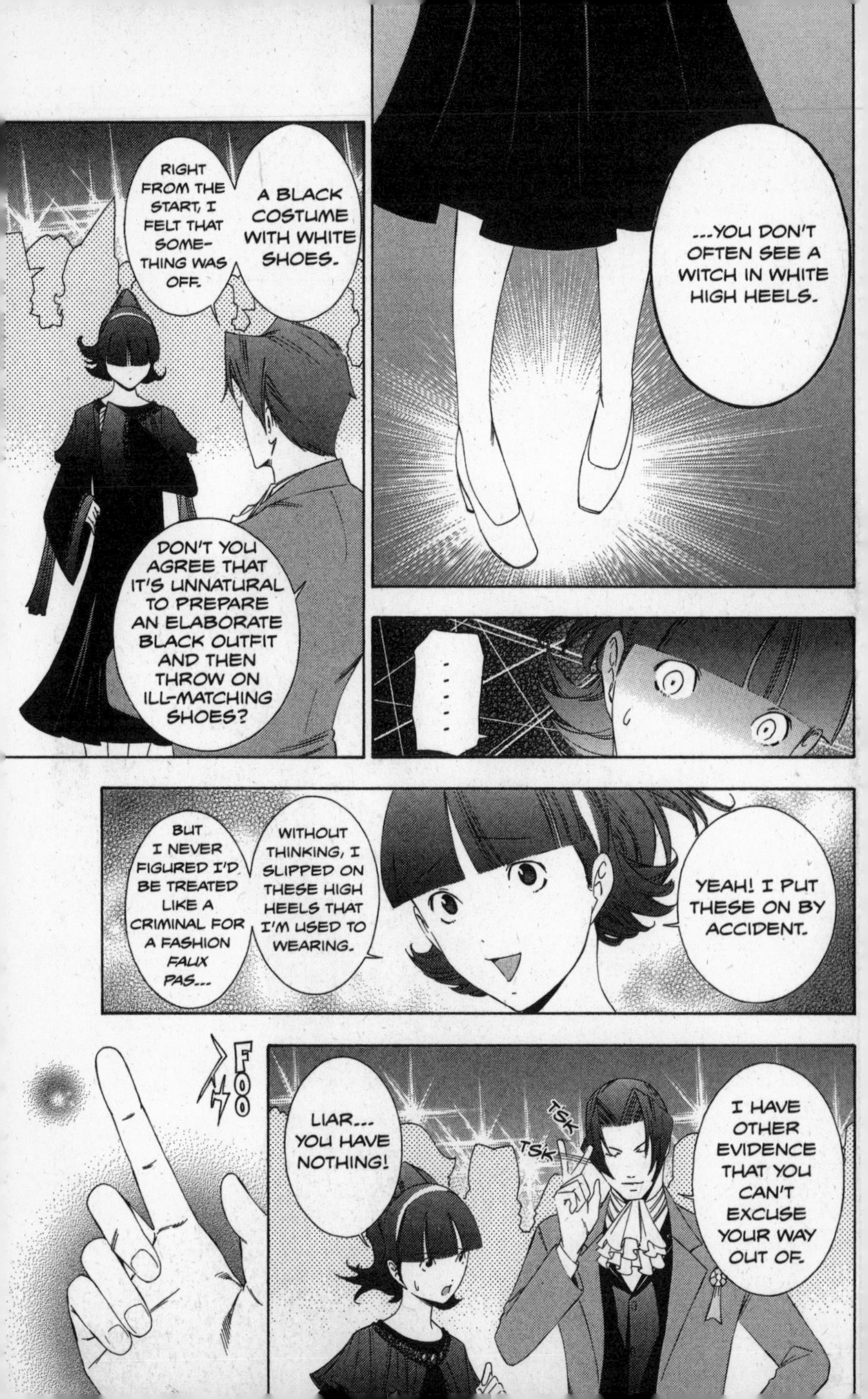
...YOU DON'T OFTEN SEE A WITCH IN WHITE HIGH HEELS.
......
A BLACK COSTUME WITH WHITE SHOES.
RIGHT FROM THE START, I FELT THAT SOME-THING WAS OFF.
DON'T YOU AGREE THAT IT'S UNNATURAL TO PREPARE AN ELABORATE BLACK OUTFIT AND THEN THROW ON ILL-MATCHING SHOES?
YEAH! I PUT THESE ON BY ACCIDENT.
WITHOUT THINKING, I SLIPPED ON THESE HIGH HEELS THAT I'M USED TO WEARING.
BUT I NEVER FIGURED I'D BE TREATED LIKE A CRIMINAL FOR A FASHION *FAUX PAS*...
I HAVE OTHER EVIDENCE THAT YOU CAN'T EXCUSE YOUR WAY OUT OF.
TSK
TSK
LIAR... YOU HAVE NOTHING!
FOO

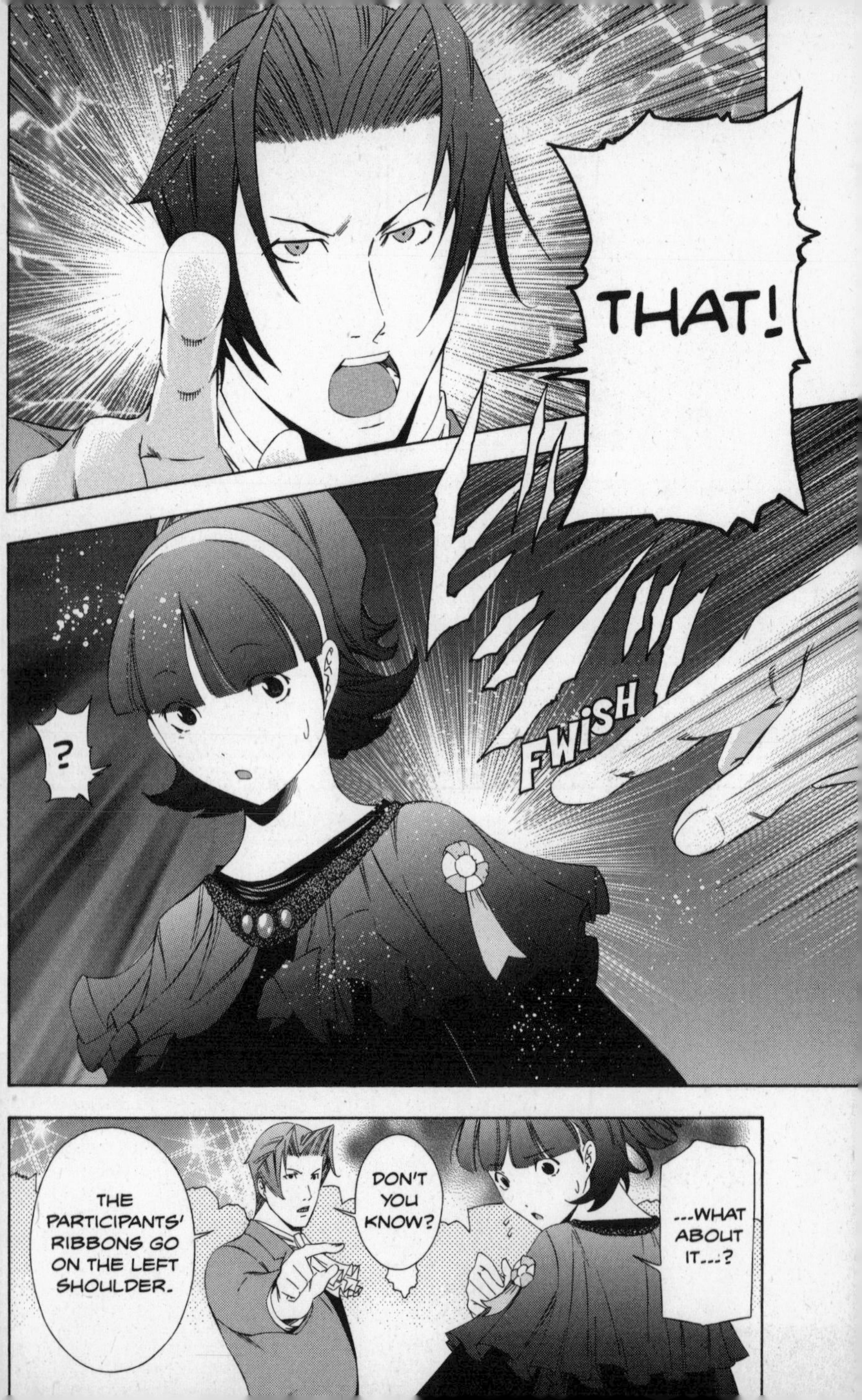
THAT!
FWISH
?
...WHAT ABOUT IT...?
DON'T YOU KNOW?
THE PARTICIPANTS' RIBBONS GO ON THE LEFT SHOULDER.

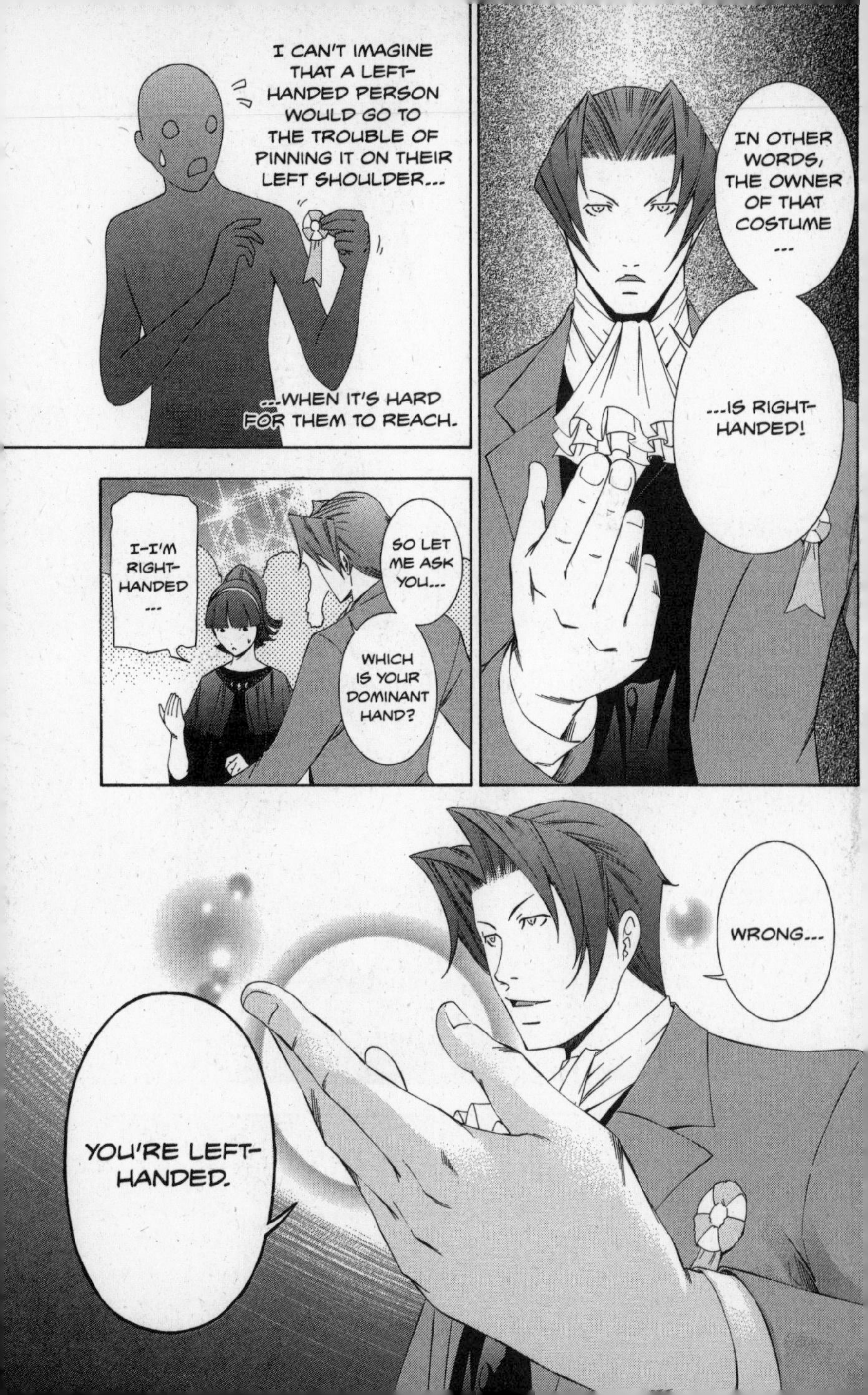
IN OTHER WORDS, THE OWNER OF THAT COSTUME ...
...IS RIGHT-HANDED!
I CAN'T IMAGINE THAT A LEFT-HANDED PERSON WOULD GO TO THE TROUBLE OF PINNING IT ON THEIR LEFT SHOULDER...
...WHEN IT'S HARD FOR THEM TO REACH.
SO LET ME ASK YOU...
WHICH IS YOUR DOMINANT HAND?
I-I'M RIGHT-HANDED ...
WRONG...
YOU'RE LEFT-HANDED.

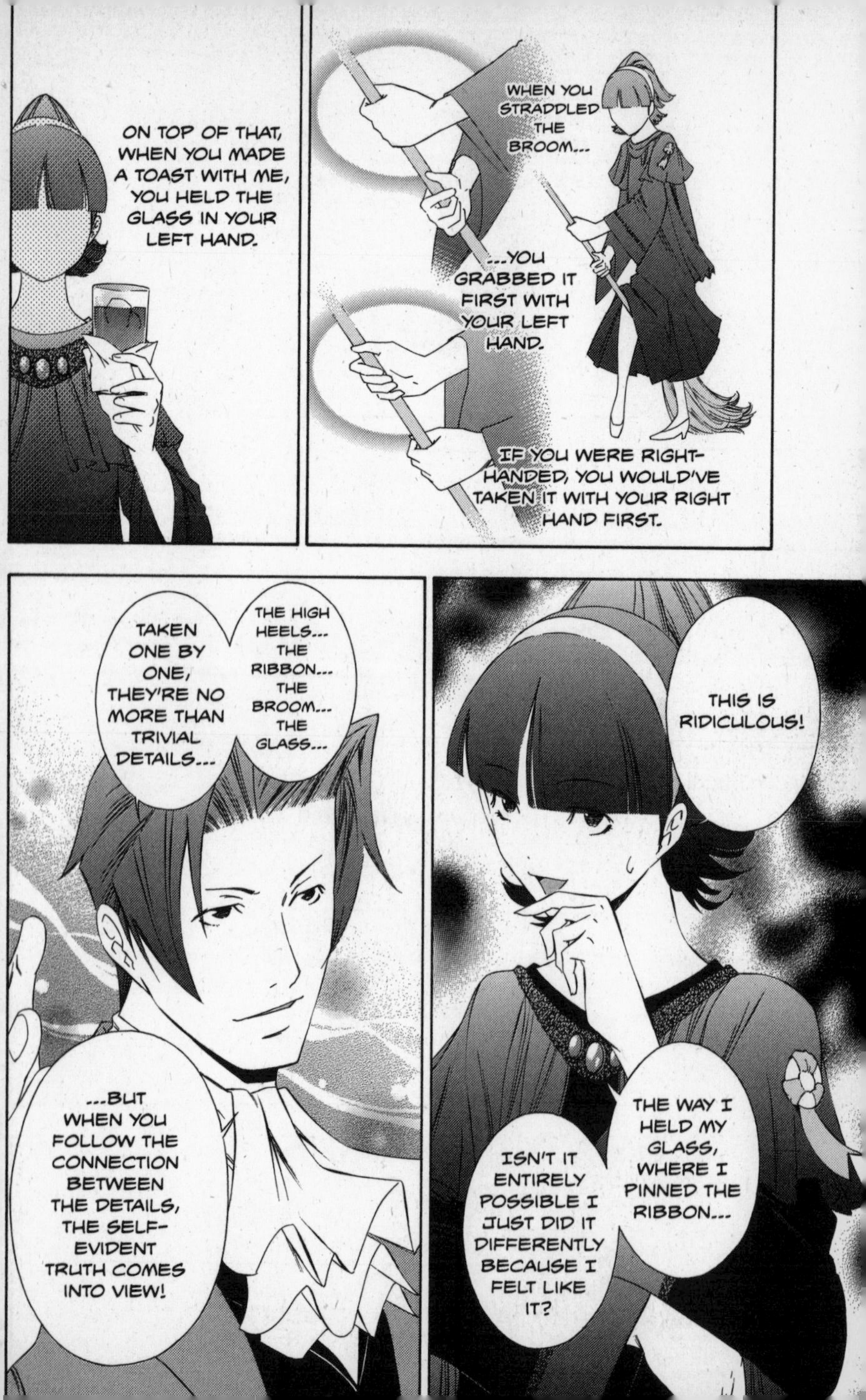
WHEN YOU STRADDLED THE BROOM...
...YOU GRABBED IT FIRST WITH YOUR LEFT HAND.
IF YOU WERE RIGHT-HANDED, YOU WOULD'VE TAKEN IT WITH YOUR RIGHT HAND FIRST.
ON TOP OF THAT, WHEN YOU MADE A TOAST WITH ME, YOU HELD THE GLASS IN YOUR LEFT HAND.
THIS IS RIDICULOUS!
THE WAY I HELD MY GLASS, WHERE I PINNED THE RIBBON...
ISN'T IT ENTIRELY POSSIBLE I JUST DID IT DIFFERENTLY BECAUSE I FELT LIKE IT?
THE HIGH HEELS... THE RIBBON... THE BROOM... THE GLASS...
TAKEN ONE BY ONE, THEY'RE NO MORE THAN TRIVIAL DETAILS...
...BUT WHEN YOU FOLLOW THE CONNECTION BETWEEN THE DETAILS, THE SELF-EVIDENT TRUTH COMES INTO VIEW!

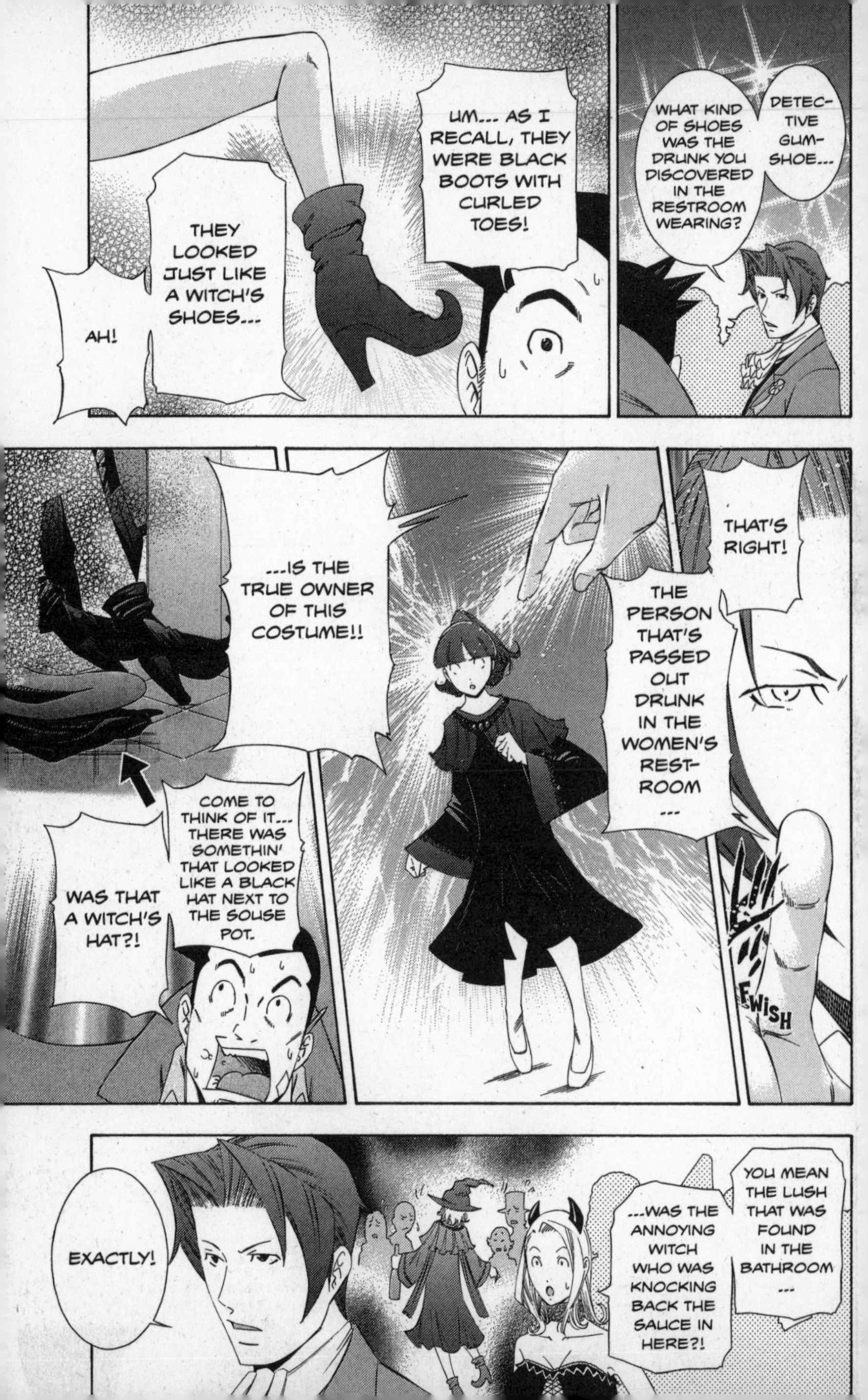
DETECTIVE GUMSHOE...
WHAT KIND OF SHOES WAS THE DRUNK YOU DISCOVERED IN THE RESTROOM WEARING?
UM... AS I RECALL, THEY WERE BLACK BOOTS WITH CURLED TOES!
THEY LOOKED JUST LIKE A WITCH'S SHOES...
AH!
THAT'S RIGHT!
THE PERSON THAT'S PASSED OUT DRUNK IN THE WOMEN'S RESTROOM ...
FWISH
...IS THE TRUE OWNER OF THIS COSTUME!!
COME TO THINK OF IT... THERE WAS SOMETHIN' THAT LOOKED LIKE A BLACK HAT NEXT TO THE SOUSE POT.
WAS THAT A WITCH'S HAT?!
YOU MEAN THE LUSH THAT WAS FOUND IN THE BATHROOM ...
...WAS THE ANNOYING WITCH WHO WAS KNOCKING BACK THE SAUCE IN HERE?!
EXACTLY!

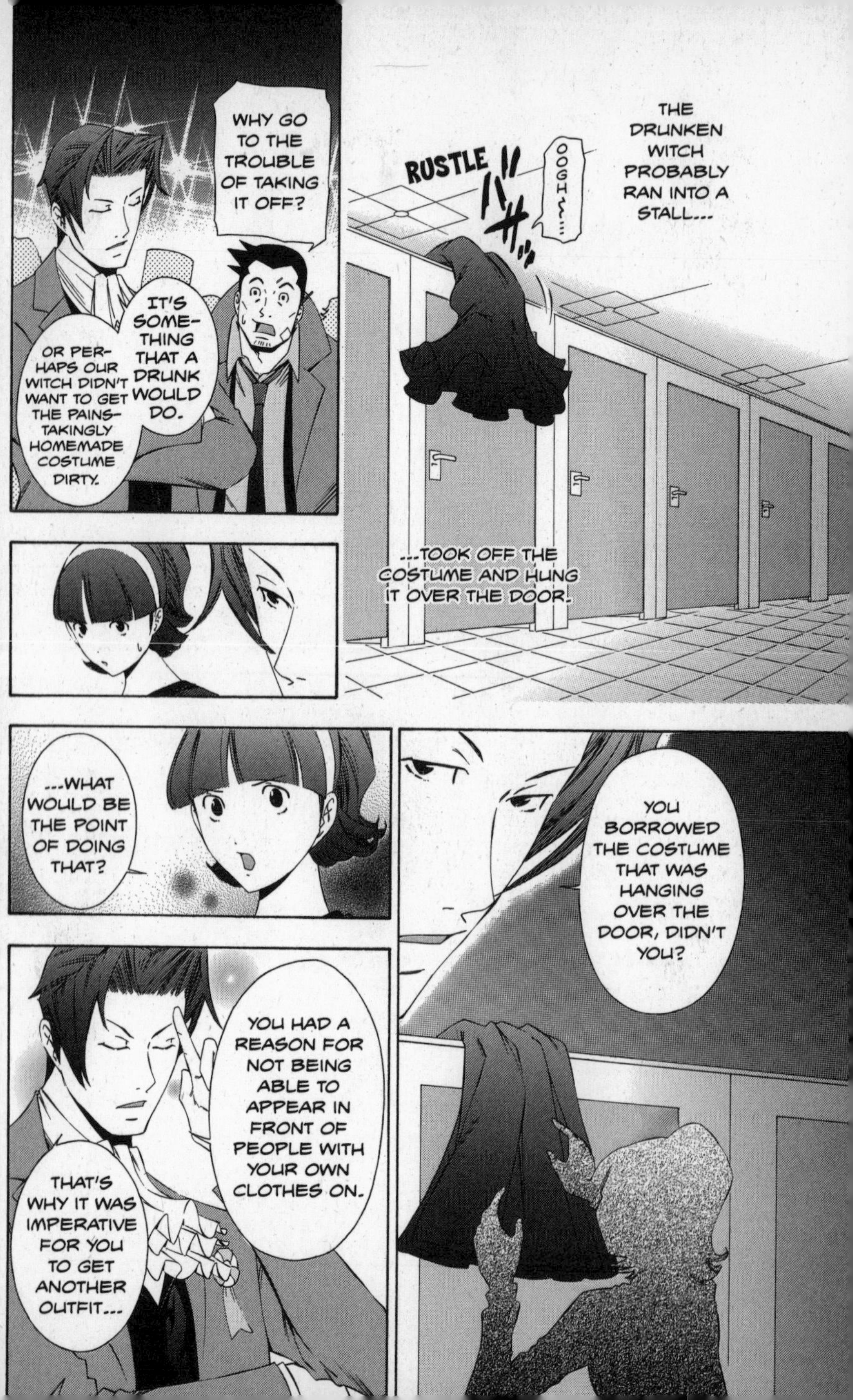
THE DRUNKEN WITCH PROBABLY RAN INTO A STALL...
RUSTLE
OOGH~...
...TOOK OFF THE COSTUME AND HUNG IT OVER THE DOOR.
WHY GO TO THE TROUBLE OF TAKING IT OFF?
IT'S SOMETHING THAT A DRUNK WOULD DO.
OR PERHAPS OUR WITCH DIDN'T WANT TO GET THE PAINSTAKINGLY HOMEMADE COSTUME DIRTY.
YOU BORROWED THE COSTUME THAT WAS HANGING OVER THE DOOR, DIDN'T YOU?
...WHAT WOULD BE THE POINT OF DOING THAT?
YOU HAD A REASON FOR NOT BEING ABLE TO APPEAR IN FRONT OF PEOPLE WITH YOUR OWN CLOTHES ON.
THAT'S WHY IT WAS IMPERATIVE FOR YOU TO GET ANOTHER OUTFIT...

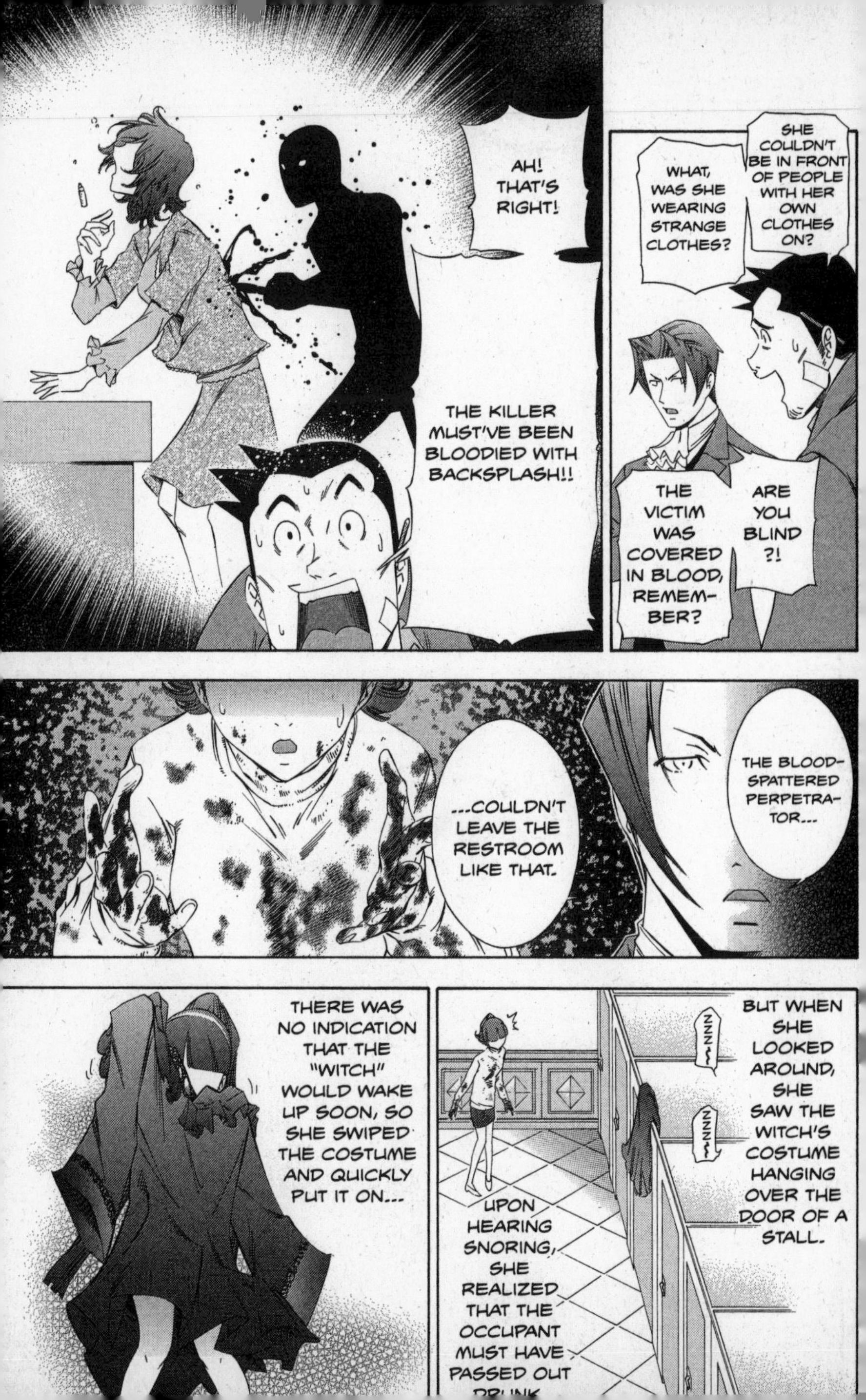

SHE COULDN'T BE IN FRONT OF PEOPLE WITH HER OWN CLOTHES ON?
WHAT, WAS SHE WEARING STRANGE CLOTHES?
ARE YOU BLIND ?!
THE VICTIM WAS COVERED IN BLOOD, REMEM-BER?
AH! THAT'S RIGHT!
THE KILLER MUST'VE BEEN BLOODIED WITH BACKSPLASH!!
THE BLOOD-SPATTERED PERPETRA-TOR...
...COULDN'T LEAVE THE RESTROOM LIKE THAT.
BUT WHEN SHE LOOKED AROUND, SHE SAW THE WITCH'S COSTUME HANGING OVER THE DOOR OF A STALL.
ZZZ~
ZZZ~
UPON HEARING SNORING, SHE REALIZED THAT THE OCCUPANT MUST HAVE PASSED OUT
THERE WAS NO INDICATION THAT THE "WITCH" WOULD WAKE UP SOON, SO SHE SWIPED THE COSTUME AND QUICKLY PUT IT ON...

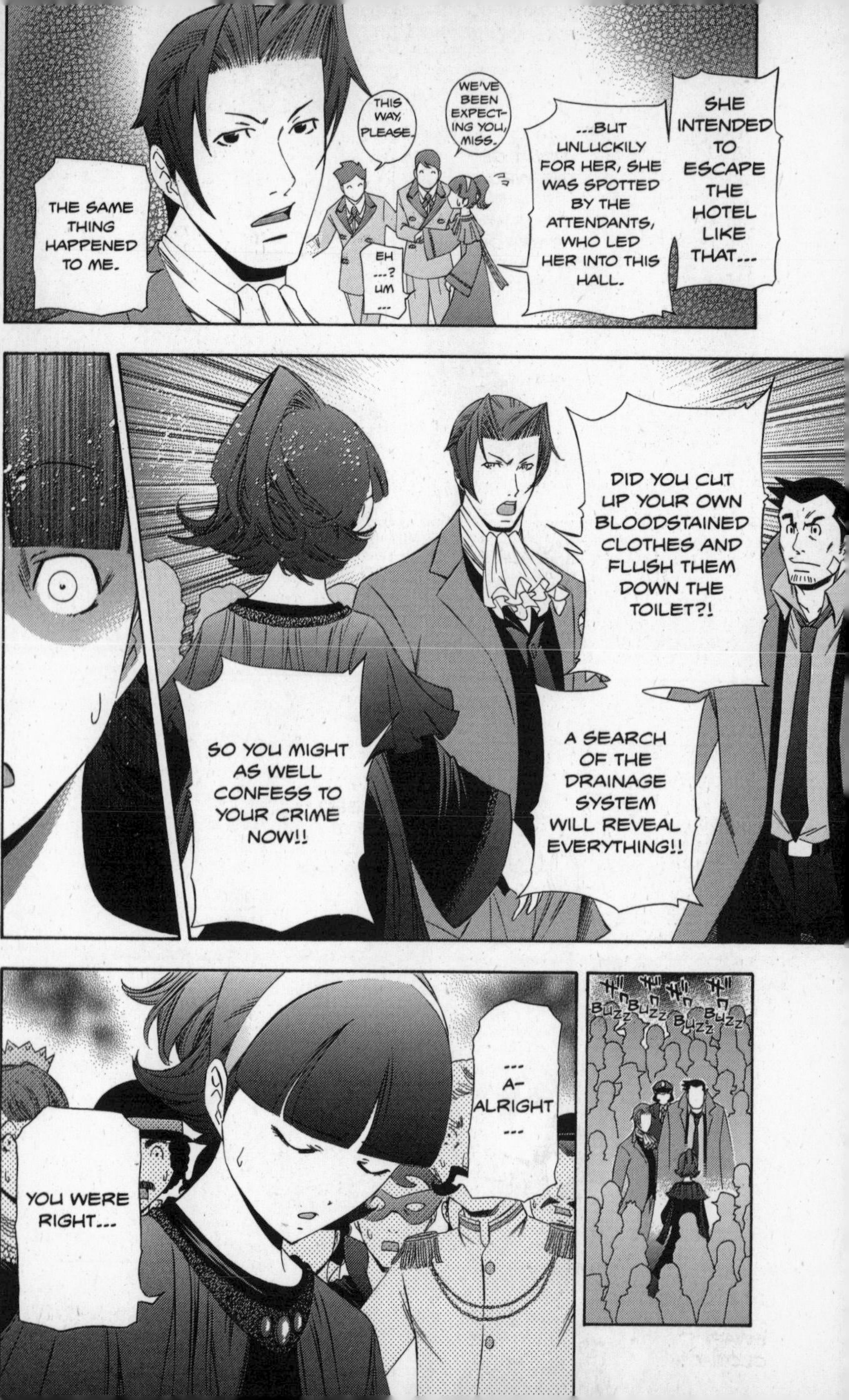
SHE INTENDED TO ESCAPE THE HOTEL LIKE THAT...
...BUT UNLUCKILY FOR HER, SHE WAS SPOTTED BY THE ATTENDANTS, WHO LED HER INTO THIS HALL.
WE'VE BEEN EXPECTING YOU, MISS.
THIS WAY, PLEASE.
EH ...? UM ...
THE SAME THING HAPPENED TO ME.
DID YOU CUT UP YOUR OWN BLOODSTAINED CLOTHES AND FLUSH THEM DOWN THE TOILET?!
A SEARCH OF THE DRAINAGE SYSTEM WILL REVEAL EVERYTHING!!
SO YOU MIGHT AS WELL CONFESS TO YOUR CRIME NOW!!
Buzz Buzz Buzz Buzz
... A-ALRIGHT ...
YOU WERE RIGHT...

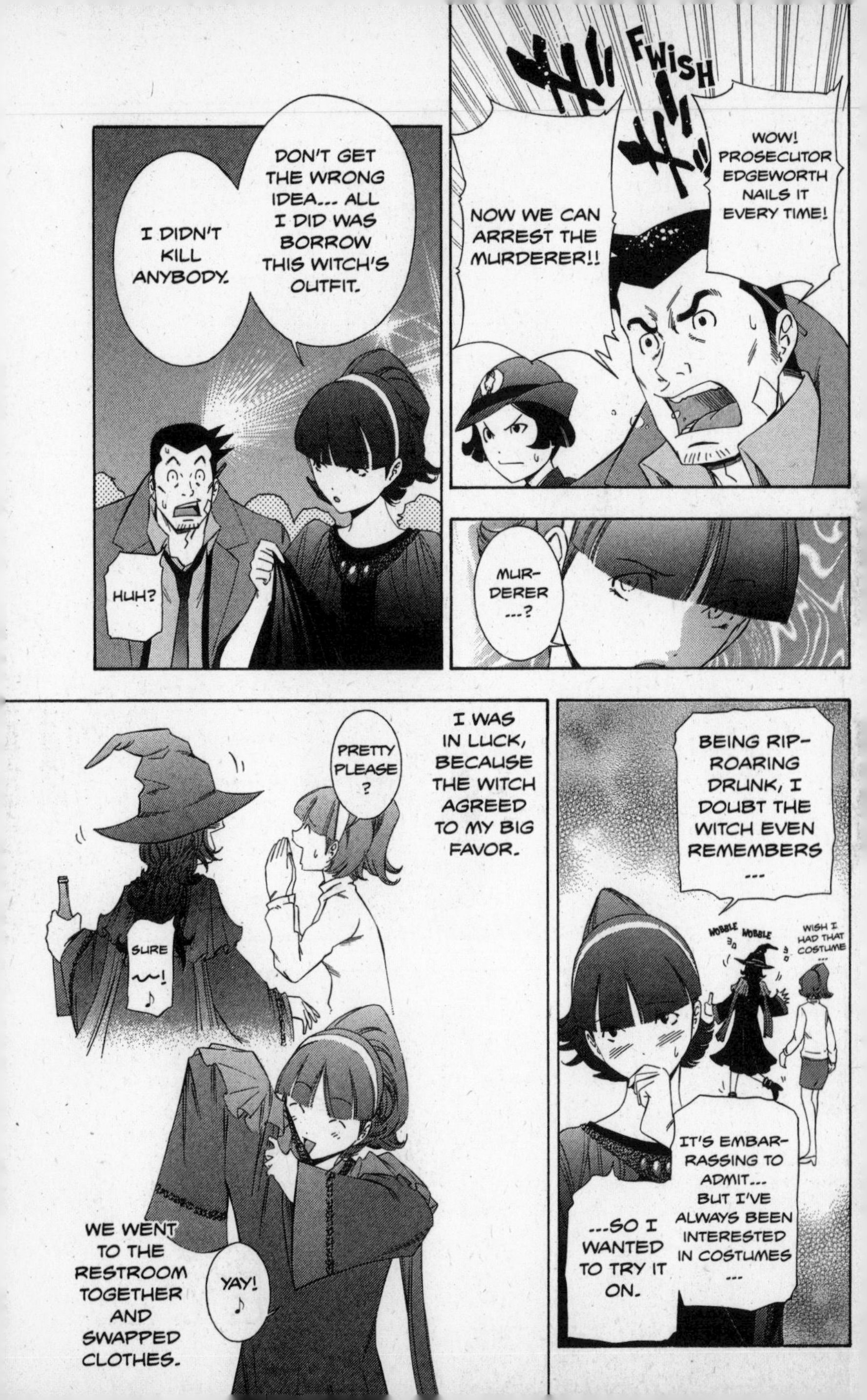
FWISH
WOW! PROSECUTOR EDGEWORTH NAILS IT EVERY TIME!
NOW WE CAN ARREST THE MURDERER!!
MUR-DERER...?
DON'T GET THE WRONG IDEA... ALL I DID WAS BORROW THIS WITCH'S OUTFIT.
I DIDN'T KILL ANYBODY.
HUH?
BEING RIP-ROARING DRUNK, I DOUBT THE WITCH EVEN REMEMBERS...
WISH I HAD THAT COSTUME...
WOBBLE WOBBLE
IT'S EMBAR-RASSING TO ADMIT... BUT I'VE ALWAYS BEEN INTERESTED IN COSTUMES...
...SO I WANTED TO TRY IT ON.
I WAS IN LUCK, BECAUSE THE WITCH AGREED TO MY BIG FAVOR.
PRETTY PLEASE?
SURE ~~! ♪
WE WENT TO THE RESTROOM TOGETHER AND SWAPPED CLOTHES.
YAY! ♪

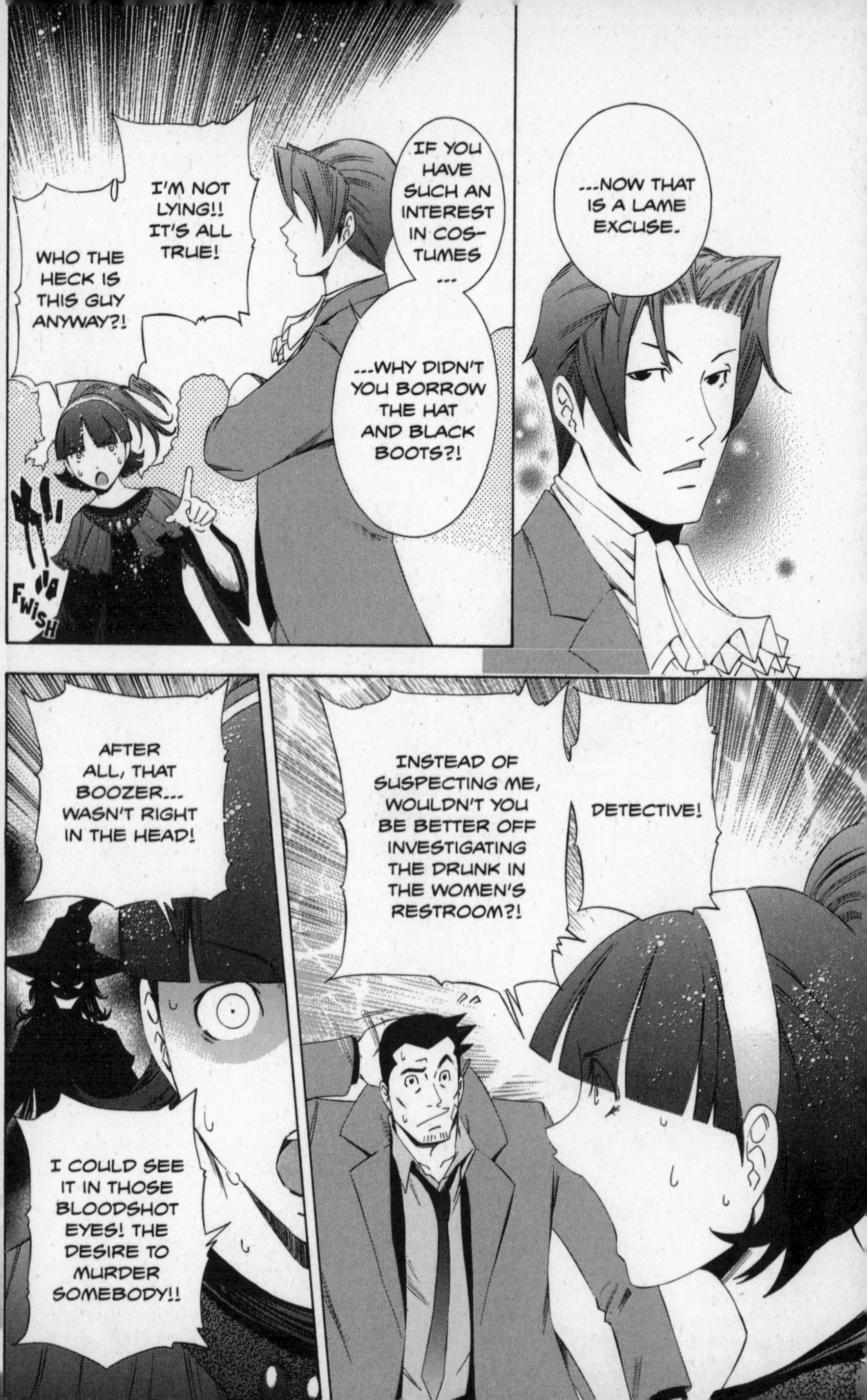
---NOW THAT IS A LAME EXCUSE.
IF YOU HAVE SUCH AN INTEREST IN COS-TUMES ---
---WHY DIDN'T YOU BORROW THE HAT AND BLACK BOOTS?!
I'M NOT LYING!! IT'S ALL TRUE!
WHO THE HECK IS THIS GUY ANYWAY?!
FWISH
DETECTIVE!
INSTEAD OF SUSPECTING ME, WOULDN'T YOU BE BETTER OFF INVESTIGATING THE DRUNK IN THE WOMEN'S RESTROOM?!
AFTER ALL, THAT BOOZER... WASN'T RIGHT IN THE HEAD!
I COULD SEE IT IN THOSE BLOODSHOT EYES! THE DESIRE TO MURDER SOMEBODY!!

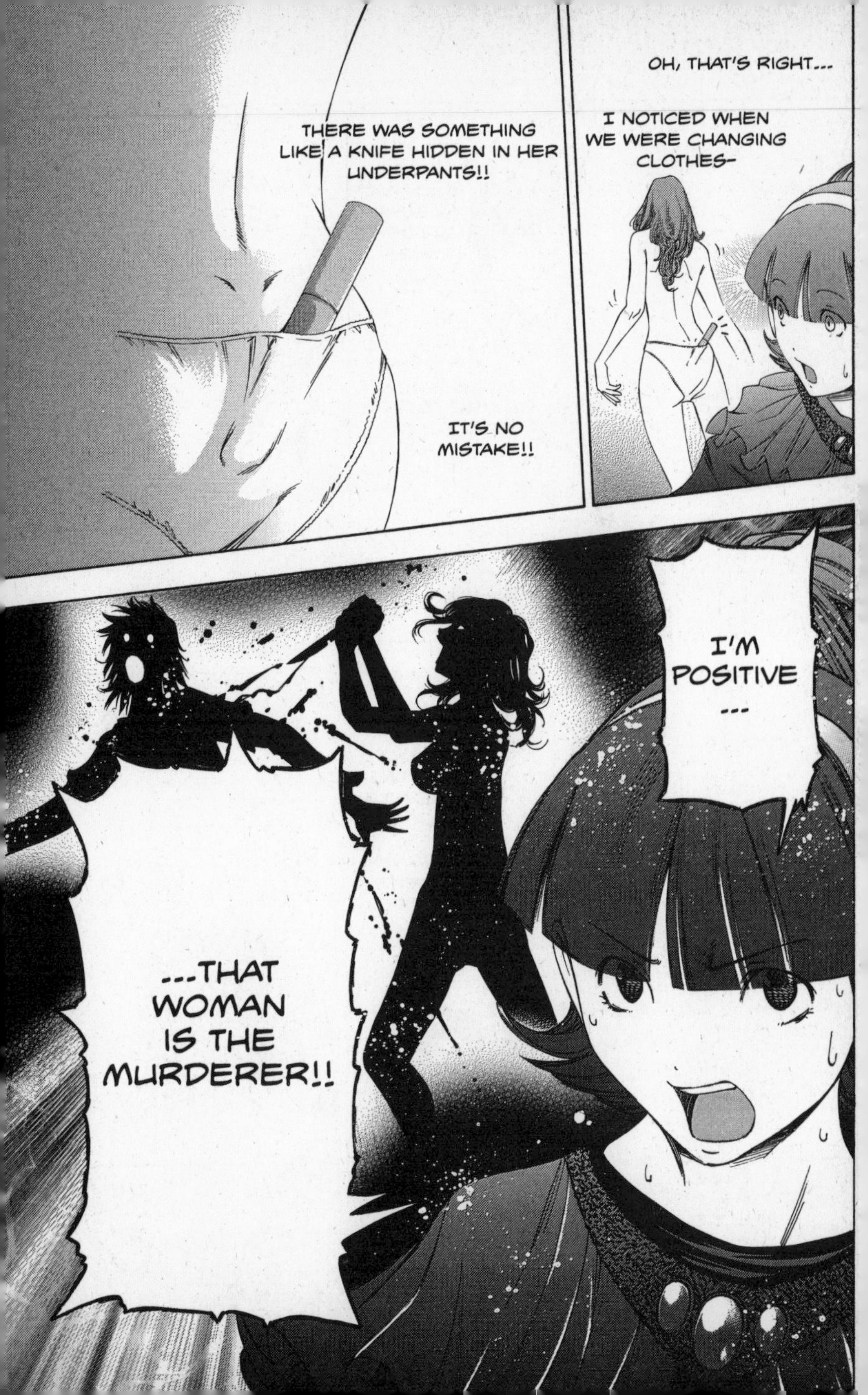
OH, THAT'S RIGHT...
I NOTICED WHEN WE WERE CHANGING CLOTHES-
THERE WAS SOMETHING LIKE A KNIFE HIDDEN IN HER UNDERPANTS!!
IT'S NO MISTAKE!!
I'M POSITIVE ---
---THAT WOMAN IS THE MURDERER!!

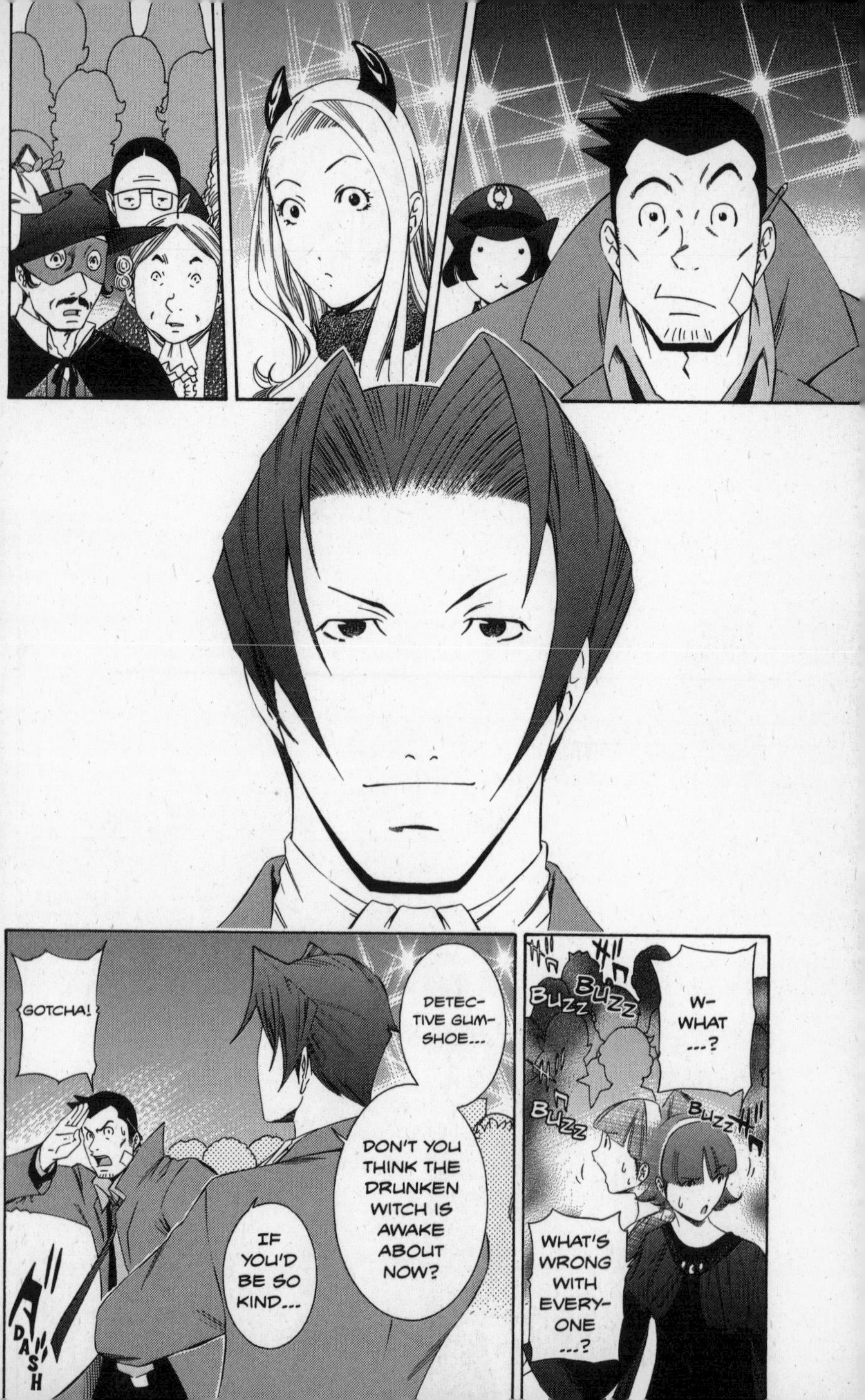
W-WHAT ...?
BUZZ BUZZ
BUZZ
BUZZ
WHAT'S WRONG WITH EVERYONE ...?
DETECTIVE GUMSHOE...
DON'T YOU THINK THE DRUNKEN WITCH IS AWAKE ABOUT NOW?
IF YOU'D BE SO KIND...
GOTCHA!
DASH

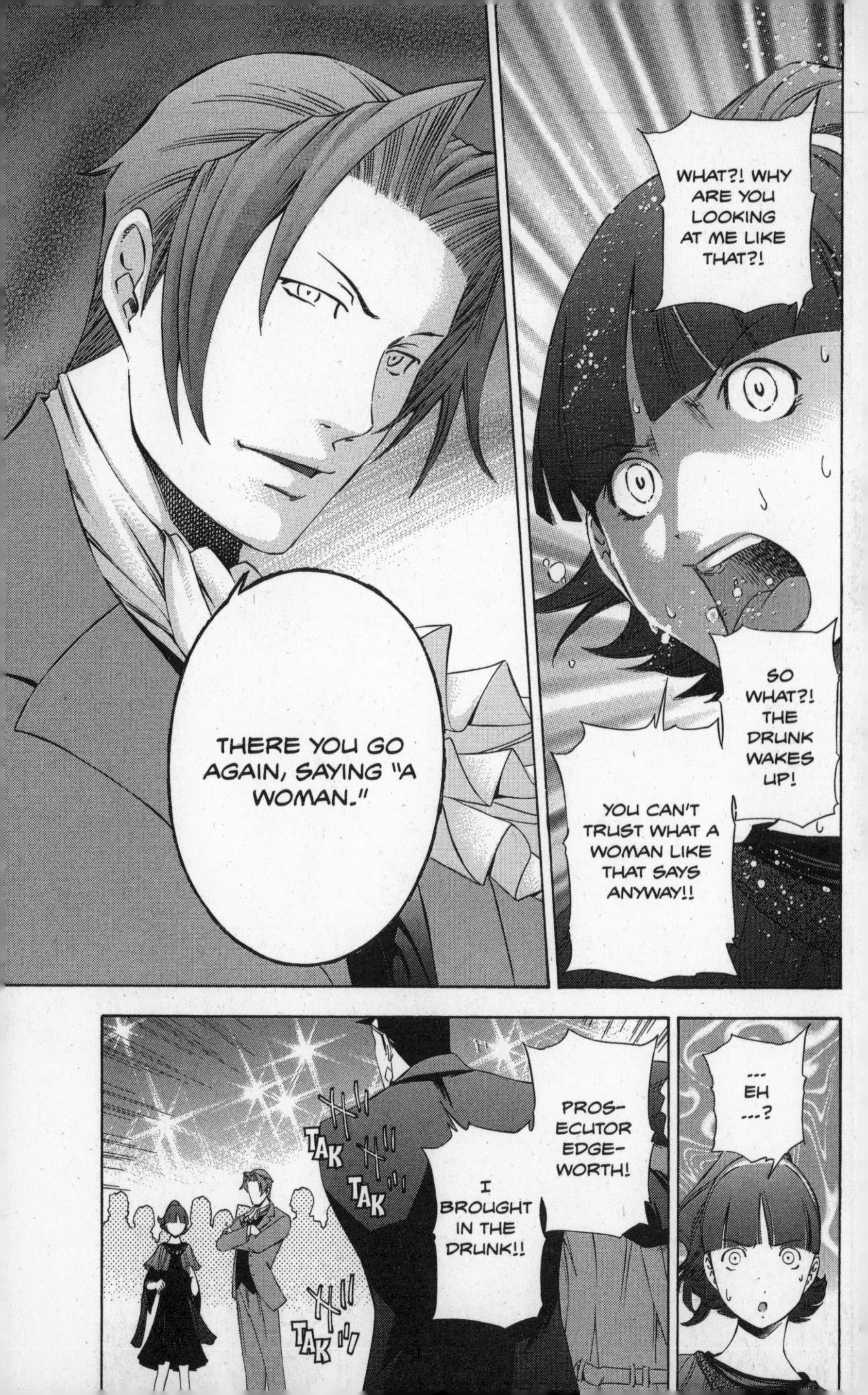
WHAT?! WHY ARE YOU LOOKING AT ME LIKE THAT?!
SO WHAT?! THE DRUNK WAKES UP!
YOU CAN'T TRUST WHAT A WOMAN LIKE THAT SAYS ANYWAY!!
THERE YOU GO AGAIN, SAYING "A WOMAN."
...EH...?
PROSECUTOR EDGEWORTH!
I BROUGHT IN THE DRUNK!!
TAK
TAK
TAK

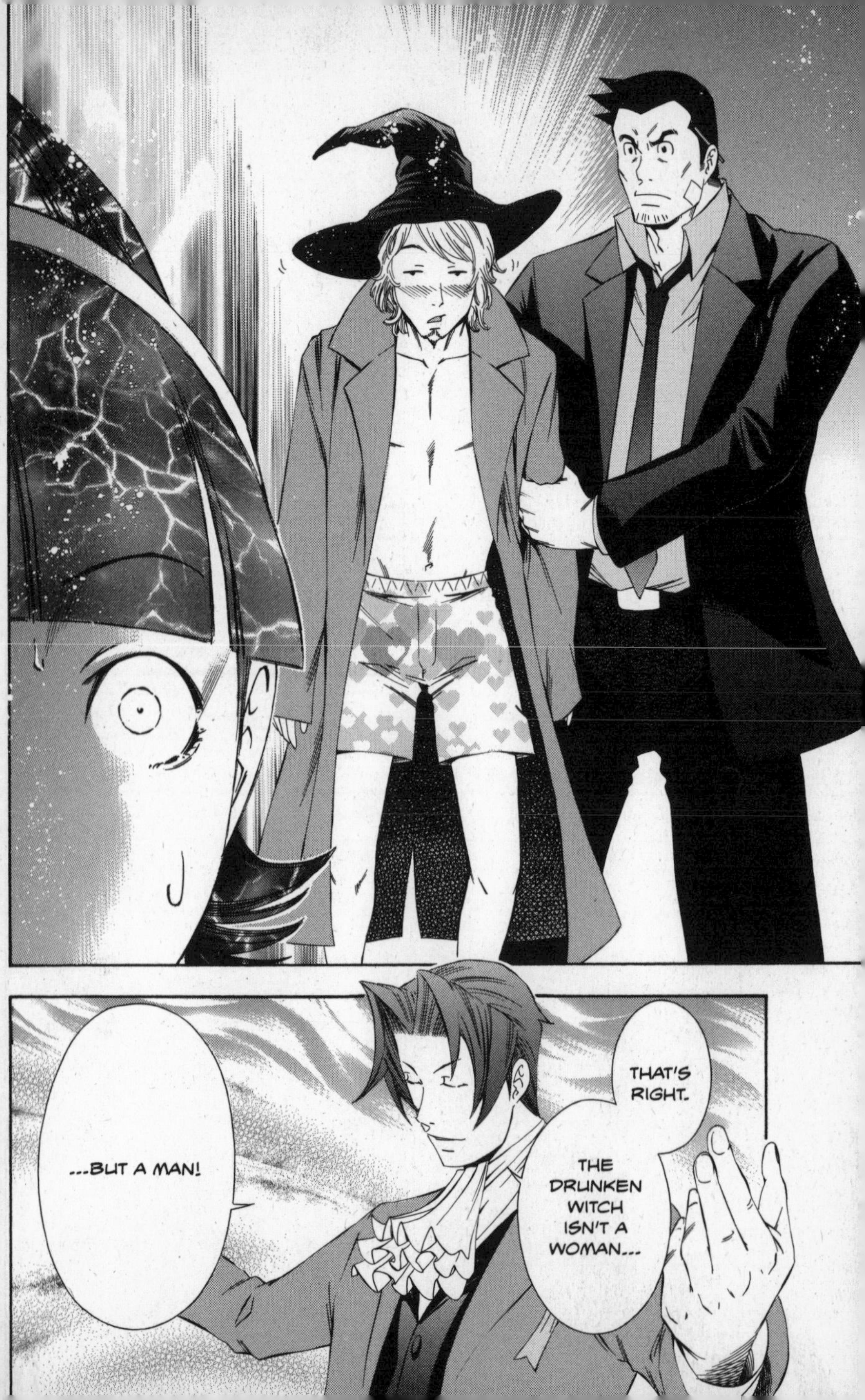
THAT'S RIGHT.
THE DRUNKEN WITCH ISN'T A WOMAN...
...BUT A MAN!

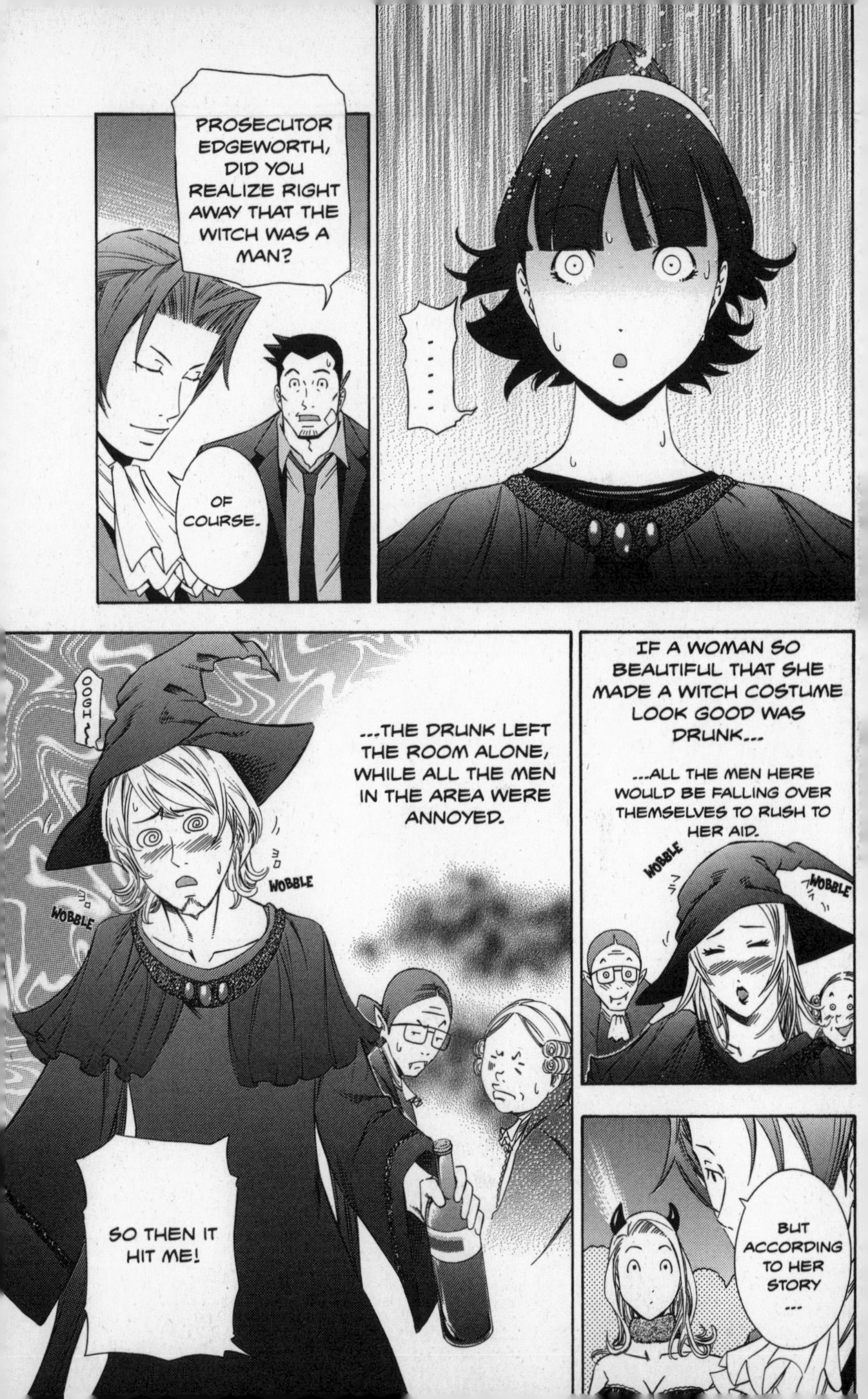
......
PROSECUTOR EDGEWORTH, DID YOU REALIZE RIGHT AWAY THAT THE WITCH WAS A MAN?
OF COURSE.
IF A WOMAN SO BEAUTIFUL THAT SHE MADE A WITCH COSTUME LOOK GOOD WAS DRUNK...
...ALL THE MEN HERE WOULD BE FALLING OVER THEMSELVES TO RUSH TO HER AID.
WOBBLE
WOBBLE
BUT ACCORDING TO HER STORY ...
...THE DRUNK LEFT THE ROOM ALONE, WHILE ALL THE MEN IN THE AREA WERE ANNOYED.
OOGH~
WOBBLE
WOBBLE
SO THEN IT HIT ME!

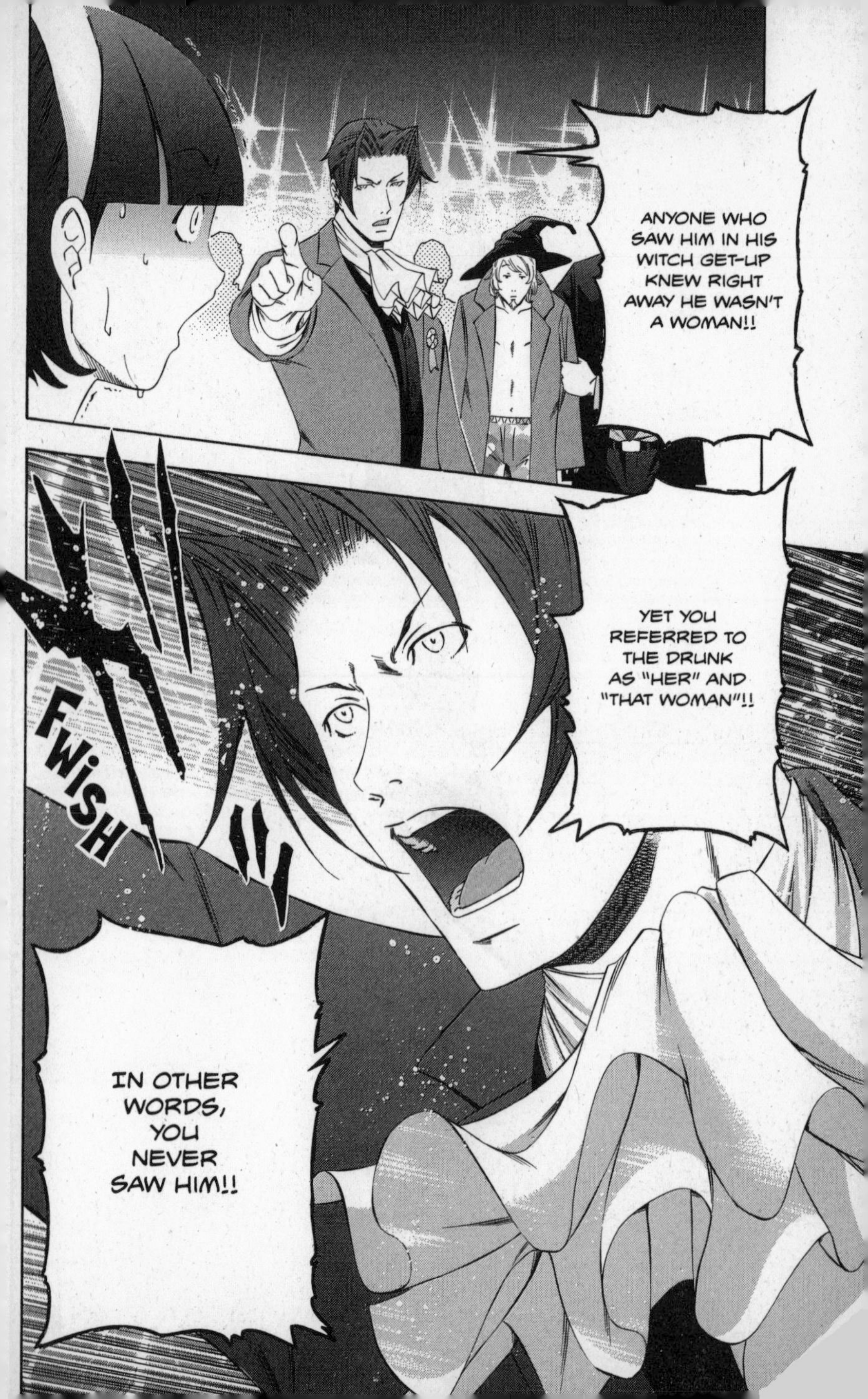
ANYONE WHO SAW HIM IN HIS WITCH GET-UP KNEW RIGHT AWAY HE WASN'T A WOMAN!!
YET YOU REFERRED TO THE DRUNK AS "HER" AND "THAT WOMAN"!!
FWISH
IN OTHER WORDS, YOU NEVER SAW HIM!!

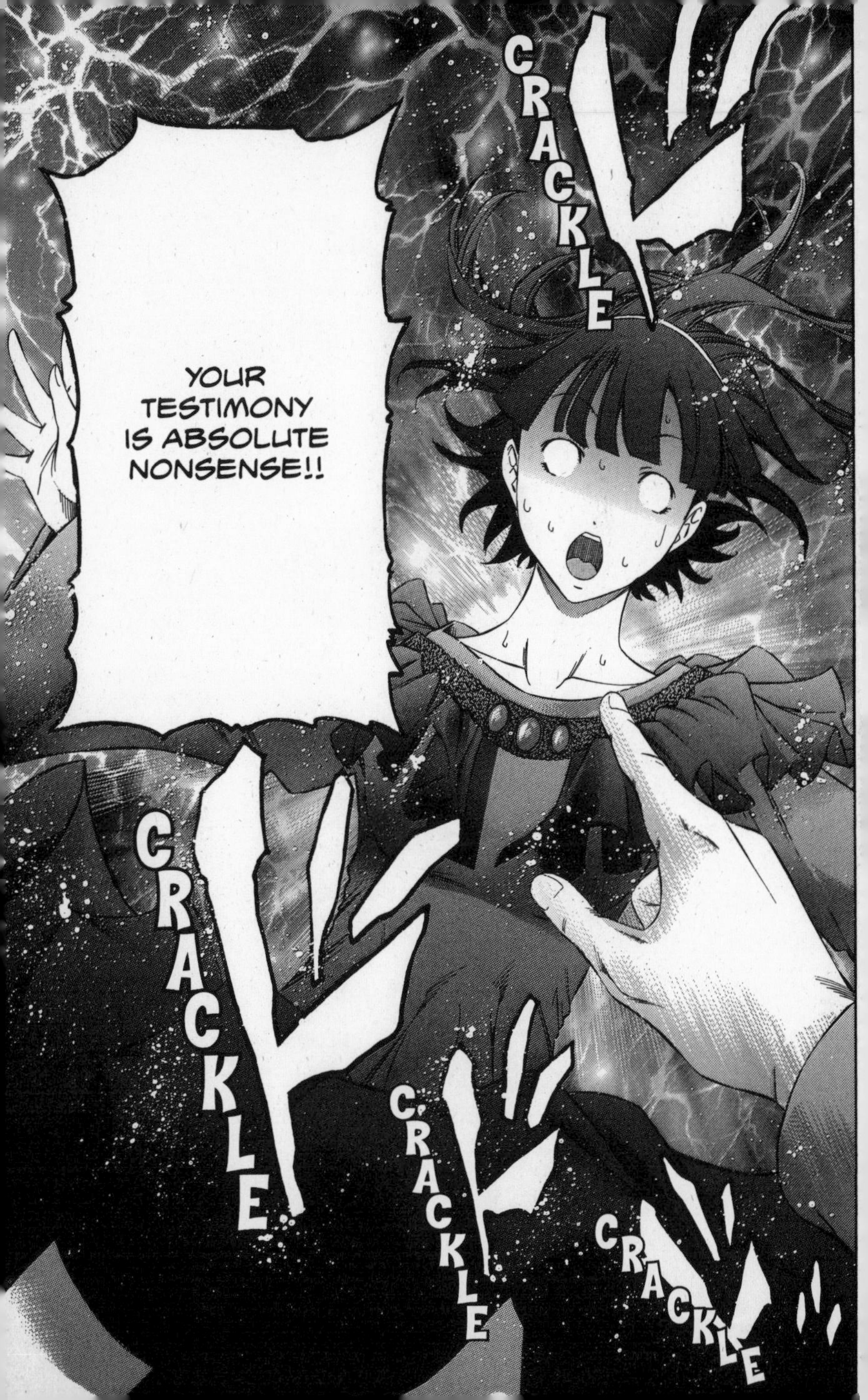
CRACKLE
YOUR TESTIMONY IS ABSOLUTE NONSENSE!!
CRACKLE
CRACKLE
CRACKLE

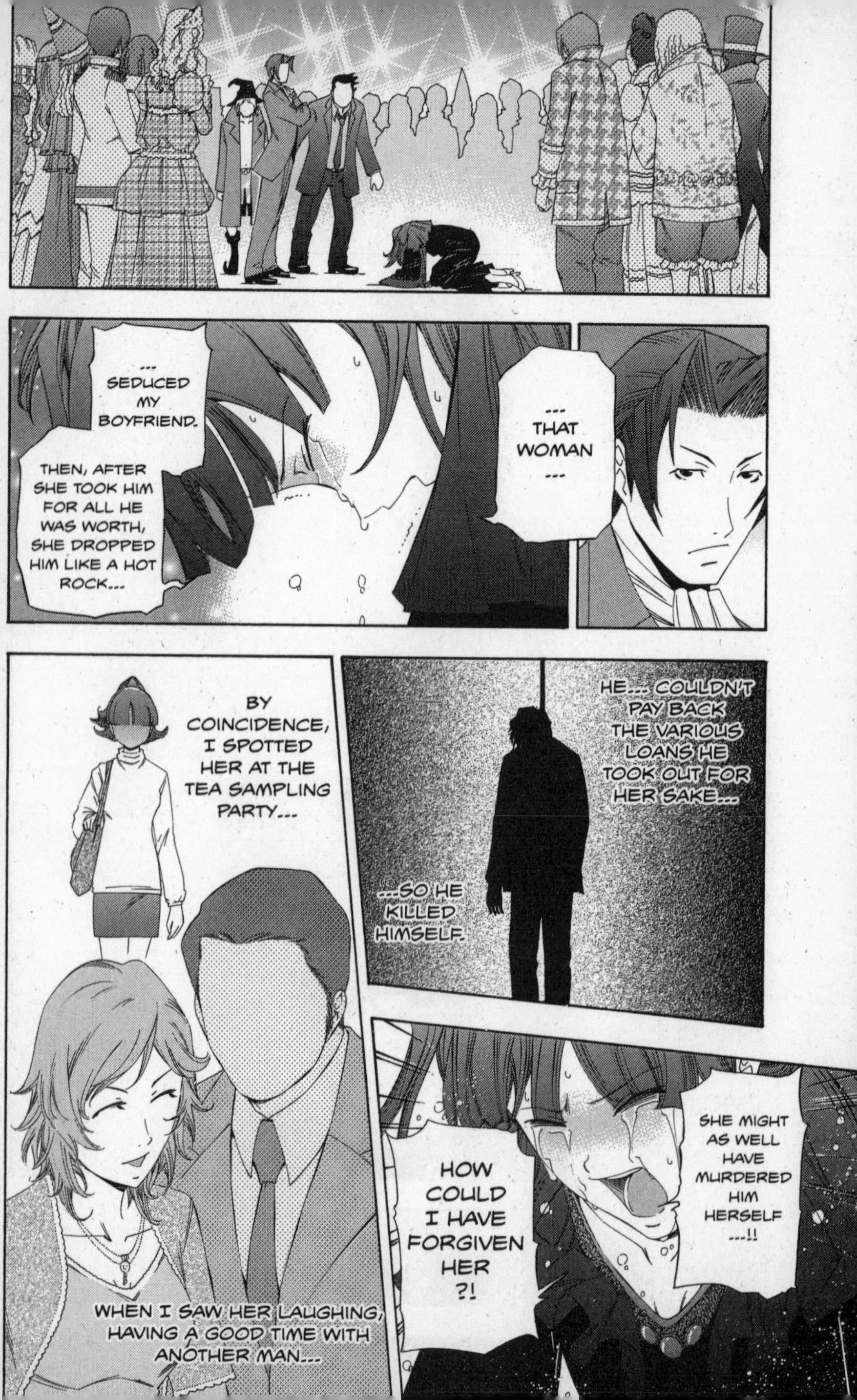
--- THAT WOMAN ---
--- SEDUCED MY BOYFRIEND.
THEN, AFTER SHE TOOK HIM FOR ALL HE WAS WORTH, SHE DROPPED HIM LIKE A HOT ROCK...
HE... COULDN'T PAY BACK THE VARIOUS LOANS HE TOOK OUT FOR HER SAKE...
...SO HE KILLED HIMSELF.
SHE MIGHT AS WELL HAVE MURDERED HIM HERSELF ---!!
HOW COULD I HAVE FORGIVEN HER ?!
BY COINCIDENCE, I SPOTTED HER AT THE TEA SAMPLING PARTY...
WHEN I SAW HER LAUGHING, HAVING A GOOD TIME WITH ANOTHER MAN...

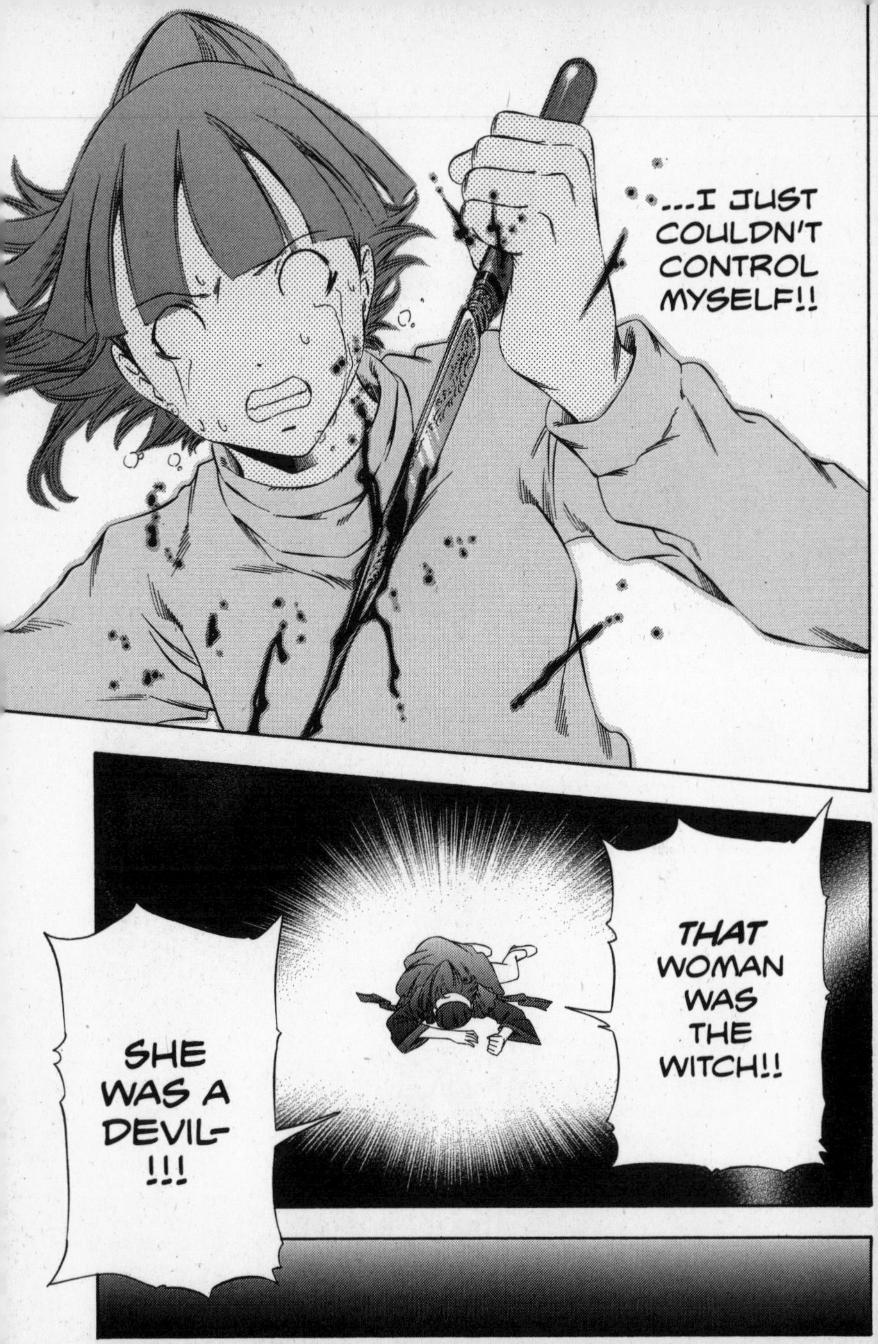
...I JUST COULDN'T CONTROL MYSELF!!
THAT WOMAN WAS THE WITCH!!
SHE WAS A DEVIL-!!!

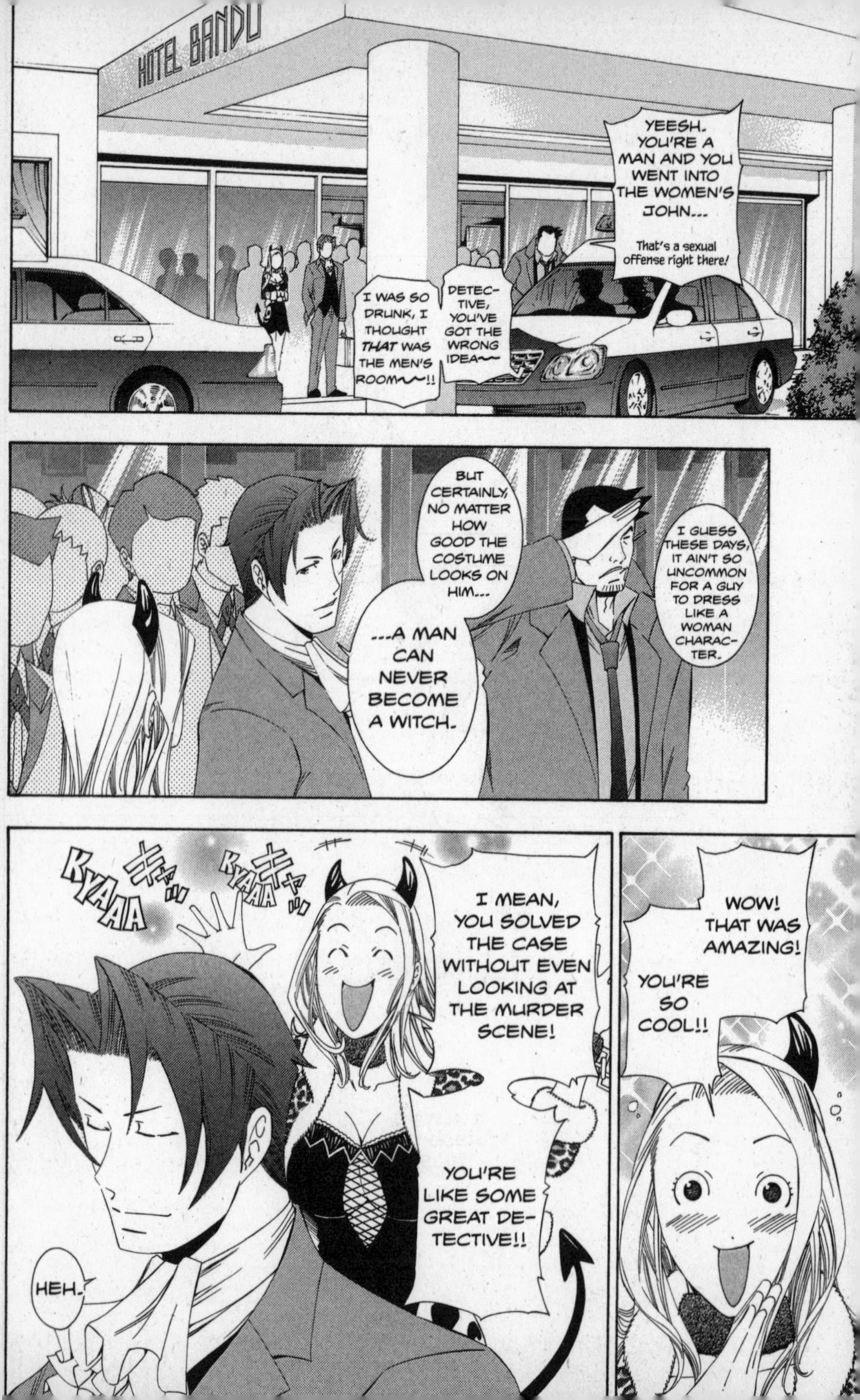
HOTEL BANDU
YEESH. YOU'RE A MAN AND YOU WENT INTO THE WOMEN'S JOHN...
That's a sexual offense right there!
DETECTIVE, YOU'VE GOT THE WRONG IDEA~~
I WAS SO DRUNK, I THOUGHT *THAT* WAS THE MEN'S ROOM~~!!
I GUESS THESE DAYS, IT AIN'T SO UNCOMMON FOR A GUY TO DRESS LIKE A WOMAN CHARACTER.
BUT CERTAINLY, NO MATTER HOW GOOD THE COSTUME LOOKS ON HIM...
...A MAN CAN NEVER BECOME A WITCH.
WOW! THAT WAS AMAZING!
YOU'RE SO COOL!!
I MEAN, YOU SOLVED THE CASE WITHOUT EVEN LOOKING AT THE MURDER SCENE!
KYAAA
KYAAA
YOU'RE LIKE SOME GREAT DETECTIVE!!
HEH.

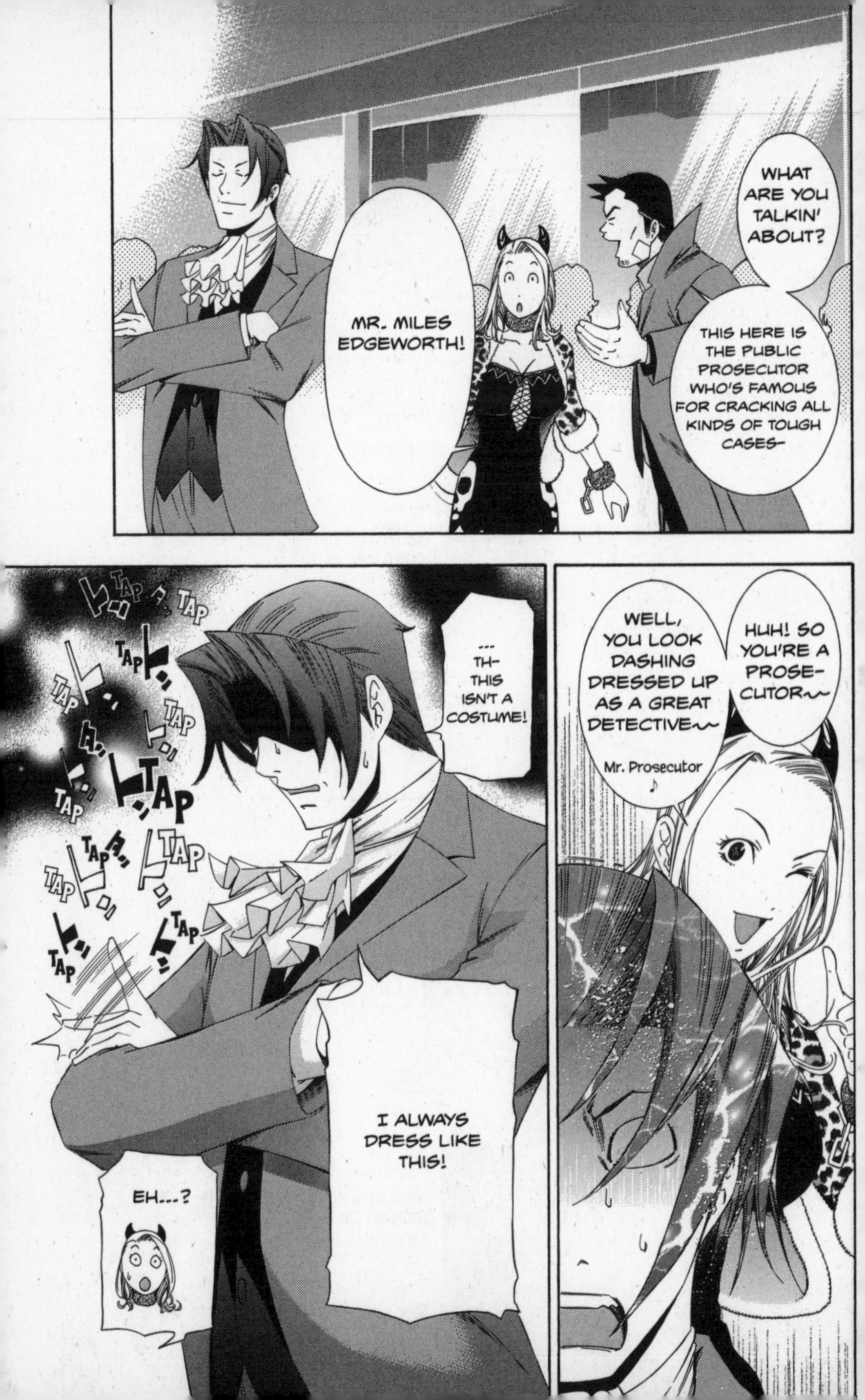
WHAT ARE YOU TALKIN' ABOUT?
THIS HERE IS THE PUBLIC PROSECUTOR WHO'S FAMOUS FOR CRACKING ALL KINDS OF TOUGH CASES—
MR. MILES EDGEWORTH!
HUH! SO YOU'RE A PROSE-CUTOR~~
WELL, YOU LOOK DASHING DRESSED UP AS A GREAT DETECTIVE~~
Mr. Prosecutor ♪
...TH-THIS ISN'T A COSTUME!
I ALWAYS DRESS LIKE THIS!
TAP TAP TAP TAP TAP TAP TAP TAP TAP TAP TAP TAP
EH...?

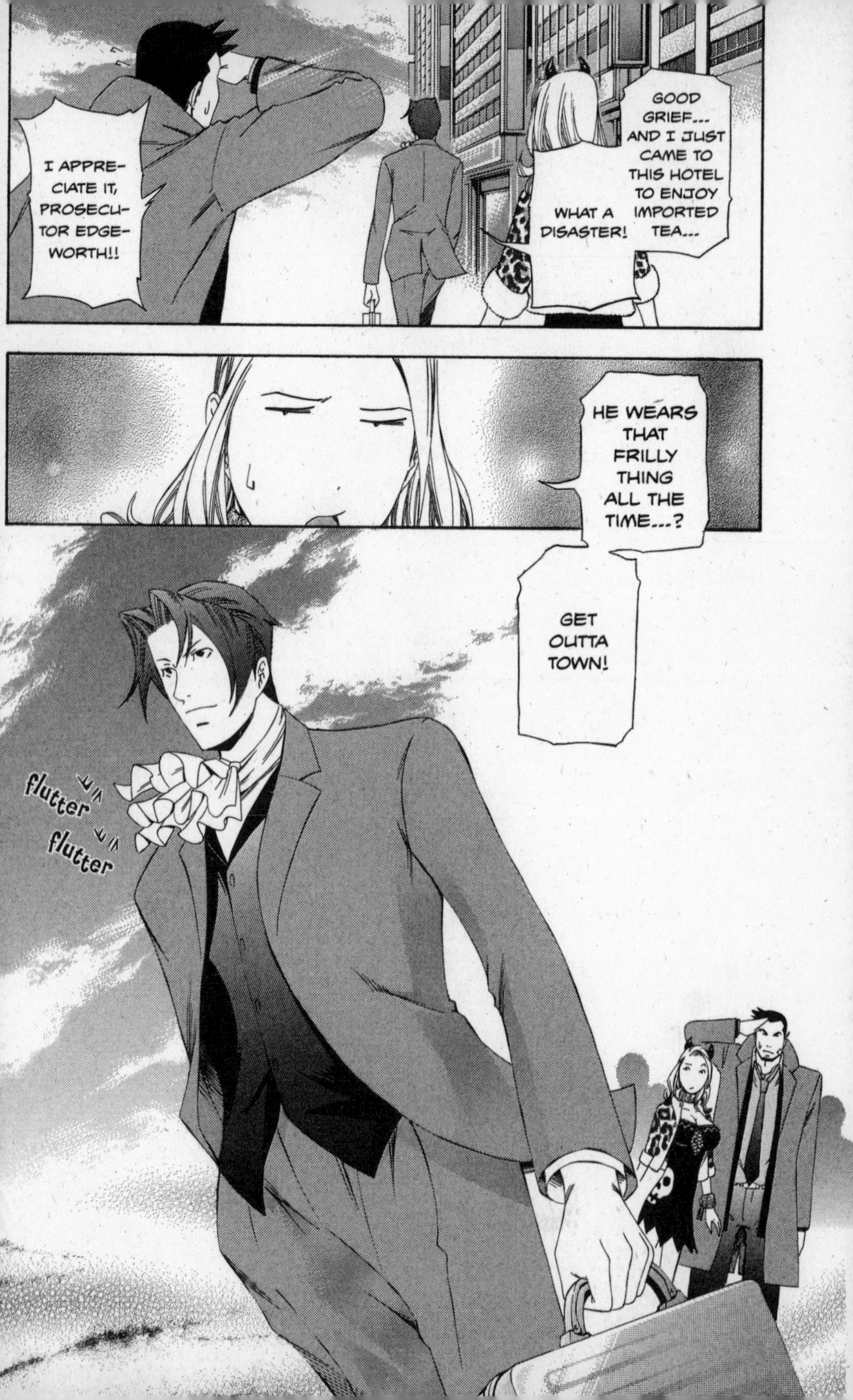
GOOD GRIEF... AND I JUST CAME TO THIS HOTEL TO ENJOY IMPORTED TEA...
WHAT A DISASTER!
I APPRECIATE IT, PROSECUTOR EDGEWORTH!!
HE WEARS THAT FRILLY THING ALL THE TIME...?
GET OUTTA TOWN!
flutter flutter

Ace Miles Edgewort
Attorney
INVESTIGATIONS™

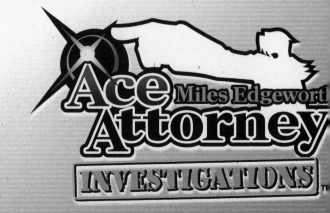

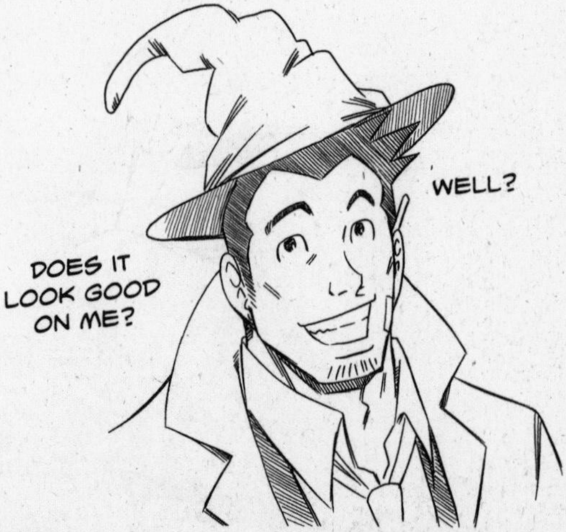
WELL?
DOES IT LOOK GOOD ON ME?

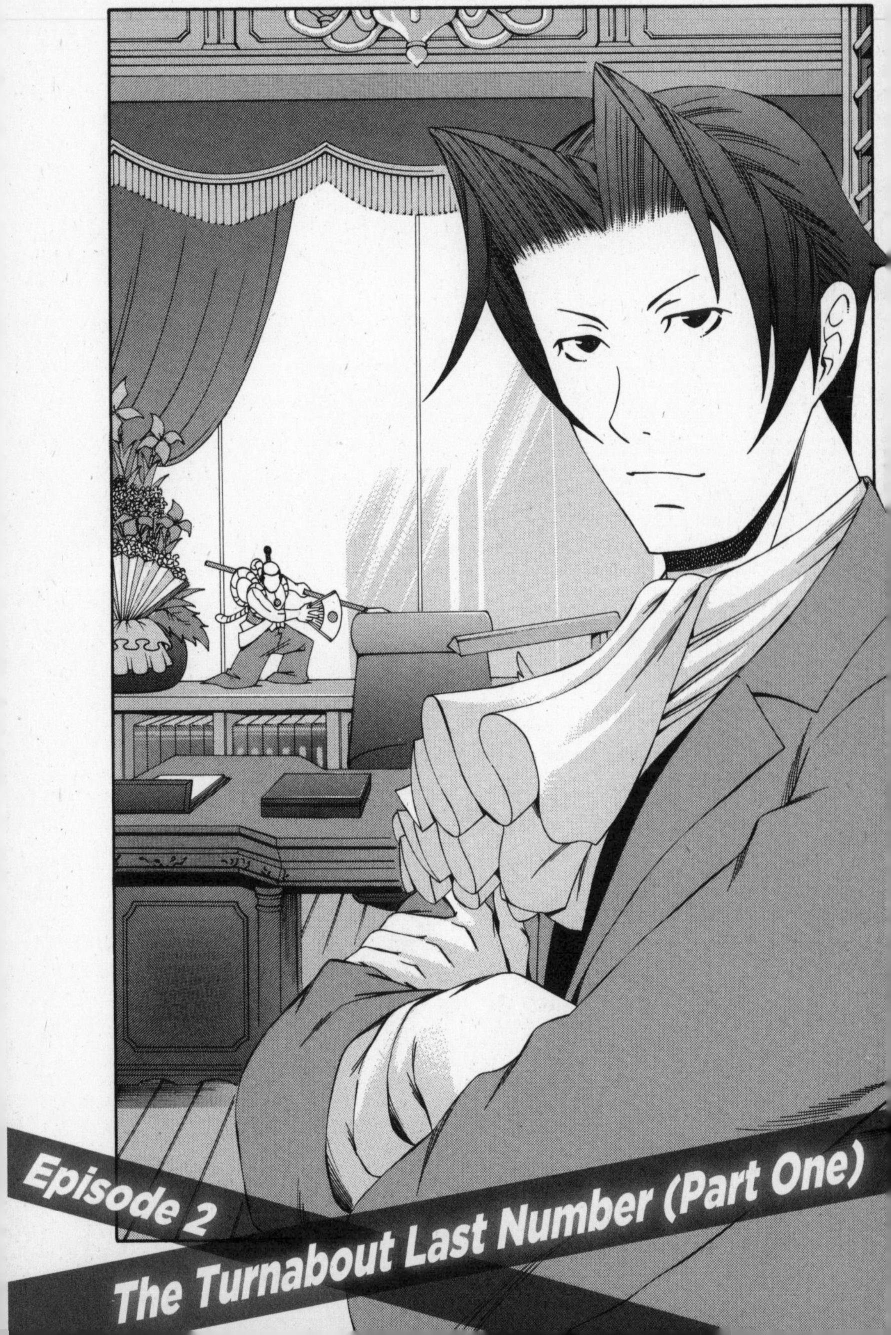
Episode 2
The Turnabout Last Number (Part One)

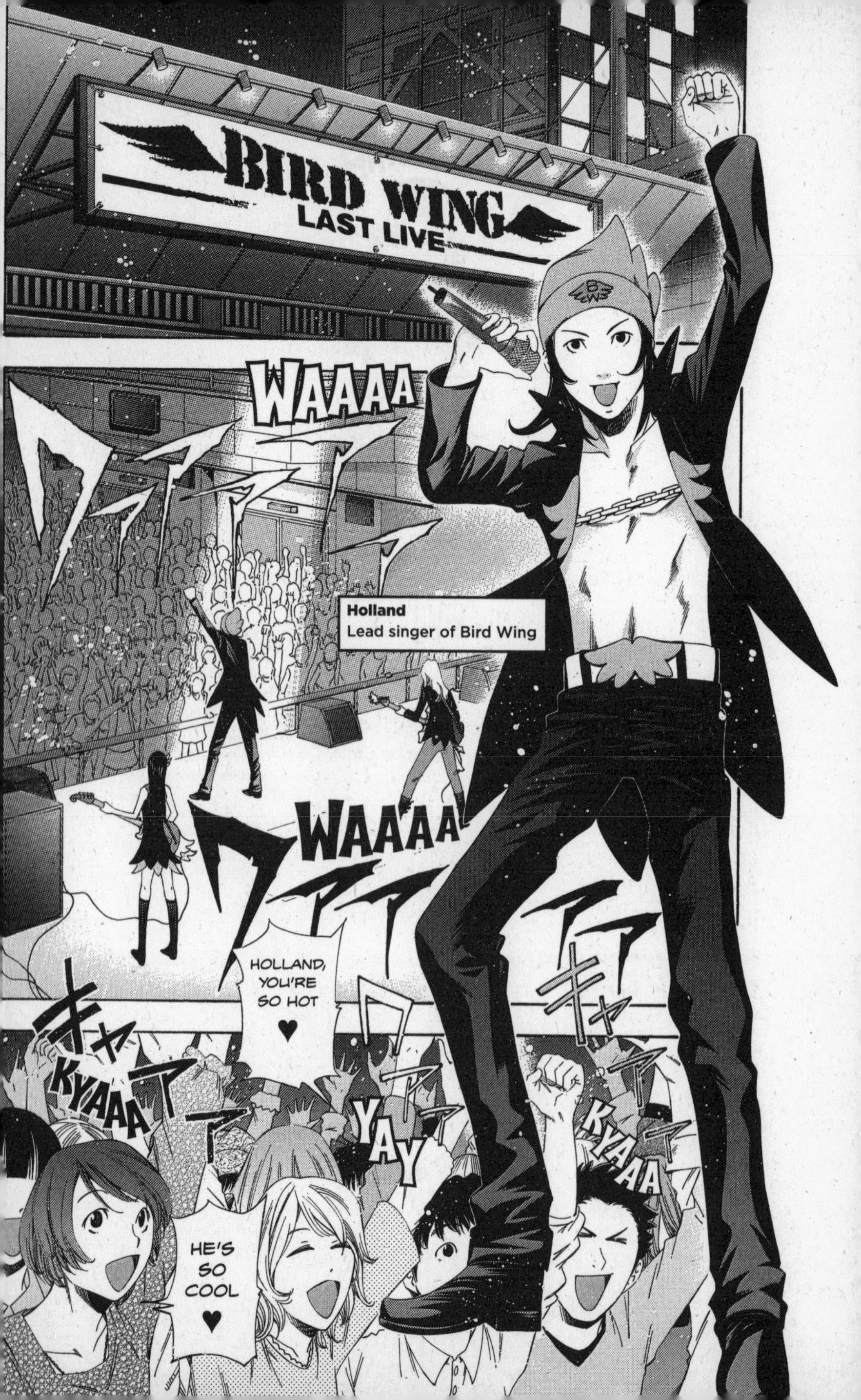
BIRD WING
LAST LIVE
WAAAA
Holland
Lead singer of Bird Wing
WAAAA
KYAAA
HOLLAND, YOU'RE SO HOT ♥
YAY
KYAAA
HE'S SO COOL ♥

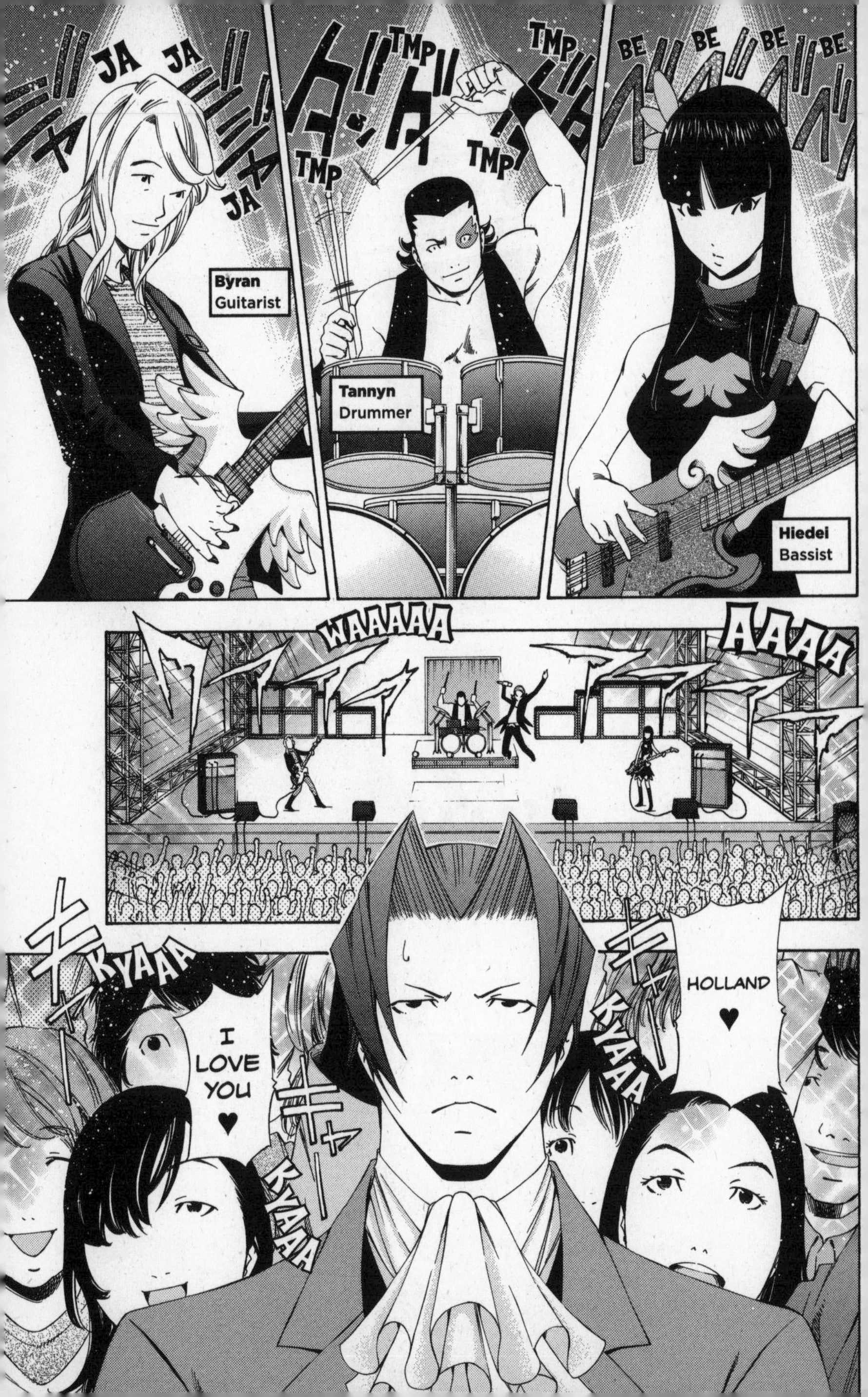
BE BE BE BE
Hiedei
Bassist
TMP TMP TMP TMP
Tannyn
Drummer
JA JA JA
Byran
Guitarist
AAAA
WAAAAA
KYAAA
HOLLAND ♥
KYAAA
I LOVE YOU ♥
KYAAA

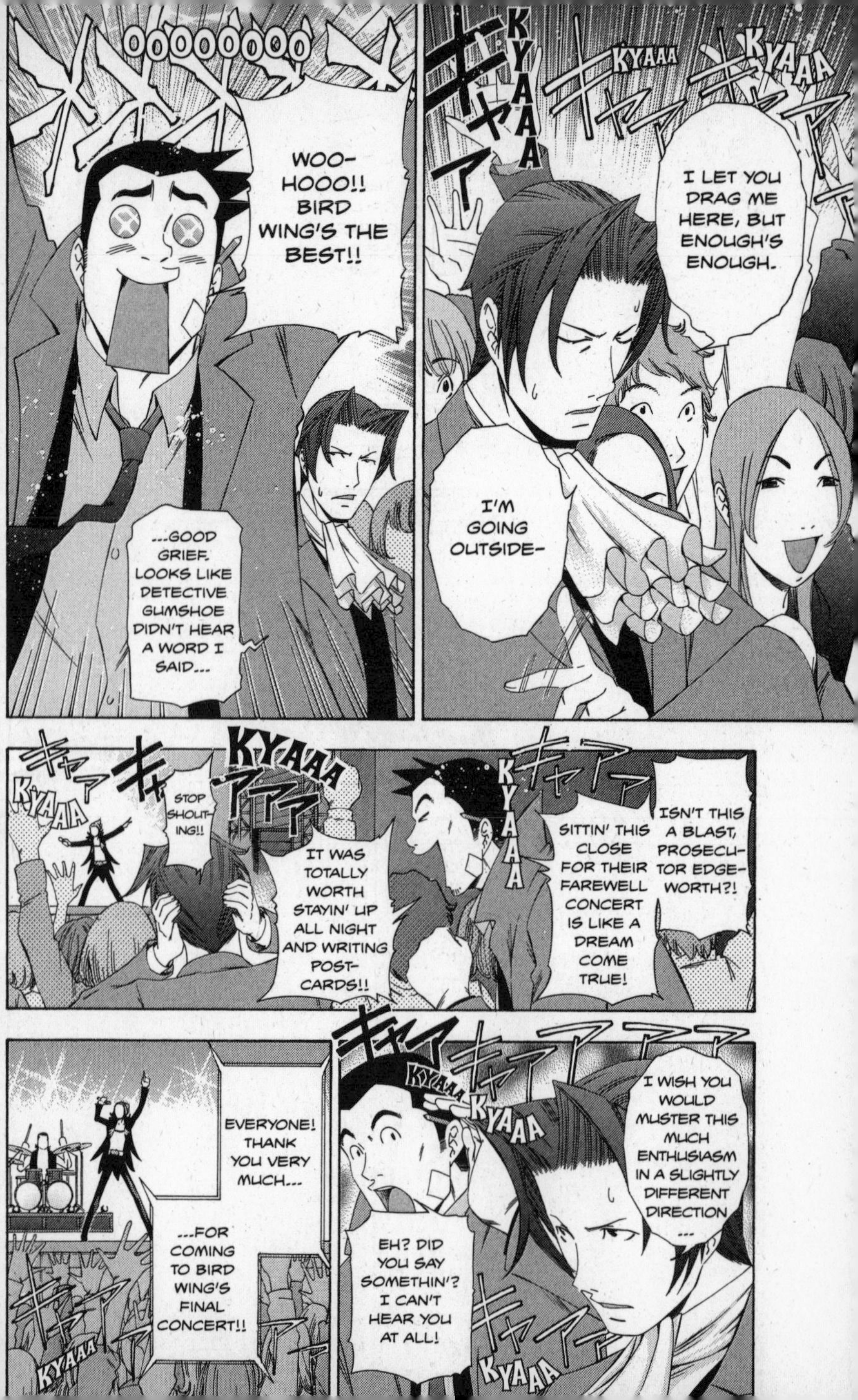
KYAAA
KYAAA
KYAAA
KYAAA
I LET YOU DRAG ME HERE, BUT ENOUGH'S ENOUGH.
I'M GOING OUTSIDE-
OOOOOOOOO
WOO-HOOO!! BIRD WING'S THE BEST!!
...GOOD GRIEF. LOOKS LIKE DETECTIVE GUMSHOE DIDN'T HEAR A WORD I SAID...
KYAAA
ISN'T THIS A BLAST, PROSECUTOR EDGEWORTH?!
SITTIN' THIS CLOSE FOR THEIR FAREWELL CONCERT IS LIKE A DREAM COME TRUE!
IT WAS TOTALLY WORTH STAYIN' UP ALL NIGHT AND WRITING POSTCARDS!!
KYAAA
STOP SHOUTING!!
KYAAA
KYAAA
KYAAA
I WISH YOU WOULD MUSTER THIS MUCH ENTHUSIASM IN A SLIGHTLY DIFFERENT DIRECTION...
EH? DID YOU SAY SOMETHIN'? I CAN'T HEAR YOU AT ALL!
KYAAA
EVERYONE! THANK YOU VERY MUCH...
...FOR COMING TO BIRD WING'S FINAL CONCERT!!
KYAAA

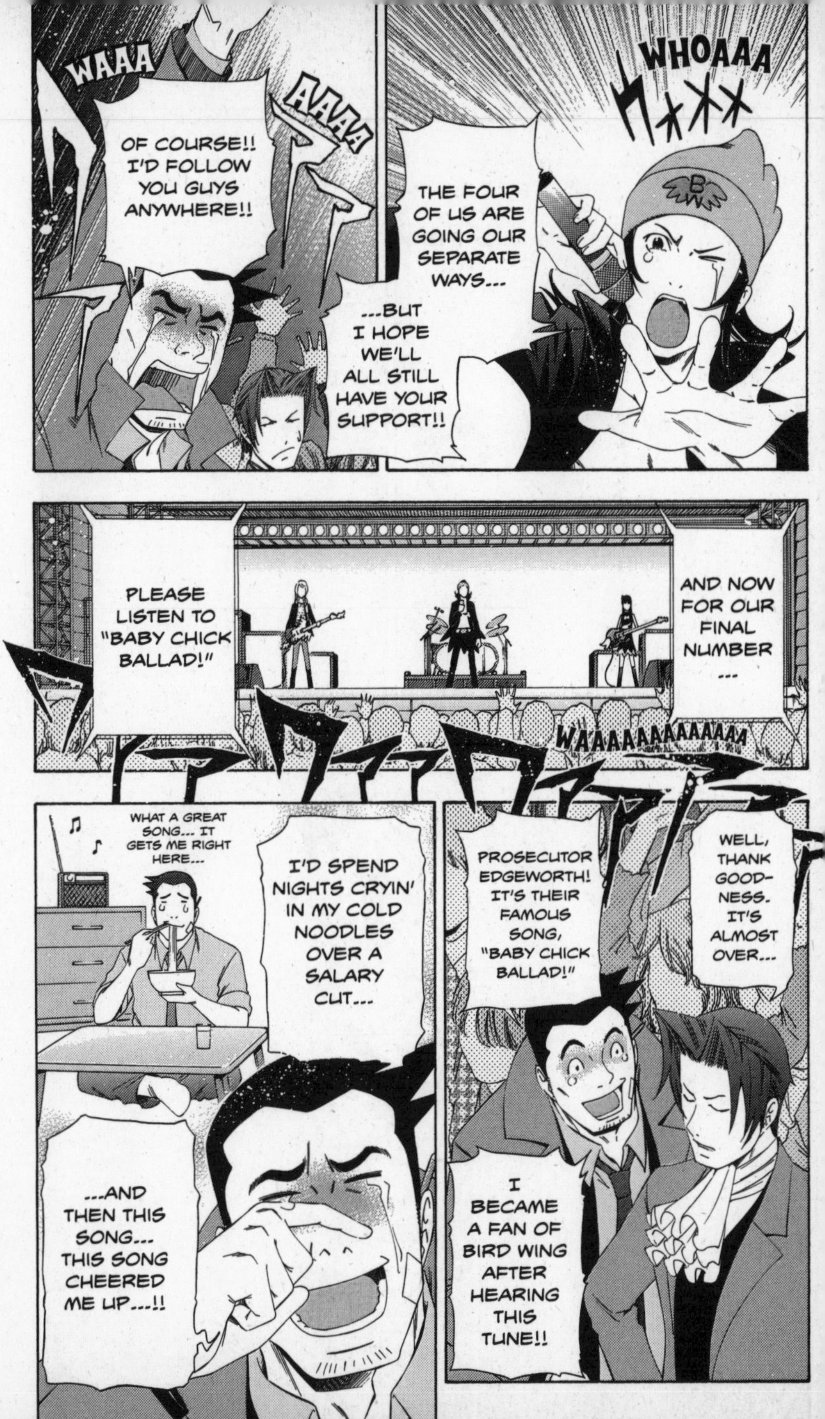
WHOAAA
THE FOUR OF US ARE GOING OUR SEPARATE WAYS...
...BUT I HOPE WE'LL ALL STILL HAVE YOUR SUPPORT!!
WAAA
AAAA
OF COURSE!! I'D FOLLOW YOU GUYS ANYWHERE!!
AND NOW FOR OUR FINAL NUMBER ...
PLEASE LISTEN TO "BABY CHICK BALLAD!"
WAAAAAAAAAAAA
WELL, THANK GOOD-NESS. IT'S ALMOST OVER...
PROSECUTOR EDGEWORTH! IT'S THEIR FAMOUS SONG, "BABY CHICK BALLAD!"
I BECAME A FAN OF BIRD WING AFTER HEARING THIS TUNE!!
I'D SPEND NIGHTS CRYIN' IN MY COLD NOODLES OVER A SALARY CUT...
WHAT A GREAT SONG... IT GETS ME RIGHT HERE...
...AND THEN THIS SONG... THIS SONG CHEERED ME UP...!!

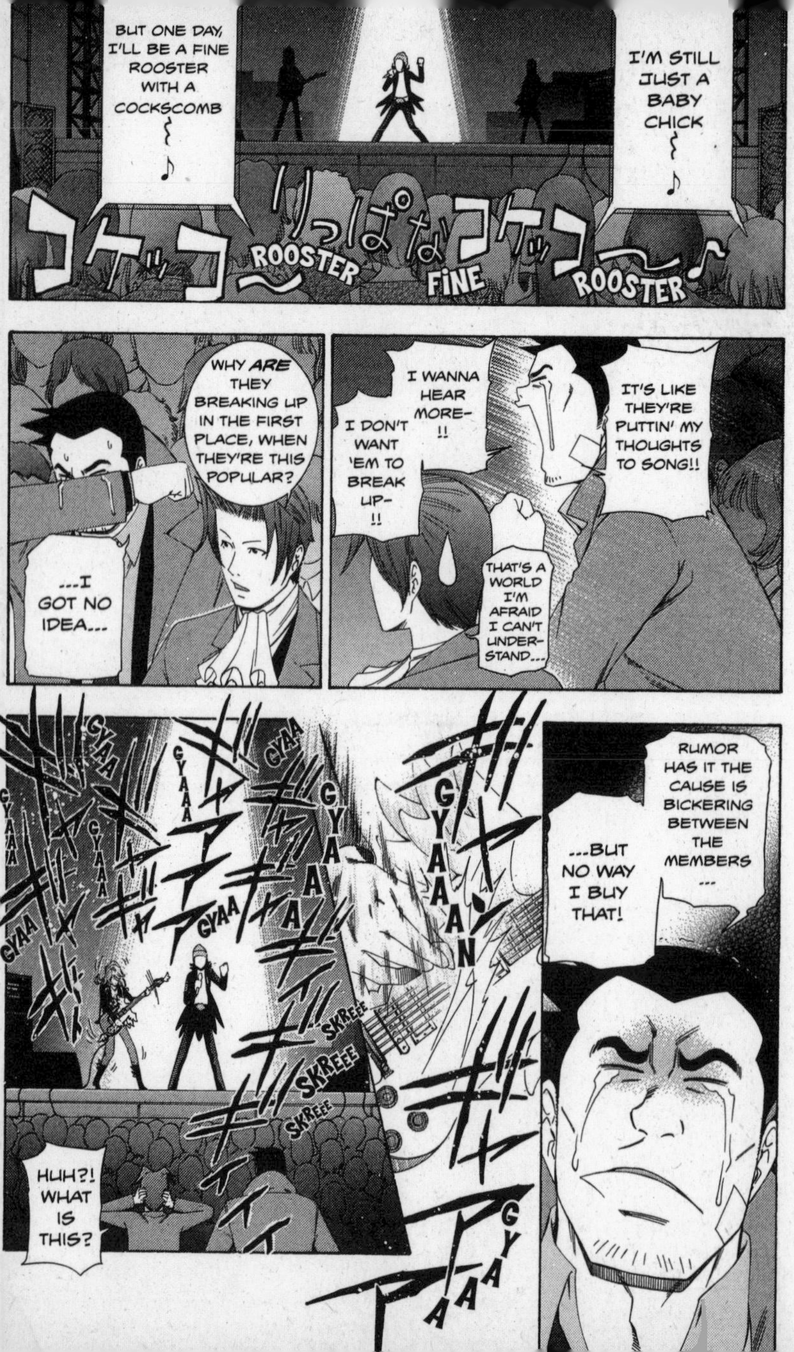

I'M STILL JUST A BABY CHICK ~ ♪
BUT ONE DAY, I'LL BE A FINE ROOSTER WITH A COCKSCOMB ~ ♪
コケッコ〜 りっぱなコケッコ〜♪
ROOSTER
FINE
ROOSTER
IT'S LIKE THEY'RE PUTTIN' MY THOUGHTS TO SONG!!
I WANNA HEAR MORE-!!
I DON'T WANT 'EM TO BREAK UP-!!
THAT'S A WORLD I'M AFRAID I CAN'T UNDERSTAND...
WHY *ARE* THEY BREAKING UP IN THE FIRST PLACE, WHEN THEY'RE THIS POPULAR?
...I GOT NO IDEA...
RUMOR HAS IT THE CAUSE IS BICKERING BETWEEN THE MEMBERS...
...BUT NO WAY I BUY THAT!
GYAAAN
GYAAA
GYAA
SKREEE
SKREEE
SKREEE
HUH?! WHAT IS THIS?

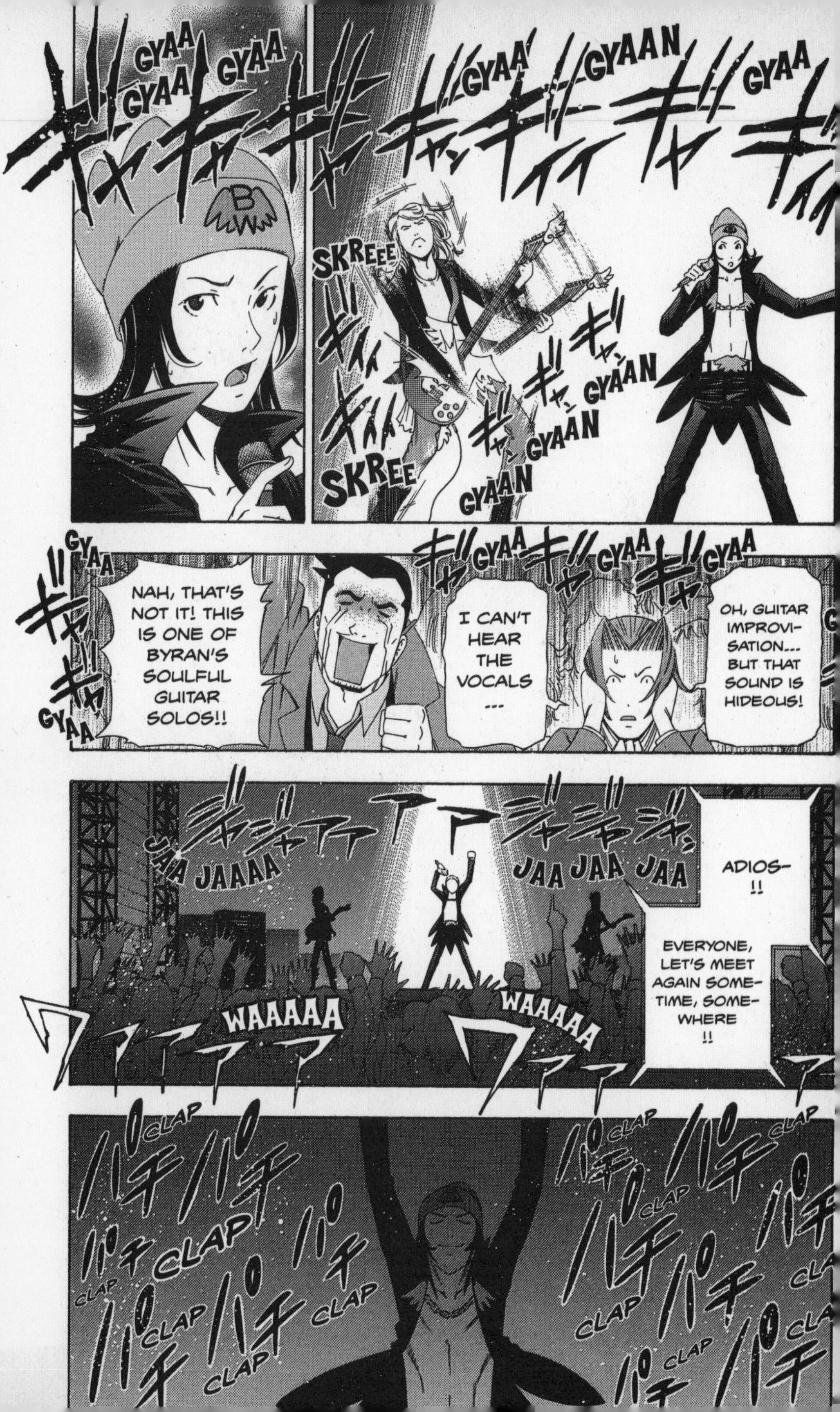
GYAA
GYAAN
GYAA
SKREEE
GYAAN
GYAAN
SKREE
GYAAN
GYAA
GYAA
GYAA
GYAA
GYAA
GYAA
OH, GUITAR IMPROVI-SATION... BUT THAT SOUND IS HIDEOUS!
I CAN'T HEAR THE VOCALS ...
NAH, THAT'S NOT IT! THIS IS ONE OF BYRAN'S SOULFUL GUITAR SOLOS!!
GYAA
GYAA
ADIOS-!!
EVERYONE, LET'S MEET AGAIN SOME-TIME, SOME-WHERE!!
JAA JAA JAA
JAA JAAAA
WAAAAA
WAAAAA
CLAP
CLAP
CLAP

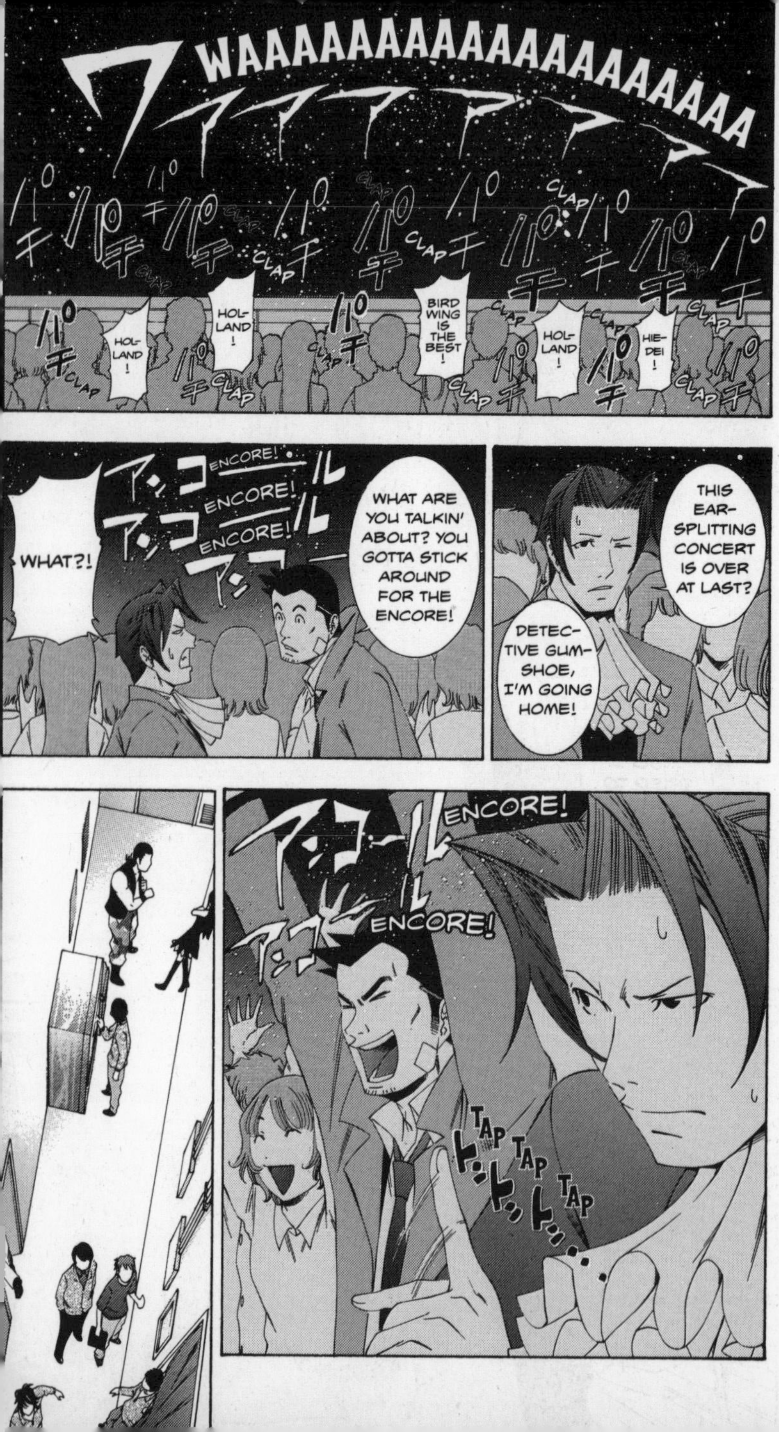
WAAAAAAAAAAAAAAAAAAAA
CLAP CLAP CLAP CLAP CLAP
HIE-DEI!
HOL-LAND!
BIRD WING IS THE BEST!
HOL-LAND!
HOL-LAND!
CLAP CLAP CLAP CLAP
THIS EAR-SPLITTING CONCERT IS OVER AT LAST?
DETECTIVE GUMSHOE, I'M GOING HOME!
ENCORE!
ENCORE!
ENCORE!
WHAT ARE YOU TALKIN' ABOUT? YOU GOTTA STICK AROUND FOR THE ENCORE!
WHAT?!
ENCORE!
ENCORE!
TAP TAP TAP

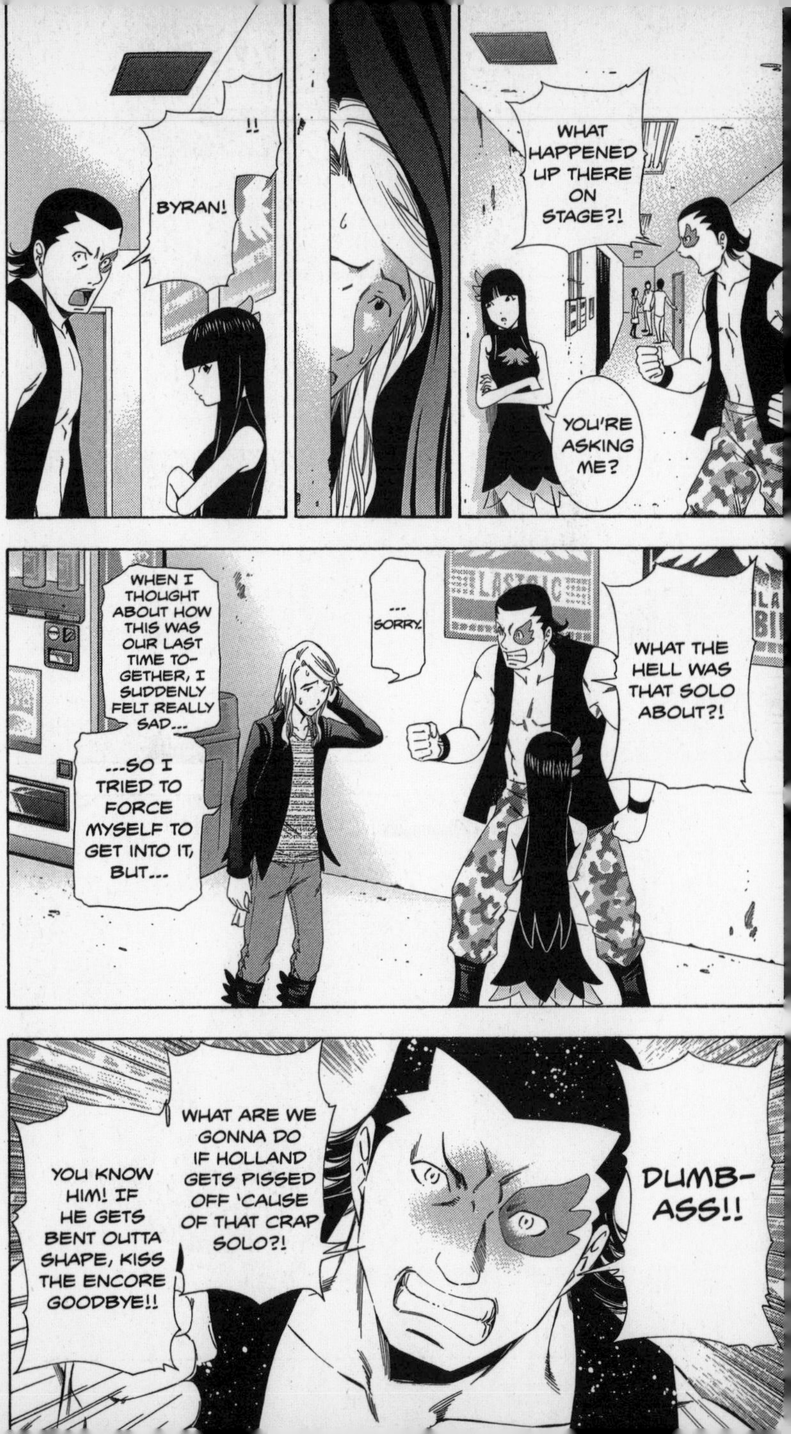
WHAT HAPPENED UP THERE ON STAGE?!
YOU'RE ASKING ME?
!! BYRAN!
WHAT THE HELL WAS THAT SOLO ABOUT?!
... SORRY.
WHEN I THOUGHT ABOUT HOW THIS WAS OUR LAST TIME TO-GETHER, I SUDDENLY FELT REALLY SAD...
...SO I TRIED TO FORCE MYSELF TO GET INTO IT, BUT...
DUMB-ASS!!
WHAT ARE WE GONNA DO IF HOLLAND GETS PISSED OFF 'CAUSE OF THAT CRAP SOLO?!
YOU KNOW HIM! IF HE GETS BENT OUTTA SHAPE, KISS THE ENCORE GOODBYE!!

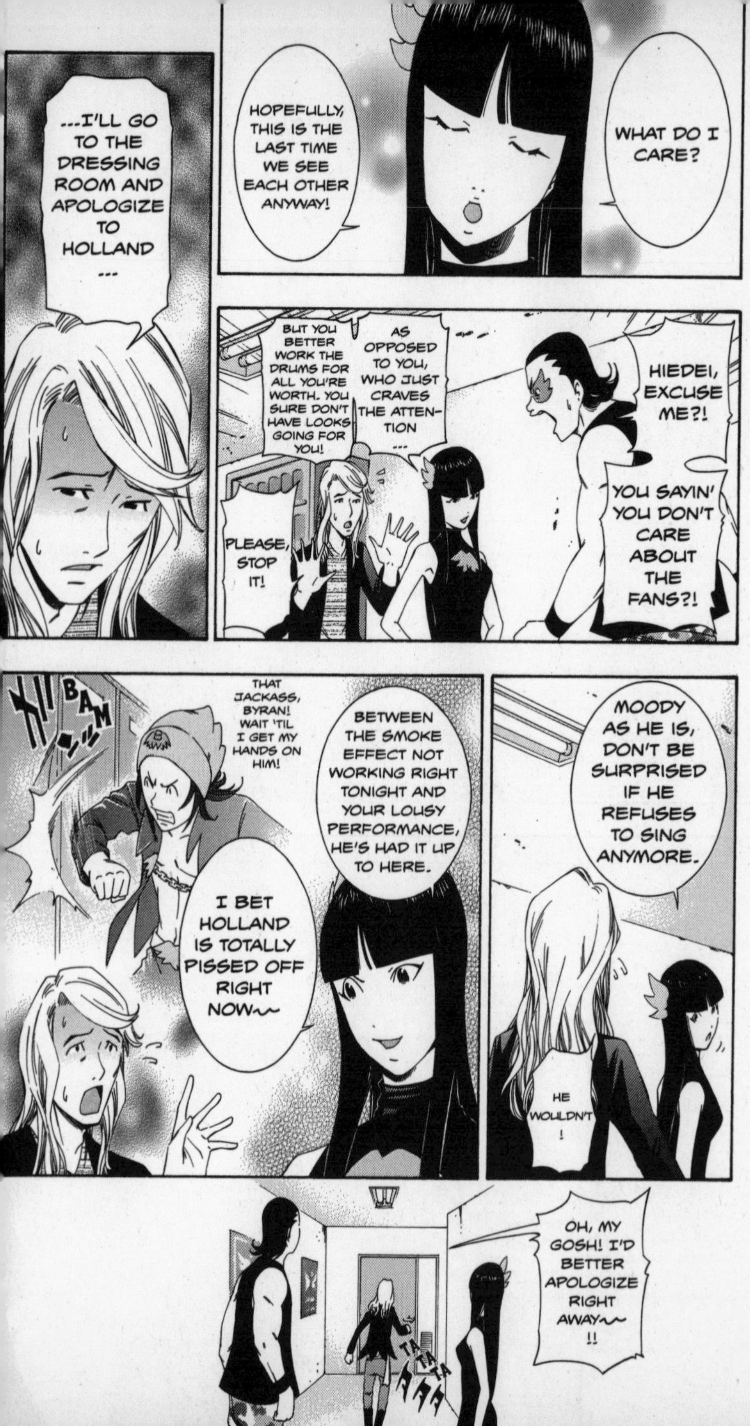
WHAT DO I CARE?
HOPEFULLY, THIS IS THE LAST TIME WE SEE EACH OTHER ANYWAY!
HIEDEI, EXCUSE ME?!
YOU SAYIN' YOU DON'T CARE ABOUT THE FANS?!
AS OPPOSED TO YOU, WHO JUST CRAVES THE ATTENTION ...
BUT YOU BETTER WORK THE DRUMS FOR ALL YOU'RE WORTH. YOU SURE DON'T HAVE LOOKS GOING FOR YOU!
PLEASE, STOP IT!
...I'LL GO TO THE DRESSING ROOM AND APOLOGIZE TO HOLLAND ...
MOODY AS HE IS, DON'T BE SURPRISED IF HE REFUSES TO SING ANYMORE.
HE WOULDN'T !
BETWEEN THE SMOKE EFFECT NOT WORKING RIGHT TONIGHT AND YOUR LOUSY PERFORMANCE, HE'S HAD IT UP TO HERE.
THAT JACKASS, BYRAN! WAIT 'TIL I GET MY HANDS ON HIM!
BAM
I BET HOLLAND IS TOTALLY PISSED OFF RIGHT NOW~
OH, MY GOSH! I'D BETTER APOLOGIZE RIGHT AWAY~ !!
TA TA TA TA

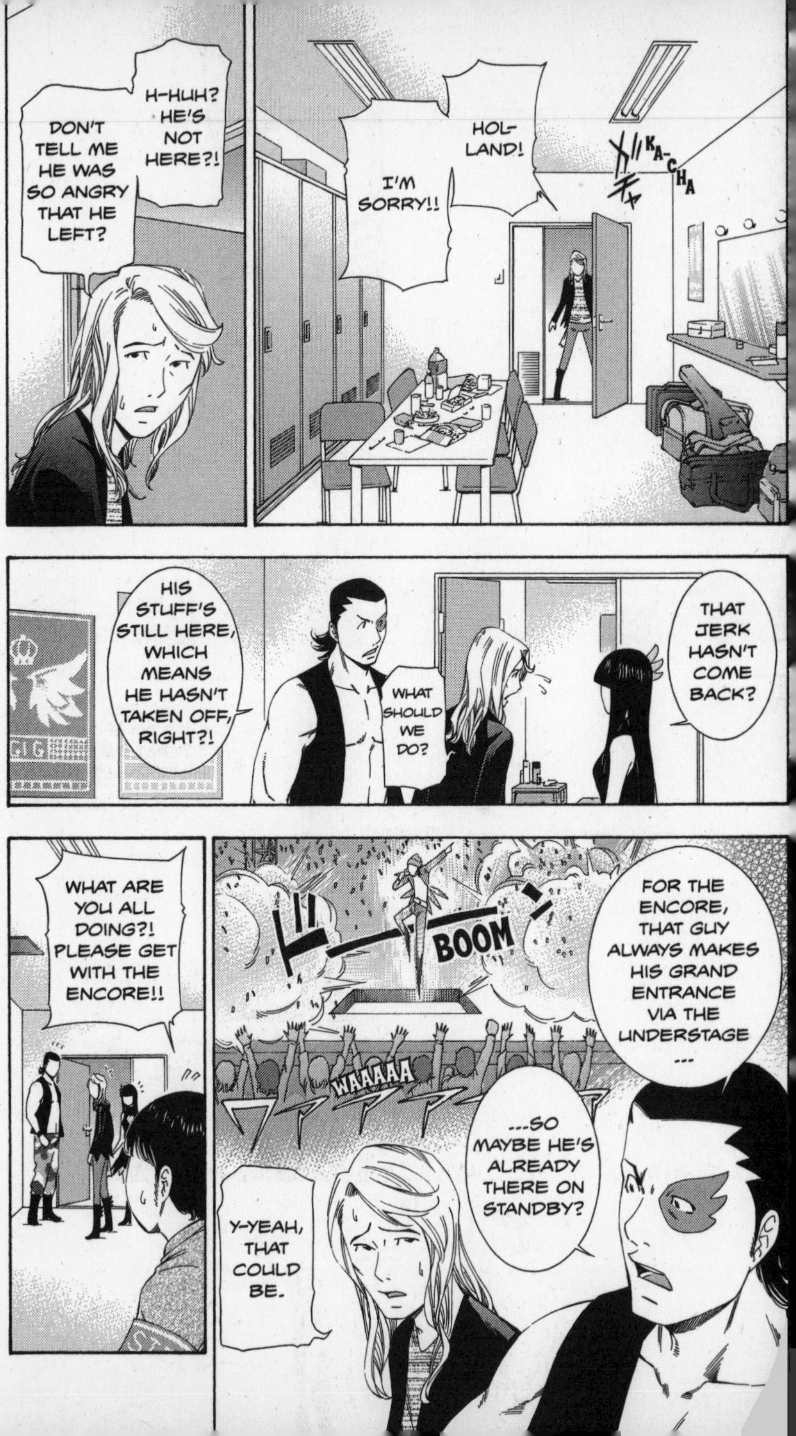
HOL-LAND!
I'M SORRY!!
KA-CHA
H-HUH? HE'S NOT HERE?!
DON'T TELL ME HE WAS SO ANGRY THAT HE LEFT?
THAT JERK HASN'T COME BACK?
WHAT SHOULD WE DO?
HIS STUFF'S STILL HERE, WHICH MEANS HE HASN'T TAKEN OFF, RIGHT?!
FOR THE ENCORE, THAT GUY ALWAYS MAKES HIS GRAND ENTRANCE VIA THE UNDERSTAGE ---
BOOM
WAAAAA
---SO MAYBE HE'S ALREADY THERE ON STANDBY?
Y-YEAH, THAT COULD BE.
WHAT ARE YOU ALL DOING?! PLEASE GET WITH THE ENCORE!!

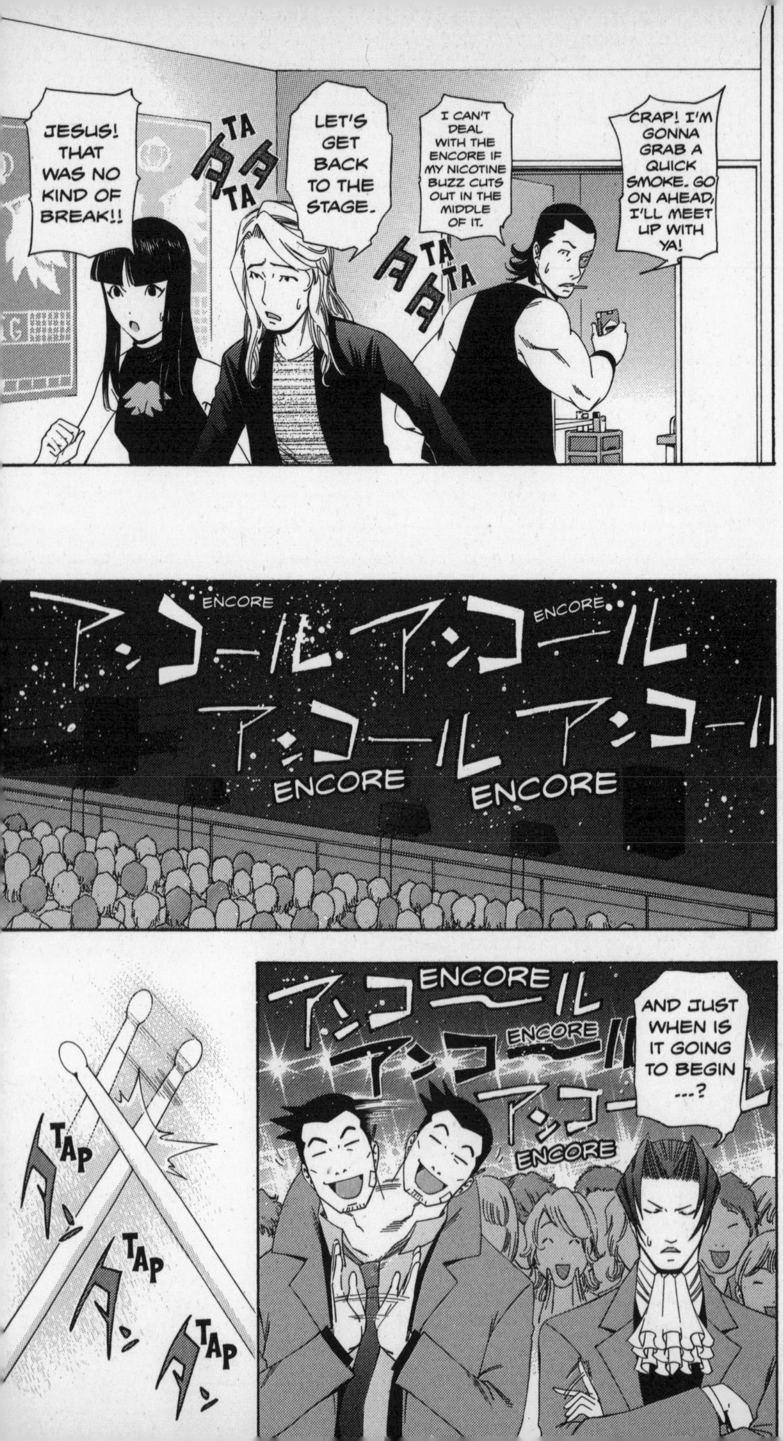
CRAP! I'M GONNA GRAB A QUICK SMOKE. GO ON AHEAD, I'LL MEET UP WITH YA!
I CAN'T DEAL WITH THE ENCORE IF MY NICOTINE BUZZ CUTS OUT IN THE MIDDLE OF IT.
TA TA TA
LET'S GET BACK TO THE STAGE.
TA TA TA
JESUS! THAT WAS NO KIND OF BREAK!!
アンコール ENCORE アンコール ENCORE
アンコール ENCORE アンコール ENCORE
アンコール ENCORE
アンコール ENCORE
アンコール ENCORE
AND JUST WHEN IS IT GOING TO BEGIN ...?
TAP
TAP
TAP

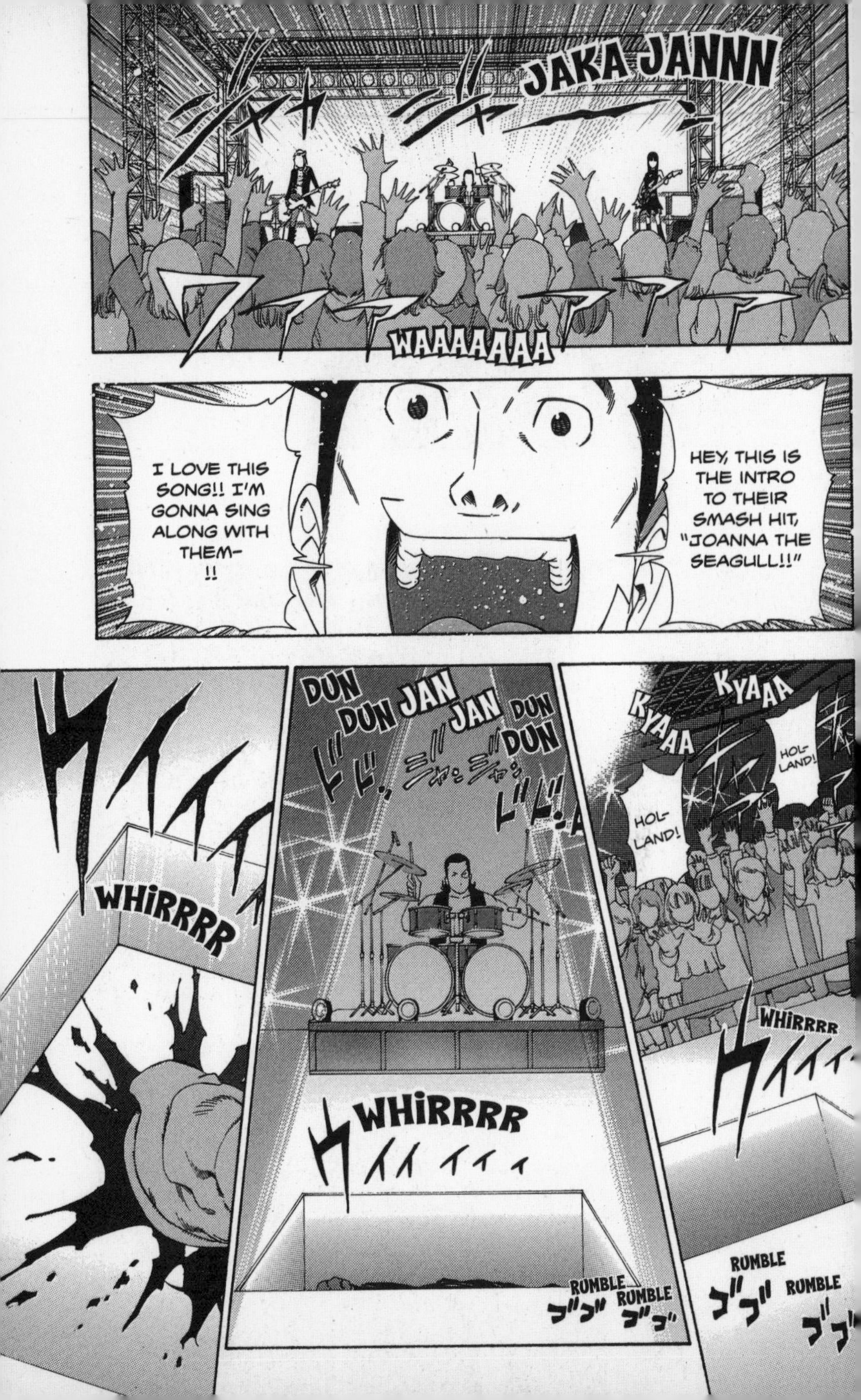
JAKA JANNN
WAAAAAAA
HEY, THIS IS THE INTRO TO THEIR SMASH HIT, "JOANNA THE SEAGULL!!"
I LOVE THIS SONG!! I'M GONNA SING ALONG WITH THEM-!!
KYAAA
KYAAA
HOL-LAND!
HOL-LAND!
WHIRRRR
RUMBLE
RUMBLE
DUN DUN JAN JAN DUN DUN
WHIRRRR
RUMBLE
RUMBLE
WHIRRRR

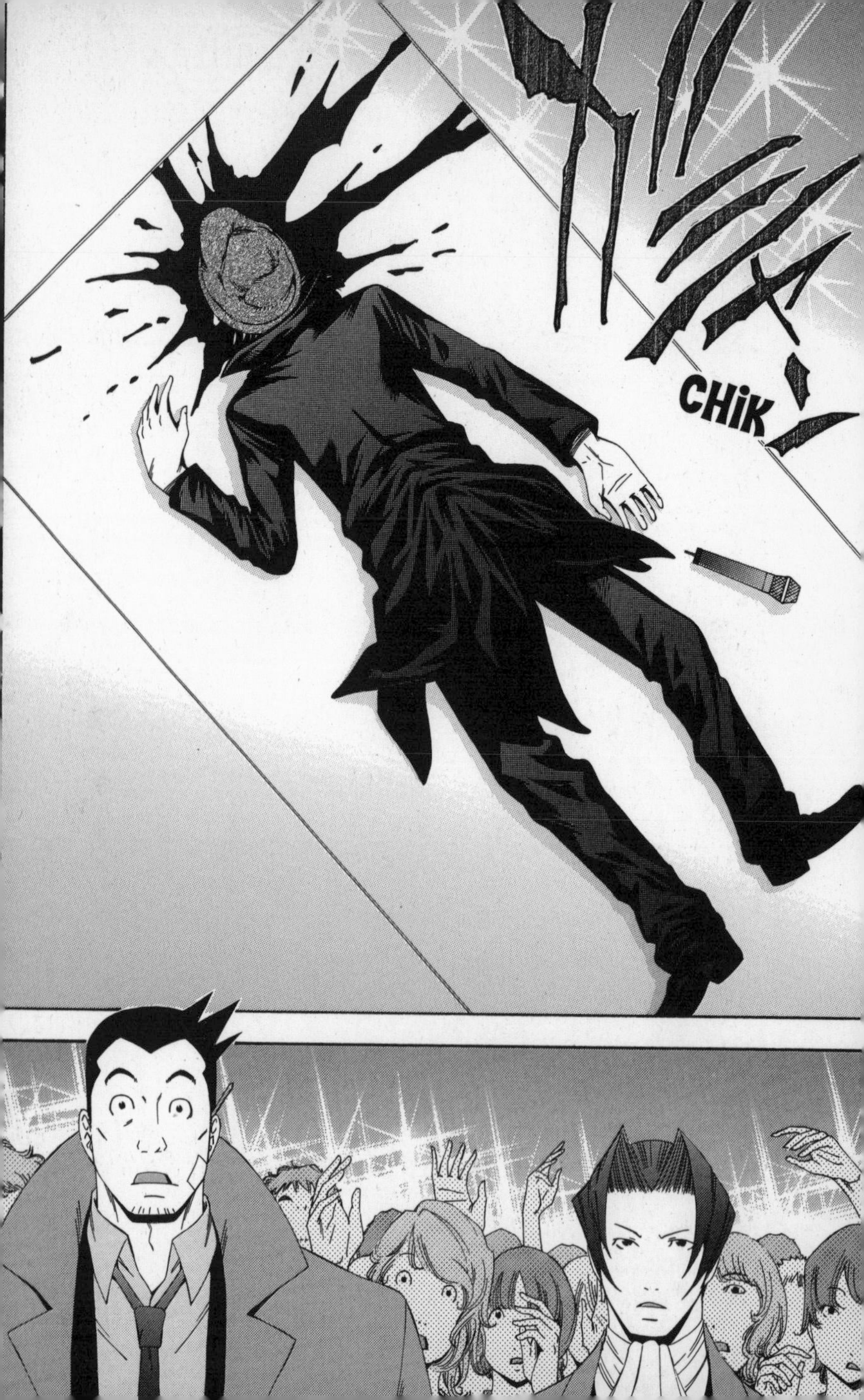
CHIK

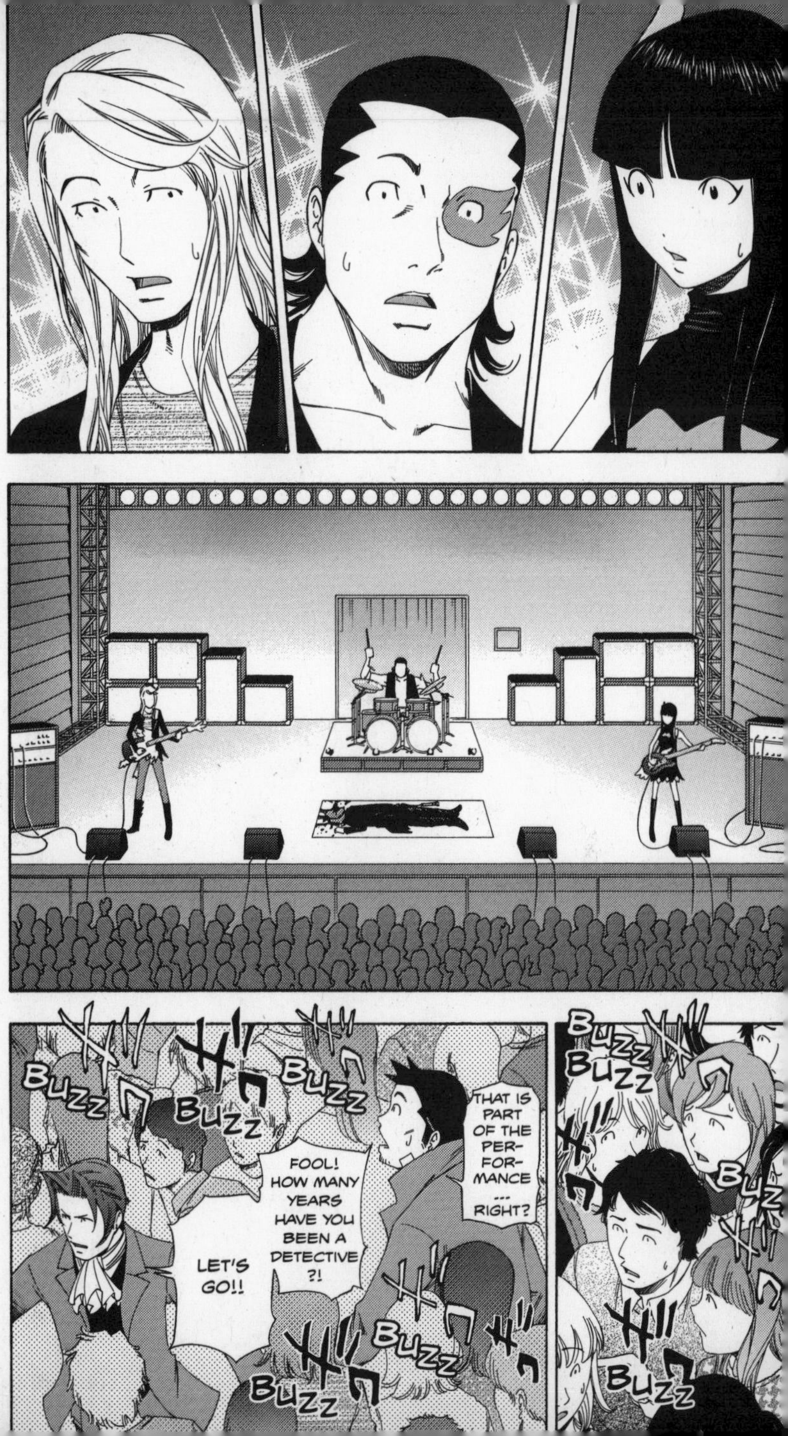

Buzz
Buzz
Buzz
Buzz
THAT IS PART OF THE PER-FORMANCE ... RIGHT?
FOOL! HOW MANY YEARS HAVE YOU BEEN A DETECTIVE ?!
LET'S GO!!
Buzz
Buzz
Buzz
Buzz
Buzz

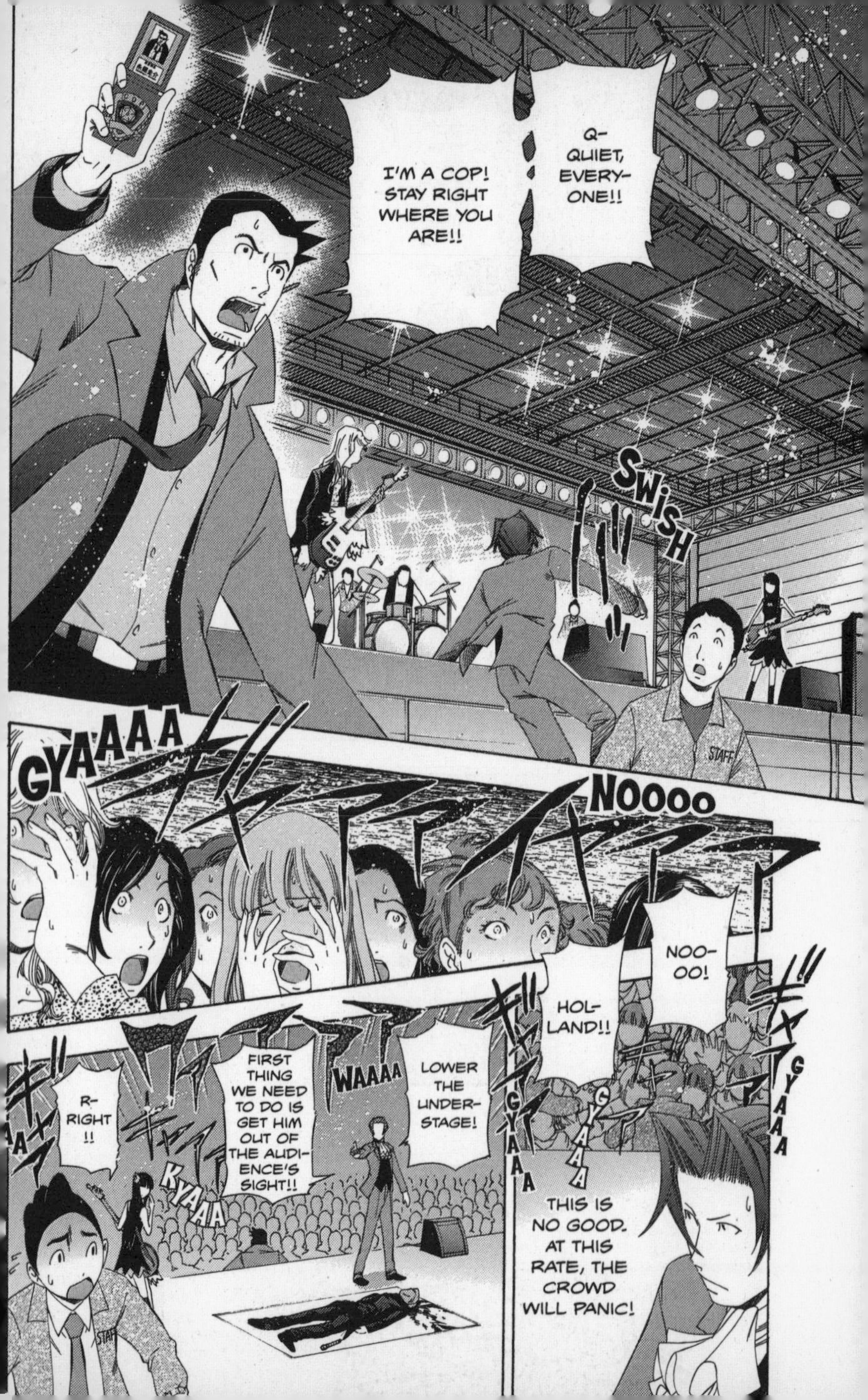
Q- QUIET, EVERYONE!!
I'M A COP! STAY RIGHT WHERE YOU ARE!!
SWISH
NOOOO
GYAAAA
NOO-OO!
HOL-LAND!!
GYAAAA
GYAAA
GYAAA
THIS IS NO GOOD. AT THIS RATE, THE CROWD WILL PANIC!
LOWER THE UNDER-STAGE!
WAAAA
FIRST THING WE NEED TO DO IS GET HIM OUT OF THE AUDIENCE'S SIGHT!!
KYAAA
R- RIGHT !!

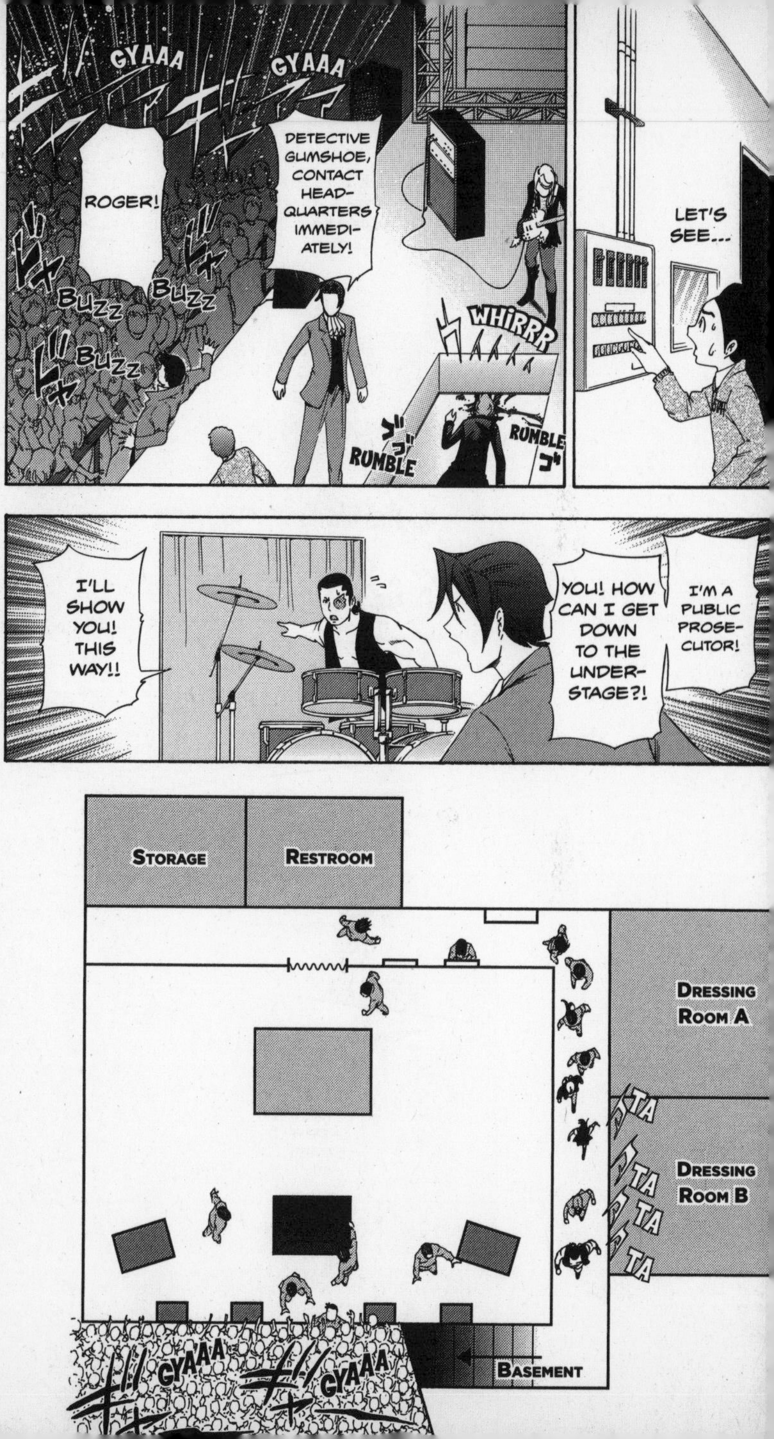
LET'S SEE...
GYAAA
GYAAA
DETECTIVE GUMSHOE, CONTACT HEAD-QUARTERS IMMEDI-ATELY!
ROGER!
BUZZ
BUZZ
BUZZ
WHIRRR
RUMBLE
RUMBLE
I'M A PUBLIC PROSE-CUTOR!
YOU! HOW CAN I GET DOWN TO THE UNDER-STAGE?!
I'LL SHOW YOU! THIS WAY!!
RESTROOM
STORAGE
DRESSING ROOM A
DRESSING ROOM B
TA
TA
TA
TA
BASEMENT
GYAAA
GYAAA

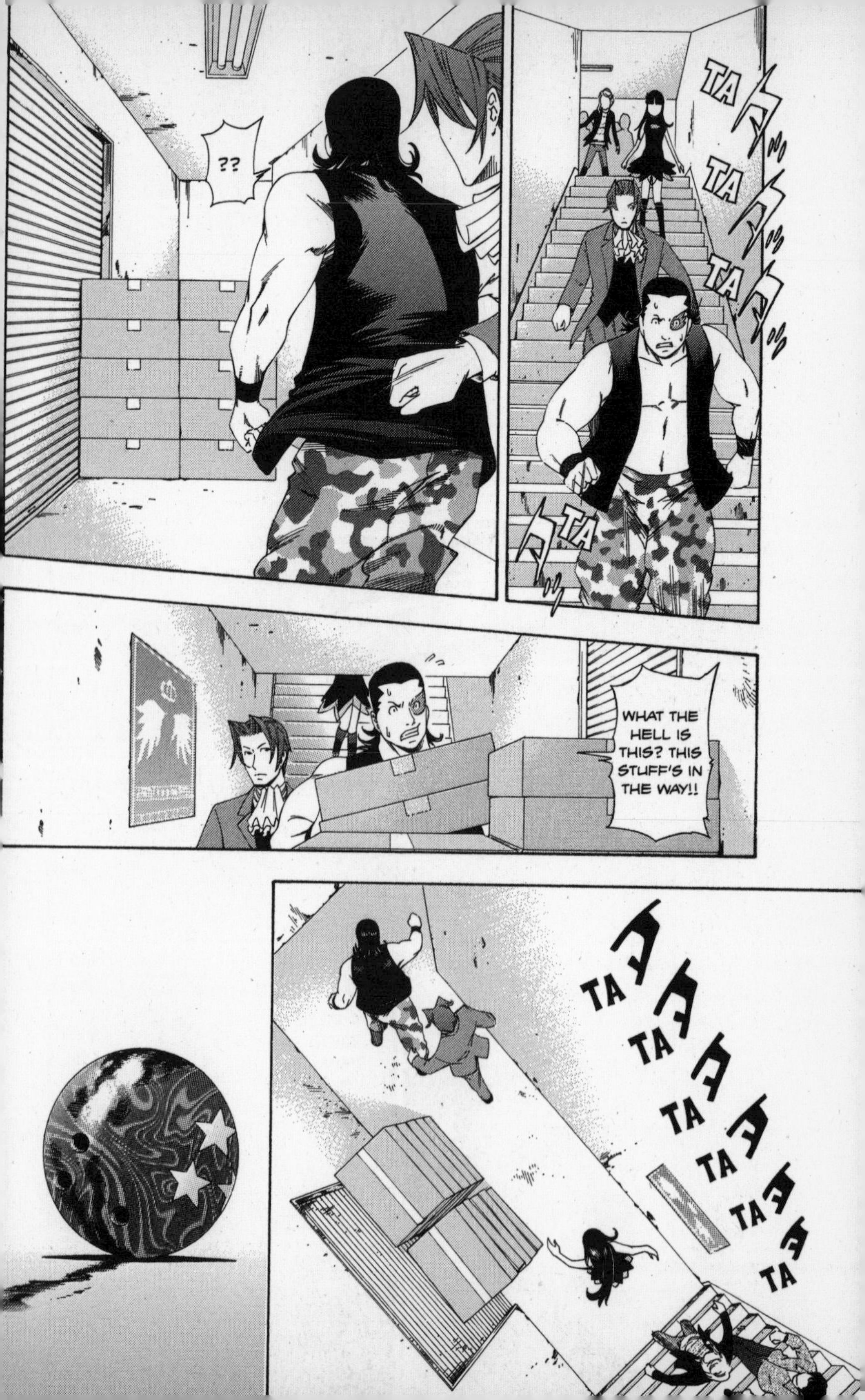
TA
TA
TA
TA
??
WHAT THE HELL IS THIS? THIS STUFF'S IN THE WAY!!
TA
TA
TA
TA
TA
TA
TA

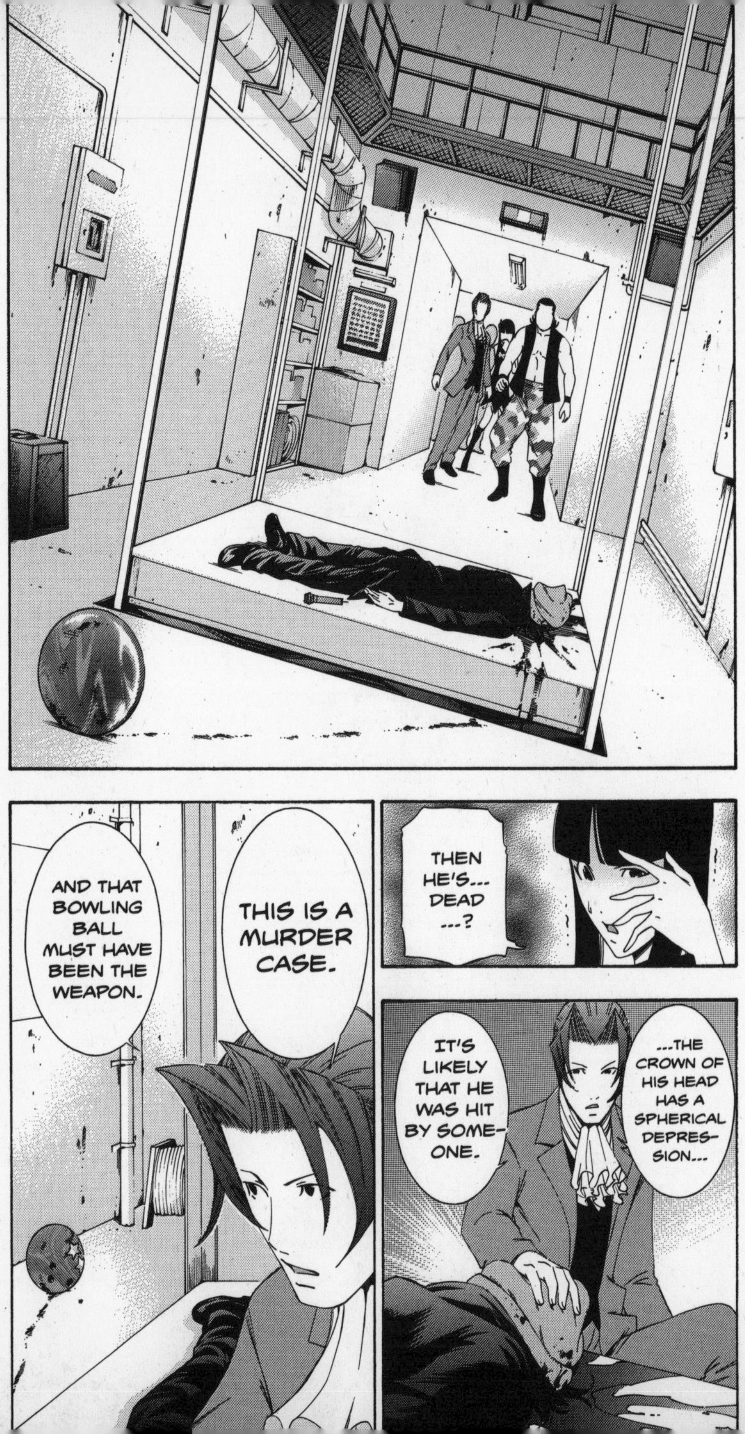
THEN HE'S... DEAD ...?
...THE CROWN OF HIS HEAD HAS A SPHERICAL DEPRES-SION...
IT'S LIKELY THAT HE WAS HIT BY SOME-ONE.
THIS IS A MURDER CASE.
AND THAT BOWLING BALL MUST HAVE BEEN THE WEAPON.

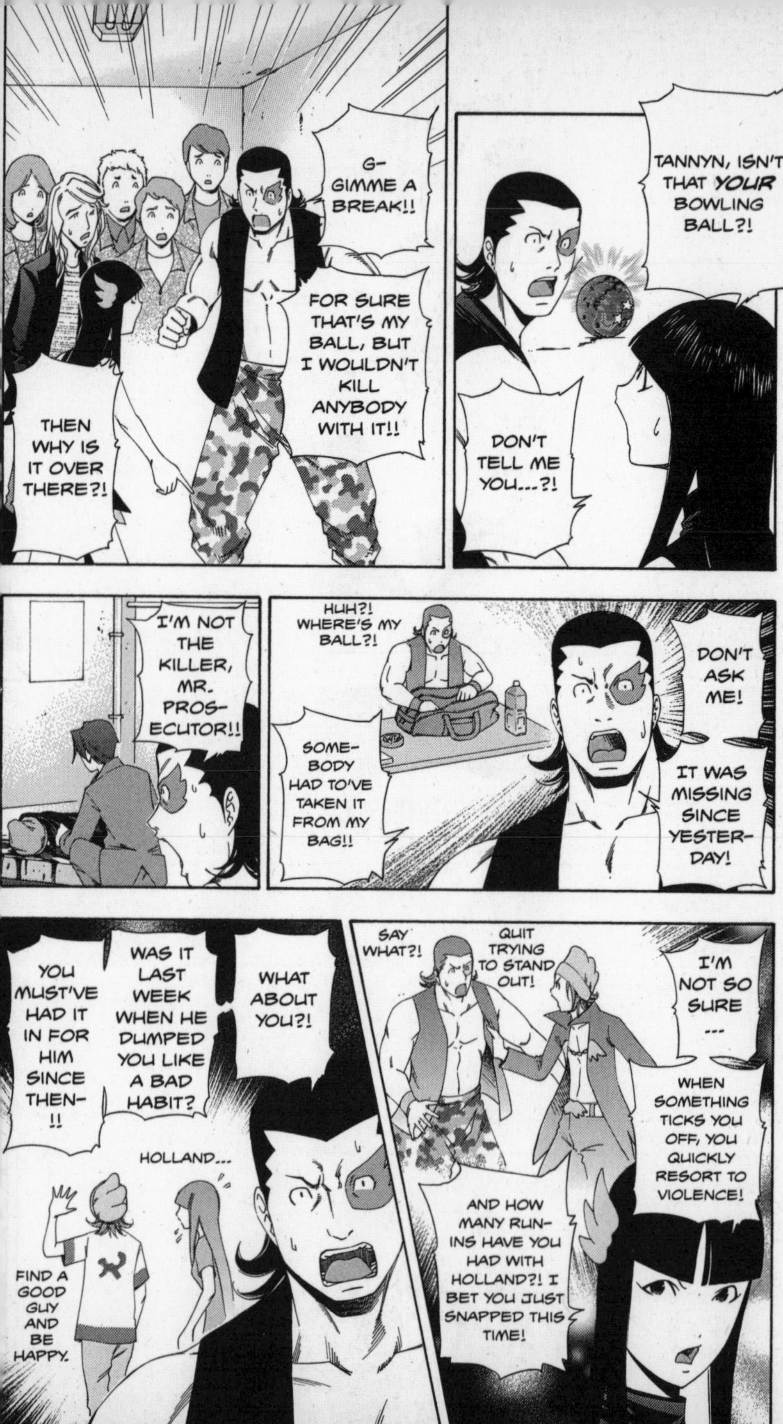
TANNYN, ISN'T THAT *YOUR* BOWLING BALL?!
DON'T TELL ME YOU...?!
G-GIMME A BREAK!!
FOR SURE THAT'S MY BALL, BUT I WOULDN'T KILL ANYBODY WITH IT!!
THEN WHY IS IT OVER THERE?!
DON'T ASK ME!
IT WAS MISSING SINCE YESTERDAY!
HUH?! WHERE'S MY BALL?!
SOMEBODY HAD TO'VE TAKEN IT FROM MY BAG!!
I'M NOT THE KILLER, MR. PROSECUTOR!!
I'M NOT SO SURE ...
WHEN SOMETHING TICKS YOU OFF, YOU QUICKLY RESORT TO VIOLENCE!
SAY WHAT?!
QUIT TRYING TO STAND OUT!
AND HOW MANY RUN-INS HAVE YOU HAD WITH HOLLAND?! I BET YOU JUST SNAPPED THIS TIME!
WHAT ABOUT YOU?!
WAS IT LAST WEEK WHEN HE DUMPED YOU LIKE A BAD HABIT?
YOU MUST'VE HAD IT IN FOR HIM SINCE THEN-!!
HOLLAND...
FIND A GOOD GUY AND BE HAPPY.

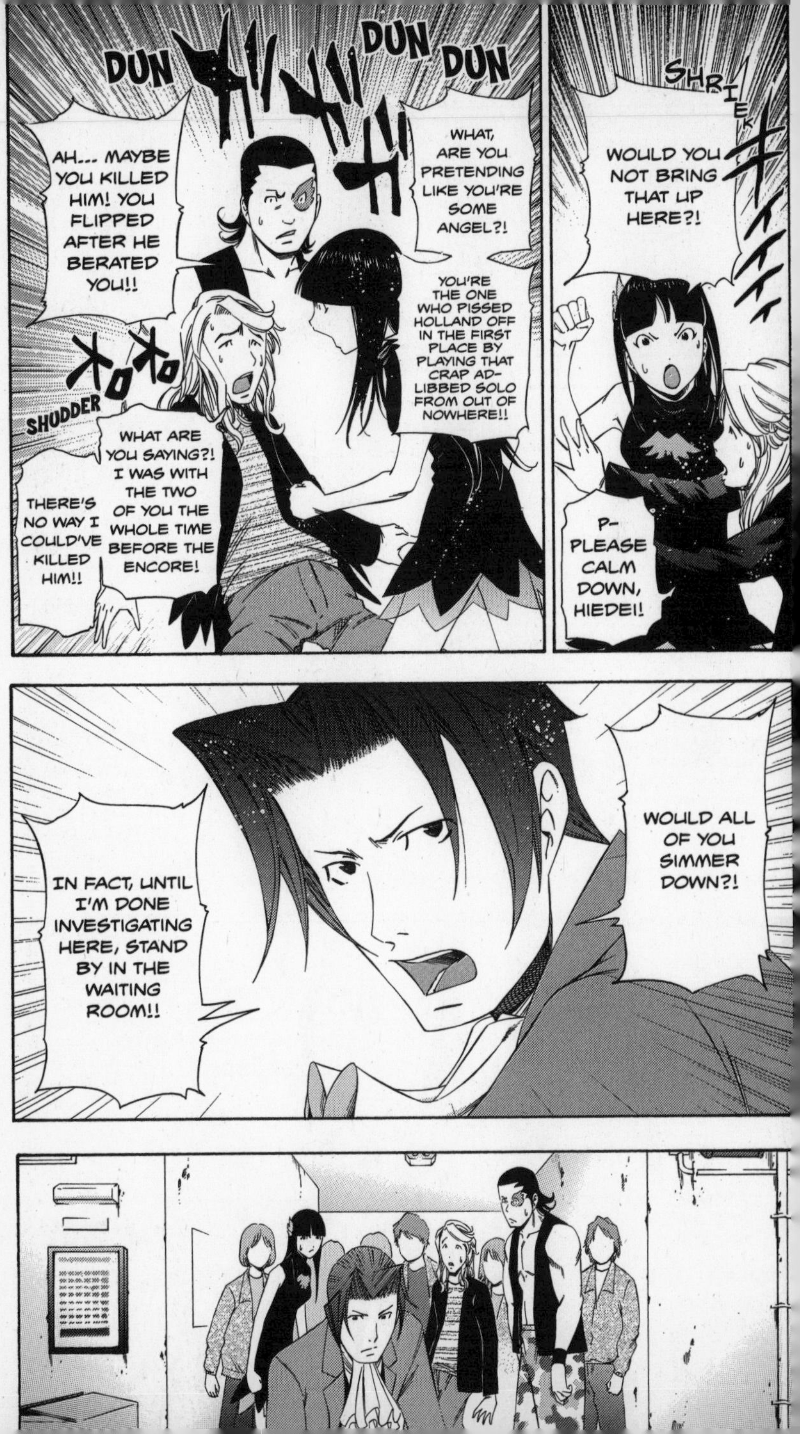
SHRIEK
WOULD YOU NOT BRING THAT UP HERE?!
P-PLEASE CALM DOWN, HIEDEI!
DUN
DUN
DUN
WHAT, ARE YOU PRETENDING LIKE YOU'RE SOME ANGEL?!
YOU'RE THE ONE WHO PISSED HOLLAND OFF IN THE FIRST PLACE BY PLAYING THAT CRAP AD-LIBBED SOLO FROM OUT OF NOWHERE!!
AH... MAYBE YOU KILLED HIM! YOU FLIPPED AFTER HE BERATED YOU!!
SHUDDER
WHAT ARE YOU SAYING?! I WAS WITH THE TWO OF YOU THE WHOLE TIME BEFORE THE ENCORE!
THERE'S NO WAY I COULD'VE KILLED HIM!!
WOULD ALL OF YOU SIMMER DOWN?!
IN FACT, UNTIL I'M DONE INVESTIGATING HERE, STAND BY IN THE WAITING ROOM!!

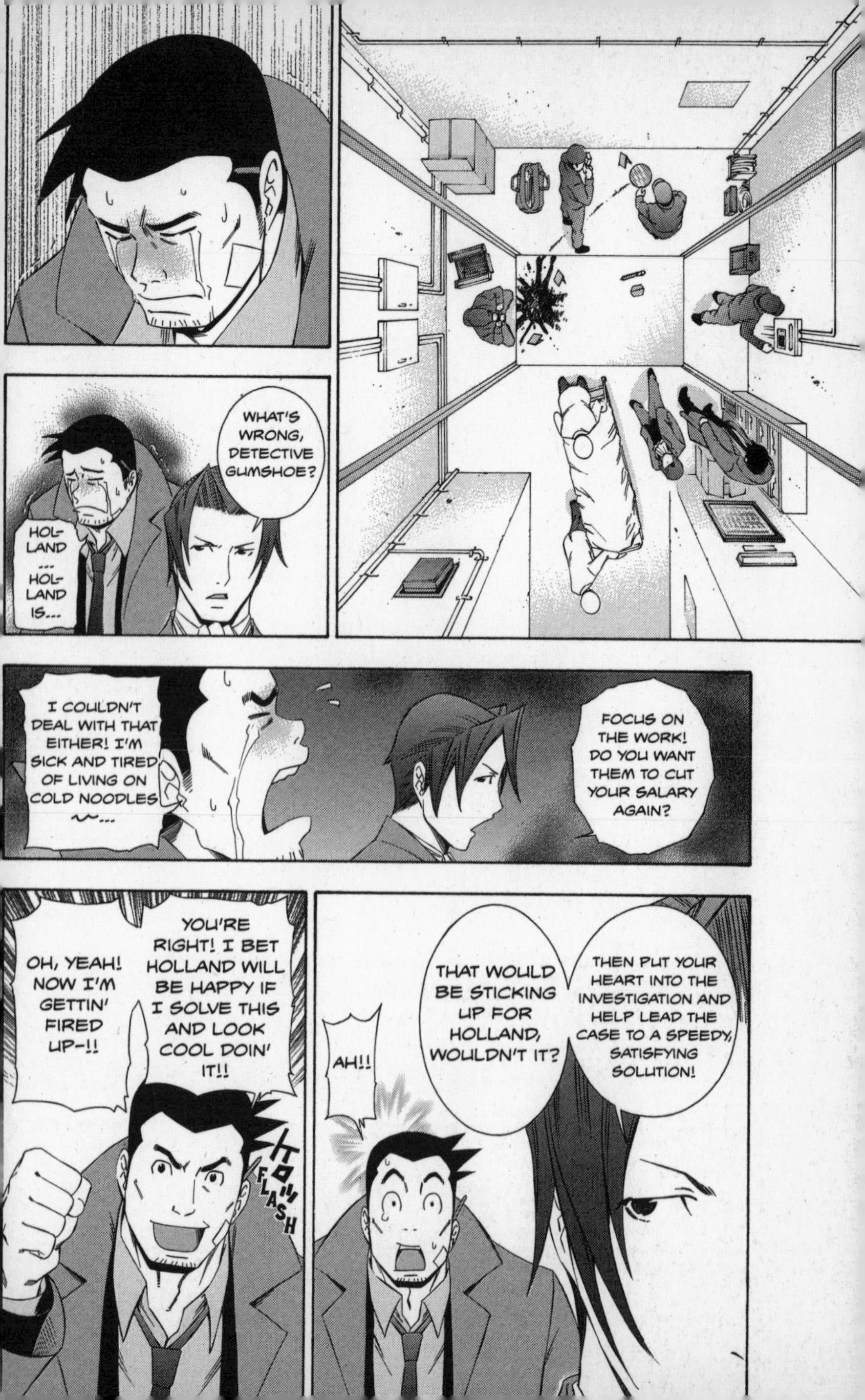
WHAT'S WRONG, DETECTIVE GUMSHOE?
HOL-LAND ... HOL-LAND IS...
I COULDN'T DEAL WITH THAT EITHER! I'M SICK AND TIRED OF LIVING ON COLD NOODLES ~...
FOCUS ON THE WORK! DO YOU WANT THEM TO CUT YOUR SALARY AGAIN?
THEN PUT YOUR HEART INTO THE INVESTIGATION AND HELP LEAD THE CASE TO A SPEEDY, SATISFYING SOLUTION!
THAT WOULD BE STICKING UP FOR HOLLAND, WOULDN'T IT?
AH!!
YOU'RE RIGHT! I BET HOLLAND WILL BE HAPPY IF I SOLVE THIS AND LOOK COOL DOIN' IT!!
OH, YEAH! NOW I'M GETTIN' FIRED UP-!!
FLASH

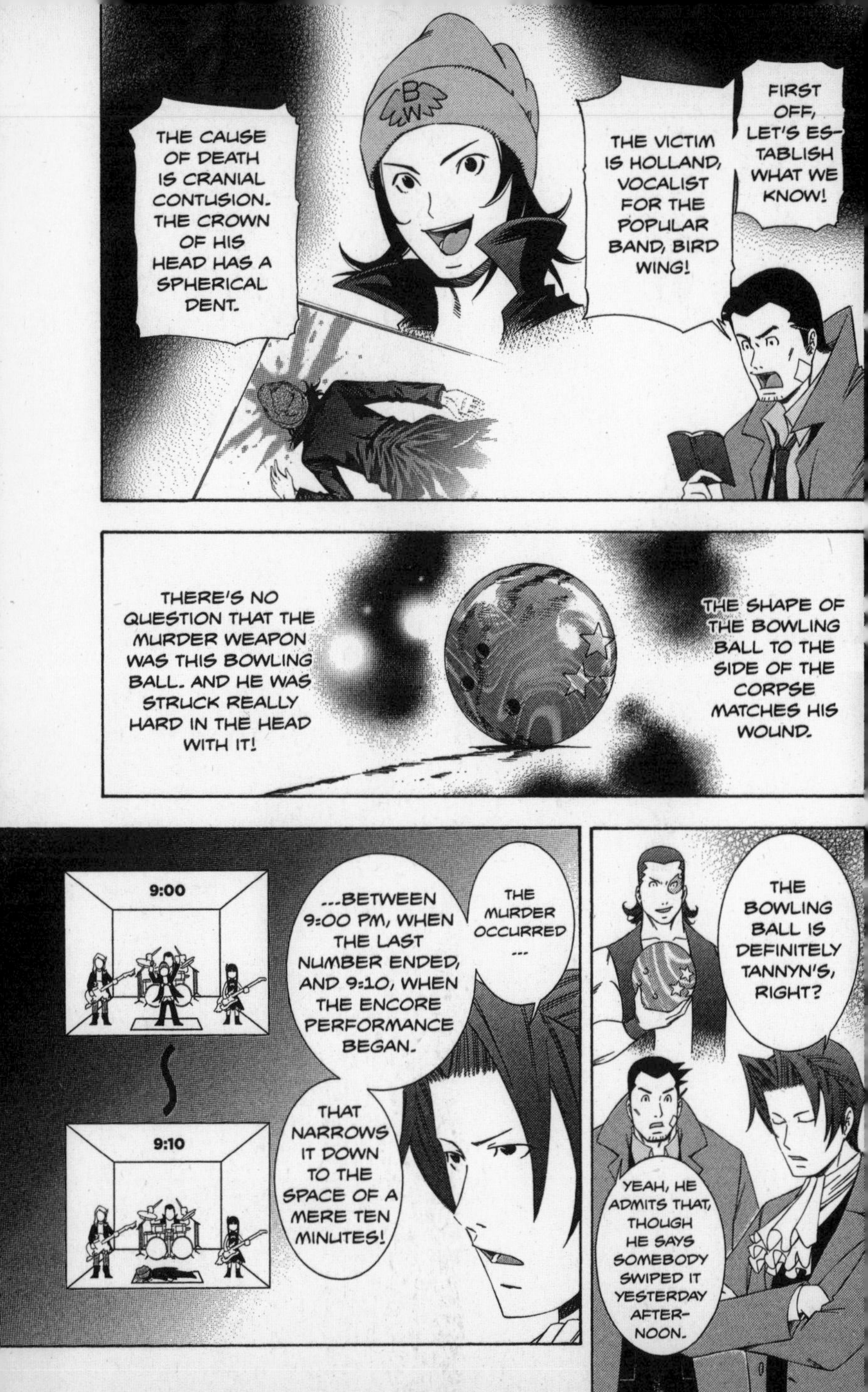
FIRST OFF, LET'S ESTABLISH WHAT WE KNOW!
THE VICTIM IS HOLLAND, VOCALIST FOR THE POPULAR BAND, BIRD WING!
THE CAUSE OF DEATH IS CRANIAL CONTUSION. THE CROWN OF HIS HEAD HAS A SPHERICAL DENT.
THE SHAPE OF THE BOWLING BALL TO THE SIDE OF THE CORPSE MATCHES HIS WOUND.
THERE'S NO QUESTION THAT THE MURDER WEAPON WAS THIS BOWLING BALL. AND HE WAS STRUCK REALLY HARD IN THE HEAD WITH IT!
THE BOWLING BALL IS DEFINITELY TANNYN'S, RIGHT?
YEAH, HE ADMITS THAT, THOUGH HE SAYS SOMEBODY SWIPED IT YESTERDAY AFTERNOON.
THE MURDER OCCURRED ...
...BETWEEN 9:00 PM, WHEN THE LAST NUMBER ENDED, AND 9:10, WHEN THE ENCORE PERFORMANCE BEGAN.
9:00
9:10
THAT NARROWS IT DOWN TO THE SPACE OF A MERE TEN MINUTES!

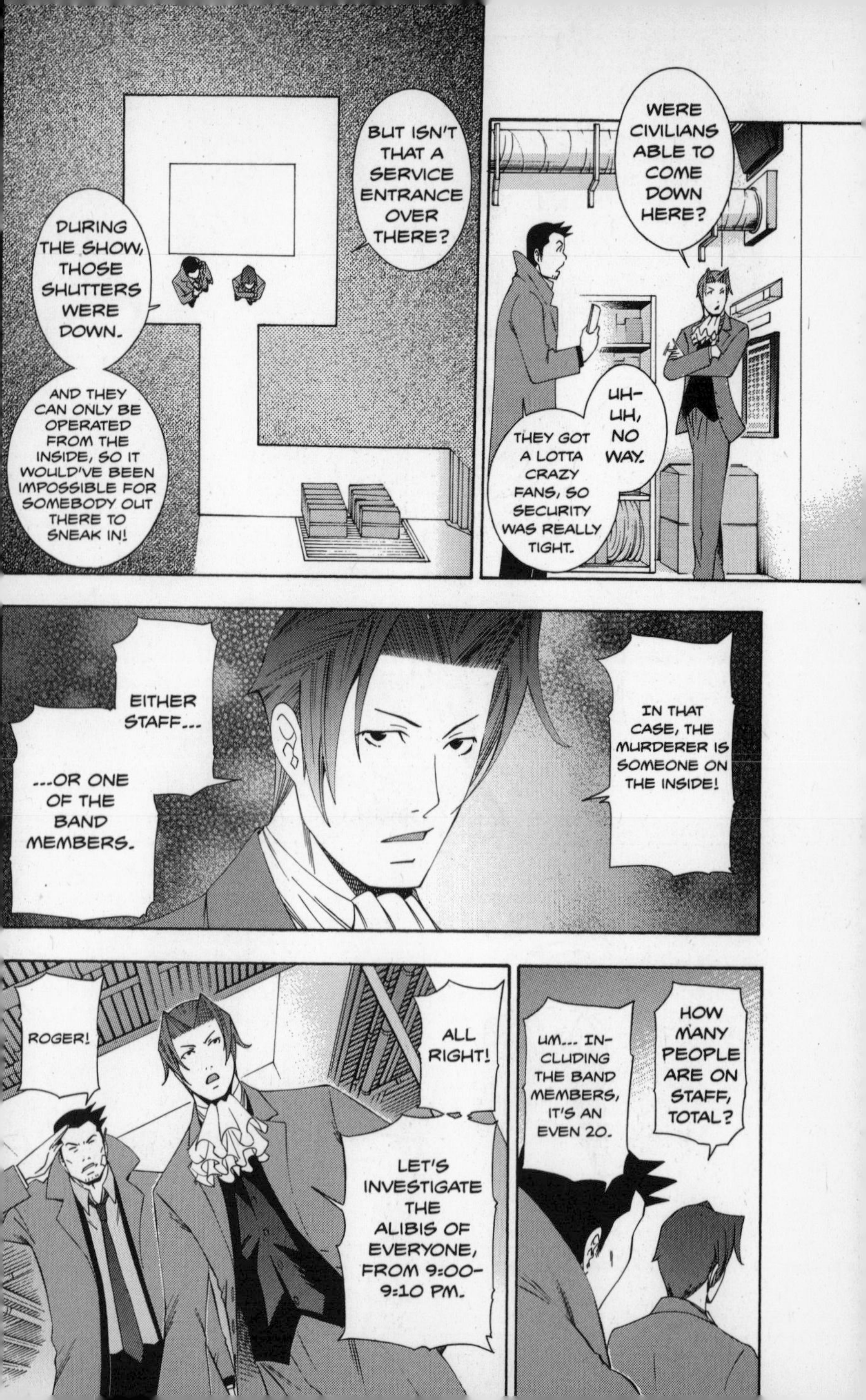
WERE CIVILIANS ABLE TO COME DOWN HERE?
UH-UH, NO WAY.
THEY GOT A LOTTA CRAZY FANS, SO SECURITY WAS REALLY TIGHT.
BUT ISN'T THAT A SERVICE ENTRANCE OVER THERE?
DURING THE SHOW, THOSE SHUTTERS WERE DOWN.
AND THEY CAN ONLY BE OPERATED FROM THE INSIDE, SO IT WOULD'VE BEEN IMPOSSIBLE FOR SOMEBODY OUT THERE TO SNEAK IN!
IN THAT CASE, THE MURDERER IS SOMEONE ON THE INSIDE!
EITHER STAFF...
...OR ONE OF THE BAND MEMBERS.
HOW MANY PEOPLE ARE ON STAFF, TOTAL?
UM... IN-CLUDING THE BAND MEMBERS, IT'S AN EVEN 20.
ALL RIGHT!
LET'S INVESTIGATE THE ALIBIS OF EVERYONE, FROM 9:00-9:10 PM.
ROGER!

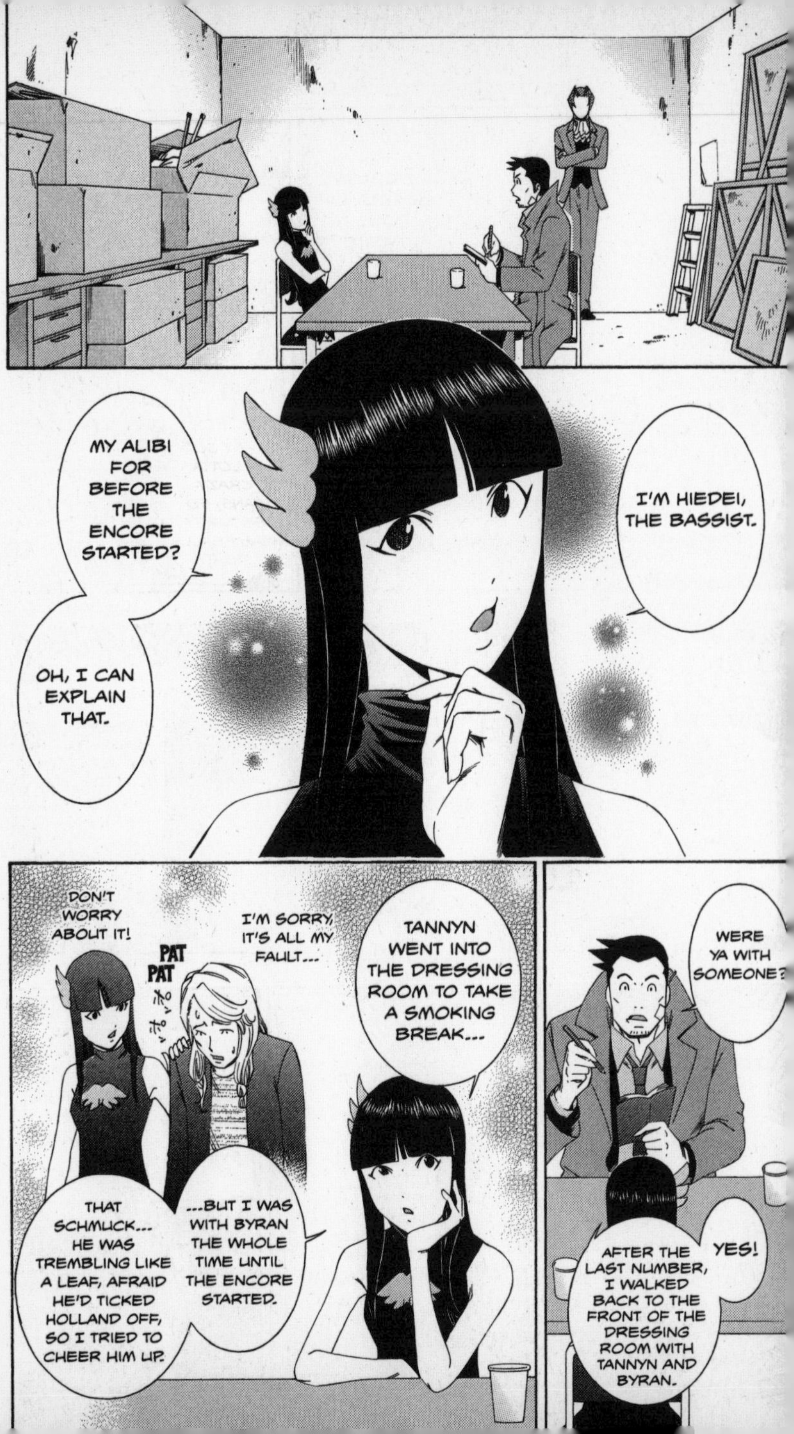
I'M HIEDEI, THE BASSIST.
MY ALIBI FOR BEFORE THE ENCORE STARTED?
OH, I CAN EXPLAIN THAT.
WERE YA WITH SOMEONE?
YES!
AFTER THE LAST NUMBER, I WALKED BACK TO THE FRONT OF THE DRESSING ROOM WITH TANNYN AND BYRAN.
TANNYN WENT INTO THE DRESSING ROOM TO TAKE A SMOKING BREAK...
...BUT I WAS WITH BYRAN THE WHOLE TIME UNTIL THE ENCORE STARTED.
I'M SORRY, IT'S ALL MY FAULT...
PAT PAT
DON'T WORRY ABOUT IT!
THAT SCHMUCK... HE WAS TREMBLING LIKE A LEAF, AFRAID HE'D TICKED HOLLAND OFF, SO I TRIED TO CHEER HIM UP.

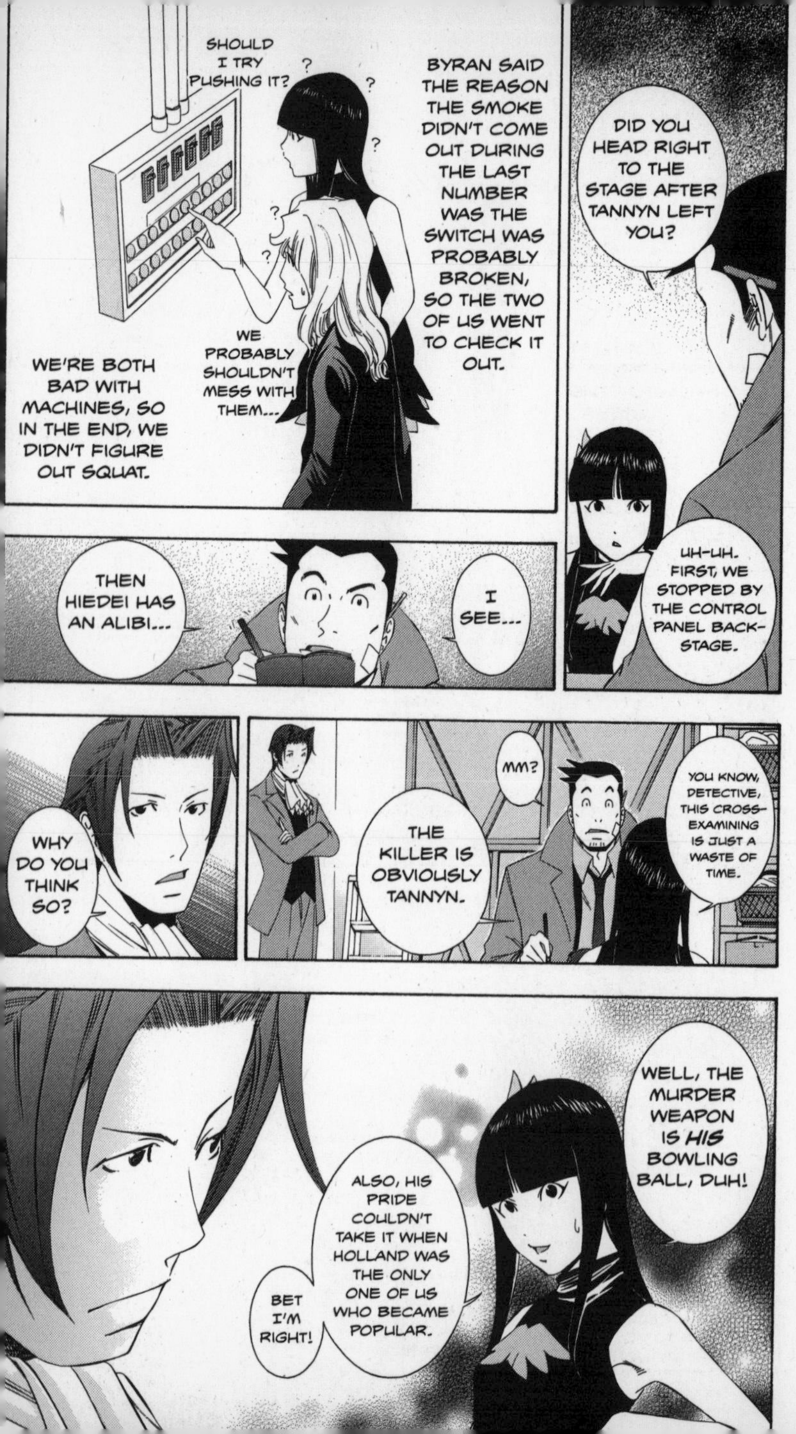
BYRAN SAID THE REASON THE SMOKE DIDN'T COME OUT DURING THE LAST NUMBER WAS THE SWITCH WAS PROBABLY BROKEN, SO THE TWO OF US WENT TO CHECK IT OUT.
SHOULD I TRY PUSHING IT?
WE PROBABLY SHOULDN'T MESS WITH THEM...
WE'RE BOTH BAD WITH MACHINES, SO IN THE END, WE DIDN'T FIGURE OUT SQUAT.
DID YOU HEAD RIGHT TO THE STAGE AFTER TANNYN LEFT YOU?
UH-UH. FIRST, WE STOPPED BY THE CONTROL PANEL BACK-STAGE.
I SEE...
THEN HIEDEI HAS AN ALIBI...
YOU KNOW, DETECTIVE, THIS CROSS-EXAMINING IS JUST A WASTE OF TIME.
MM?
THE KILLER IS OBVIOUSLY TANNYN.
WHY DO YOU THINK SO?
WELL, THE MURDER WEAPON IS *HIS* BOWLING BALL, DUH!
ALSO, HIS PRIDE COULDN'T TAKE IT WHEN HOLLAND WAS THE ONLY ONE OF US WHO BECAME POPULAR.
BET I'M RIGHT!

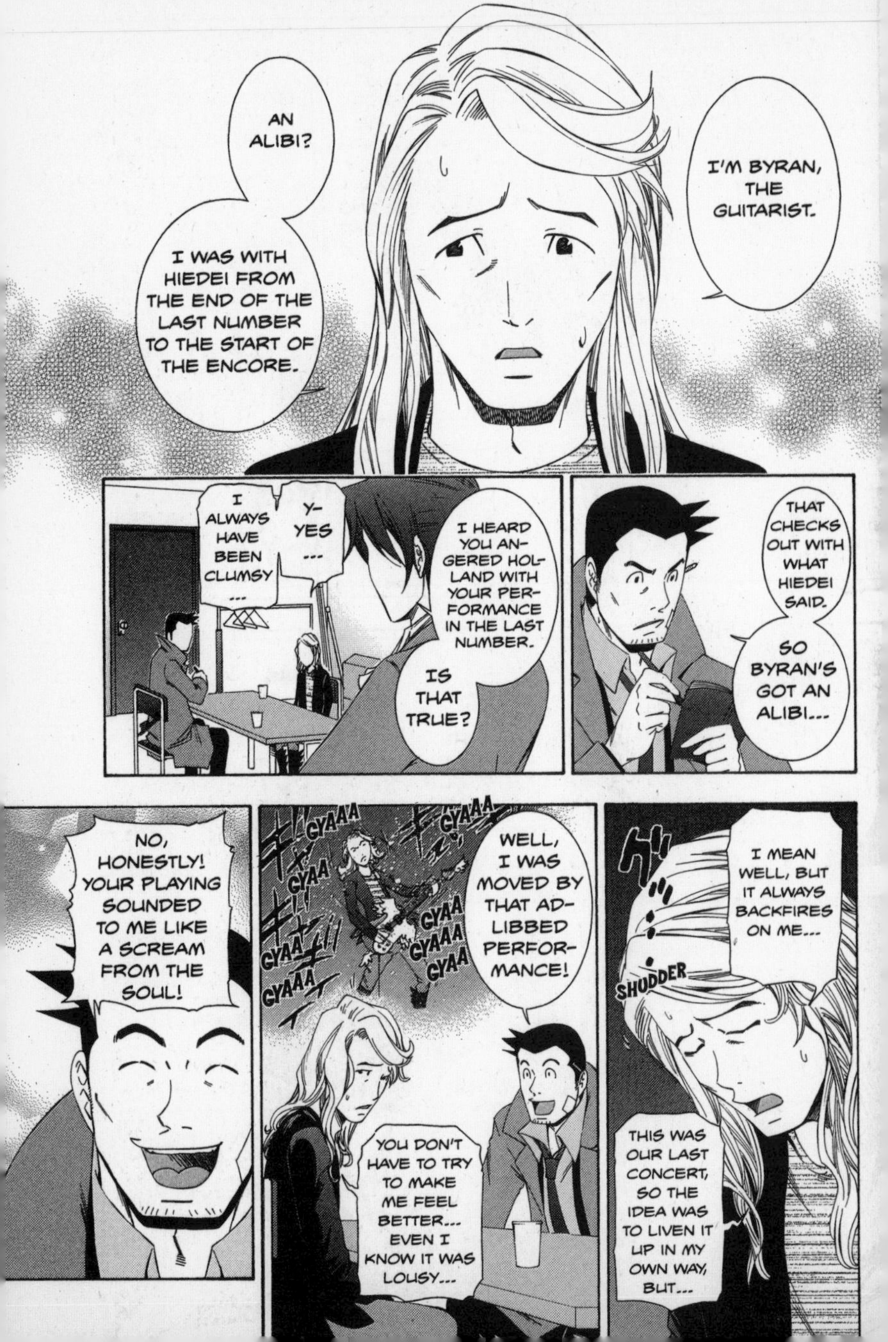
I'M BYRAN, THE GUITARIST.
AN ALIBI?
I WAS WITH HIEDEI FROM THE END OF THE LAST NUMBER TO THE START OF THE ENCORE.
THAT CHECKS OUT WITH WHAT HIEDEI SAID.
SO BYRAN'S GOT AN ALIBI...
I HEARD YOU ANGERED HOLLAND WITH YOUR PERFORMANCE IN THE LAST NUMBER.
IS THAT TRUE?
Y-YES...
I ALWAYS HAVE BEEN CLUMSY...
I MEAN WELL, BUT IT ALWAYS BACKFIRES ON ME...
SHUDDER
THIS WAS OUR LAST CONCERT, SO THE IDEA WAS TO LIVEN IT UP IN MY OWN WAY, BUT...
GYAAA GYAAA GYAA GYAA GYAAA GYAAA GYAA GYAAA GYAA GYAAA
WELL, I WAS MOVED BY THAT AD-LIBBED PERFORMANCE!
YOU DON'T HAVE TO TRY TO MAKE ME FEEL BETTER... EVEN I KNOW IT WAS LOUSY...
NO, HONESTLY! YOUR PLAYING SOUNDED TO ME LIKE A SCREAM FROM THE SOUL!

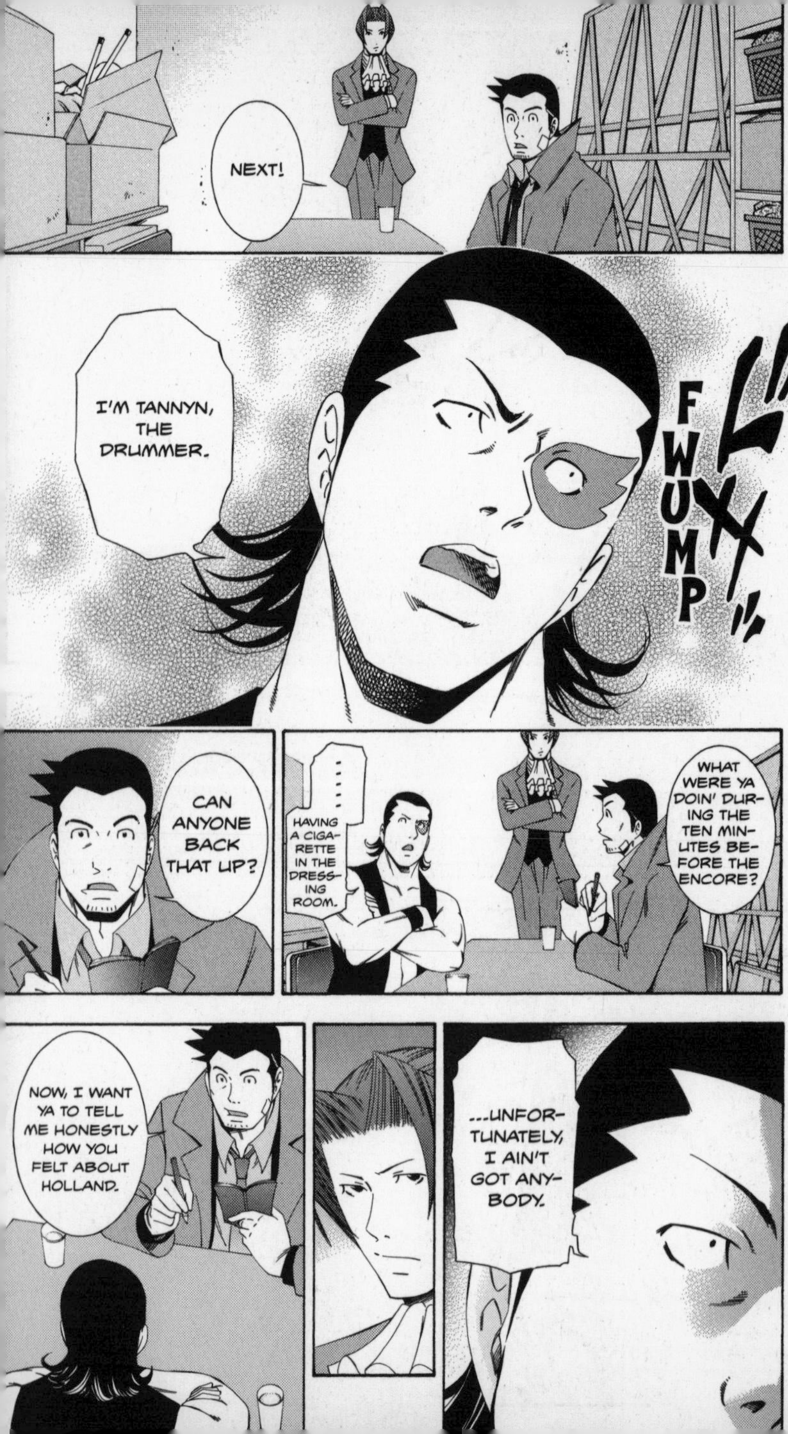
NEXT!
I'M TANNYN, THE DRUMMER.
FWUMP
WHAT WERE YA DOIN' DURING THE TEN MINUTES BEFORE THE ENCORE?
......
HAVING A CIGARETTE IN THE DRESSING ROOM.
CAN ANYONE BACK THAT UP?
...UNFORTUNATELY, I AIN'T GOT ANYBODY.
NOW, I WANT YA TO TELL ME HONESTLY HOW YOU FELT ABOUT HOLLAND.

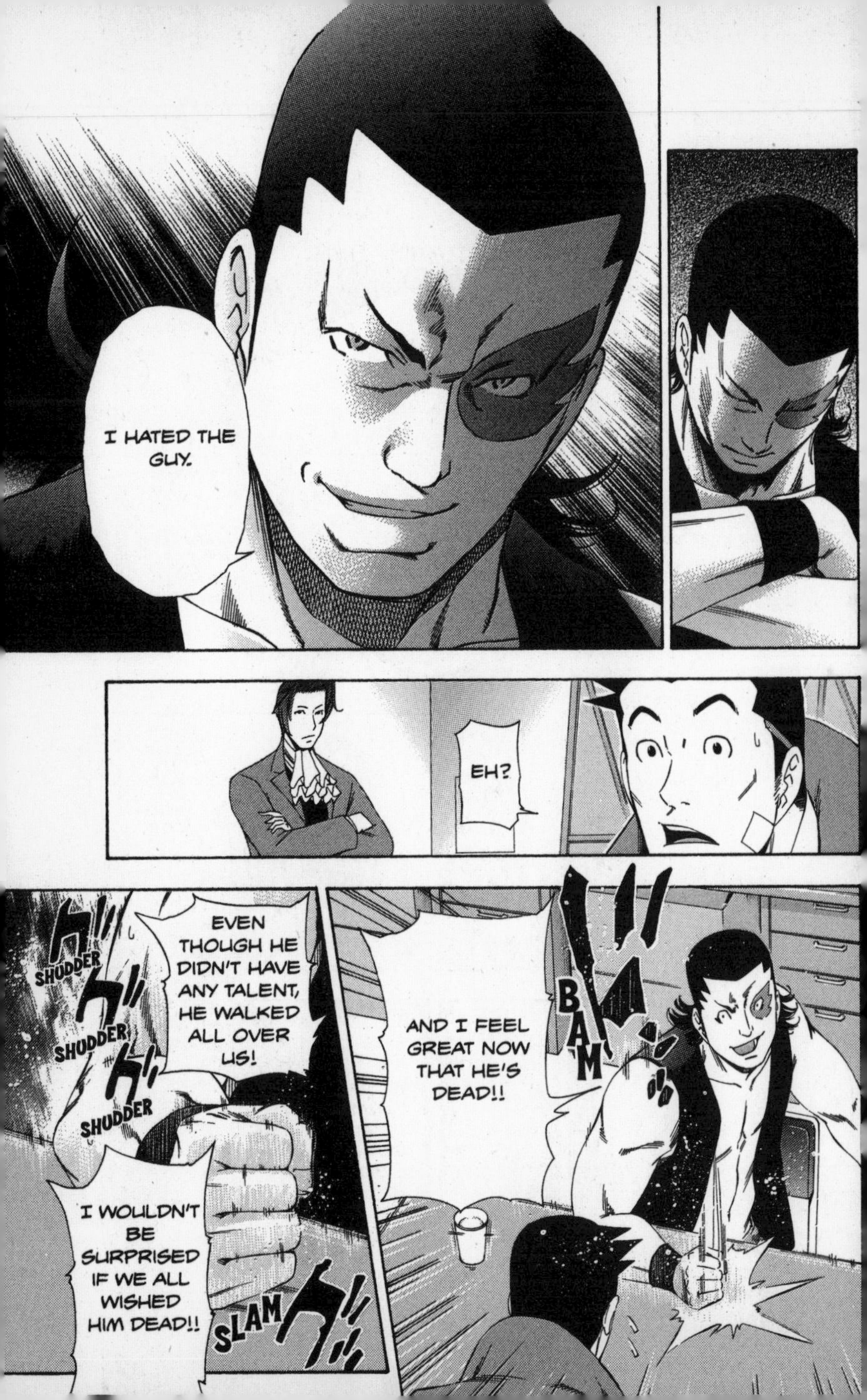
I HATED THE GUY.
EH?
BAM
AND I FEEL GREAT NOW THAT HE'S DEAD!!
EVEN THOUGH HE DIDN'T HAVE ANY TALENT, HE WALKED ALL OVER US!
SHUDDER
SHUDDER
SHUDDER
I WOULDN'T BE SURPRISED IF WE ALL WISHED HIM DEAD!!
SLAM

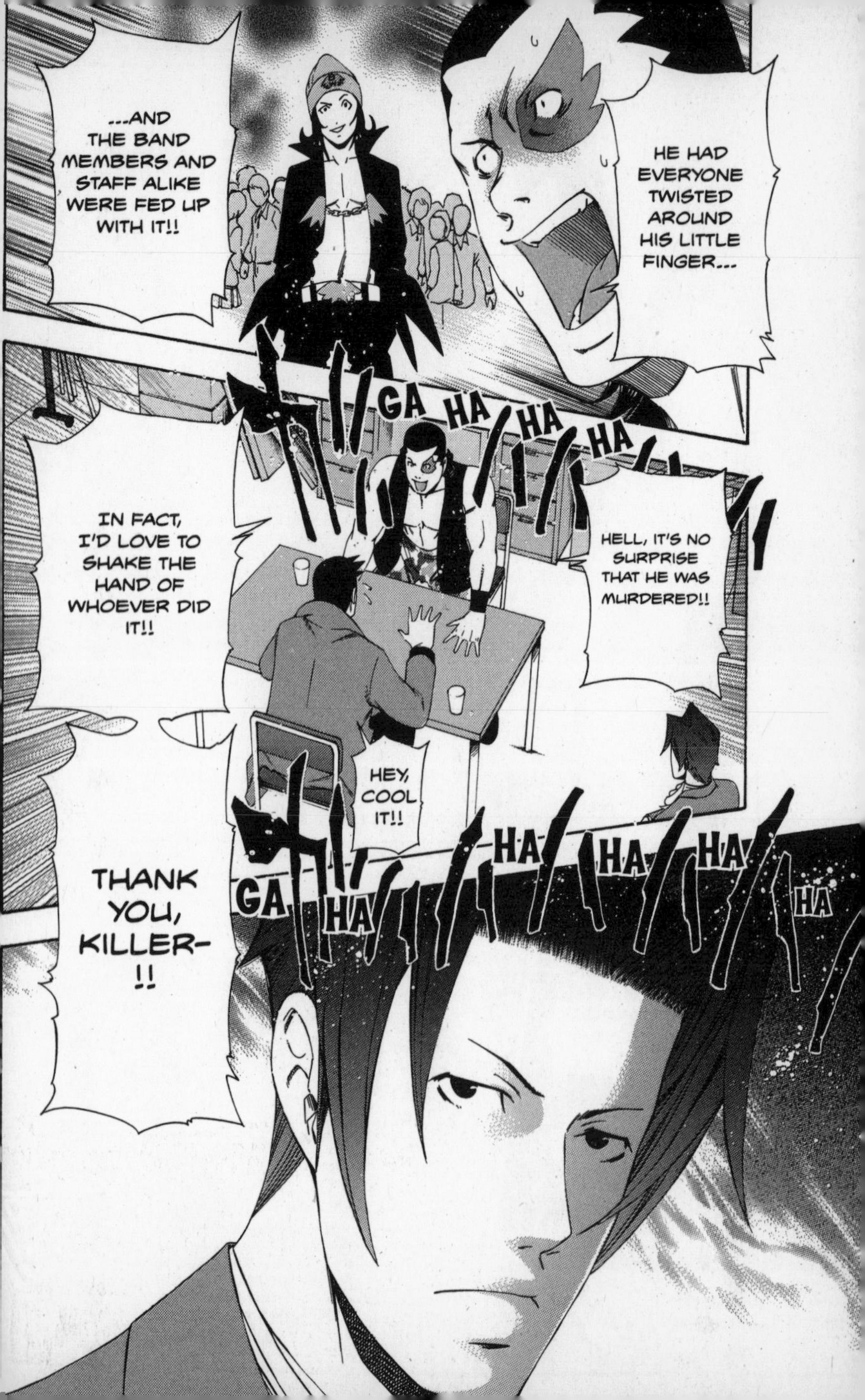
HE HAD EVERYONE TWISTED AROUND HIS LITTLE FINGER...
...AND THE BAND MEMBERS AND STAFF ALIKE WERE FED UP WITH IT!!
GA HA HA HA
HELL, IT'S NO SURPRISE THAT HE WAS MURDERED!!
IN FACT, I'D LOVE TO SHAKE THE HAND OF WHOEVER DID IT!!
HEY, COOL IT!!
GA HA HA HA HA HA
THANK YOU, KILLER-!!

Ace Attorney
Miles Edgeworth
INVESTIGATIONS

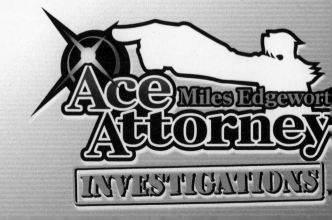

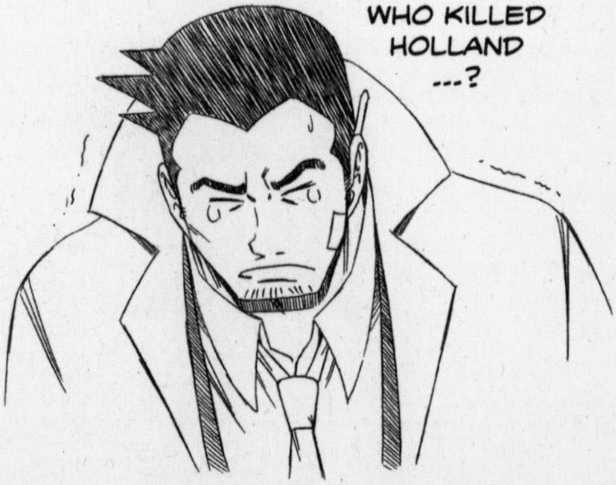
WHO KILLED HOLLAND ---?

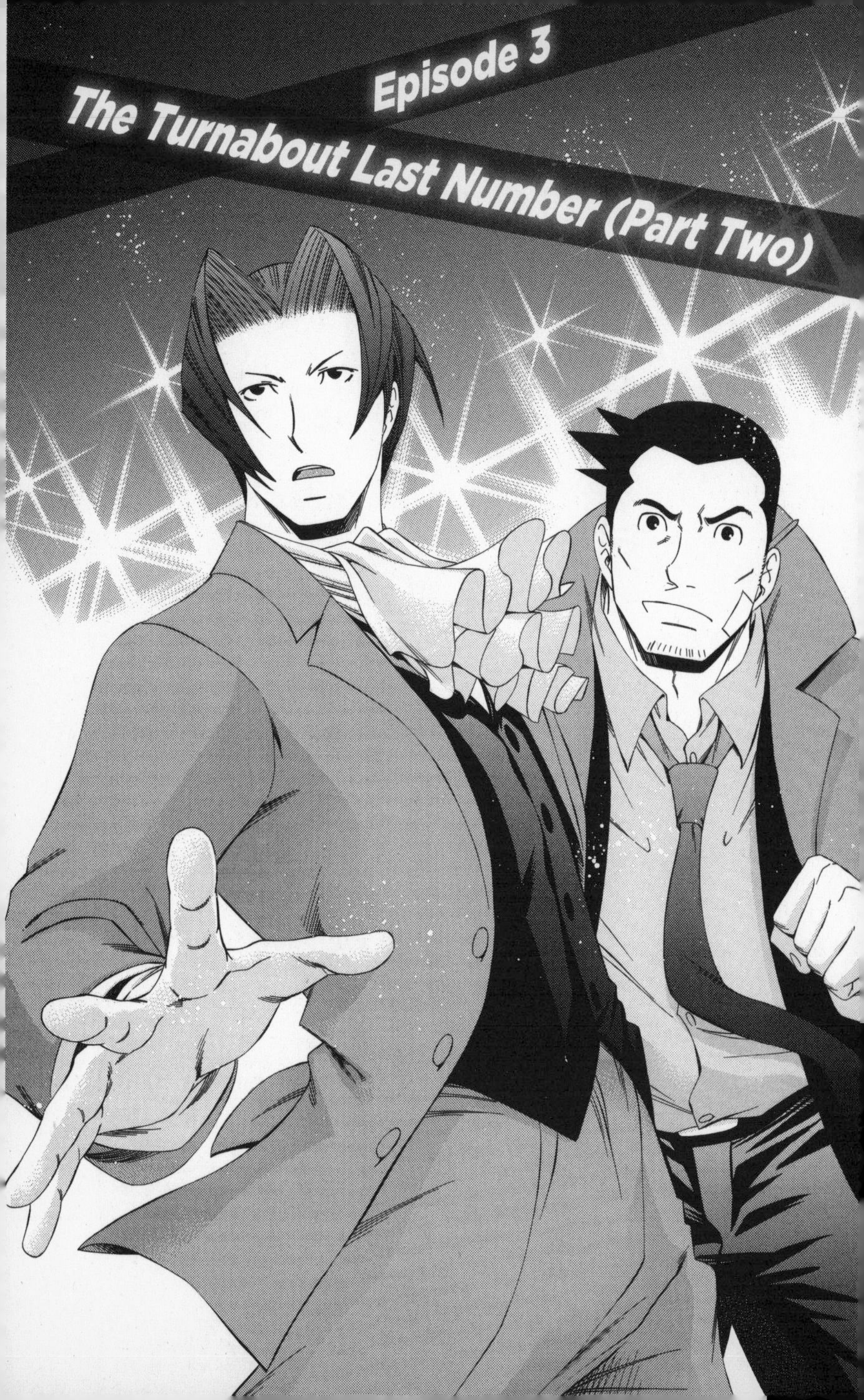
Episode 3
The Turnabout Last Number (Part Two)

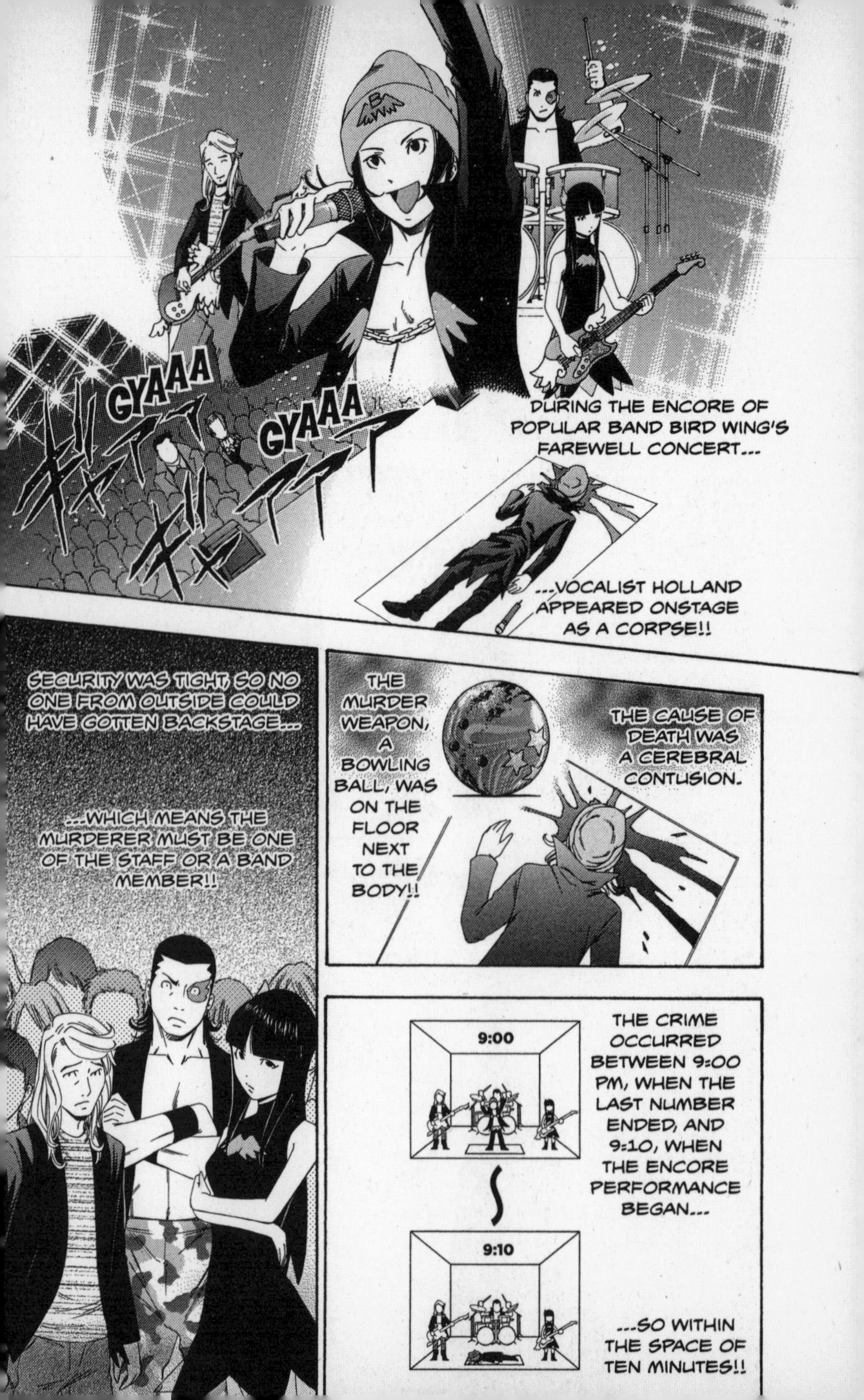

DURING THE ENCORE OF POPULAR BAND BIRD WING'S FAREWELL CONCERT...
GYAAA
GYAAA
...VOCALIST HOLLAND APPEARED ONSTAGE AS A CORPSE!!
THE CAUSE OF DEATH WAS A CEREBRAL CONTUSION.
THE MURDER WEAPON, A BOWLING BALL, WAS ON THE FLOOR NEXT TO THE BODY!!
THE CRIME OCCURRED BETWEEN 9:00 PM, WHEN THE LAST NUMBER ENDED, AND 9:10, WHEN THE ENCORE PERFORMANCE BEGAN...
9:00
9:10
...SO WITHIN THE SPACE OF TEN MINUTES!!
SECURITY WAS TIGHT, SO NO ONE FROM OUTSIDE COULD HAVE GOTTEN BACKSTAGE...
...WHICH MEANS THE MURDERER MUST BE ONE OF THE STAFF OR A BAND MEMBER!!

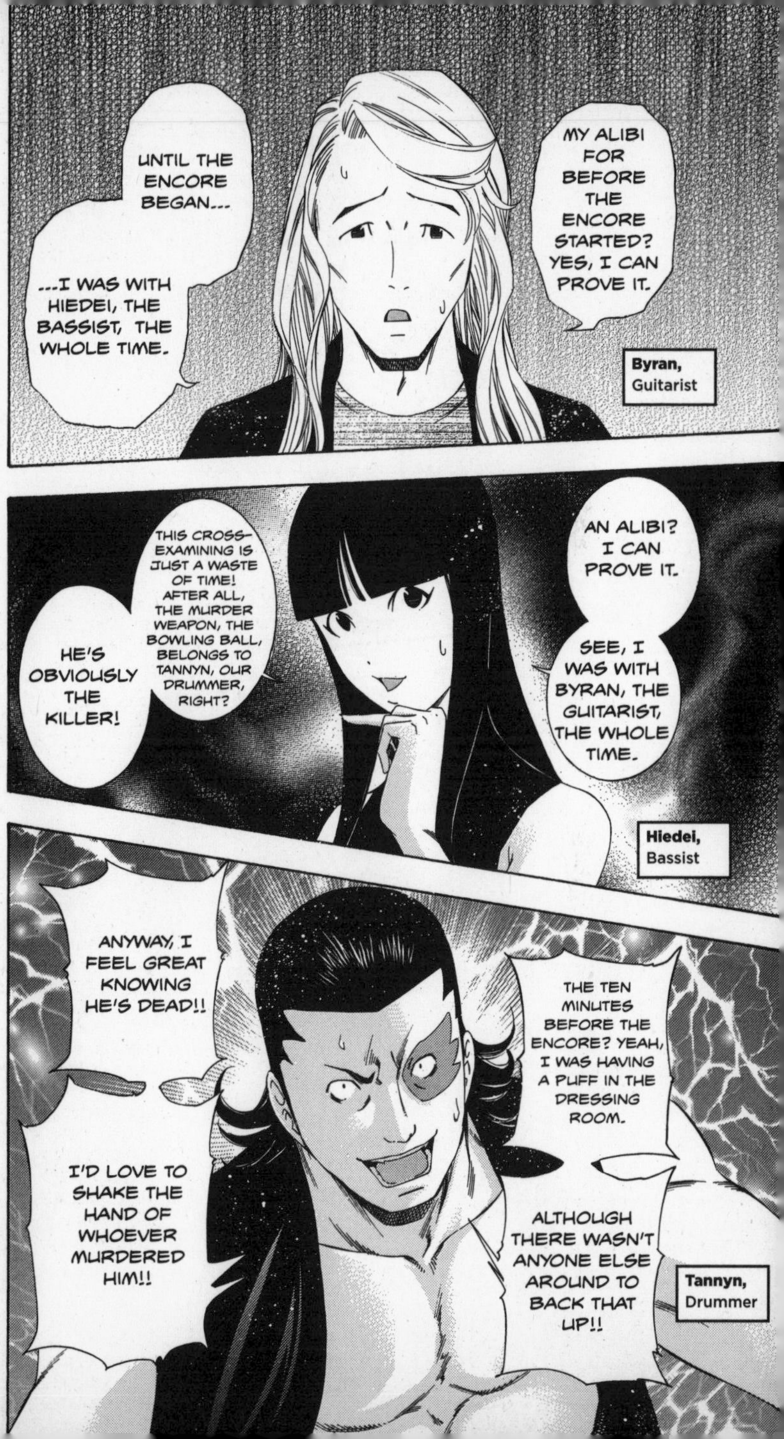
MY ALIBI FOR BEFORE THE ENCORE STARTED? YES, I CAN PROVE IT.
UNTIL THE ENCORE BEGAN...
...I WAS WITH HIEDEI, THE BASSIST, THE WHOLE TIME.
Byran, Guitarist
AN ALIBI? I CAN PROVE IT.
SEE, I WAS WITH BYRAN, THE GUITARIST, THE WHOLE TIME.
THIS CROSS-EXAMINING IS JUST A WASTE OF TIME! AFTER ALL, THE MURDER WEAPON, THE BOWLING BALL, BELONGS TO TANNYN, OUR DRUMMER, RIGHT?
HE'S OBVIOUSLY THE KILLER!
Hiedei, Bassist
THE TEN MINUTES BEFORE THE ENCORE? YEAH, I WAS HAVING A PUFF IN THE DRESSING ROOM.
ALTHOUGH THERE WASN'T ANYONE ELSE AROUND TO BACK THAT UP!!
ANYWAY, I FEEL GREAT KNOWING HE'S DEAD!!
I'D LOVE TO SHAKE THE HAND OF WHOEVER MURDERED HIM!!
Tannyn, Drummer

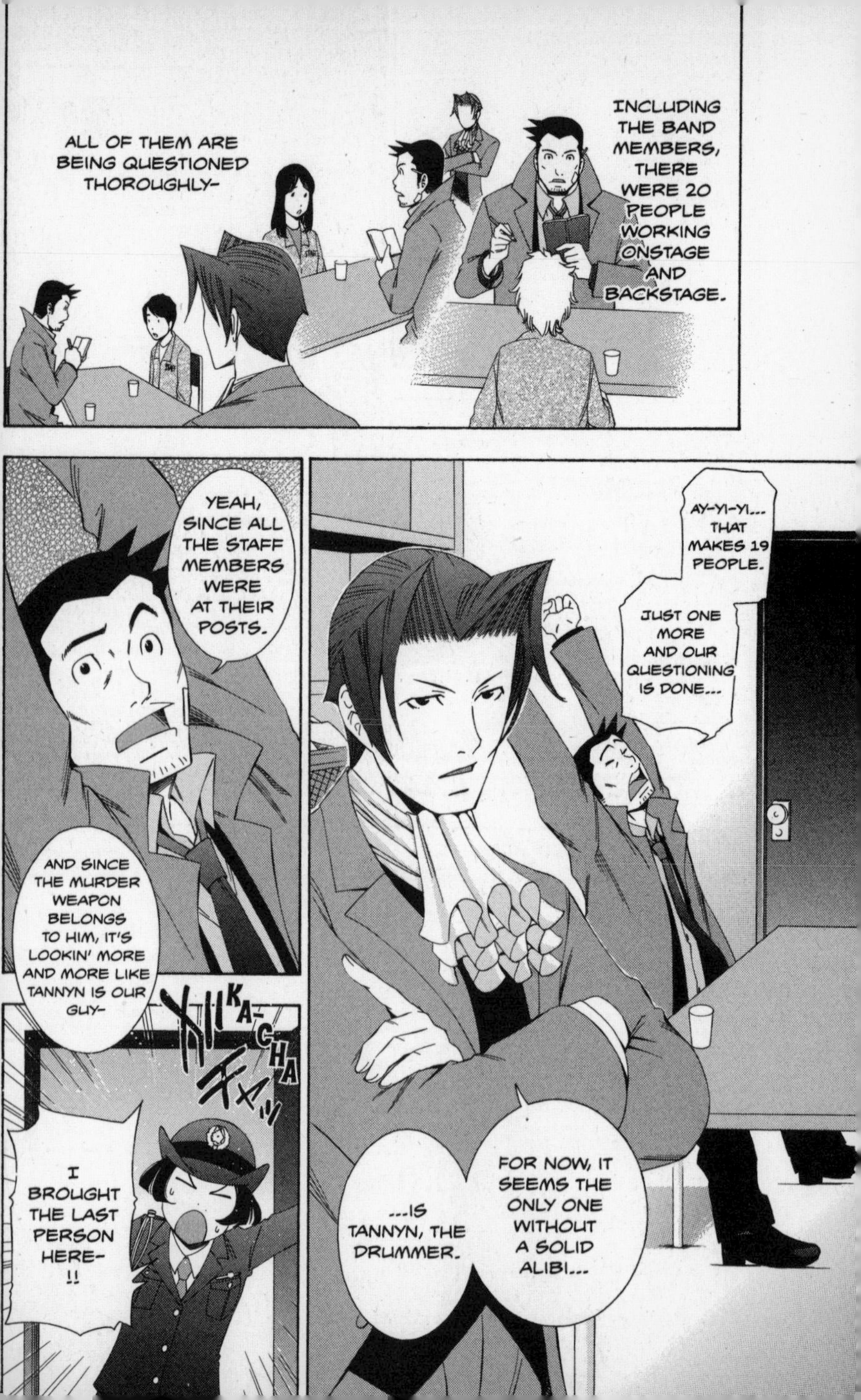
INCLUDING THE BAND MEMBERS, THERE WERE 20 PEOPLE WORKING ONSTAGE AND BACKSTAGE.
ALL OF THEM ARE BEING QUESTIONED THOROUGHLY-
AY-YI-YI... THAT MAKES 19 PEOPLE.
JUST ONE MORE AND OUR QUESTIONING IS DONE...
FOR NOW, IT SEEMS THE ONLY ONE WITHOUT A SOLID ALIBI...
...IS TANNYN, THE DRUMMER.
YEAH, SINCE ALL THE STAFF MEMBERS WERE AT THEIR POSTS.
AND SINCE THE MURDER WEAPON BELONGS TO HIM, IT'S LOOKIN' MORE AND MORE LIKE TANNYN IS OUR GUY-
KA-CHA
I BROUGHT THE LAST PERSON HERE-!!

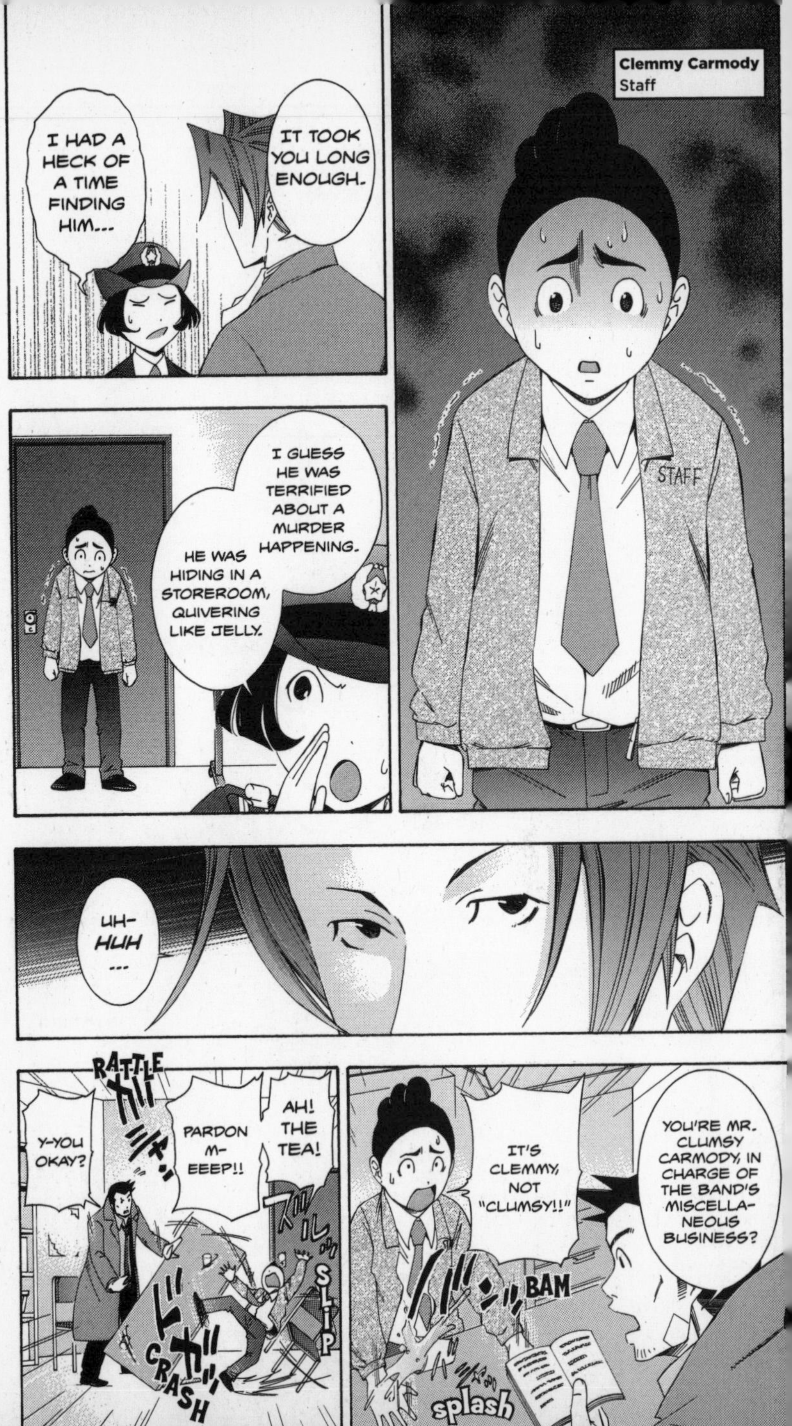
Clemmy Carmody
Staff
STAFF
IT TOOK YOU LONG ENOUGH.
I HAD A HECK OF A TIME FINDING HIM...
I GUESS HE WAS TERRIFIED ABOUT A MURDER HAPPENING.
HE WAS HIDING IN A STOREROOM, QUIVERING LIKE JELLY.
UH-HUH...
YOU'RE MR. CLUMSY CARMODY, IN CHARGE OF THE BAND'S MISCELLANEOUS BUSINESS?
IT'S CLEMMY, NOT "CLUMSY!!"
BAM
splash
AH! THE TEA!
RATTLE
PARDON M-EEEP!!
Y-YOU OKAY?
SLIP
CRASH

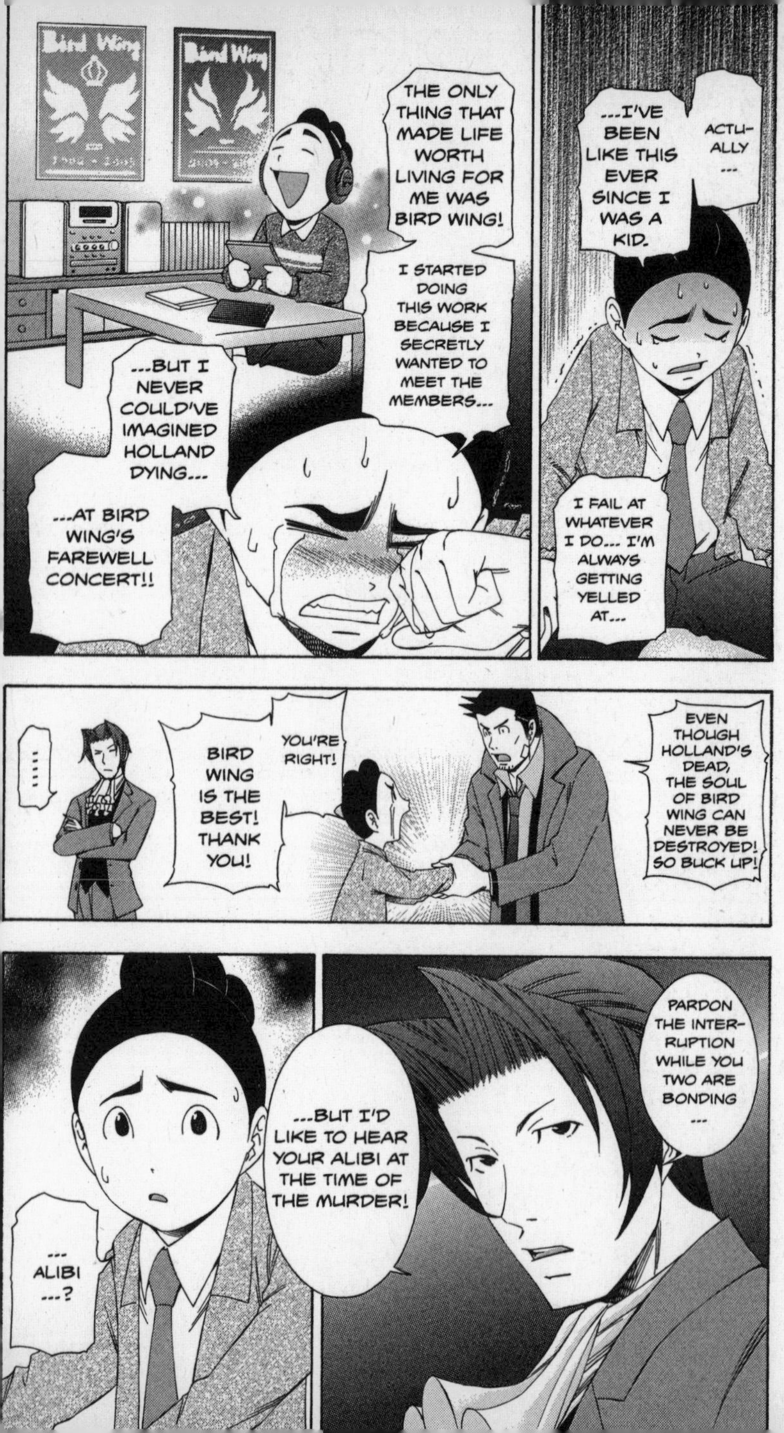
ACTU-ALLY ...
...I'VE BEEN LIKE THIS EVER SINCE I WAS A KID.
I FAIL AT WHATEVER I DO... I'M ALWAYS GETTING YELLED AT...
THE ONLY THING THAT MADE LIFE WORTH LIVING FOR ME WAS BIRD WING!
Bird Wing
Bird Wing
I STARTED DOING THIS WORK BECAUSE I SECRETLY WANTED TO MEET THE MEMBERS...
...BUT I NEVER COULD'VE IMAGINED HOLLAND DYING...
...AT BIRD WING'S FAREWELL CONCERT!!
EVEN THOUGH HOLLAND'S DEAD, THE SOUL OF BIRD WING CAN NEVER BE DESTROYED! SO BUCK UP!
YOU'RE RIGHT!
BIRD WING IS THE BEST! THANK YOU!
......
PARDON THE INTER-RUPTION WHILE YOU TWO ARE BONDING ...
...BUT I'D LIKE TO HEAR YOUR ALIBI AT THE TIME OF THE MURDER!
...ALIBI...?

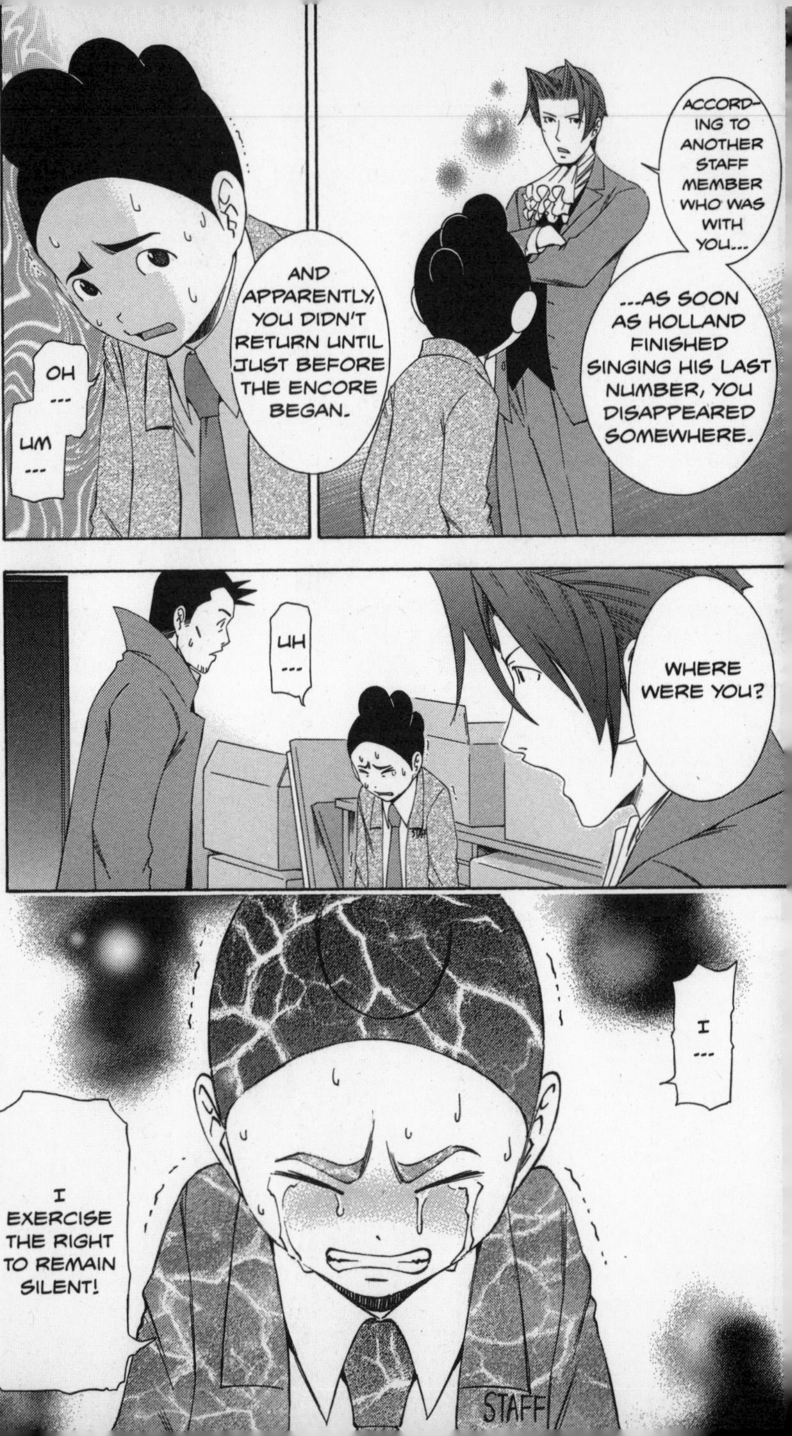
ACCORD-ING TO ANOTHER STAFF MEMBER WHO WAS WITH YOU...
...AS SOON AS HOLLAND FINISHED SINGING HIS LAST NUMBER, YOU DISAPPEARED SOMEWHERE.
AND APPARENTLY, YOU DIDN'T RETURN UNTIL JUST BEFORE THE ENCORE BEGAN.
OH... UM...
WHERE WERE YOU?
UH...
I...
I EXERCISE THE RIGHT TO REMAIN SILENT!
STAFF

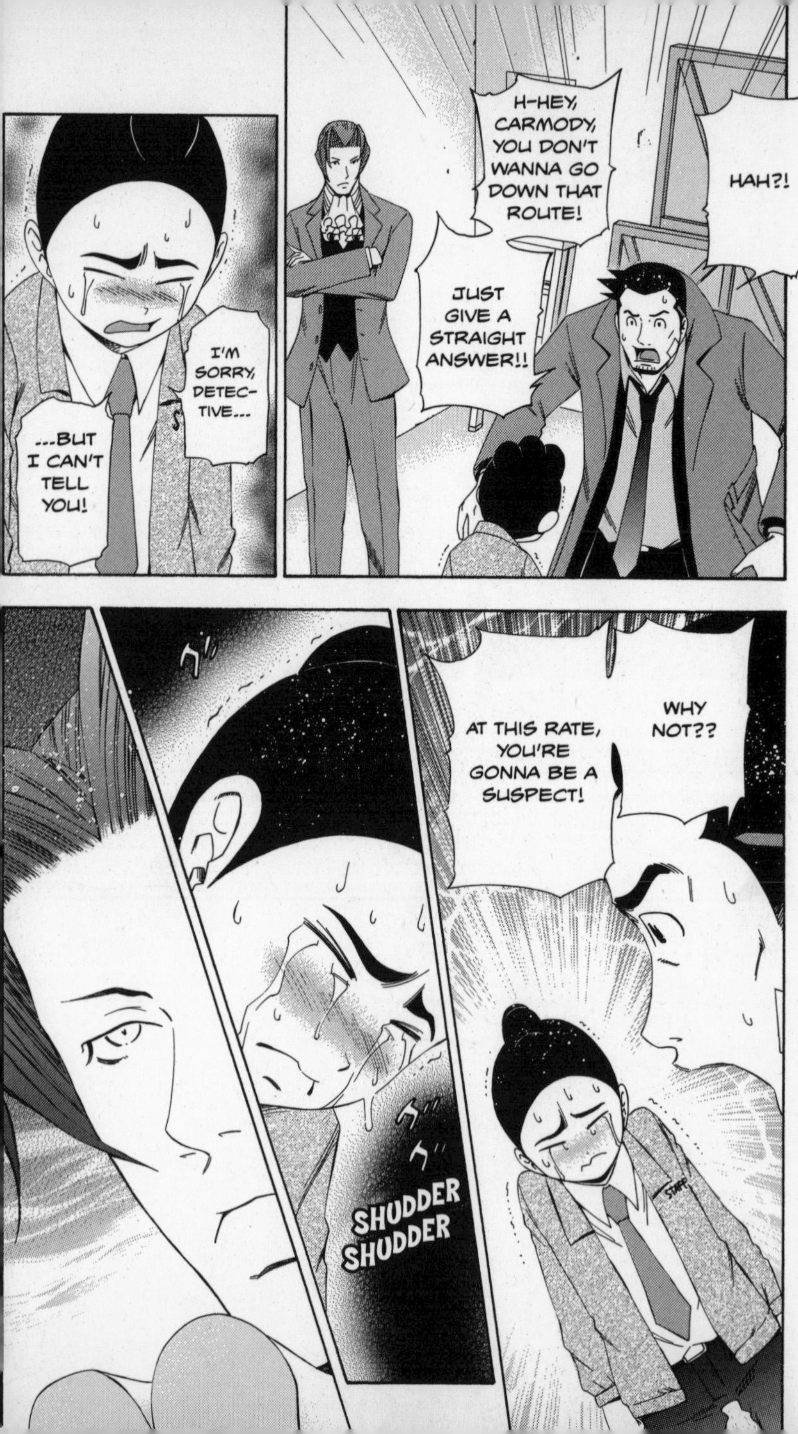
HAH?!
H-HEY, CARMODY, YOU DON'T WANNA GO DOWN THAT ROUTE!
JUST GIVE A STRAIGHT ANSWER!!
I'M SORRY, DETECTIVE...
...BUT I CAN'T TELL YOU!
WHY NOT??
AT THIS RATE, YOU'RE GONNA BE A SUSPECT!
SHUDDER SHUDDER

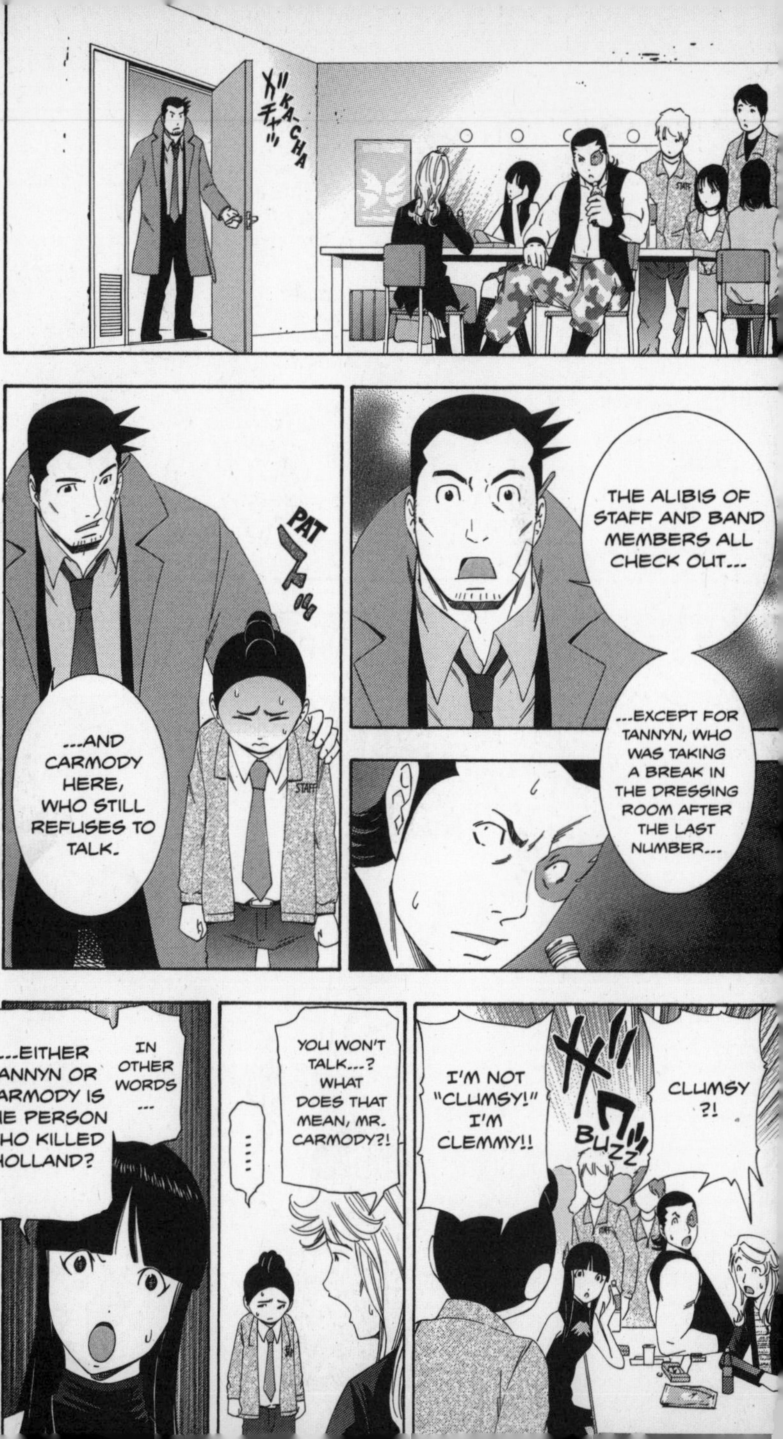
KA-CHA
THE ALIBIS OF STAFF AND BAND MEMBERS ALL CHECK OUT...
...EXCEPT FOR TANNYN, WHO WAS TAKING A BREAK IN THE DRESSING ROOM AFTER THE LAST NUMBER...
PAT
...AND CARMODY HERE, WHO STILL REFUSES TO TALK.
CLUMSY ?!
BUZZ
I'M NOT "CLUMSY!" I'M CLEMMY!!
YOU WON'T TALK...? WHAT DOES THAT MEAN, MR. CARMODY?!
.....
IN OTHER WORDS ...
...EITHER TANNYN OR CARMODY IS THE PERSON WHO KILLED HOLLAND?

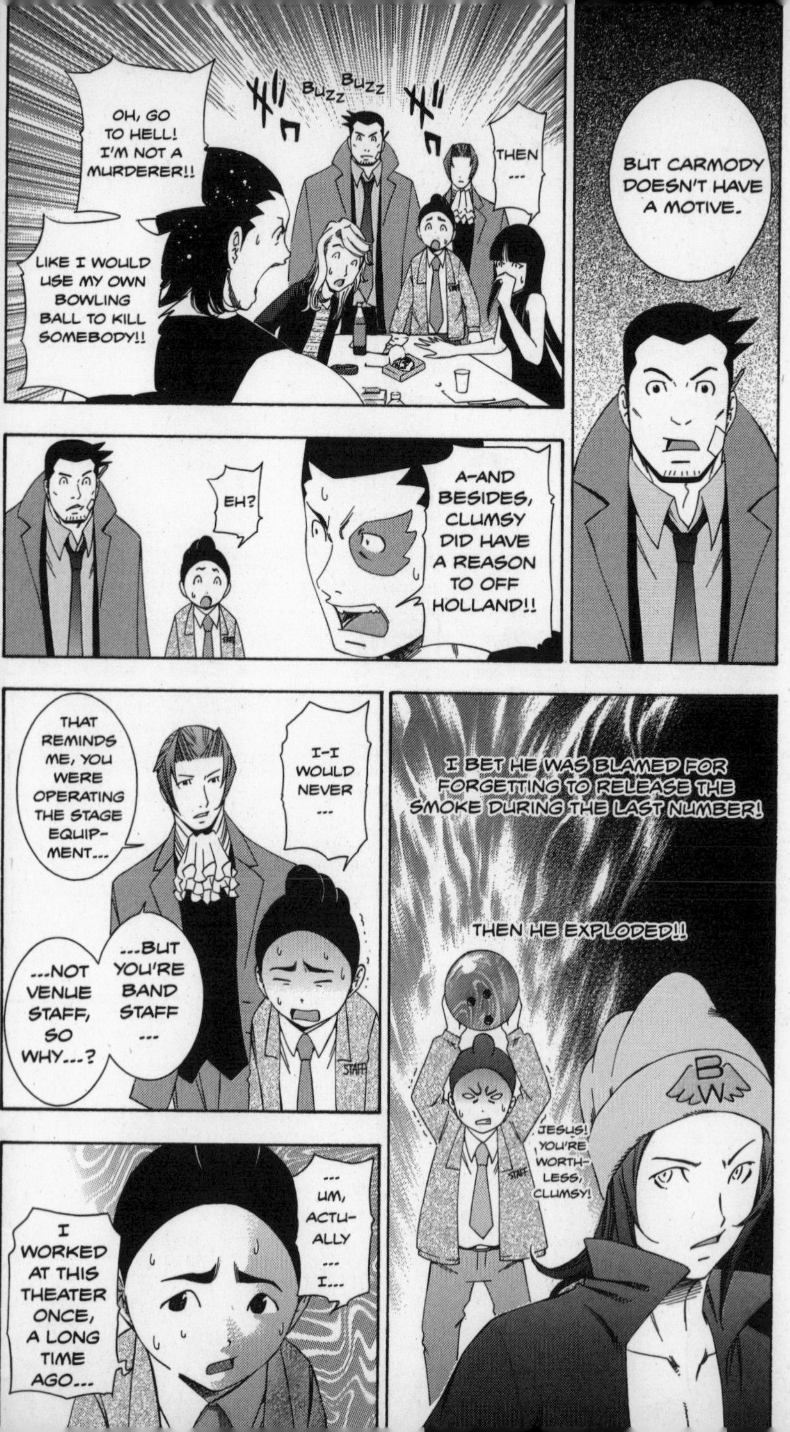
BUT CARMODY DOESN'T HAVE A MOTIVE.
BUZZ BUZZ
THEN ---
OH, GO TO HELL! I'M NOT A MURDERER!!
LIKE I WOULD USE MY OWN BOWLING BALL TO KILL SOMEBODY!!
A-AND BESIDES, CLUMSY DID HAVE A REASON TO OFF HOLLAND!!
EH?
I BET HE WAS BLAMED FOR FORGETTING TO RELEASE THE SMOKE DURING THE LAST NUMBER!
THEN HE EXPLODED!!
JESUS! YOU'RE WORTHLESS, CLUMSY!
I-I WOULD NEVER ---
THAT REMINDS ME, YOU WERE OPERATING THE STAGE EQUIPMENT...
...BUT YOU'RE BAND STAFF ---
...NOT VENUE STAFF, SO WHY...?
--- UM, ACTUALLY --- I...
I WORKED AT THIS THEATER ONCE, A LONG TIME AGO...

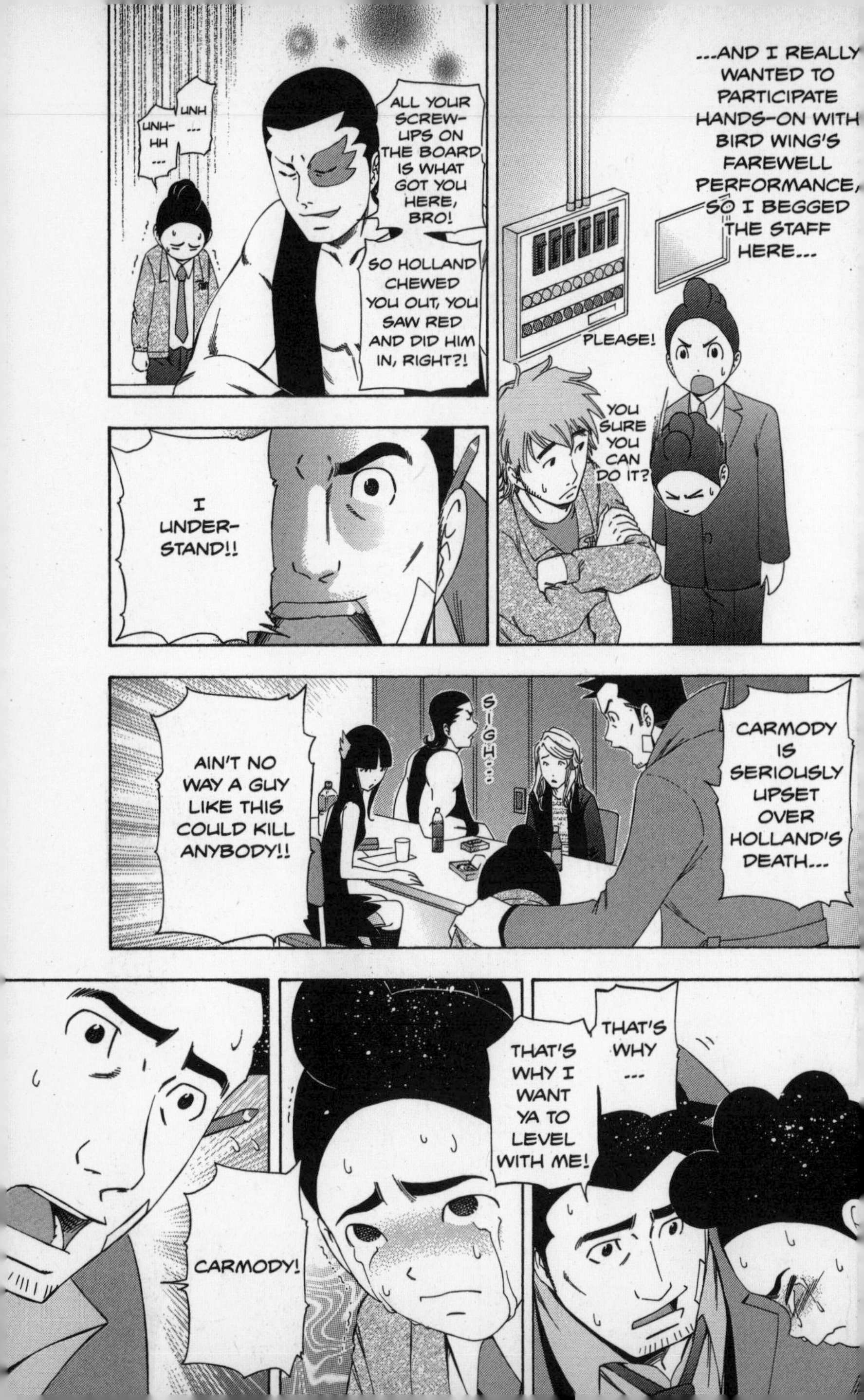
...AND I REALLY WANTED TO PARTICIPATE HANDS-ON WITH BIRD WING'S FAREWELL PERFORMANCE, SO I BEGGED THE STAFF HERE...
PLEASE!
YOU SURE YOU CAN DO IT?
ALL YOUR SCREW-UPS ON THE BOARD IS WHAT GOT YOU HERE, BRO!
SO HOLLAND CHEWED YOU OUT, YOU SAW RED AND DID HIM IN, RIGHT?!
UNH ...
UNH-HH ...
I UNDER-STAND!!
CARMODY IS SERIOUSLY UPSET OVER HOLLAND'S DEATH...
SIGH...
AIN'T NO WAY A GUY LIKE THIS COULD KILL ANYBODY!!
THAT'S WHY ...
THAT'S WHY I WANT YA TO LEVEL WITH ME!
CARMODY!

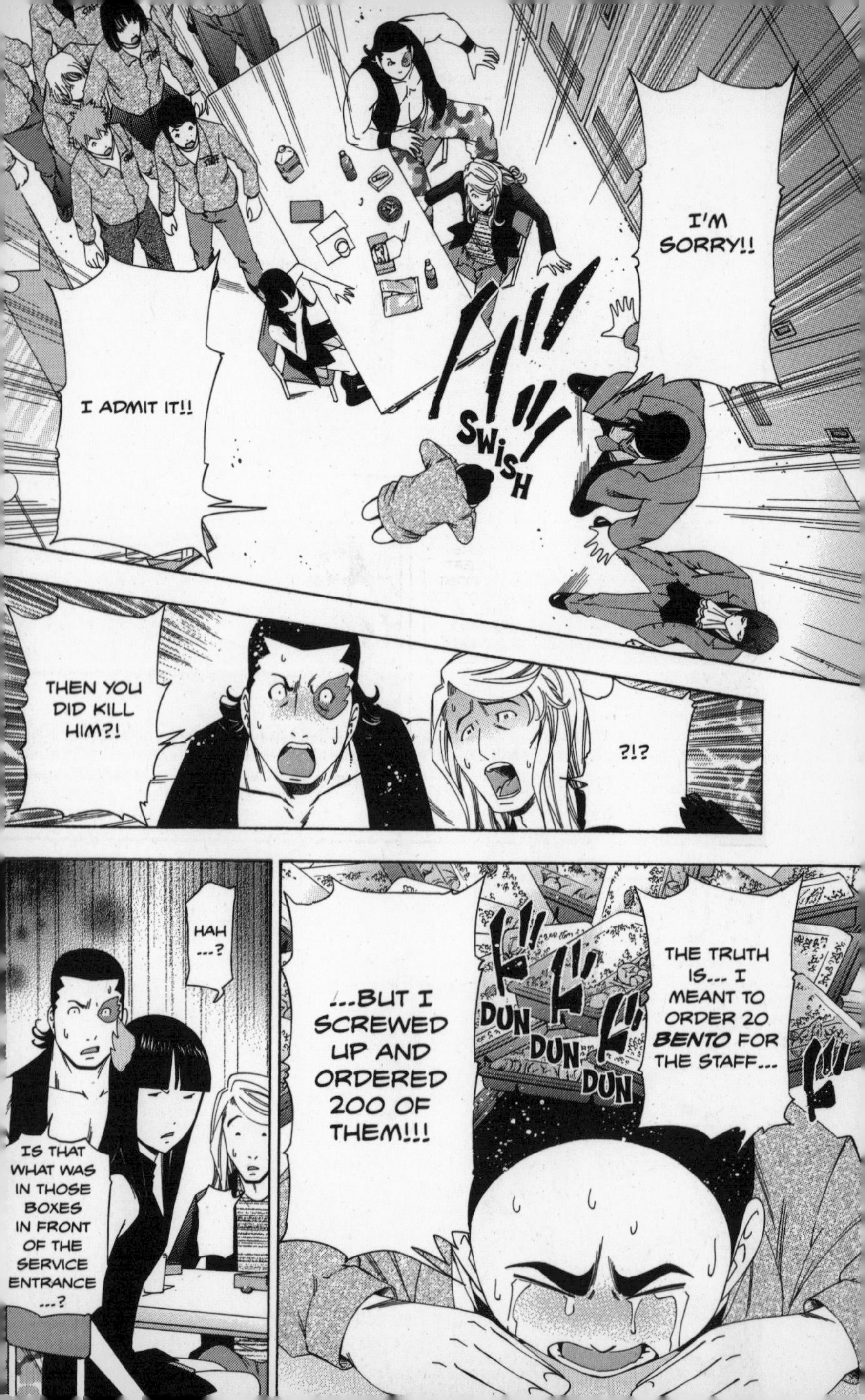
I'M SORRY!!
SWISH
I ADMIT IT!!
?!?
THEN YOU DID KILL HIM?!
THE TRUTH IS... I MEANT TO ORDER 20 *BENTO* FOR THE STAFF...
DUN DUN DUN
...BUT I SCREWED UP AND ORDERED 200 OF THEM!!!
HAH ...?
IS THAT WHAT WAS IN THOSE BOXES IN FRONT OF THE SERVICE ENTRANCE ...?

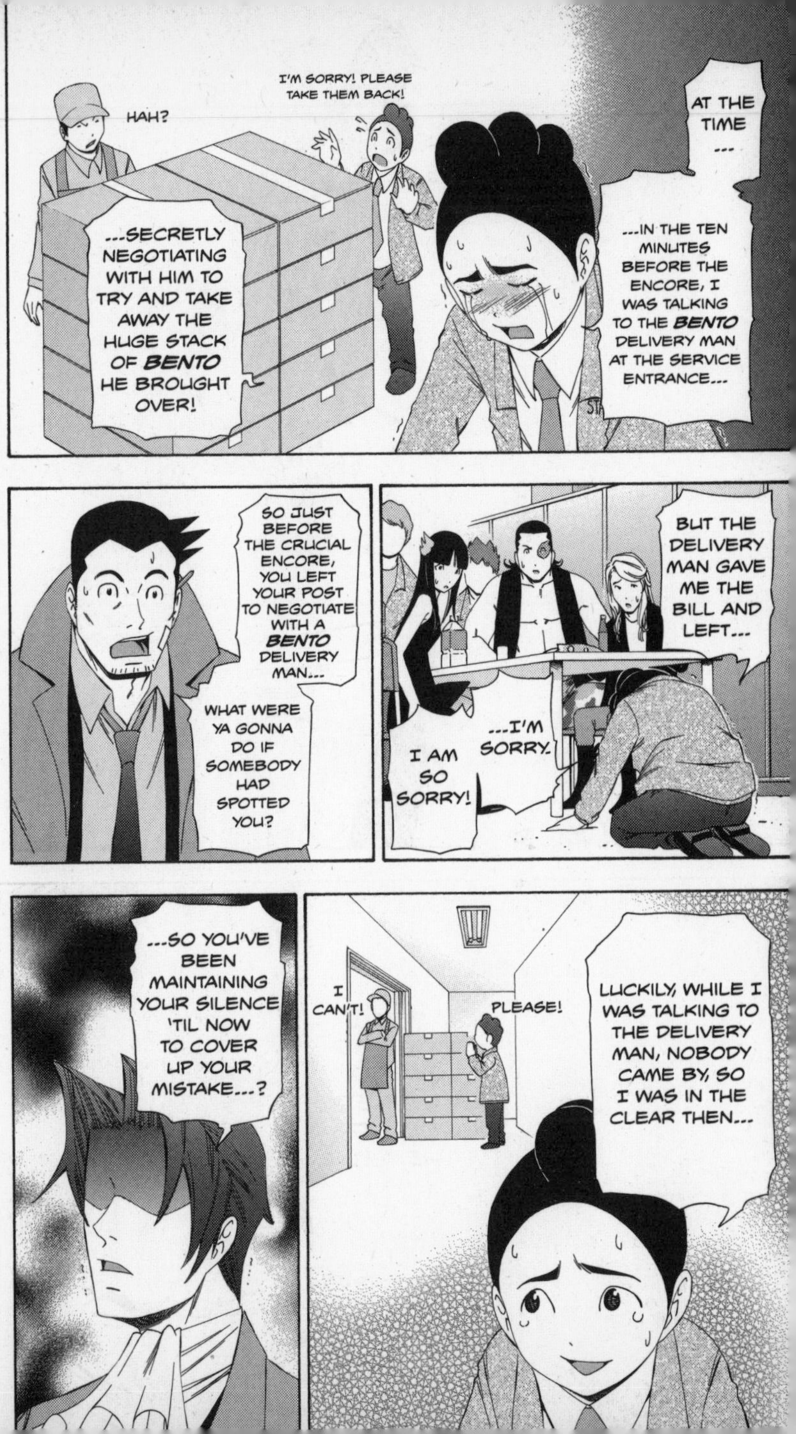
AT THE TIME ---
...IN THE TEN MINUTES BEFORE THE ENCORE, I WAS TALKING TO THE *BENTO* DELIVERY MAN AT THE SERVICE ENTRANCE...
I'M SORRY! PLEASE TAKE THEM BACK!
HAH?
...SECRETLY NEGOTIATING WITH HIM TO TRY AND TAKE AWAY THE HUGE STACK OF *BENTO* HE BROUGHT OVER!
BUT THE DELIVERY MAN GAVE ME THE BILL AND LEFT...
...I'M SORRY.
I AM SO SORRY!
SO JUST BEFORE THE CRUCIAL ENCORE, YOU LEFT YOUR POST TO NEGOTIATE WITH A *BENTO* DELIVERY MAN...
WHAT WERE YA GONNA DO IF SOMEBODY HAD SPOTTED YOU?
LUCKILY, WHILE I WAS TALKING TO THE DELIVERY MAN, NOBODY CAME BY, SO I WAS IN THE CLEAR THEN...
PLEASE!
I CAN'T!
...SO YOU'VE BEEN MAINTAINING YOUR SILENCE 'TIL NOW TO COVER UP YOUR MISTAKE...?

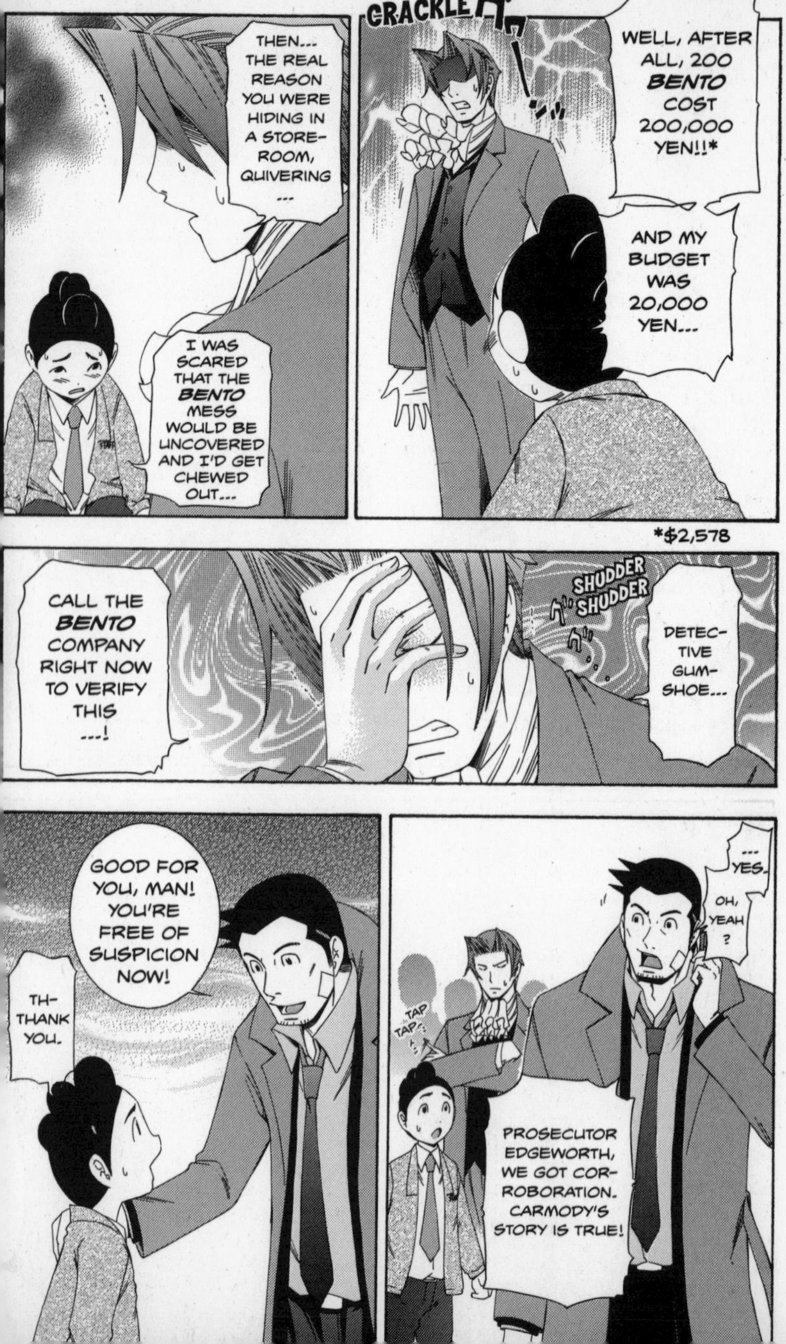
CRACKLE
WELL, AFTER ALL, 200 BENTO COST 200,000 YEN!!*
AND MY BUDGET WAS 20,000 YEN...
THEN... THE REAL REASON YOU WERE HIDING IN A STORE-ROOM, QUIVERING ...
I WAS SCARED THAT THE BENTO MESS WOULD BE UNCOVERED AND I'D GET CHEWED OUT...
SHUDDER SHUDDER
DETEC-TIVE GUM-SHOE...
CALL THE BENTO COMPANY RIGHT NOW TO VERIFY THIS ...!
...YES.
OH, YEAH?
TAP TAP
PROSECUTOR EDGEWORTH, WE GOT COR-ROBORATION. CARMODY'S STORY IS TRUE!
GOOD FOR YOU, MAN! YOU'RE FREE OF SUSPICION NOW!
TH-THANK YOU.

*$2,578

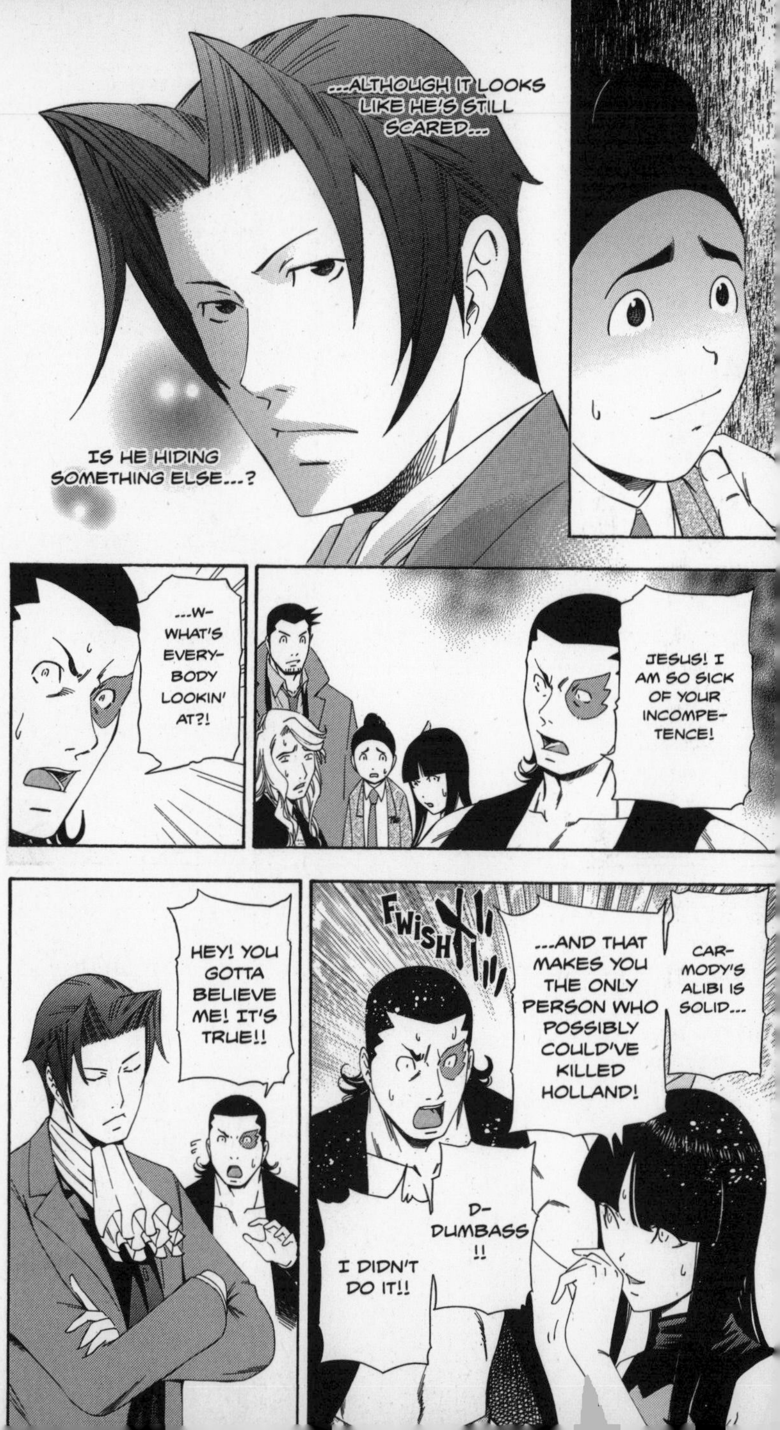
...ALTHOUGH IT LOOKS LIKE HE'S STILL SCARED...
IS HE HIDING SOMETHING ELSE...?
JESUS! I AM SO SICK OF YOUR INCOMPE-TENCE!
...W-WHAT'S EVERY-BODY LOOKIN' AT?!
CAR-MODY'S ALIBI IS SOLID...
...AND THAT MAKES YOU THE ONLY PERSON WHO POSSIBLY COULD'VE KILLED HOLLAND!
FWISH
D-DUMBASS!!
I DIDN'T DO IT!!
HEY! YOU GOTTA BELIEVE ME! IT'S TRUE!!

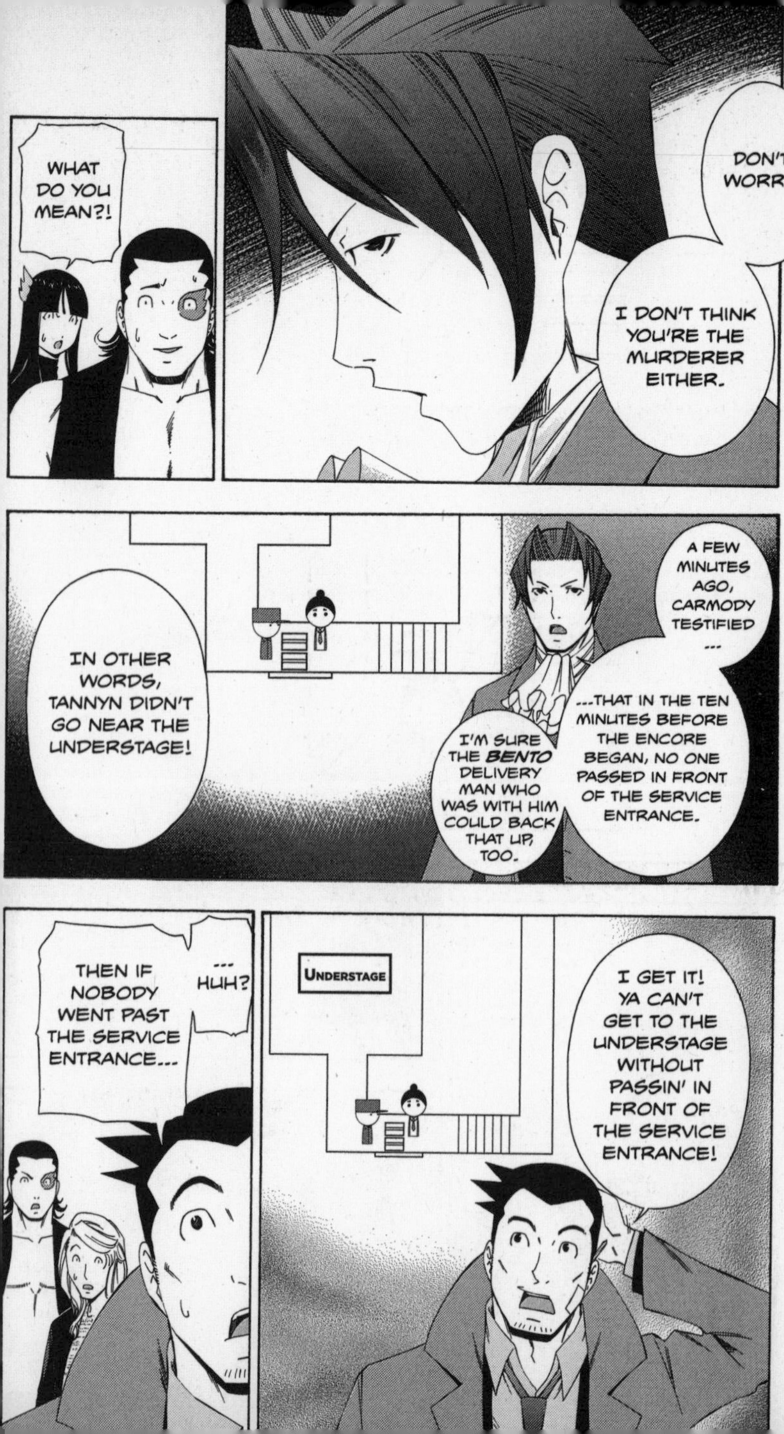
DON'T WORRY.
I DON'T THINK YOU'RE THE MURDERER EITHER.
WHAT DO YOU MEAN?!
A FEW MINUTES AGO, CARMODY TESTIFIED...
...THAT IN THE TEN MINUTES BEFORE THE ENCORE BEGAN, NO ONE PASSED IN FRONT OF THE SERVICE ENTRANCE.
I'M SURE THE *BENTO* DELIVERY MAN WHO WAS WITH HIM COULD BACK THAT UP, TOO.
IN OTHER WORDS, TANNYN DIDN'T GO NEAR THE UNDERSTAGE!
I GET IT! YA CAN'T GET TO THE UNDERSTAGE WITHOUT PASSIN' IN FRONT OF THE SERVICE ENTRANCE!
UNDERSTAGE
...HUH?
THEN IF NOBODY WENT PAST THE SERVICE ENTRANCE...

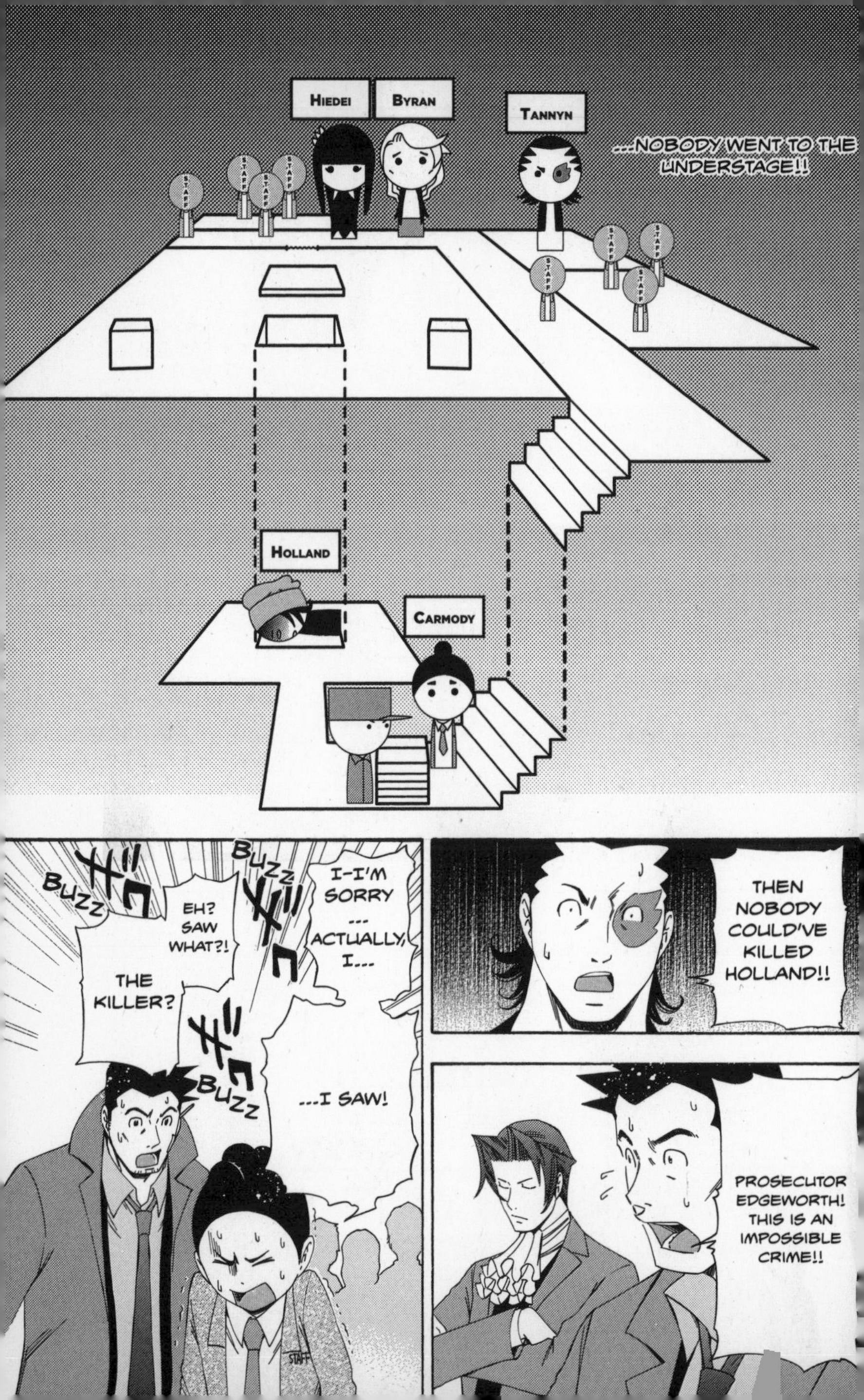
HIEDEI
BYRAN
TANNYN
...NOBODY WENT TO THE UNDERSTAGE!!
STAFF
HOLLAND
CARMODY
THEN NOBODY COULD'VE KILLED HOLLAND!!
PROSECUTOR EDGEWORTH! THIS IS AN IMPOSSIBLE CRIME!!
I-I'M SORRY --- ACTUALLY, I...
BUZZ
EH? SAW WHAT?!
BUZZ
THE KILLER?
...I SAW!
BUZZ
STAFF

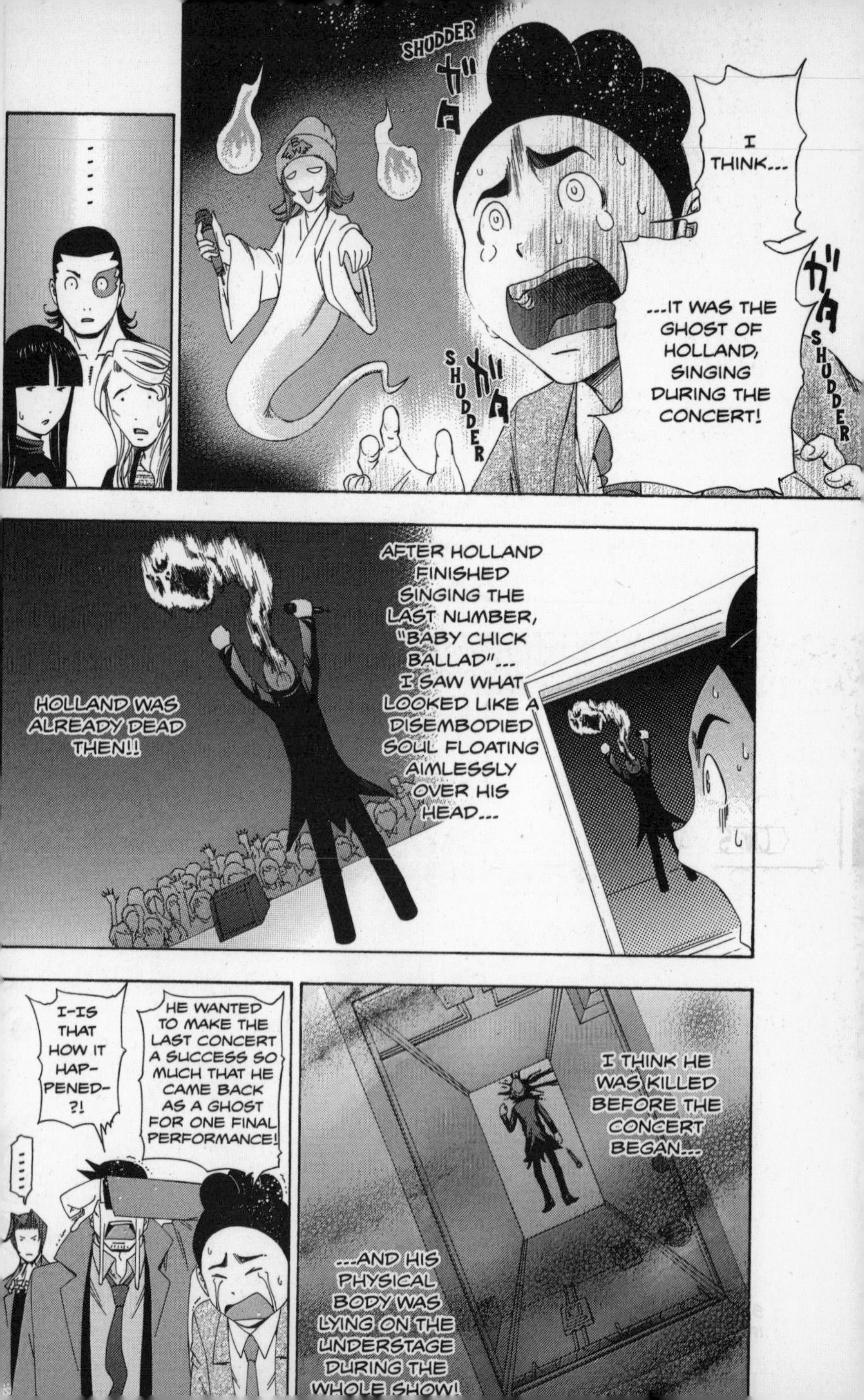

I THINK...
SHUDDER
...IT WAS THE GHOST OF HOLLAND, SINGING DURING THE CONCERT!
SHUDDER
SHUDDER
......
AFTER HOLLAND FINISHED SINGING THE LAST NUMBER, "BABY CHICK BALLAD"... I SAW WHAT LOOKED LIKE A DISEMBODIED SOUL FLOATING AIMLESSLY OVER HIS HEAD...
HOLLAND WAS ALREADY DEAD THEN!!
I THINK HE WAS KILLED BEFORE THE CONCERT BEGAN...
...AND HIS PHYSICAL BODY WAS LYING ON THE UNDERSTAGE DURING THE WHOLE SHOW!
HE WANTED TO MAKE THE LAST CONCERT A SUCCESS SO MUCH THAT HE CAME BACK AS A GHOST FOR ONE FINAL PERFORMANCE!
I-IS THAT HOW IT HAP-PENED-?!
......

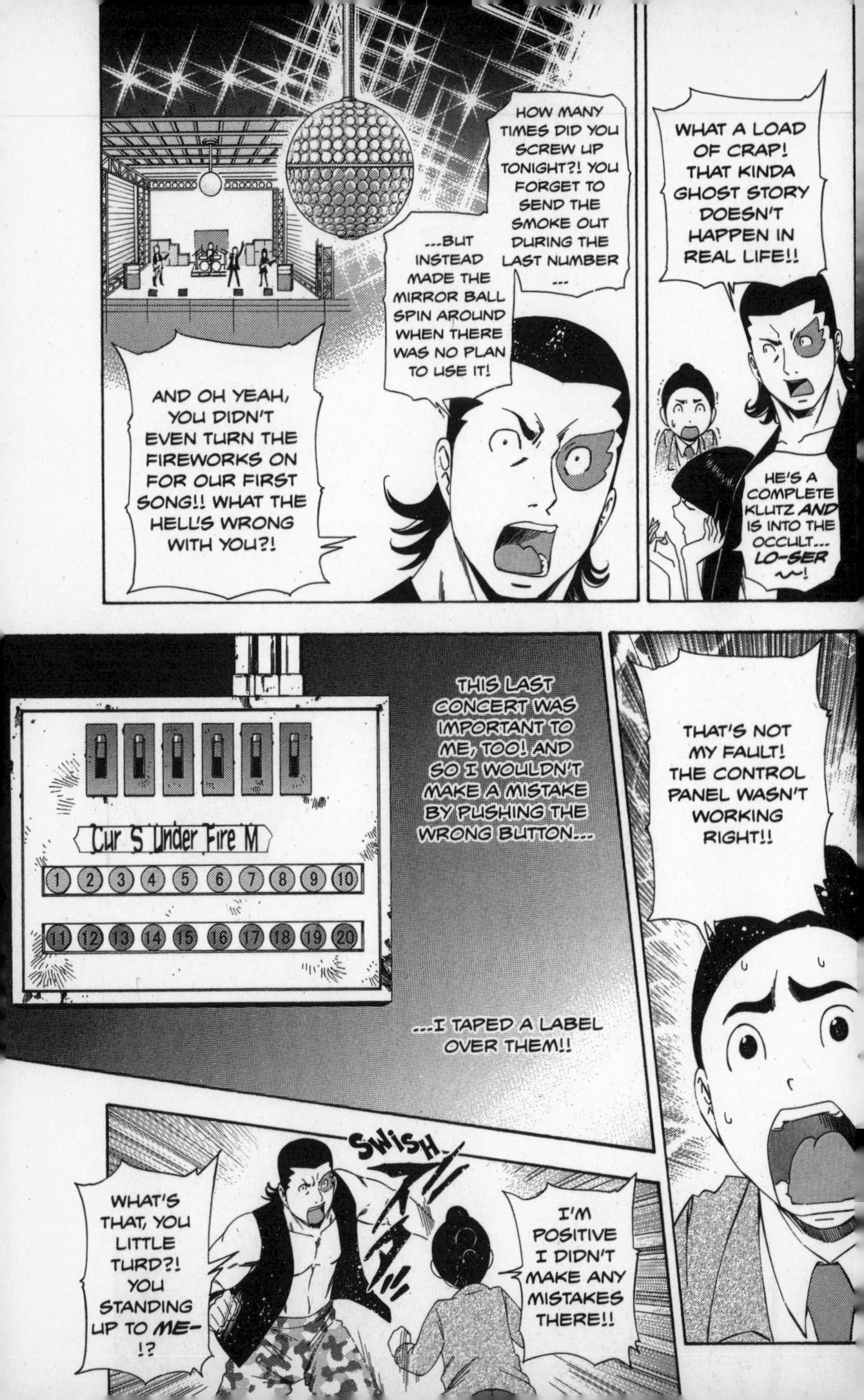
WHAT A LOAD OF CRAP! THAT KINDA GHOST STORY DOESN'T HAPPEN IN REAL LIFE!!
HE'S A COMPLETE KLUTZ *AND* IS INTO THE OCCULT... *LO-SER* ~~!
HOW MANY TIMES DID YOU SCREW UP TONIGHT?! YOU FORGET TO SEND THE SMOKE OUT DURING THE LAST NUMBER ...
...BUT INSTEAD MADE THE MIRROR BALL SPIN AROUND WHEN THERE WAS NO PLAN TO USE IT!
AND OH YEAH, YOU DIDN'T EVEN TURN THE FIREWORKS ON FOR OUR FIRST SONG!! WHAT THE HELL'S WRONG WITH YOU?!
THAT'S NOT MY FAULT! THE CONTROL PANEL WASN'T WORKING RIGHT!!
THIS LAST CONCERT WAS IMPORTANT TO ME, TOO! AND SO I WOULDN'T MAKE A MISTAKE BY PUSHING THE WRONG BUTTON...
Cur S Under Fire M
1 2 3 4 5 6 7 8 9 10
11 12 13 14 15 16 17 18 19 20
...I TAPED A LABEL OVER THEM!!
I'M POSITIVE I DIDN'T MAKE ANY MISTAKES THERE!!
SWISH
WHAT'S THAT, YOU LITTLE TURD?! YOU STANDING UP TO *ME*-!?

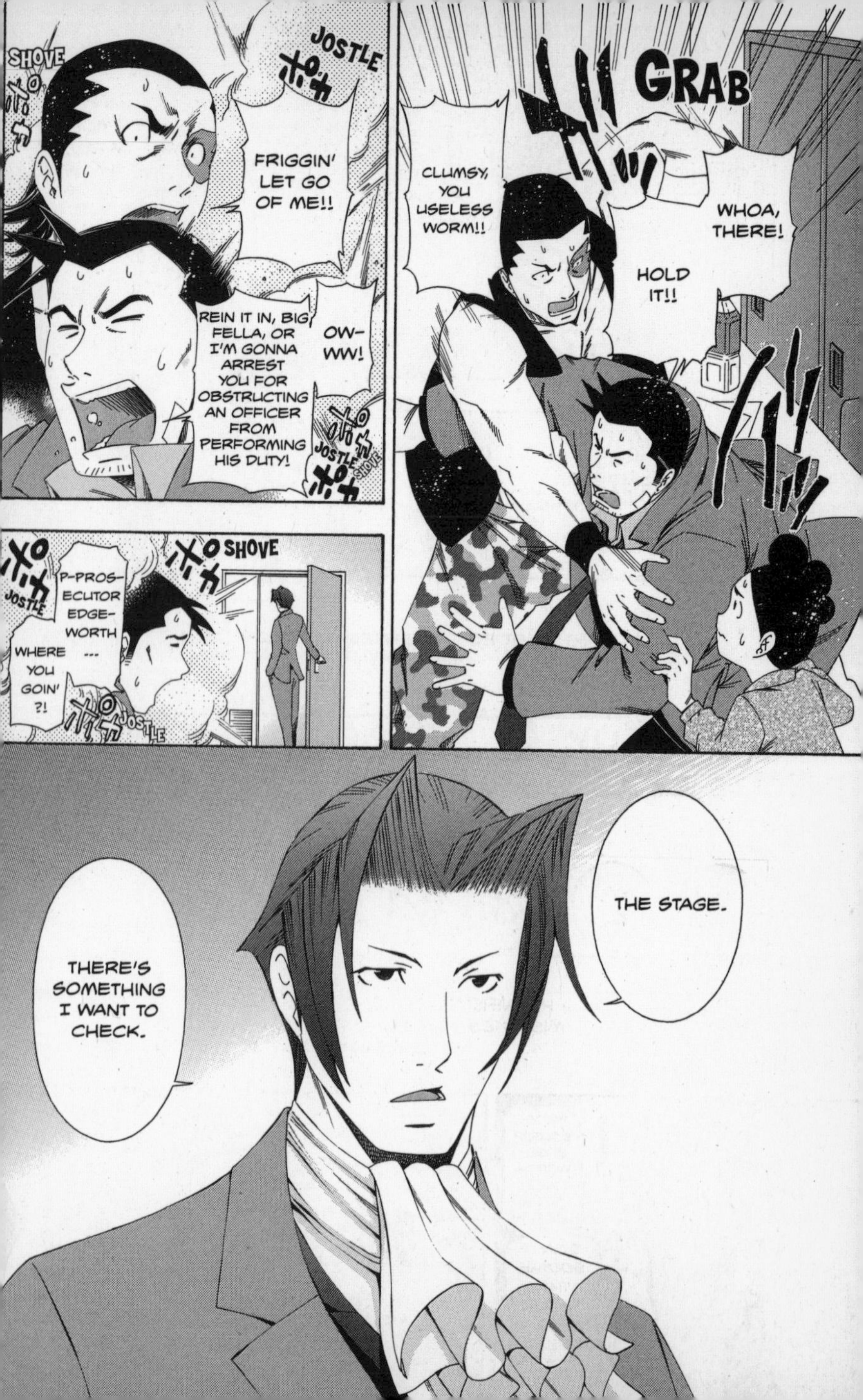
GRAB
WHOA, THERE!
HOLD IT!!
CLUMSY, YOU USELESS WORM!!
JOSTLE
FRIGGIN' LET GO OF ME!!
SHOVE
OW-WW!
REIN IT IN, BIG FELLA, OR I'M GONNA ARREST YOU FOR OBSTRUCTING AN OFFICER FROM PERFORMING HIS DUTY!
JOSTLE
SHOVE
SHOVE
P-PROSECUTOR EDGEWORTH --- WHERE YOU GOIN'?!
JOSTLE
JOSTLE
THE STAGE.
THERE'S SOMETHING I WANT TO CHECK.

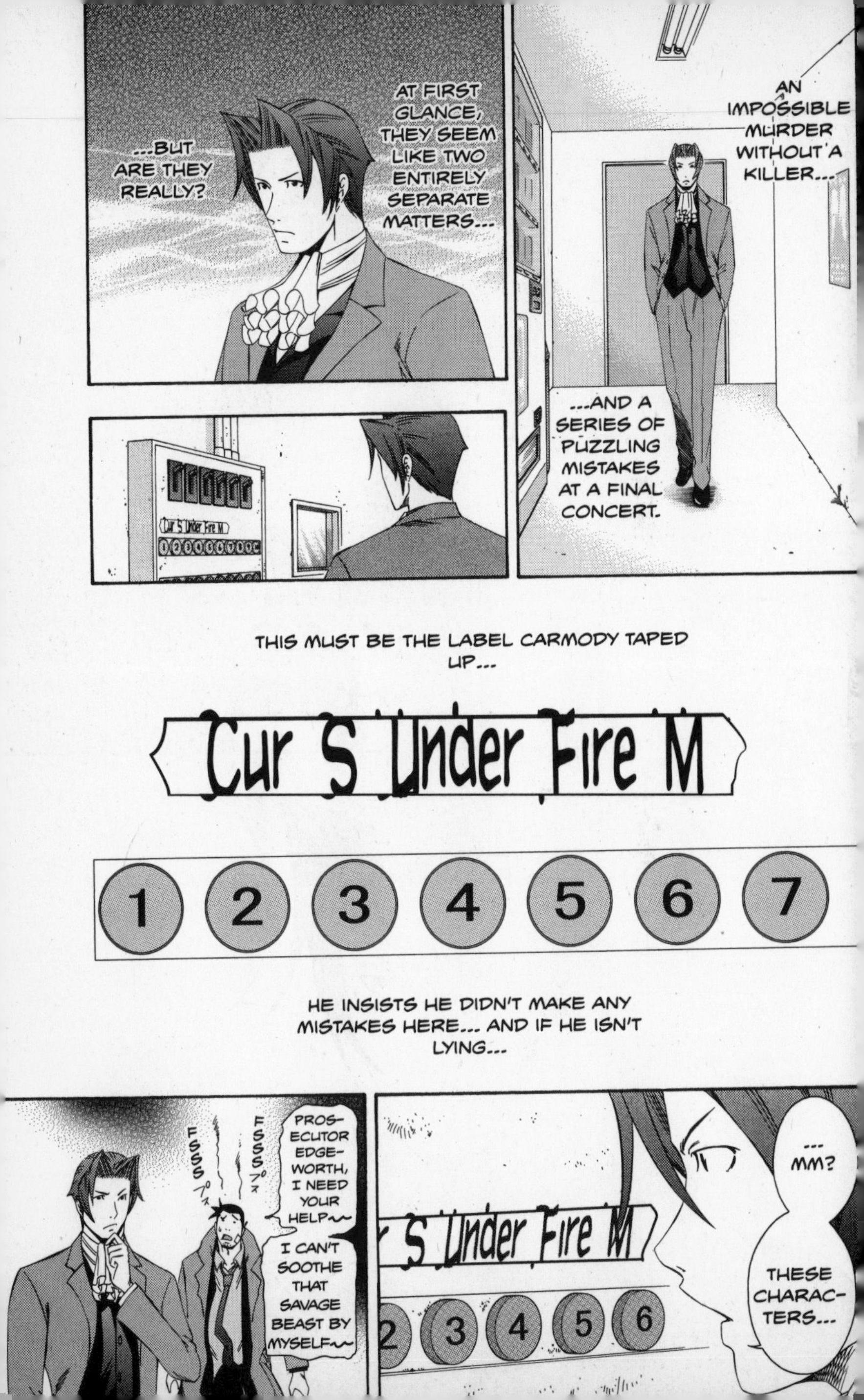
AN IMPOSSIBLE MURDER WITHOUT A KILLER...
...AND A SERIES OF PUZZLING MISTAKES AT A FINAL CONCERT.
AT FIRST GLANCE, THEY SEEM LIKE TWO ENTIRELY SEPARATE MATTERS...
...BUT ARE THEY REALLY?
THIS MUST BE THE LABEL CARMODY TAPED UP...
Cur S Under Fire M
1 2 3 4 5 6 7
HE INSISTS HE DIDN'T MAKE ANY MISTAKES HERE... AND IF HE ISN'T LYING...
... MM?
THESE CHARAC-TERS...
r S Under Fire M
2 3 4 5 6
FSSS
FSSS
PROS-ECUTOR EDGE-WORTH, I NEED YOUR HELP~
I CAN'T SOOTHE THAT SAVAGE BEAST BY MYSELF~

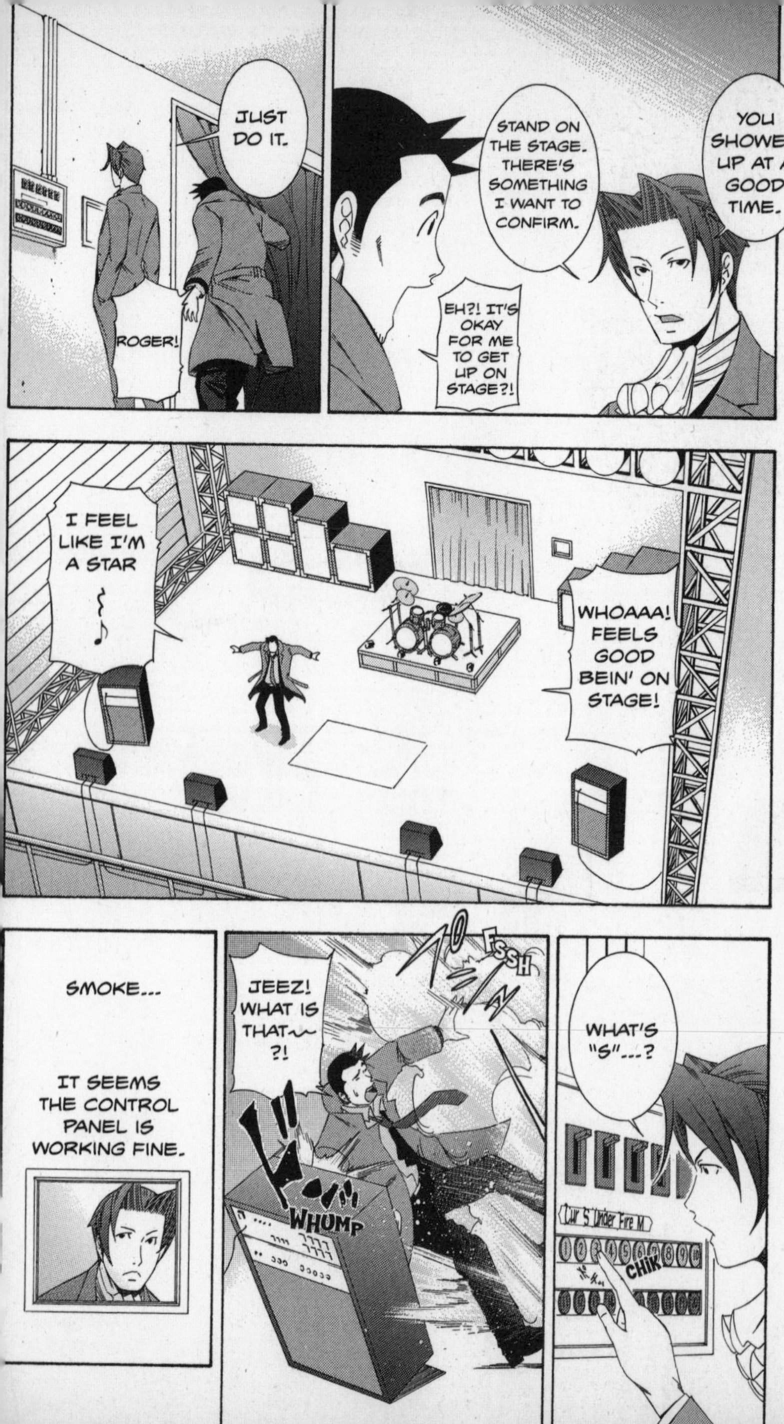
YOU SHOWED UP AT A GOOD TIME.
STAND ON THE STAGE. THERE'S SOMETHING I WANT TO CONFIRM.
EH?! IT'S OKAY FOR ME TO GET UP ON STAGE?!
JUST DO IT.
ROGER!
WHOAAA! FEELS GOOD BEIN' ON STAGE!
I FEEL LIKE I'M A STAR ♪
WHAT'S "S"...?
Cur S Under Fire M
CHIK
FSSH
JEEZ! WHAT IS THAT~~?!
WHUMP
SMOKE...
IT SEEMS THE CONTROL PANEL IS WORKING FINE.

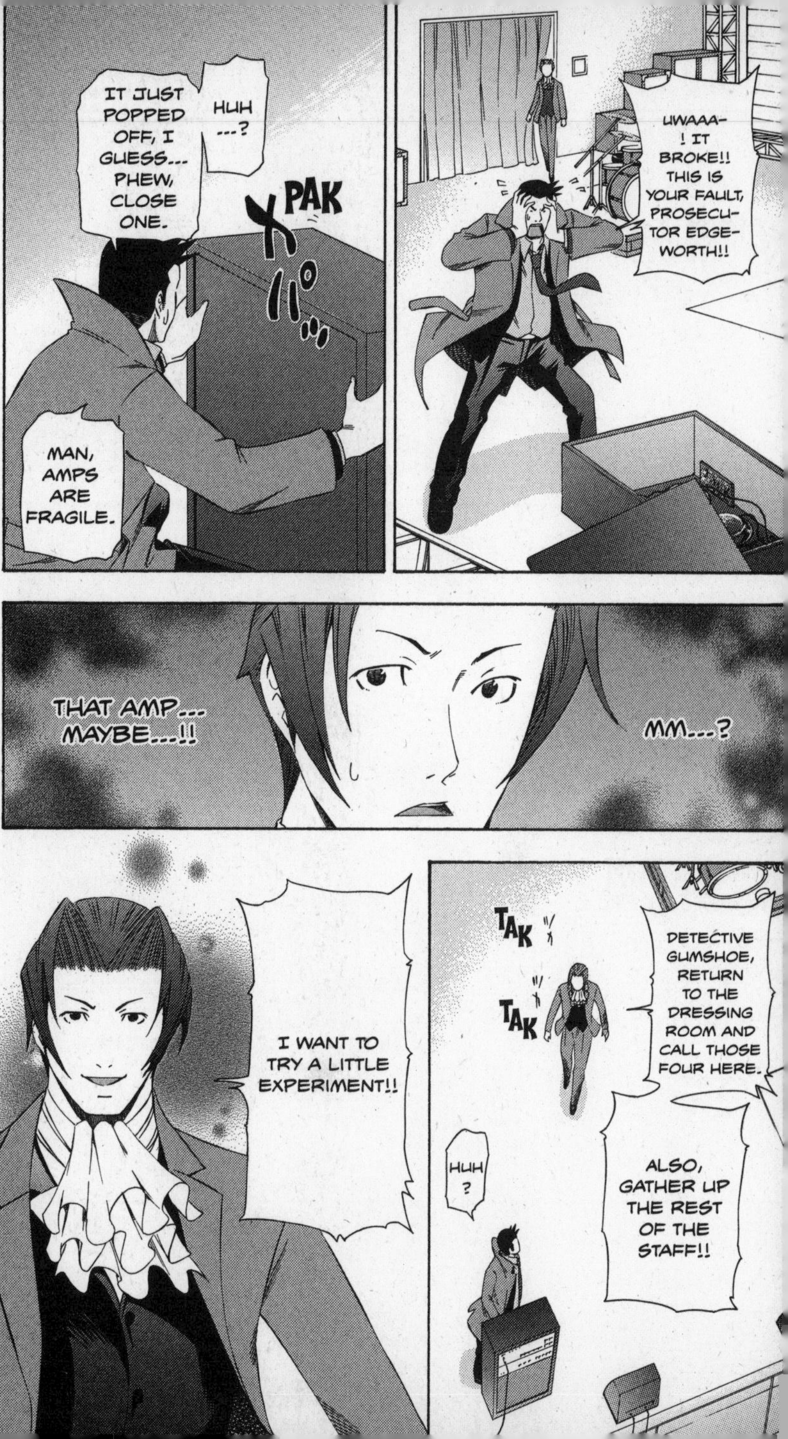
UWAAA-! IT BROKE!! THIS IS YOUR FAULT, PROSECUTOR EDGEWORTH!!
HUH ---?
IT JUST POPPED OFF, I GUESS... PHEW, CLOSE ONE.
PAK
MAN, AMPS ARE FRAGILE.
MM...?
THAT AMP... MAYBE...!!
TAK
TAK
DETECTIVE GUMSHOE, RETURN TO THE DRESSING ROOM AND CALL THOSE FOUR HERE.
ALSO, GATHER UP THE REST OF THE STAFF!!
HUH?
I WANT TO TRY A LITTLE EXPERIMENT!!

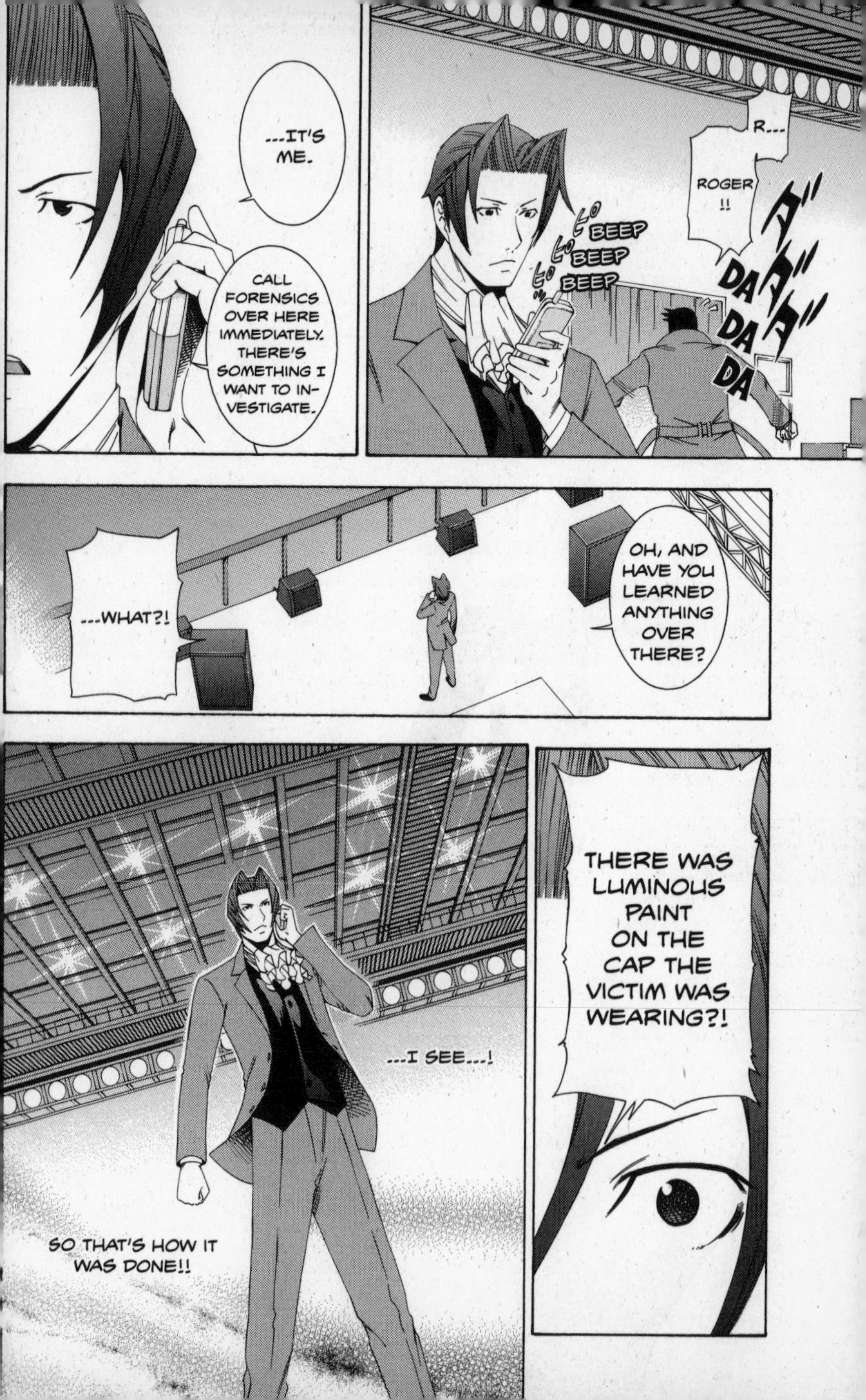
R...
ROGER !!
ダダダ
DA DA DA
ピピピ
BEEP BEEP BEEP
...IT'S ME.
CALL FORENSICS OVER HERE IMMEDIATELY. THERE'S SOMETHING I WANT TO IN-VESTIGATE.
OH, AND HAVE YOU LEARNED ANYTHING OVER THERE?
...WHAT?!
THERE WAS LUMINOUS PAINT ON THE CAP THE VICTIM WAS WEARING?!
...I SEE...!
SO THAT'S HOW IT WAS DONE!!

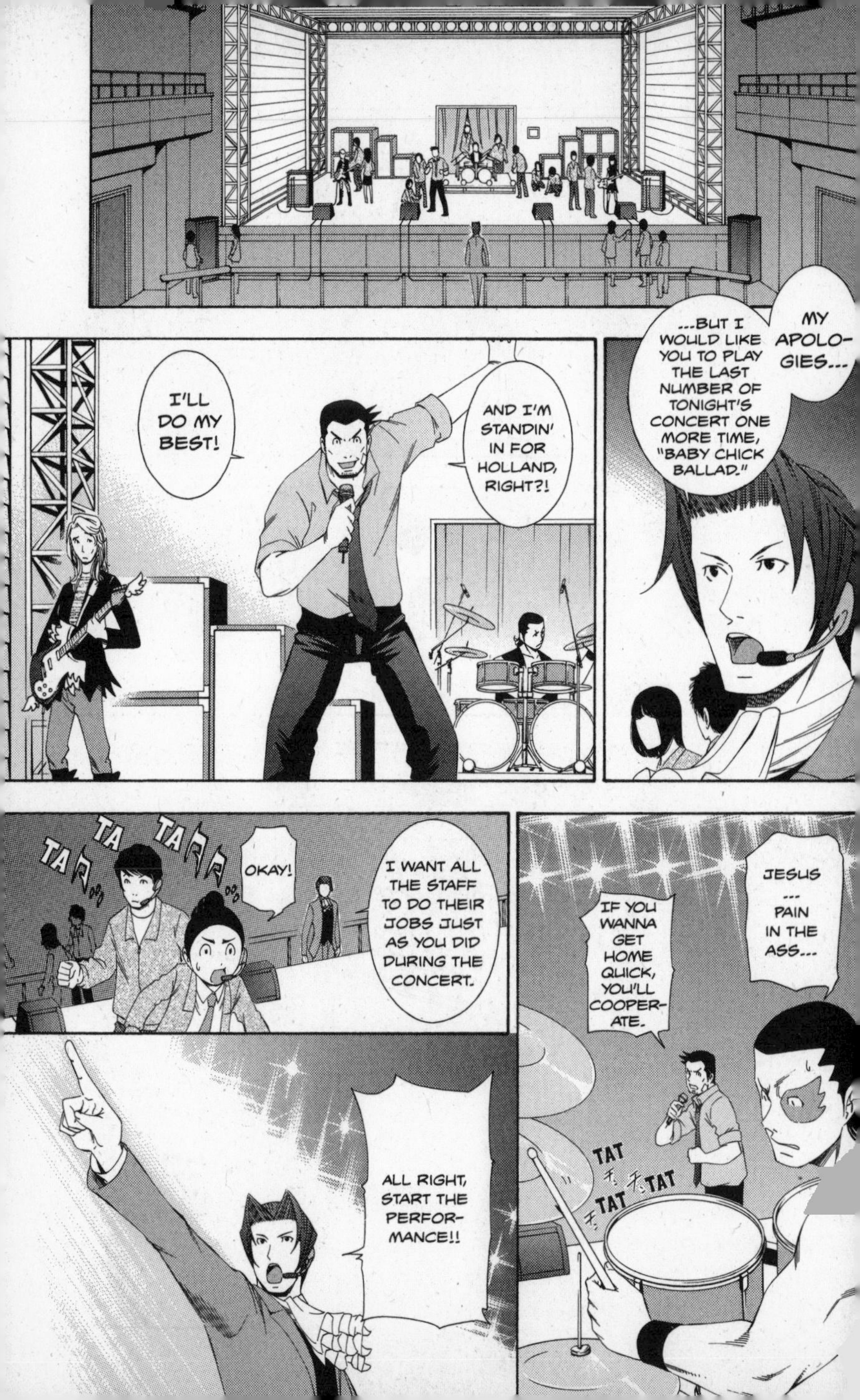
MY APOLOGIES...
...BUT I WOULD LIKE YOU TO PLAY THE LAST NUMBER OF TONIGHT'S CONCERT ONE MORE TIME, "BABY CHICK BALLAD."
AND I'M STANDIN' IN FOR HOLLAND, RIGHT?!
I'LL DO MY BEST!
JESUS ... PAIN IN THE ASS...
IF YOU WANNA GET HOME QUICK, YOU'LL COOPERATE.
TAT TAT TAT
I WANT ALL THE STAFF TO DO THEIR JOBS JUST AS YOU DID DURING THE CONCERT.
OKAY!
TA TA TA
ALL RIGHT, START THE PERFORMANCE!!

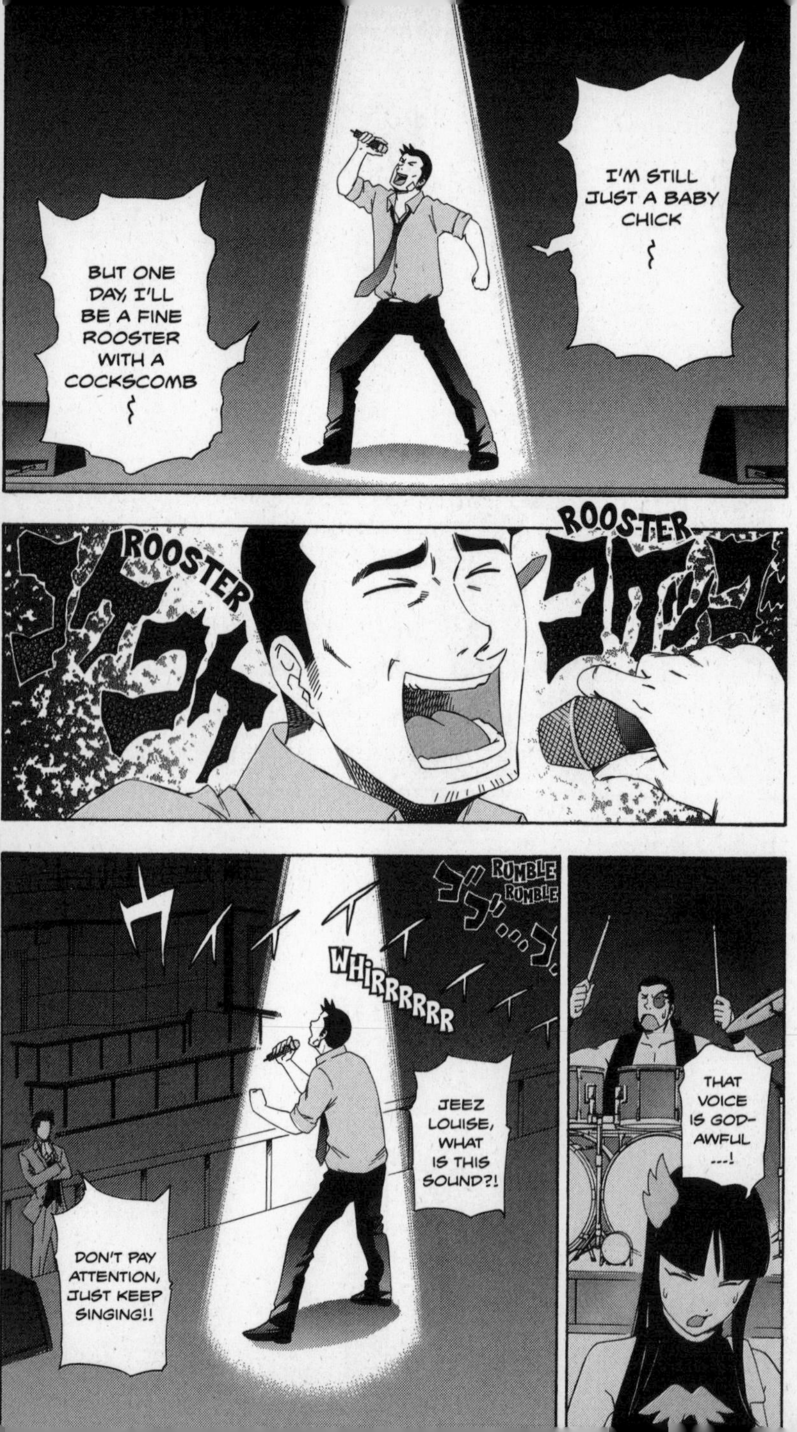
I'M STILL JUST A BABY CHICK ~
BUT ONE DAY, I'LL BE A FINE ROOSTER WITH A COCKSCOMB ~
ROOSTER
ROOSTER
THAT VOICE IS GOD-AWFUL ---!
RUMBLE RUMBLE
WHIRRRRRRR
JEEZ LOUISE, WHAT IS THIS SOUND?!
DON'T PAY ATTENTION, JUST KEEP SINGING!!

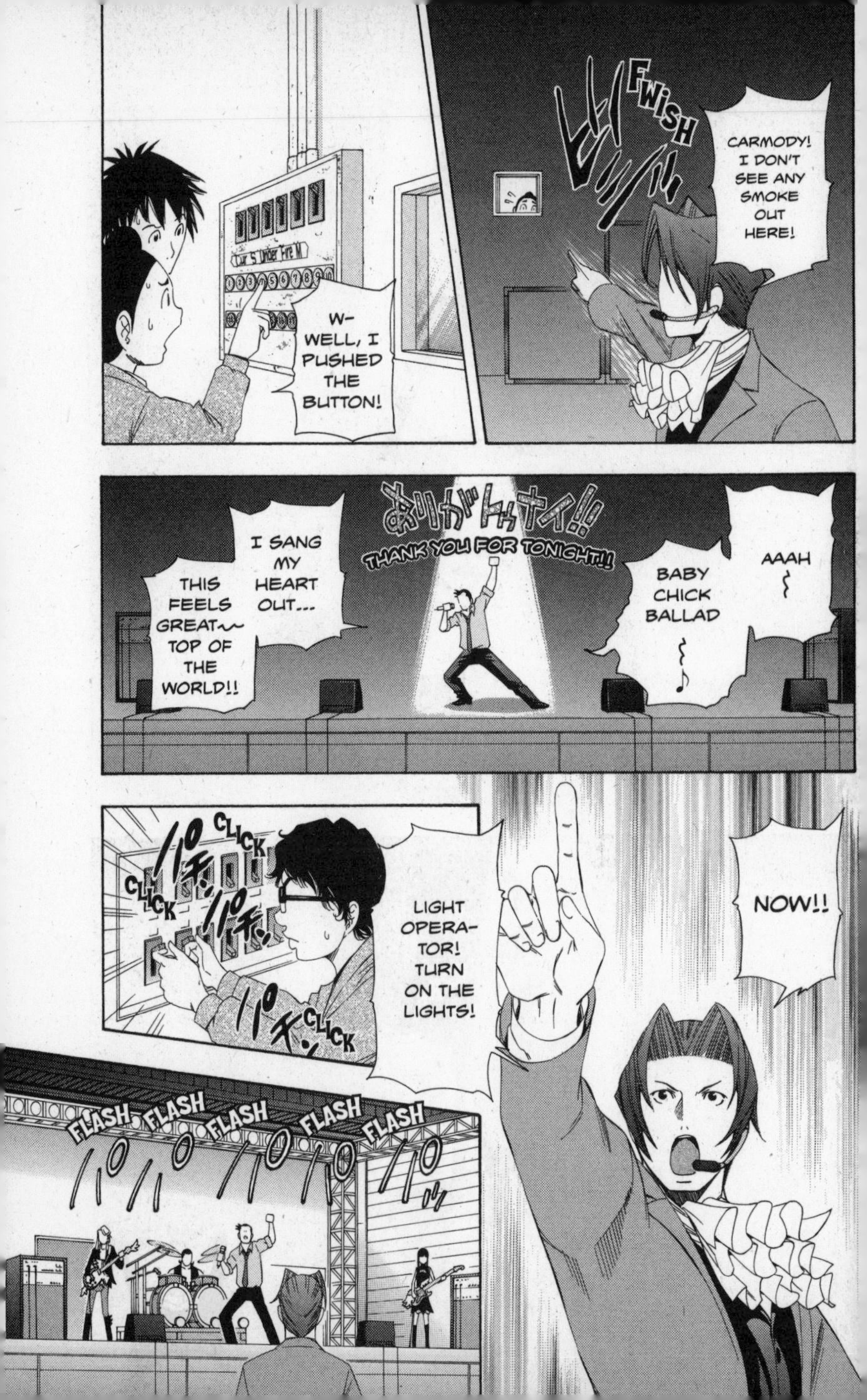

FWISH
CARMODY! I DON'T SEE ANY SMOKE OUT HERE!
W-WELL, I PUSHED THE BUTTON!
AAAH ~ BABY CHICK BALLAD ~ ♪
THANK YOU FOR TONIGHT!!
I SANG MY HEART OUT...
THIS FEELS GREAT~~ TOP OF THE WORLD!!
NOW!!
LIGHT OPERATOR! TURN ON THE LIGHTS!
CLICK
CLICK
CLICK
FLASH FLASH FLASH FLASH FLASH

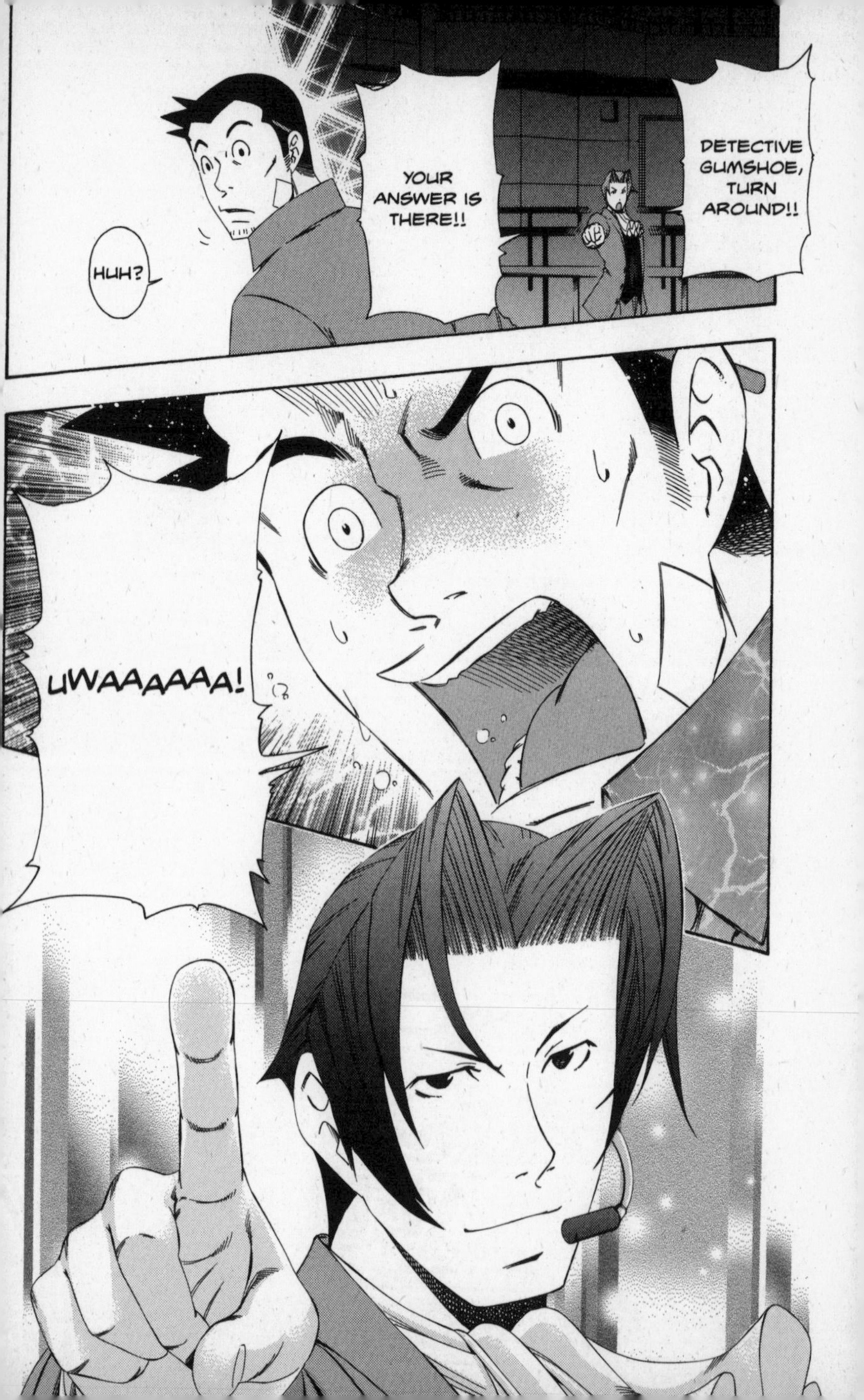
DETECTIVE GUMSHOE, TURN AROUND!!
YOUR ANSWER IS THERE!!
HUH?
UWAAAAAA!

Ace Attorney Miles Edgeworth
INVESTIGATIONS™

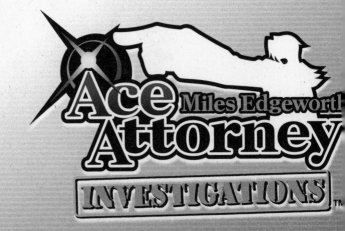

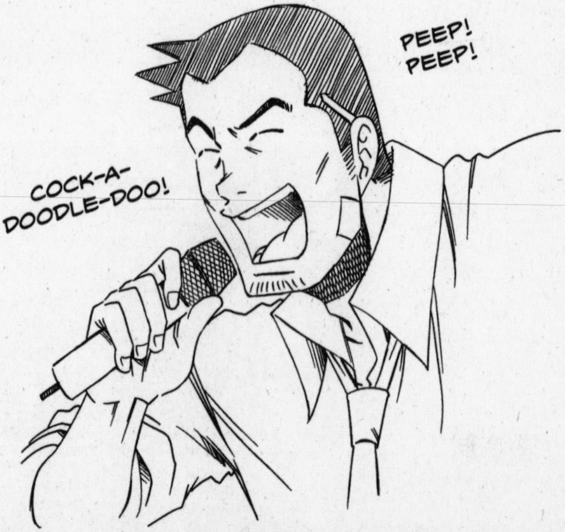
PEEP! PEEP!
COCK-A-DOODLE-DOO!

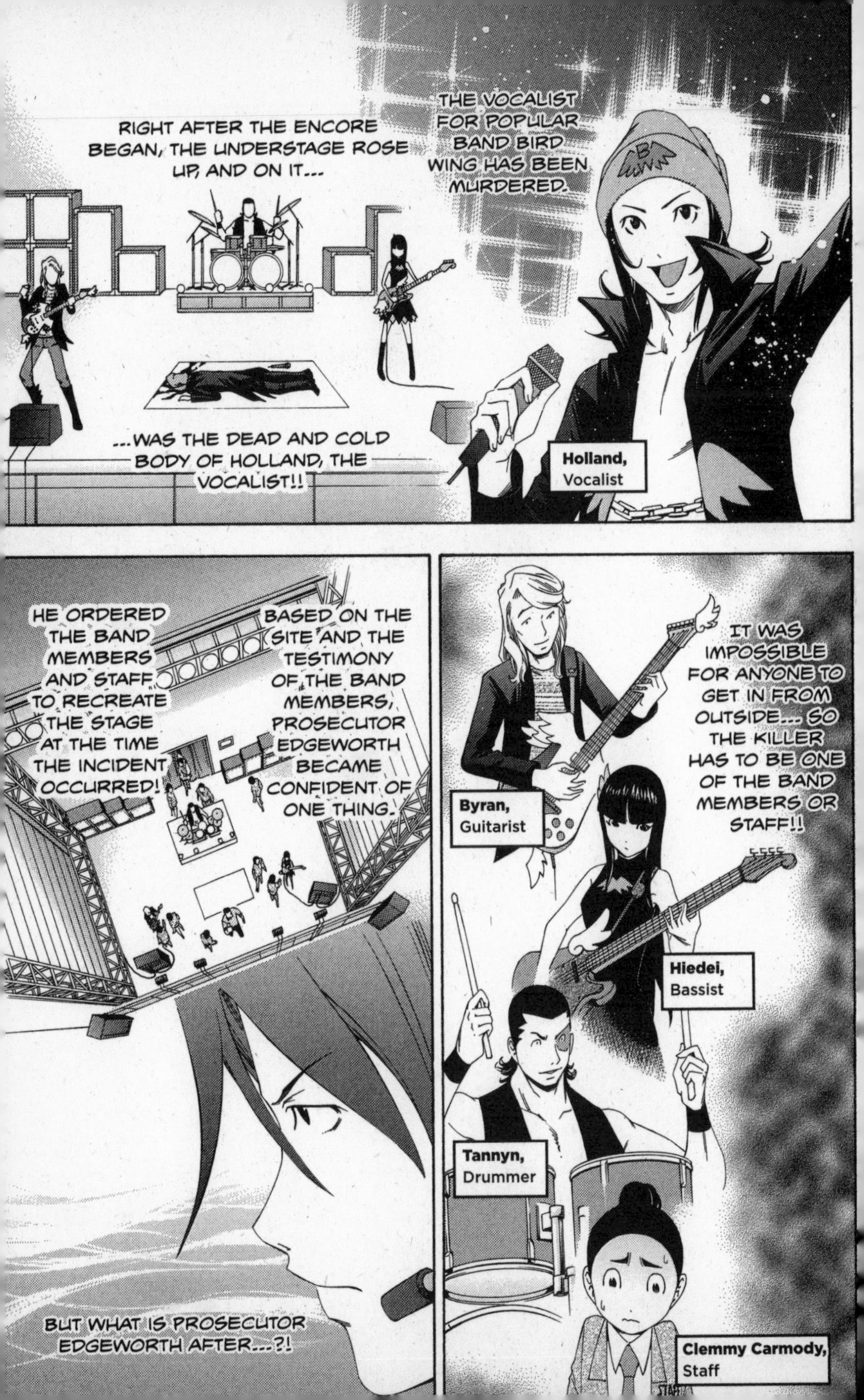
THE VOCALIST FOR POPULAR BAND BIRD WING HAS BEEN MURDERED.
Holland, Vocalist
RIGHT AFTER THE ENCORE BEGAN, THE UNDERSTAGE ROSE UP, AND ON IT...
...WAS THE DEAD AND COLD BODY OF HOLLAND, THE VOCALIST!!
IT WAS IMPOSSIBLE FOR ANYONE TO GET IN FROM OUTSIDE... SO THE KILLER HAS TO BE ONE OF THE BAND MEMBERS OR STAFF!!
Byran, Guitarist
Hiedei, Bassist
Tannyn, Drummer
Clemmy Carmody, Staff
BASED ON THE SITE AND THE TESTIMONY OF THE BAND MEMBERS, PROSECUTOR EDGEWORTH BECAME CONFIDENT OF ONE THING.
HE ORDERED THE BAND MEMBERS AND STAFF TO RECREATE THE STAGE AT THE TIME THE INCIDENT OCCURRED!
BUT WHAT IS PROSECUTOR EDGEWORTH AFTER...?!

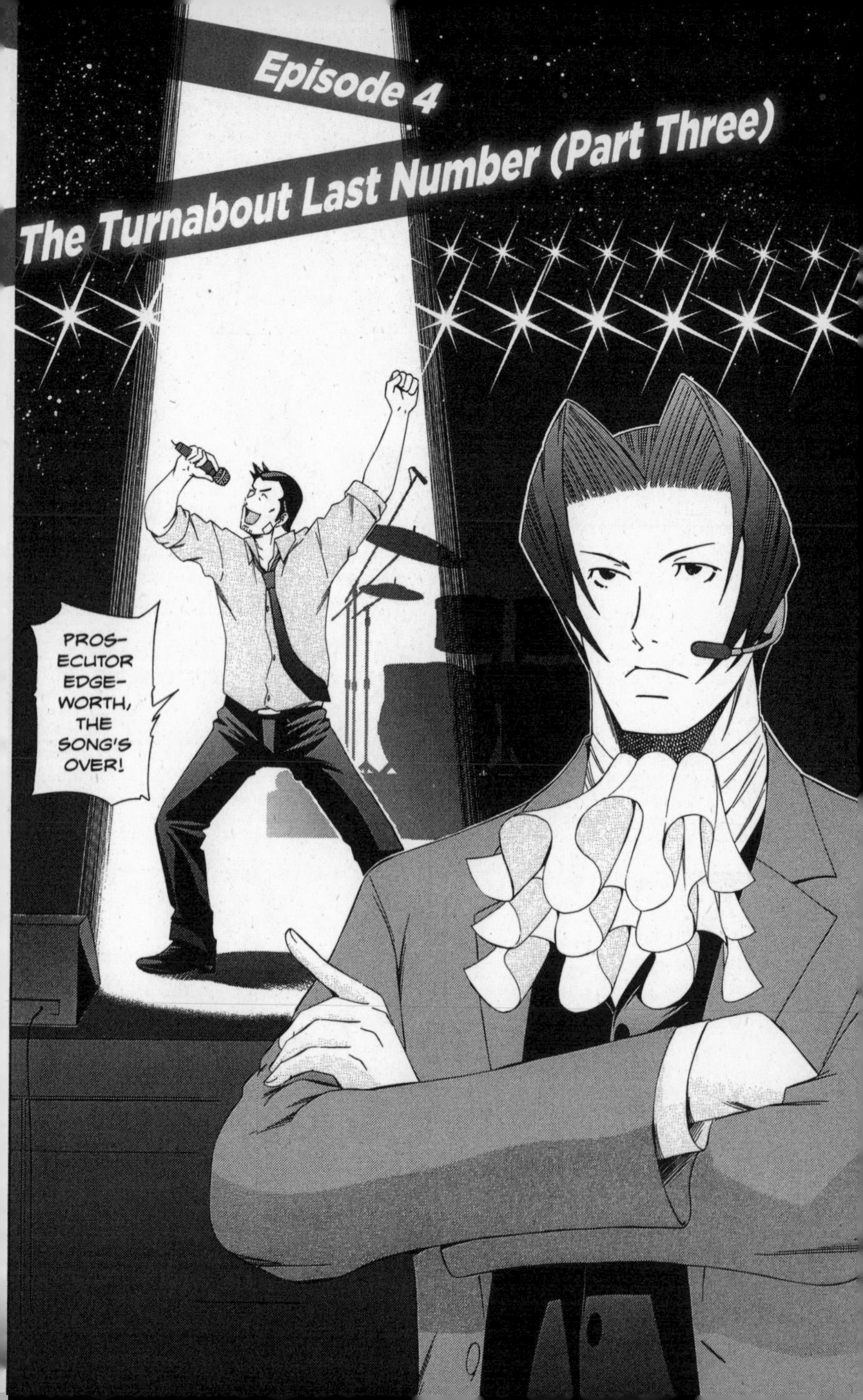
Episode 4
The Turnabout Last Number (Part Three)
PROSECUTOR EDGEWORTH, THE SONG'S OVER!

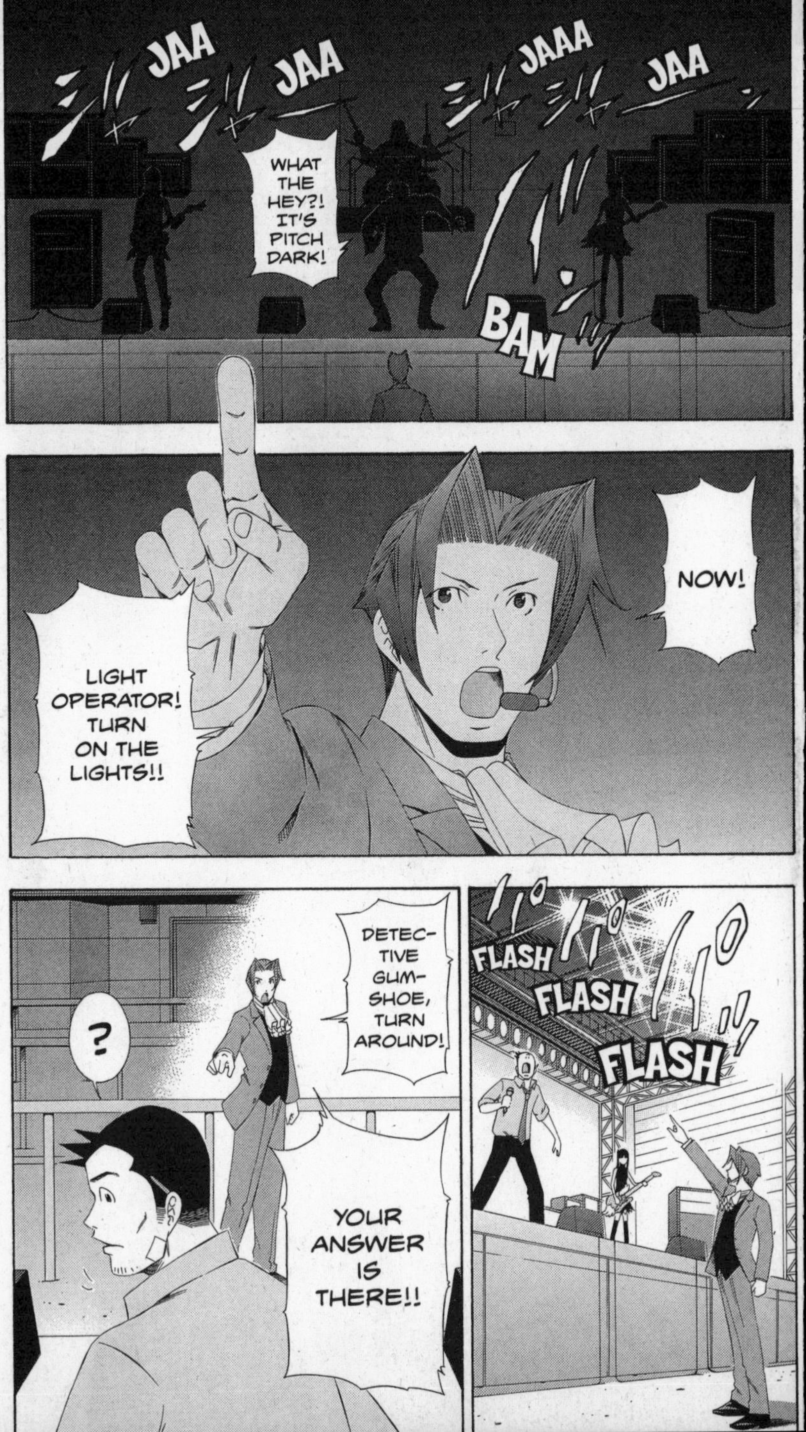
JAA
JAAA
WHAT THE HEY?! IT'S PITCH DARK!
JAA
JAA
BAM
NOW!
LIGHT OPERATOR! TURN ON THE LIGHTS!!
FLASH
FLASH
FLASH
DETEC-TIVE GUM-SHOE, TURN AROUND!
?
YOUR ANSWER IS THERE!!

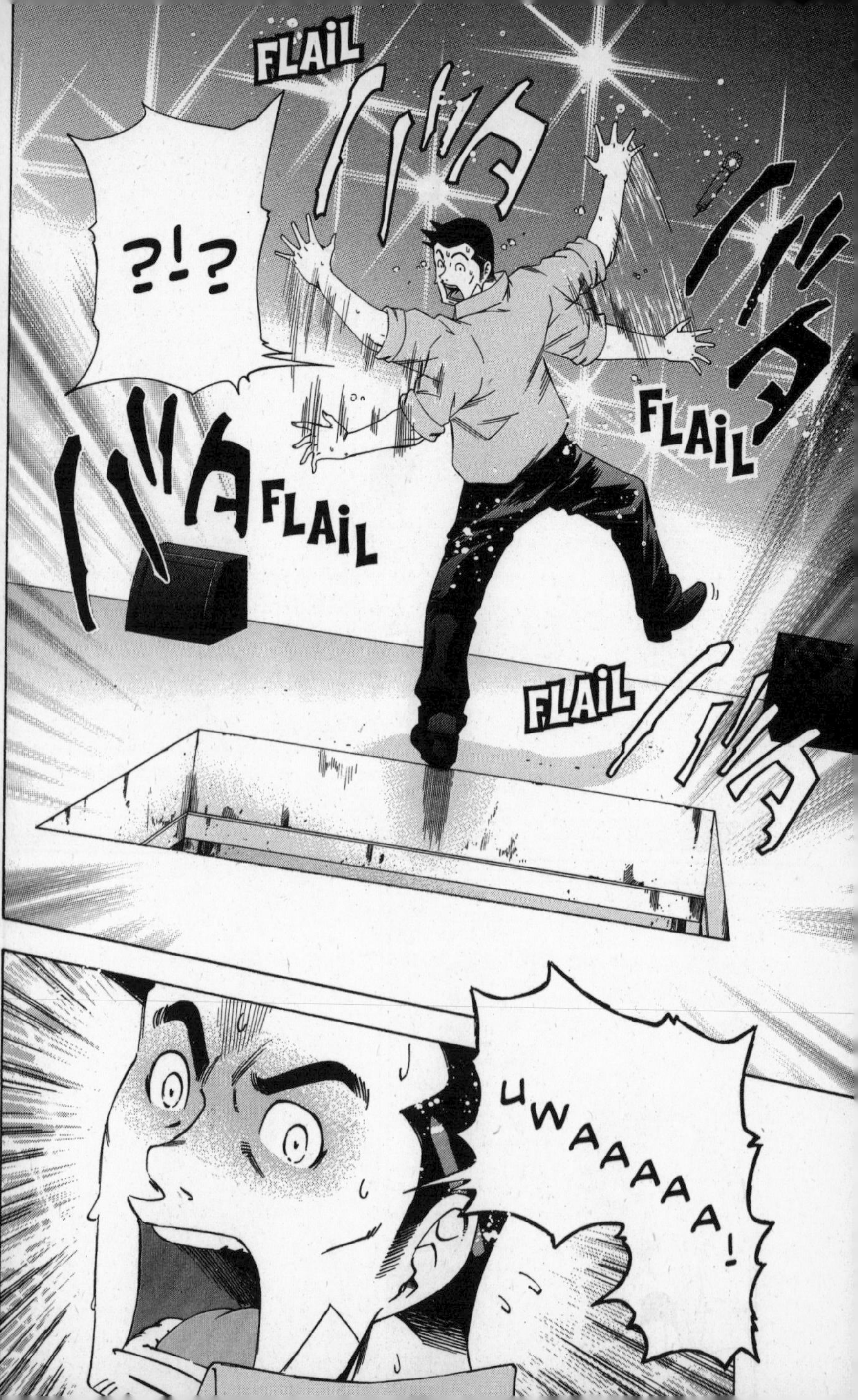
FLAIL
?!?
FLAIL
FLAIL
FLAIL
UWAAAAAA!

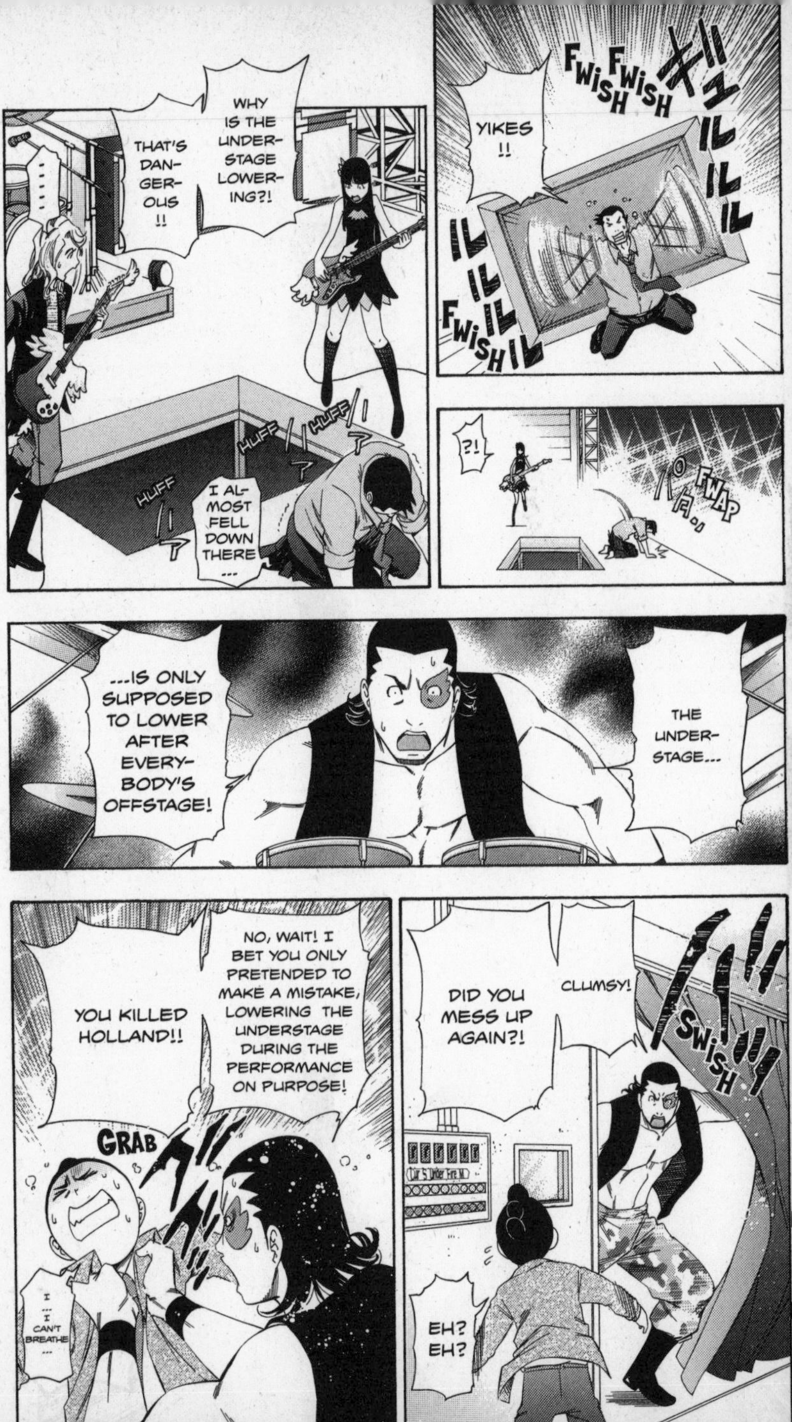
FWISH FWISH
YIKES !!
FWISH
?!
FWAP
WHY IS THE UNDER-STAGE LOWER-ING?!
THAT'S DAN-GER-OUS !!
...
HUFF HUFF
HUFF
I AL-MOST FELL DOWN THERE ...
THE UNDER-STAGE...
...IS ONLY SUPPOSED TO LOWER AFTER EVERY-BODY'S OFFSTAGE!
CLUMSY!
DID YOU MESS UP AGAIN?!
SWISH
EH? EH?
NO, WAIT! I BET YOU ONLY PRETENDED TO MAKE A MISTAKE, LOWERING THE UNDERSTAGE DURING THE PERFORMANCE ON PURPOSE!
YOU KILLED HOLLAND!!
GRAB
I ... I CAN'T BREATHE ...

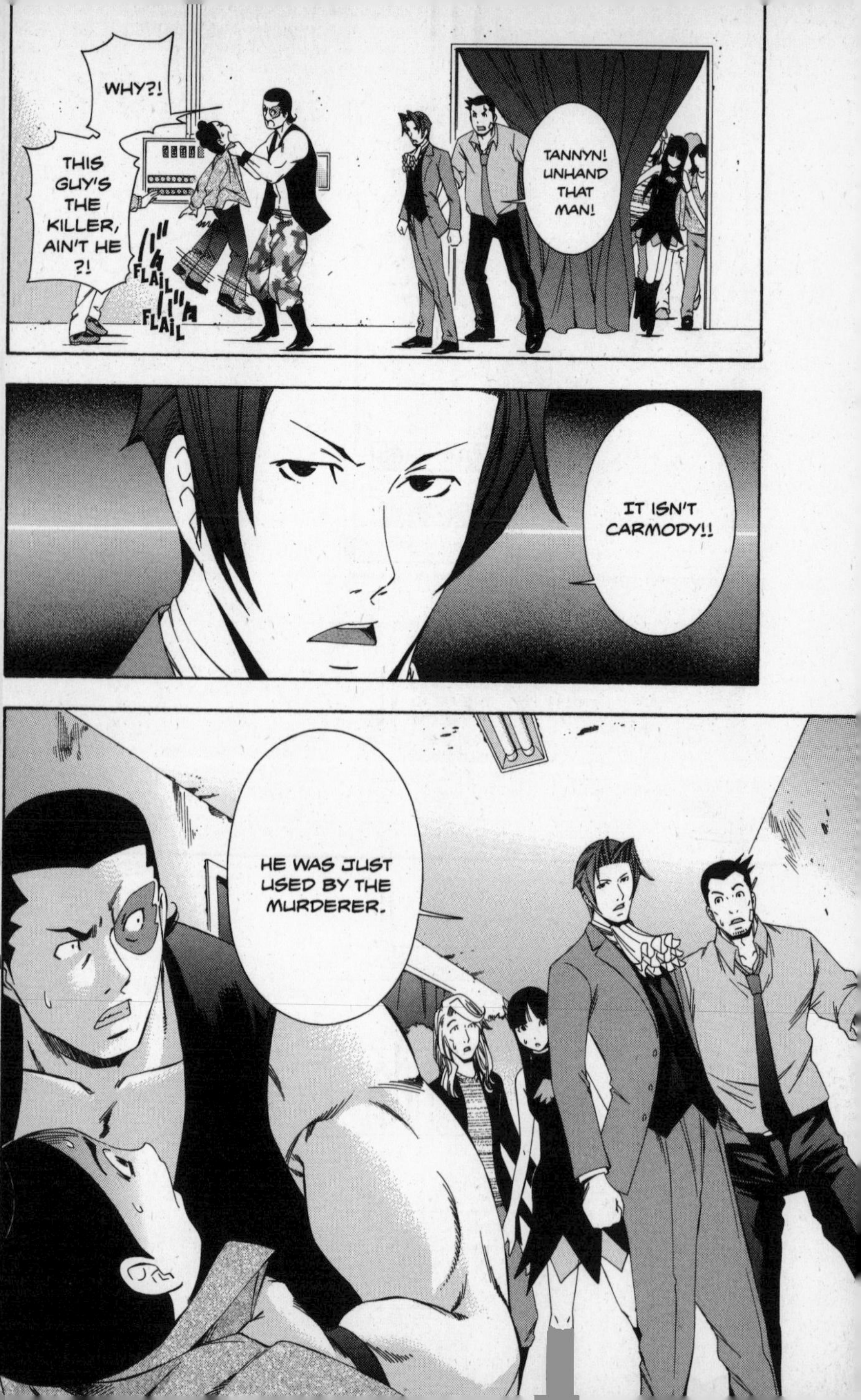
TANNYN! UNHAND THAT MAN!
WHY?!
THIS GUY'S THE KILLER, AIN'T HE ?!
FLAIL
FLAIL
IT ISN'T CARMODY!!
HE WAS JUST USED BY THE MURDERER.

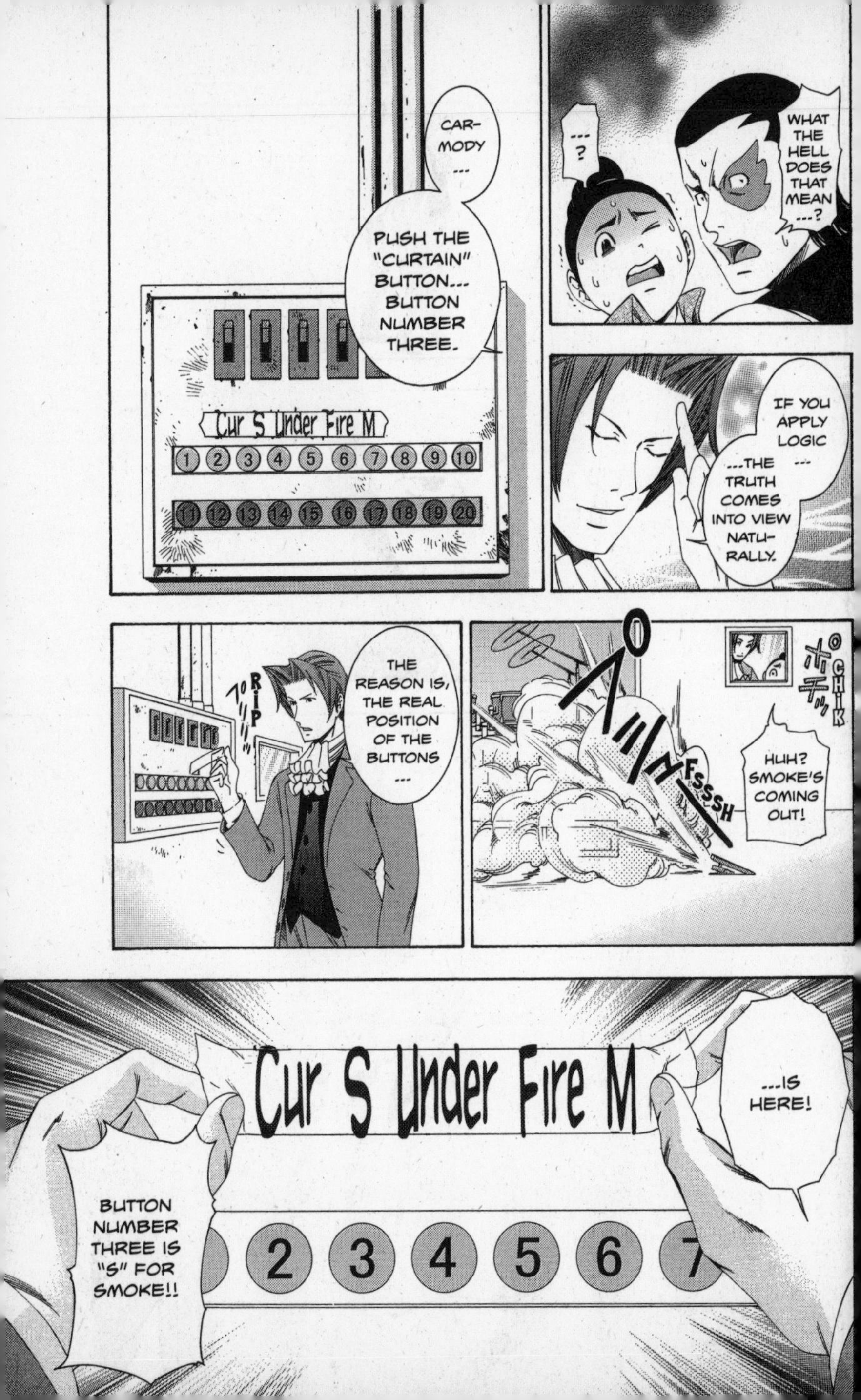
WHAT THE HELL DOES THAT MEAN ---?
---?
IF YOU APPLY LOGIC ---
---THE TRUTH COMES INTO VIEW NATU-RALLY.
CAR-MODY ---
PUSH THE "CURTAIN" BUTTON--- BUTTON NUMBER THREE.
Cur S Under Fire M
1 2 3 4 5 6 7 8 9 10
11 12 13 14 15 16 17 18 19 20
CHIK
HUH? SMOKE'S COMING OUT!
FSSSH
RIP
THE REASON IS, THE REAL POSITION OF THE BUTTONS ---
---IS HERE!
Cur S Under Fire M
2 3 4 5 6 7
BUTTON NUMBER THREE IS "S" FOR SMOKE!!

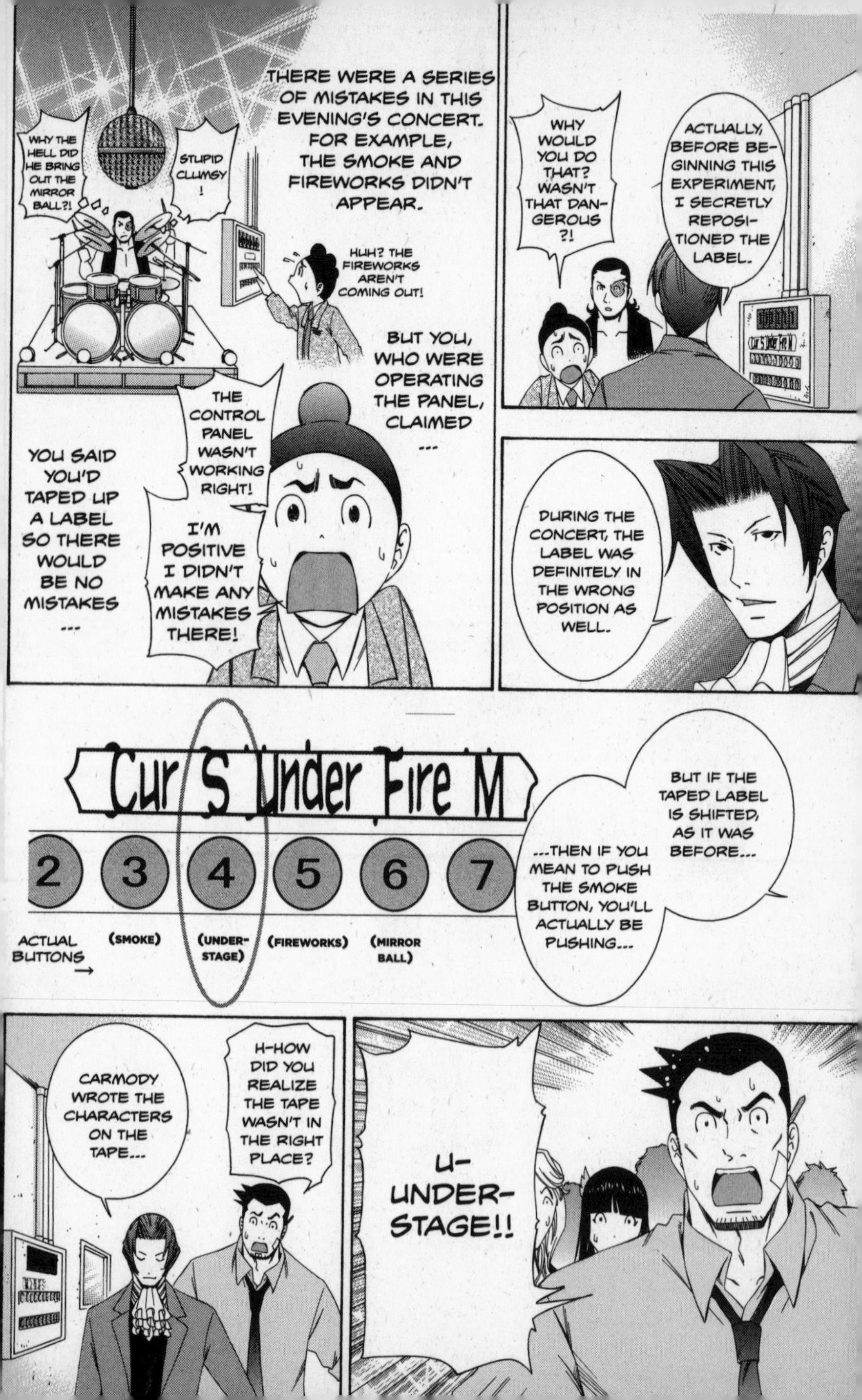
ACTUALLY, BEFORE BEGINNING THIS EXPERIMENT, I SECRETLY REPOSITIONED THE LABEL.
WHY WOULD YOU DO THAT? WASN'T THAT DANGEROUS?!
DURING THE CONCERT, THE LABEL WAS DEFINITELY IN THE WRONG POSITION AS WELL.
THERE WERE A SERIES OF MISTAKES IN THIS EVENING'S CONCERT. FOR EXAMPLE, THE SMOKE AND FIREWORKS DIDN'T APPEAR.
STUPID CLUMSY!
WHY THE HELL DID HE BRING OUT THE MIRROR BALL?!
HUH? THE FIREWORKS AREN'T COMING OUT!
BUT YOU, WHO WERE OPERATING THE PANEL, CLAIMED ---
THE CONTROL PANEL WASN'T WORKING RIGHT!
I'M POSITIVE I DIDN'T MAKE ANY MISTAKES THERE!
YOU SAID YOU'D TAPED UP A LABEL SO THERE WOULD BE NO MISTAKES ---
BUT IF THE TAPED LABEL IS SHIFTED, AS IT WAS BEFORE...
...THEN IF YOU MEAN TO PUSH THE SMOKE BUTTON, YOU'LL ACTUALLY BE PUSHING...
Cur S Under Fire M
2 3 4 5 6 7
ACTUAL BUTTONS →
(SMOKE)
(UNDER-STAGE)
(FIREWORKS)
(MIRROR BALL)
U-UNDER-STAGE!!
H-HOW DID YOU REALIZE THE TAPE WASN'T IN THE RIGHT PLACE?
CARMODY WROTE THE CHARACTERS ON THE TAPE...

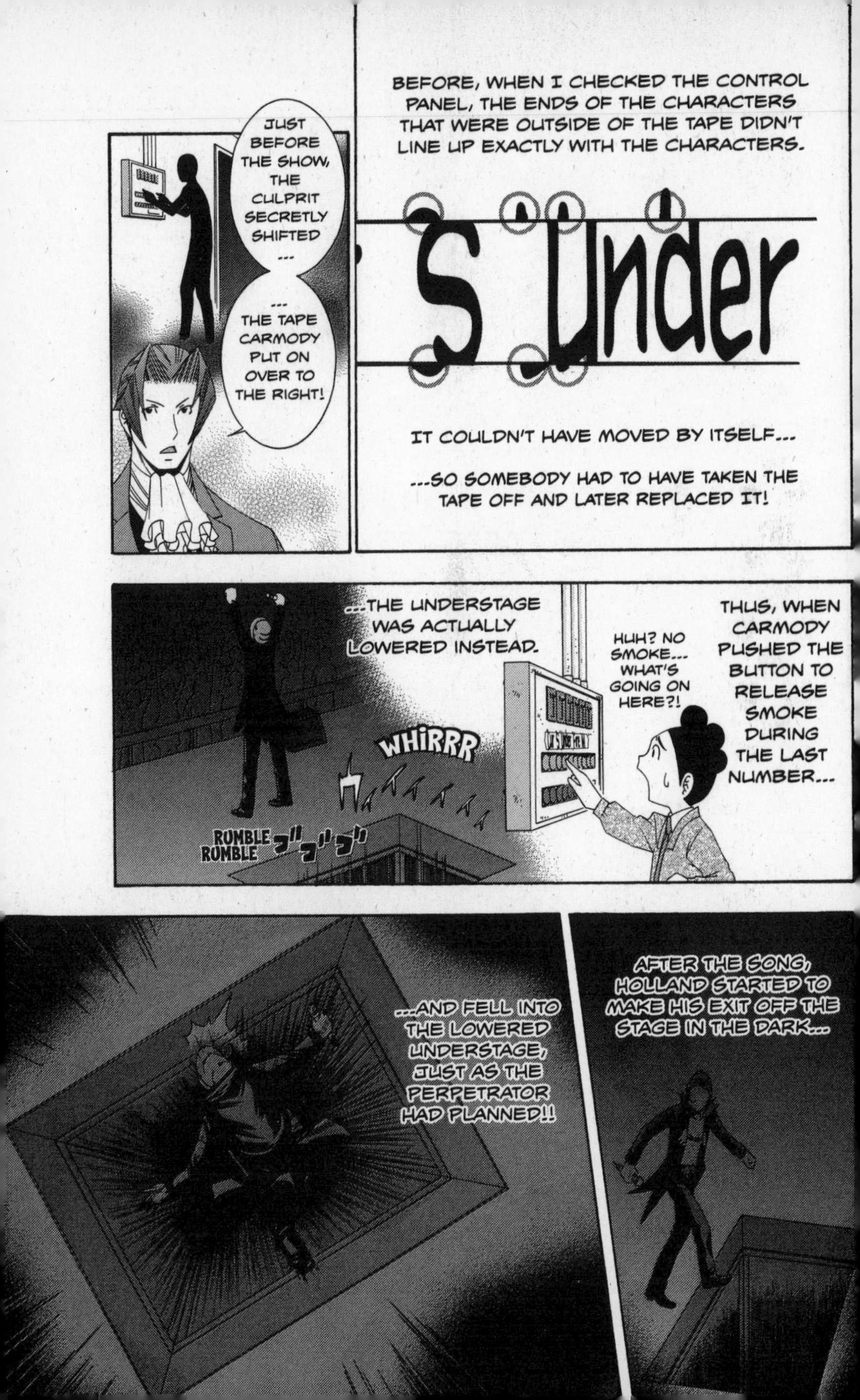
BEFORE, WHEN I CHECKED THE CONTROL PANEL, THE ENDS OF THE CHARACTERS THAT WERE OUTSIDE OF THE TAPE DIDN'T LINE UP EXACTLY WITH THE CHARACTERS.
'S Under
IT COULDN'T HAVE MOVED BY ITSELF...
...SO SOMEBODY HAD TO HAVE TAKEN THE TAPE OFF AND LATER REPLACED IT!
JUST BEFORE THE SHOW, THE CULPRIT SECRETLY SHIFTED ...
... THE TAPE CARMODY PUT ON OVER TO THE RIGHT!
THUS, WHEN CARMODY PUSHED THE BUTTON TO RELEASE SMOKE DURING THE LAST NUMBER...
HUH? NO SMOKE... WHAT'S GOING ON HERE?!
...THE UNDERSTAGE WAS ACTUALLY LOWERED INSTEAD.
WHIRRR
RUMBLE RUMBLE
AFTER THE SONG, HOLLAND STARTED TO MAKE HIS EXIT OFF THE STAGE IN THE DARK...
...AND FELL INTO THE LOWERED UNDERSTAGE, JUST AS THE PERPETRATOR HAD PLANNED!!

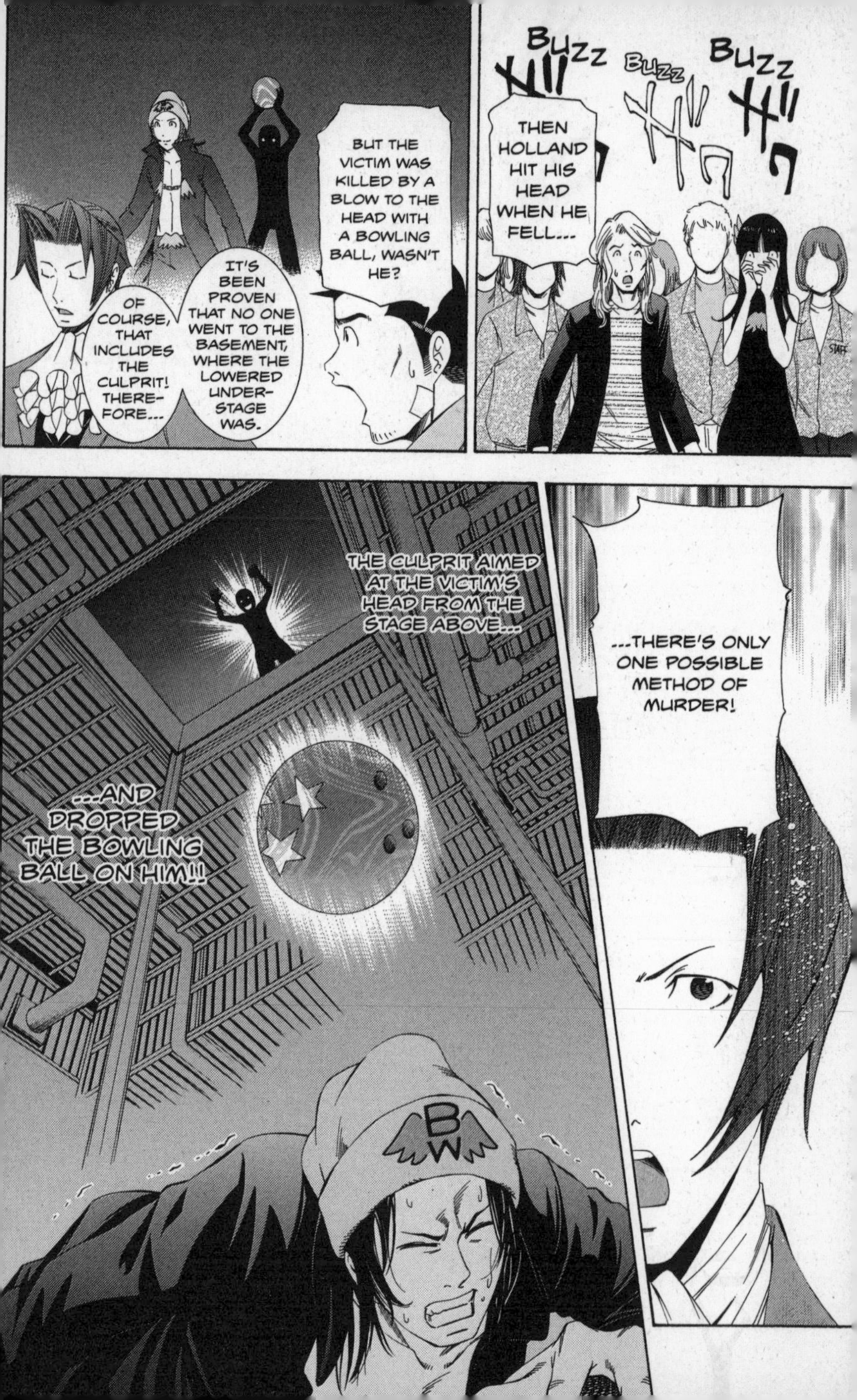
BUZZ
BUZZ
BUZZ
THEN HOLLAND HIT HIS HEAD WHEN HE FELL...
BUT THE VICTIM WAS KILLED BY A BLOW TO THE HEAD WITH A BOWLING BALL, WASN'T HE?
IT'S BEEN PROVEN THAT NO ONE WENT TO THE BASEMENT, WHERE THE LOWERED UNDER-STAGE WAS.
OF COURSE, THAT INCLUDES THE CULPRIT! THERE-FORE...
...THERE'S ONLY ONE POSSIBLE METHOD OF MURDER!
THE CULPRIT AIMED AT THE VICTIM'S HEAD FROM THE STAGE ABOVE...
...AND DROPPED THE BOWLING BALL ON HIM!!

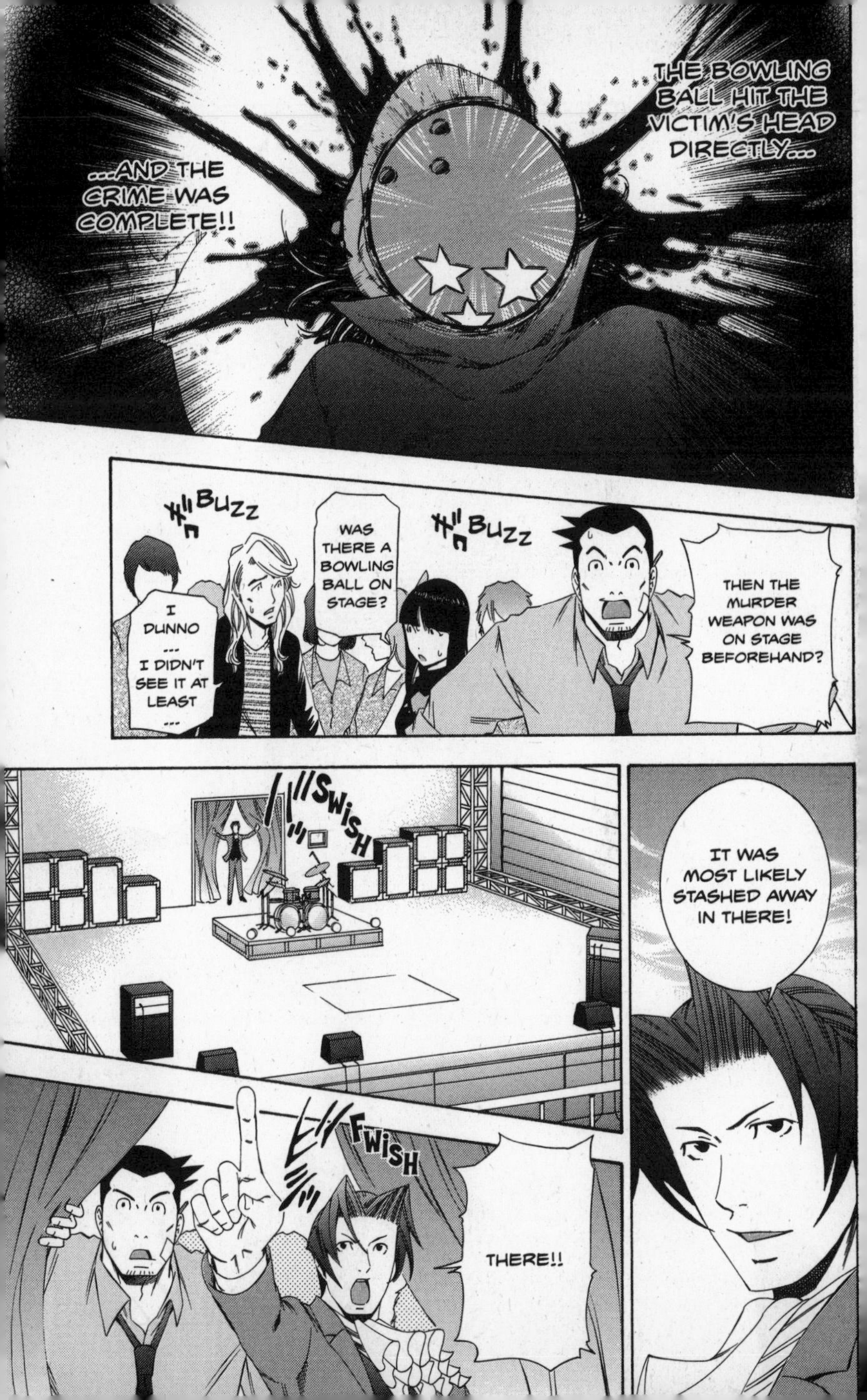
THE BOWLING BALL HIT THE VICTIM'S HEAD DIRECTLY...
...AND THE CRIME WAS COMPLETE!!
THEN THE MURDER WEAPON WAS ON STAGE BEFOREHAND?
BUZZ
WAS THERE A BOWLING BALL ON STAGE?
BUZZ
I DUNNO ... I DIDN'T SEE IT AT LEAST ...
IT WAS MOST LIKELY STASHED AWAY IN THERE!
SWISH
FWISH
THERE!!

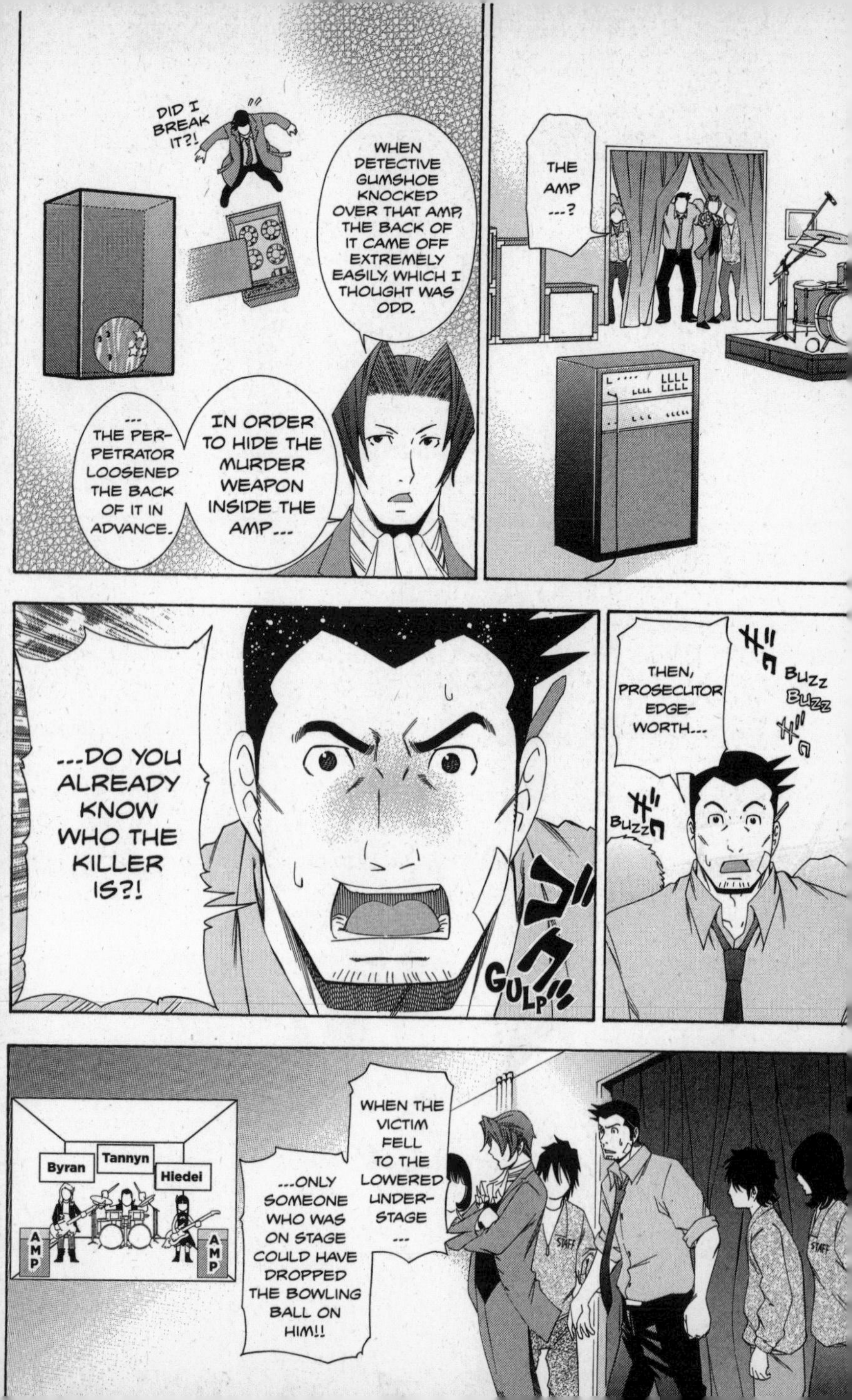
THE AMP ---?
WHEN DETECTIVE GUMSHOE KNOCKED OVER THAT AMP, THE BACK OF IT CAME OFF EXTREMELY EASILY, WHICH I THOUGHT WAS ODD.
DID I BREAK IT?!
IN ORDER TO HIDE THE MURDER WEAPON INSIDE THE AMP...
... THE PERPETRATOR LOOSENED THE BACK OF IT IN ADVANCE.
THEN, PROSECUTOR EDGEWORTH...
BUZZ BUZZ
BUZZ
...DO YOU ALREADY KNOW WHO THE KILLER IS?!
GULP!!
WHEN THE VICTIM FELL TO THE LOWERED UNDER-STAGE ---
...ONLY SOMEONE WHO WAS ON STAGE COULD HAVE DROPPED THE BOWLING BALL ON HIM!!
Byran
Tannyn
Hiedei
AMP
AMP

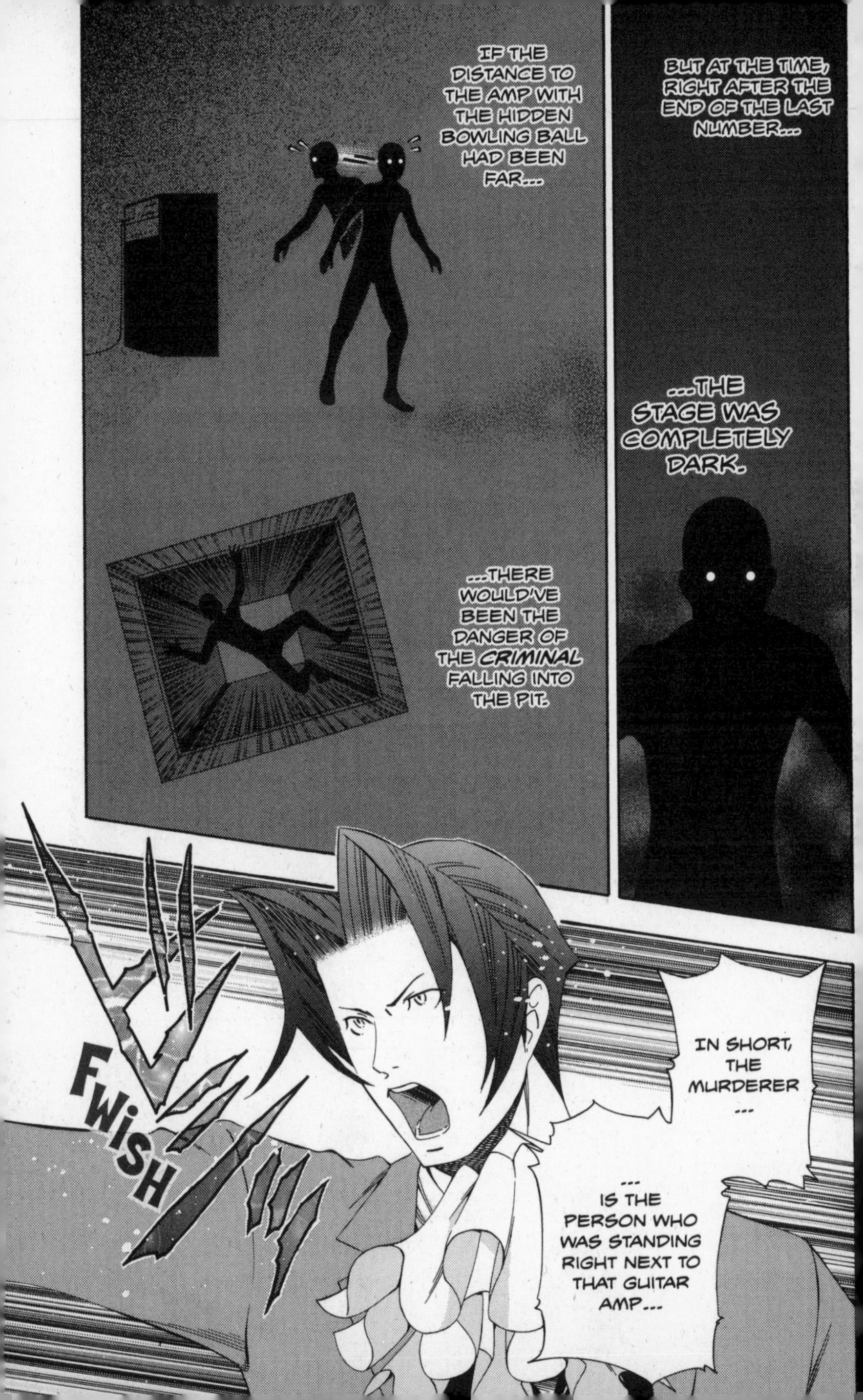
IF THE DISTANCE TO THE AMP WITH THE HIDDEN BOWLING BALL HAD BEEN FAR...
...THERE WOULD'VE BEEN THE DANGER OF THE *CRIMINAL* FALLING INTO THE PIT.
BUT AT THE TIME, RIGHT AFTER THE END OF THE LAST NUMBER...
...THE STAGE WAS COMPLETELY DARK.
FWISH
IN SHORT, THE MURDERER ...
... IS THE PERSON WHO WAS STANDING RIGHT NEXT TO THAT GUITAR AMP...

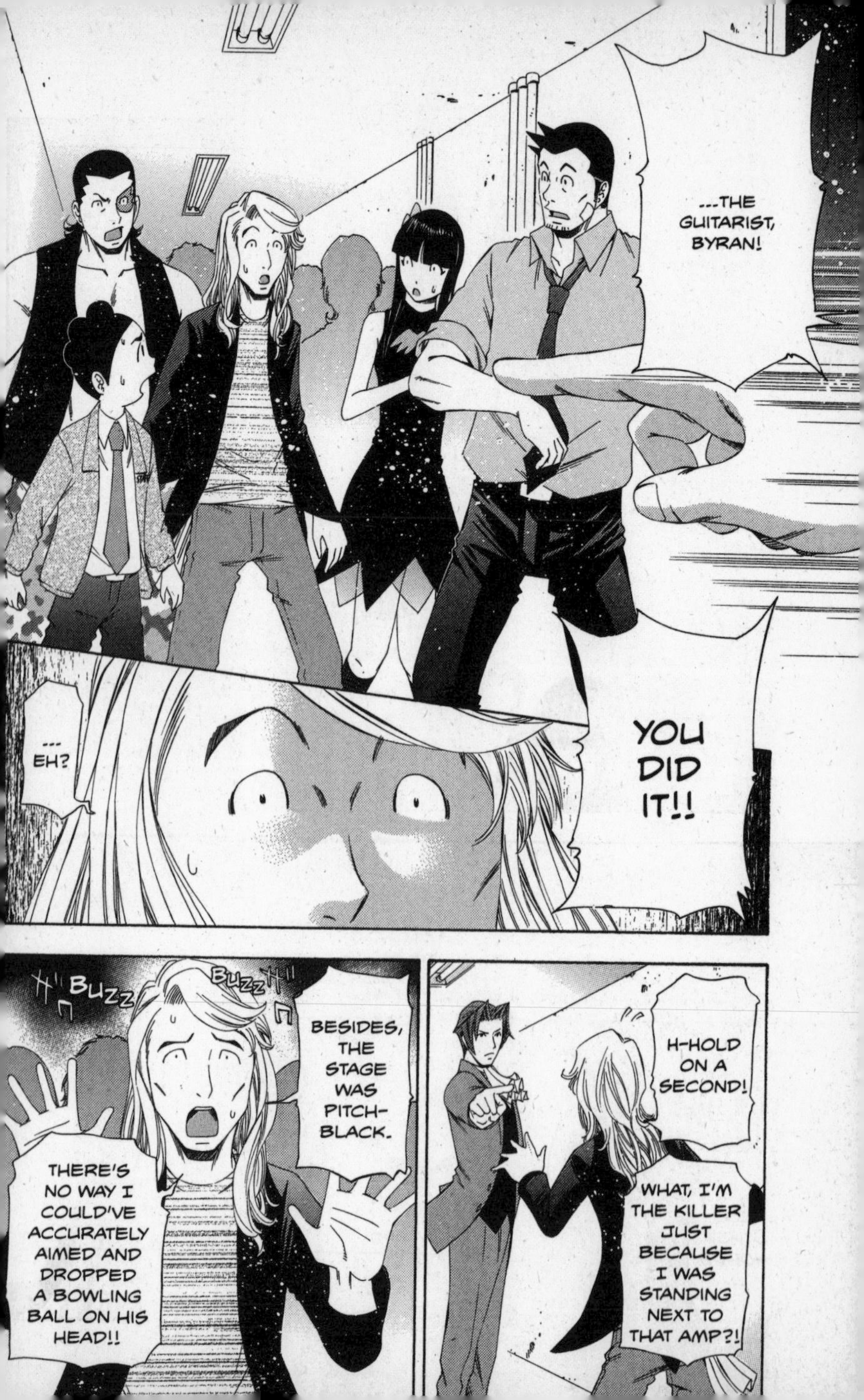
...THE GUITARIST, BYRAN!
YOU DID IT!!
...EH?
H-HOLD ON A SECOND!
WHAT, I'M THE KILLER JUST BECAUSE I WAS STANDING NEXT TO THAT AMP?!
Buzz
Buzz
BESIDES, THE STAGE WAS PITCH-BLACK.
THERE'S NO WAY I COULD'VE ACCURATELY AIMED AND DROPPED A BOWLING BALL ON HIS HEAD!!

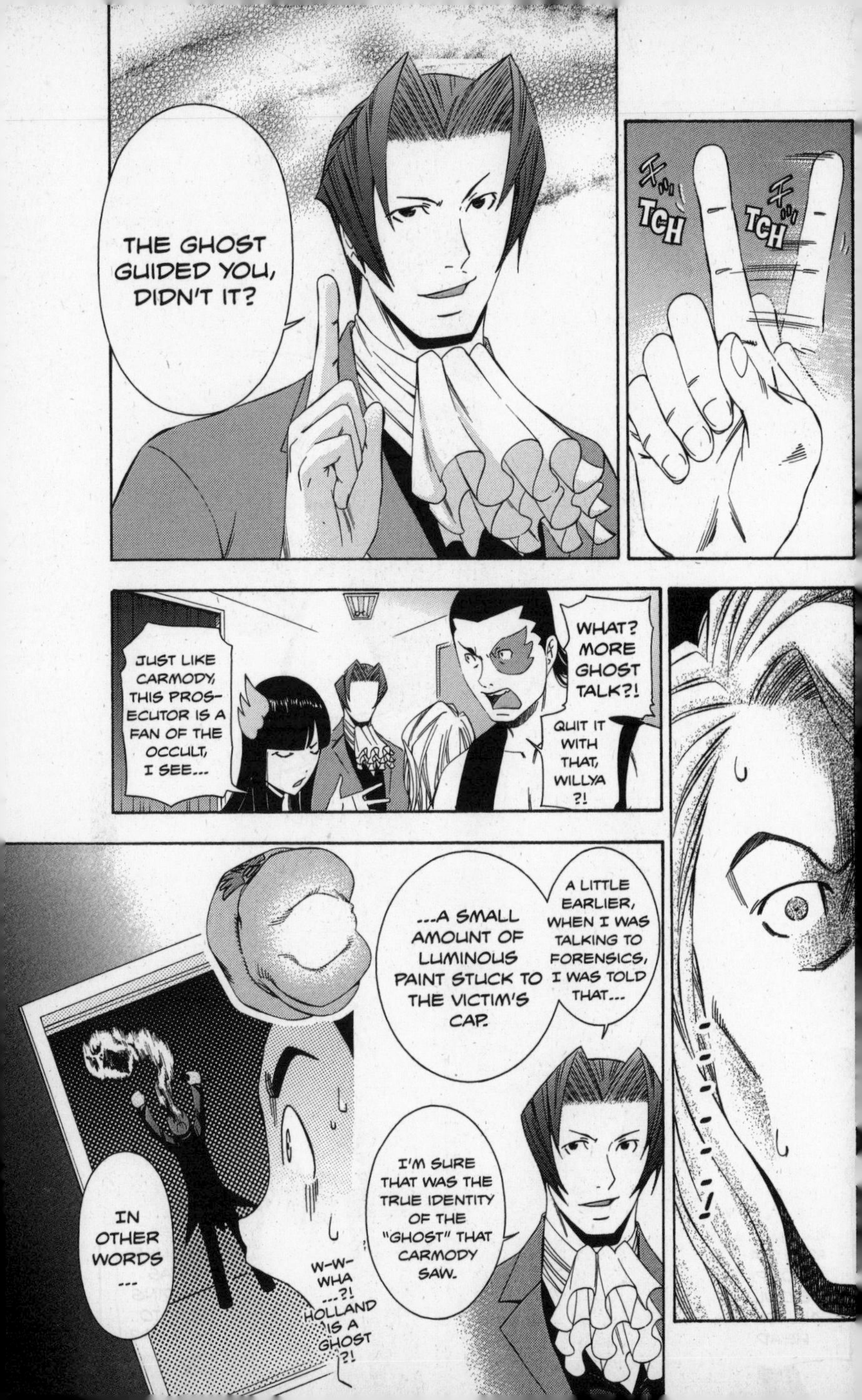
TCH
TCH
THE GHOST GUIDED YOU, DIDN'T IT?
......!
WHAT? MORE GHOST TALK?!
QUIT IT WITH THAT, WILLYA?!
JUST LIKE CARMODY, THIS PROSECUTOR IS A FAN OF THE OCCULT, I SEE...
A LITTLE EARLIER, WHEN I WAS TALKING TO FORENSICS, I WAS TOLD THAT...
...A SMALL AMOUNT OF LUMINOUS PAINT STUCK TO THE VICTIM'S CAP.
I'M SURE THAT WAS THE TRUE IDENTITY OF THE "GHOST" THAT CARMODY SAW.
W-W-WHA...?! HOLLAND IS A GHOST?!
IN OTHER WORDS...

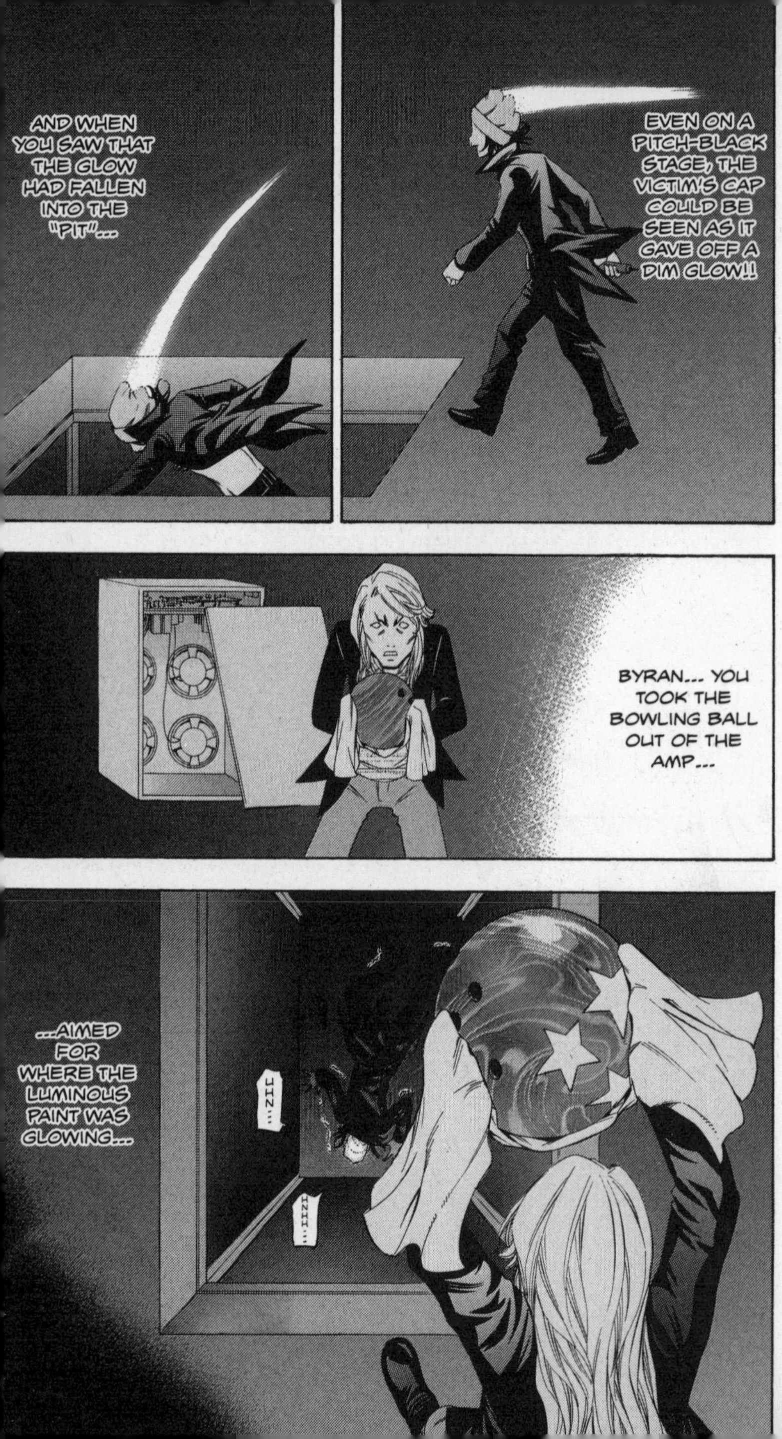
EVEN ON A PITCH-BLACK STAGE, THE VICTIM'S CAP COULD BE SEEN AS IT GAVE OFF A DIM GLOW!!
AND WHEN YOU SAW THAT THE GLOW HAD FALLEN INTO THE "PIT"...
BYRAN... YOU TOOK THE BOWLING BALL OUT OF THE AMP...
...AIMED FOR WHERE THE LUMINOUS PAINT WAS GLOWING...
UHN...
HNHH...

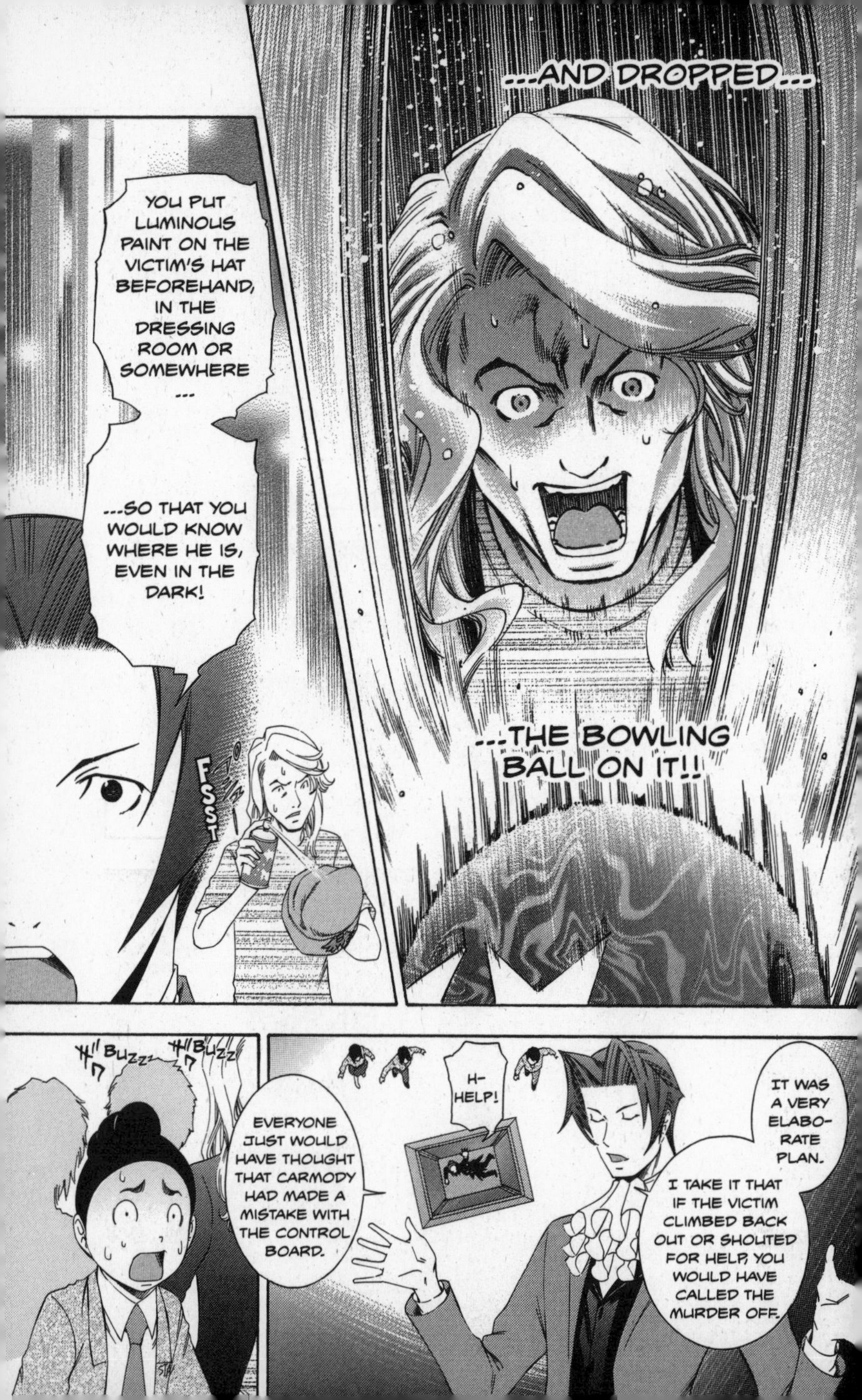
...AND DROPPED...
...THE BOWLING BALL ON IT!!
YOU PUT LUMINOUS PAINT ON THE VICTIM'S HAT BEFOREHAND, IN THE DRESSING ROOM OR SOMEWHERE ...
...SO THAT YOU WOULD KNOW WHERE HE IS, EVEN IN THE DARK!
FSST
IT WAS A VERY ELABO- RATE PLAN.
I TAKE IT THAT IF THE VICTIM CLIMBED BACK OUT OR SHOUTED FOR HELP, YOU WOULD HAVE CALLED THE MURDER OFF.
H- HELP!
EVERYONE JUST WOULD HAVE THOUGHT THAT CARMODY HAD MADE A MISTAKE WITH THE CONTROL BOARD.
BUZZZ
BUZZZ

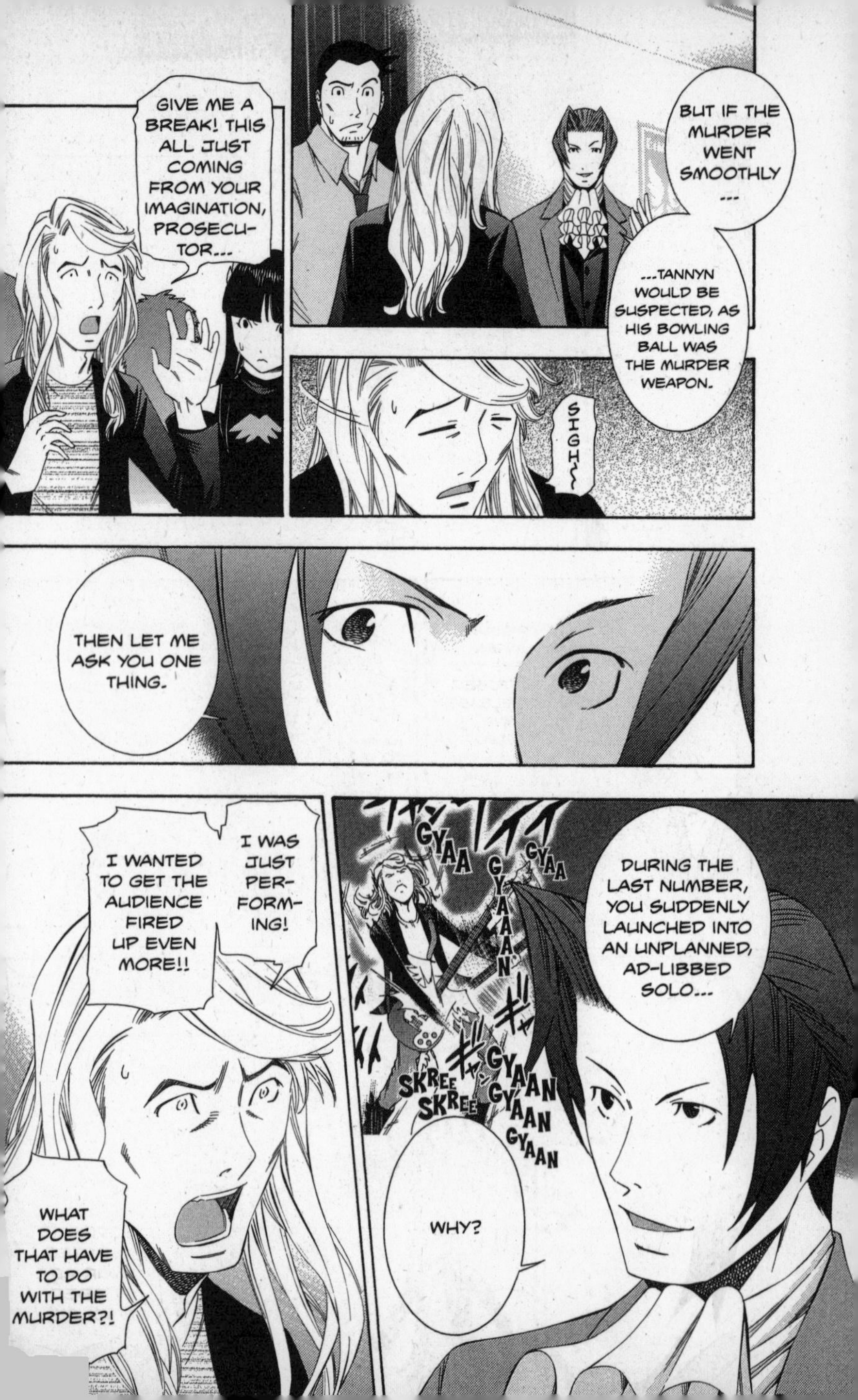
BUT IF THE MURDER WENT SMOOTHLY ...
...TANNYN WOULD BE SUSPECTED, AS HIS BOWLING BALL WAS THE MURDER WEAPON.
SIGH~
GIVE ME A BREAK! THIS ALL JUST COMING FROM YOUR IMAGINATION, PROSECUTOR...
THEN LET ME ASK YOU ONE THING.
DURING THE LAST NUMBER, YOU SUDDENLY LAUNCHED INTO AN UNPLANNED, AD-LIBBED SOLO...
GYAA GYAA GYAAAN
SKREE SKREE GYAAN GYAAN GYAAN
WHY?
I WAS JUST PERFORMING!
I WANTED TO GET THE AUDIENCE FIRED UP EVEN MORE!!
WHAT DOES THAT HAVE TO DO WITH THE MURDER?!

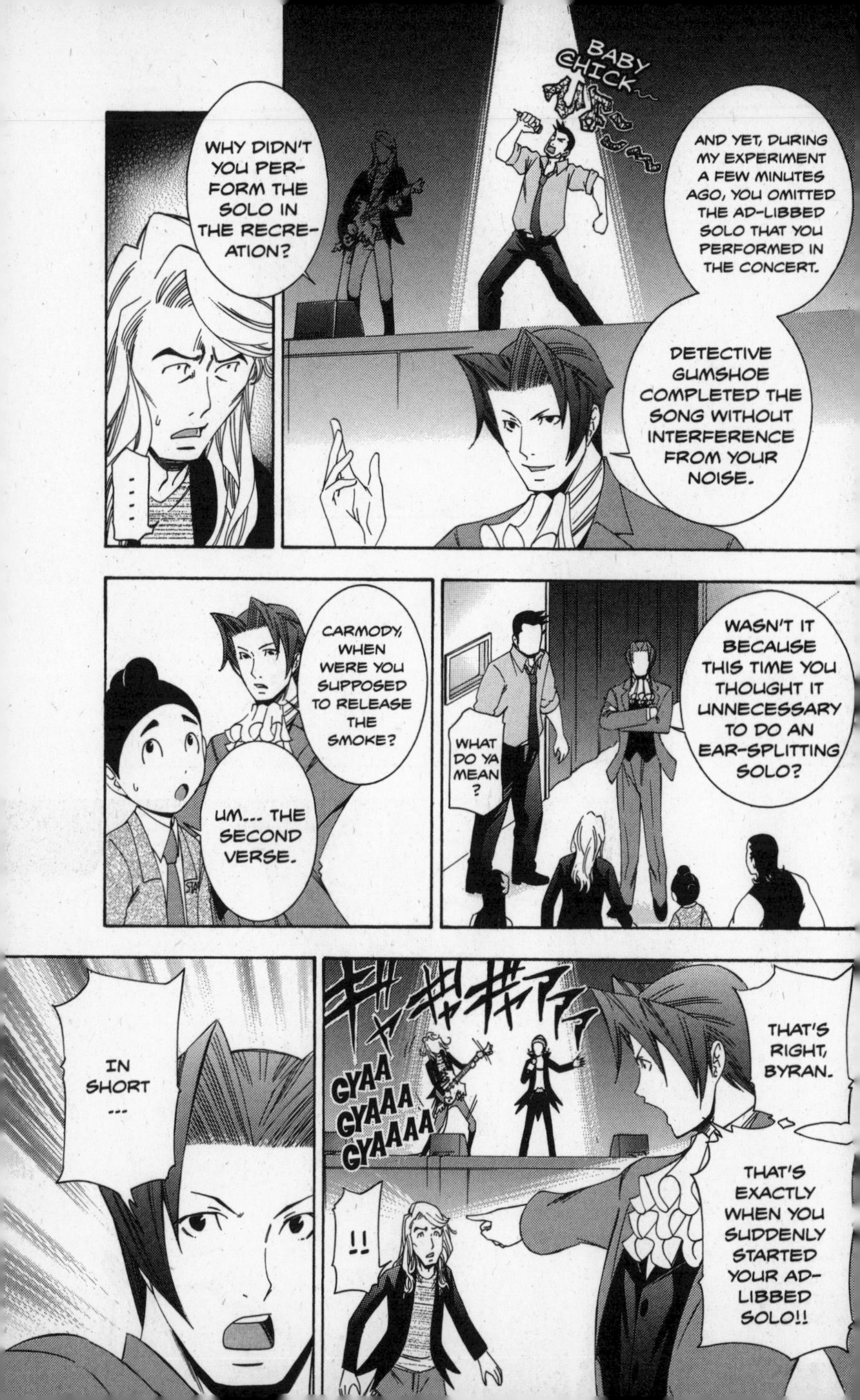
BABY CHICK~
AND YET, DURING MY EXPERIMENT A FEW MINUTES AGO, YOU OMITTED THE AD-LIBBED SOLO THAT YOU PERFORMED IN THE CONCERT.
WHY DIDN'T YOU PER-FORM THE SOLO IN THE RECRE-ATION?
DETECTIVE GUMSHOE COMPLETED THE SONG WITHOUT INTERFERENCE FROM YOUR NOISE.
WASN'T IT BECAUSE THIS TIME YOU THOUGHT IT UNNECESSARY TO DO AN EAR-SPLITTING SOLO?
WHAT DO YA MEAN?
CARMODY, WHEN WERE YOU SUPPOSED TO RELEASE THE SMOKE?
UM... THE SECOND VERSE.
THAT'S RIGHT, BYRAN.
GYAA GYAAA GYAAAA GYAAAA
THAT'S EXACTLY WHEN YOU SUDDENLY STARTED YOUR AD-LIBBED SOLO!!
!!
IN SHORT ---

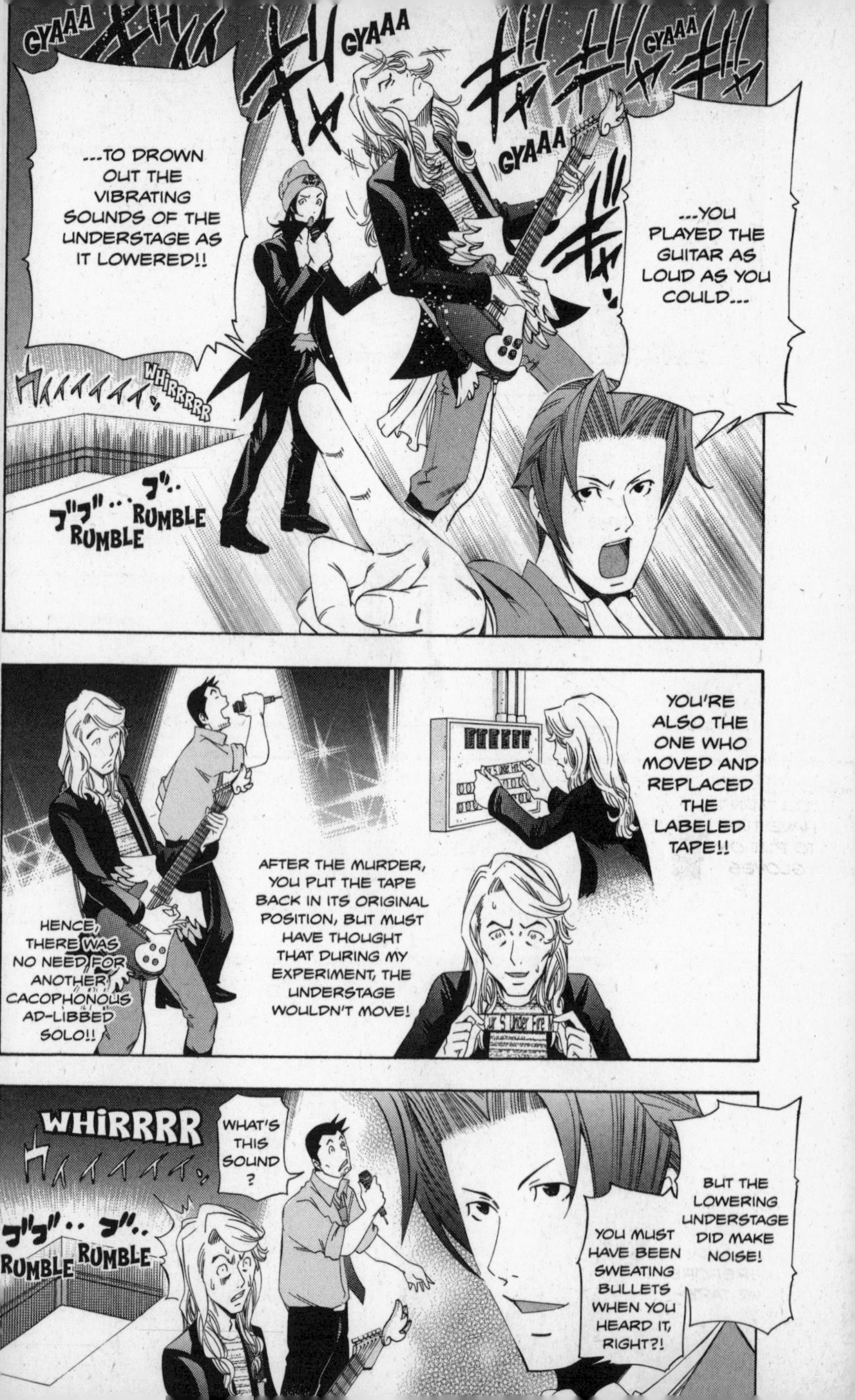
GYAAA
GYAAA
GYAAA
GYAAA
...YOU PLAYED THE GUITAR AS LOUD AS YOU COULD...
...TO DROWN OUT THE VIBRATING SOUNDS OF THE UNDERSTAGE AS IT LOWERED!!
WHIRRRRR
RUMBLE RUMBLE
YOU'RE ALSO THE ONE WHO MOVED AND REPLACED THE LABELED TAPE!!
AFTER THE MURDER, YOU PUT THE TAPE BACK IN ITS ORIGINAL POSITION, BUT MUST HAVE THOUGHT THAT DURING MY EXPERIMENT, THE UNDERSTAGE WOULDN'T MOVE!
HENCE, THERE WAS NO NEED FOR ANOTHER CACOPHONOUS AD-LIBBED SOLO!!
BUT THE LOWERING UNDERSTAGE DID MAKE NOISE!
YOU MUST HAVE BEEN SWEATING BULLETS WHEN YOU HEARD IT, RIGHT?!
WHAT'S THIS SOUND?
WHIRRRR
RUMBLE RUMBLE

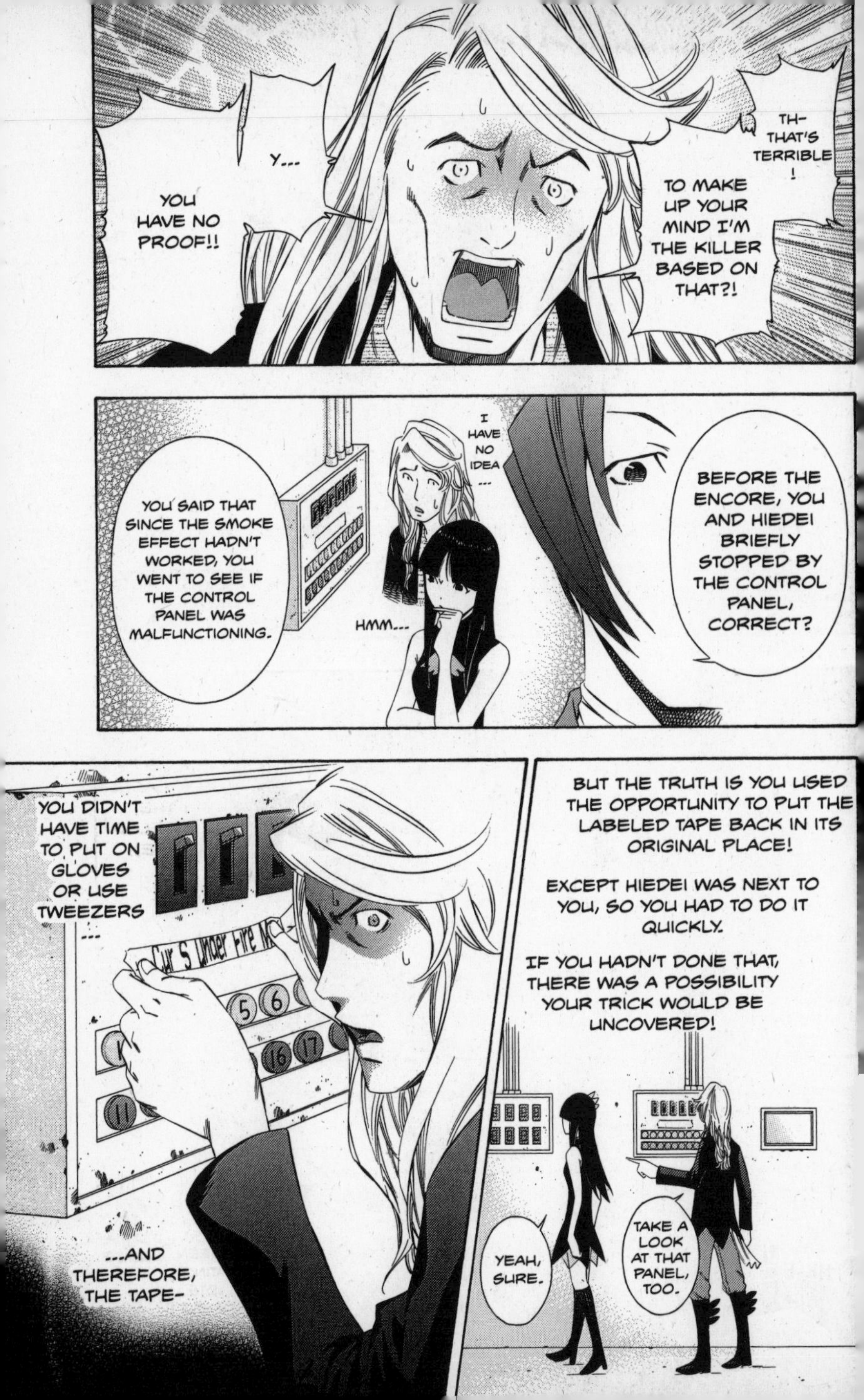
TH-THAT'S TERRIBLE!
TO MAKE UP YOUR MIND I'M THE KILLER BASED ON THAT?!
Y...
YOU HAVE NO PROOF!!
BEFORE THE ENCORE, YOU AND HIEDEI BRIEFLY STOPPED BY THE CONTROL PANEL, CORRECT?
I HAVE NO IDEA...
YOU SAID THAT SINCE THE SMOKE EFFECT HADN'T WORKED, YOU WENT TO SEE IF THE CONTROL PANEL WAS MALFUNCTIONING.
HMM...
BUT THE TRUTH IS YOU USED THE OPPORTUNITY TO PUT THE LABELED TAPE BACK IN ITS ORIGINAL PLACE!
EXCEPT HIEDEI WAS NEXT TO YOU, SO YOU HAD TO DO IT QUICKLY.
IF YOU HADN'T DONE THAT, THERE WAS A POSSIBILITY YOUR TRICK WOULD BE UNCOVERED!
TAKE A LOOK AT THAT PANEL, TOO.
YEAH, SURE.
YOU DIDN'T HAVE TIME TO PUT ON GLOVES OR USE TWEEZERS...
...AND THEREFORE, THE TAPE-

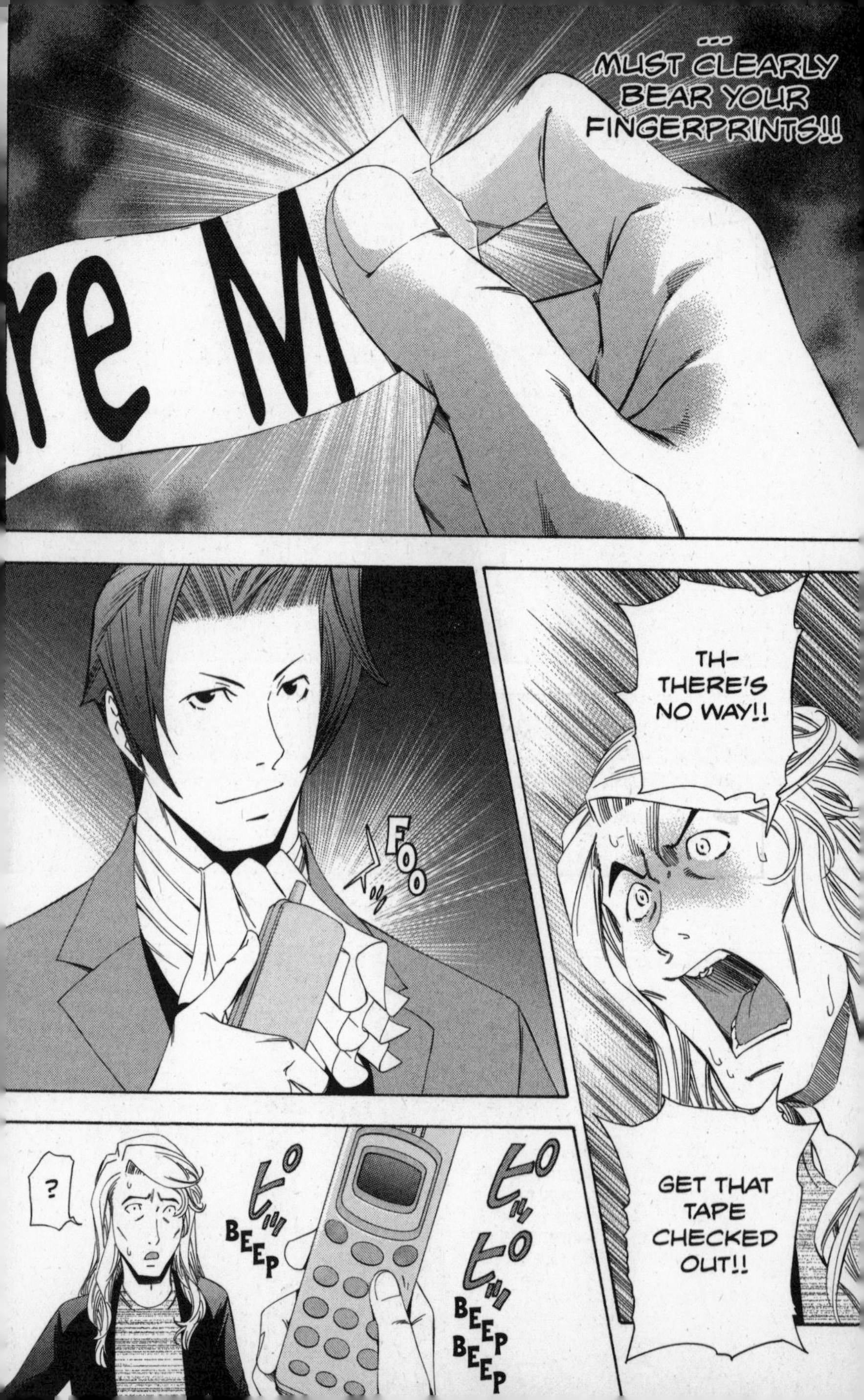
...
MUST CLEARLY BEAR YOUR FINGERPRINTS!!
re M
TH-THERE'S NO WAY!!
GET THAT TAPE CHECKED OUT!!
FOO
BEEP
BEEP BEEP
?

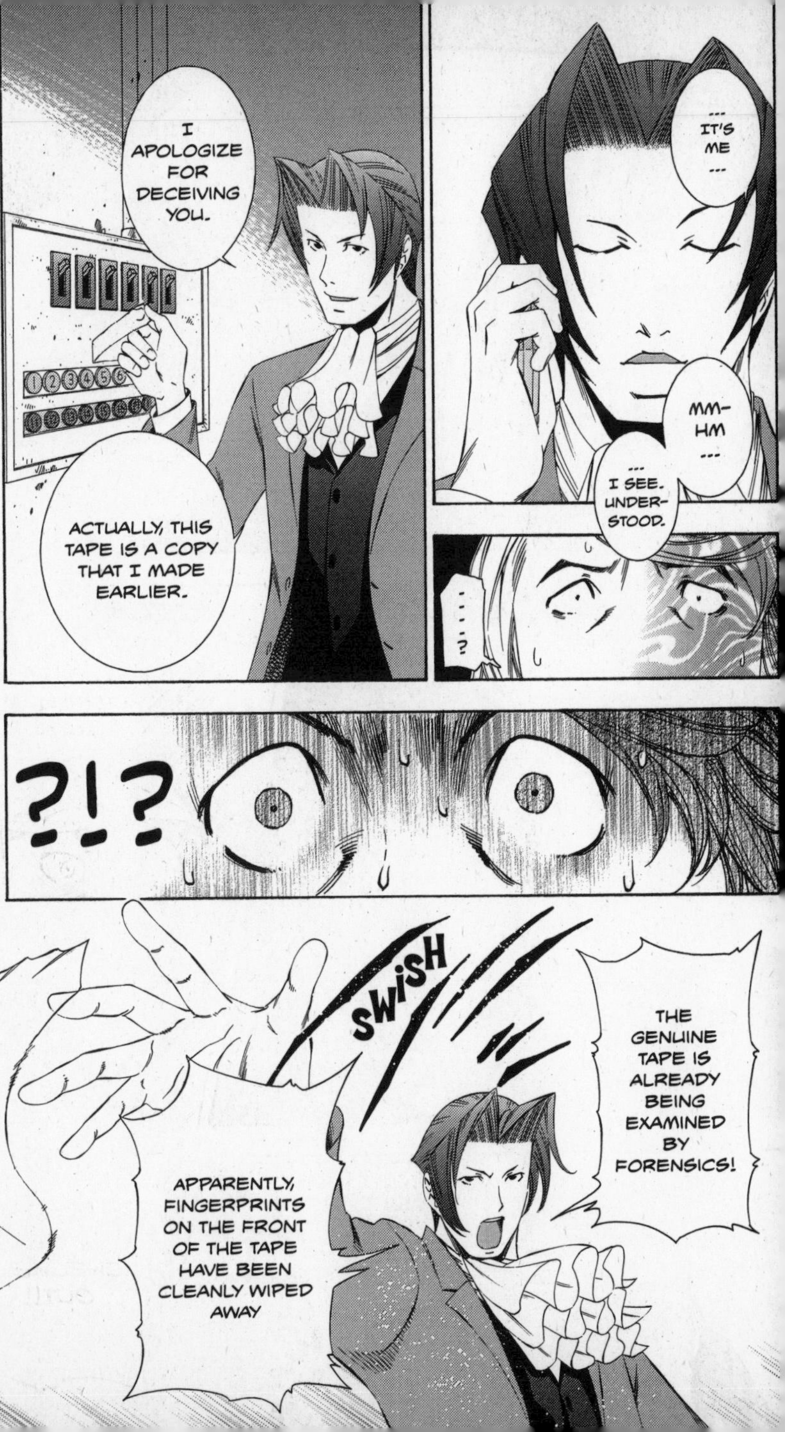

...IT'S ME...
MM-HM...
...I SEE. UNDERSTOOD.
.....?
I APOLOGIZE FOR DECEIVING YOU.
ACTUALLY, THIS TAPE IS A COPY THAT I MADE EARLIER.
?!?
SWISH
THE GENUINE TAPE IS ALREADY BEING EXAMINED BY FORENSICS!
APPARENTLY, FINGERPRINTS ON THE FRONT OF THE TAPE HAVE BEEN CLEANLY WIPED AWAY

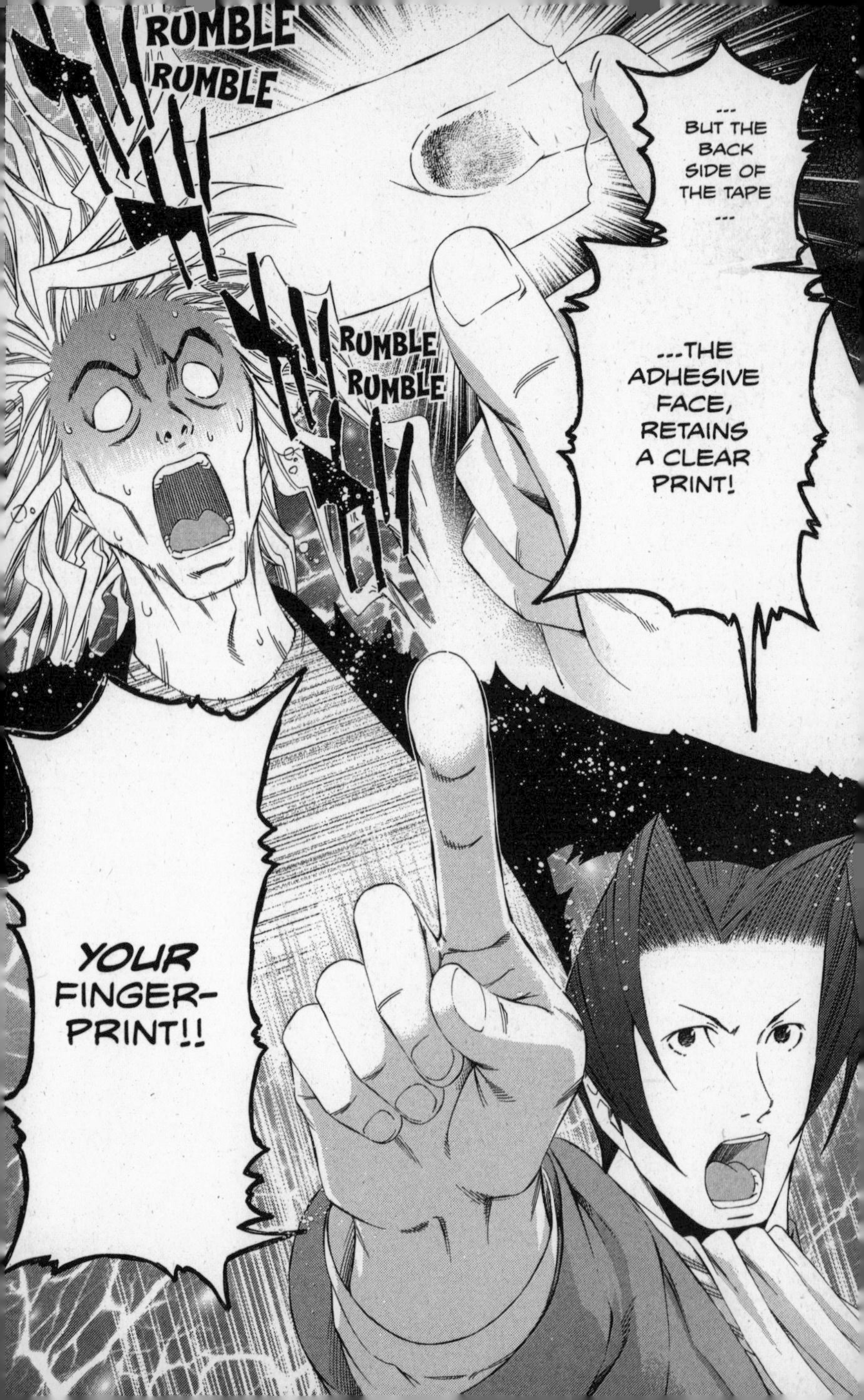
RUMBLE RUMBLE
... BUT THE BACK SIDE OF THE TAPE ...
...THE ADHESIVE FACE, RETAINS A CLEAR PRINT!
RUMBLE RUMBLE
YOUR FINGER-PRINT!!

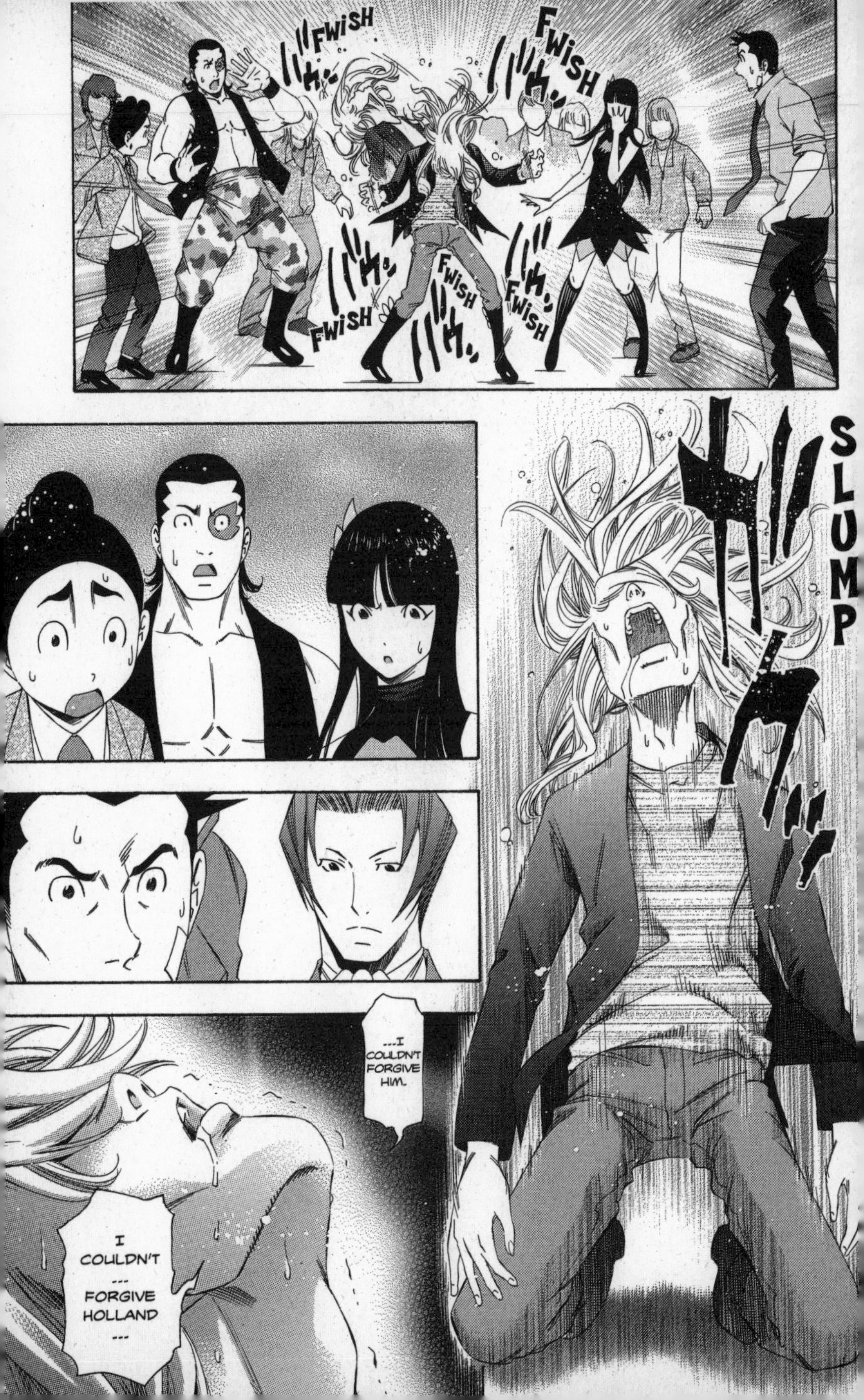
FWISH
FWISH
FWISH
FWISH
FWISH
FWISH
SLUMP
...I COULDN'T FORGIVE HIM.
I COULDN'T --- FORGIVE HOLLAND ---

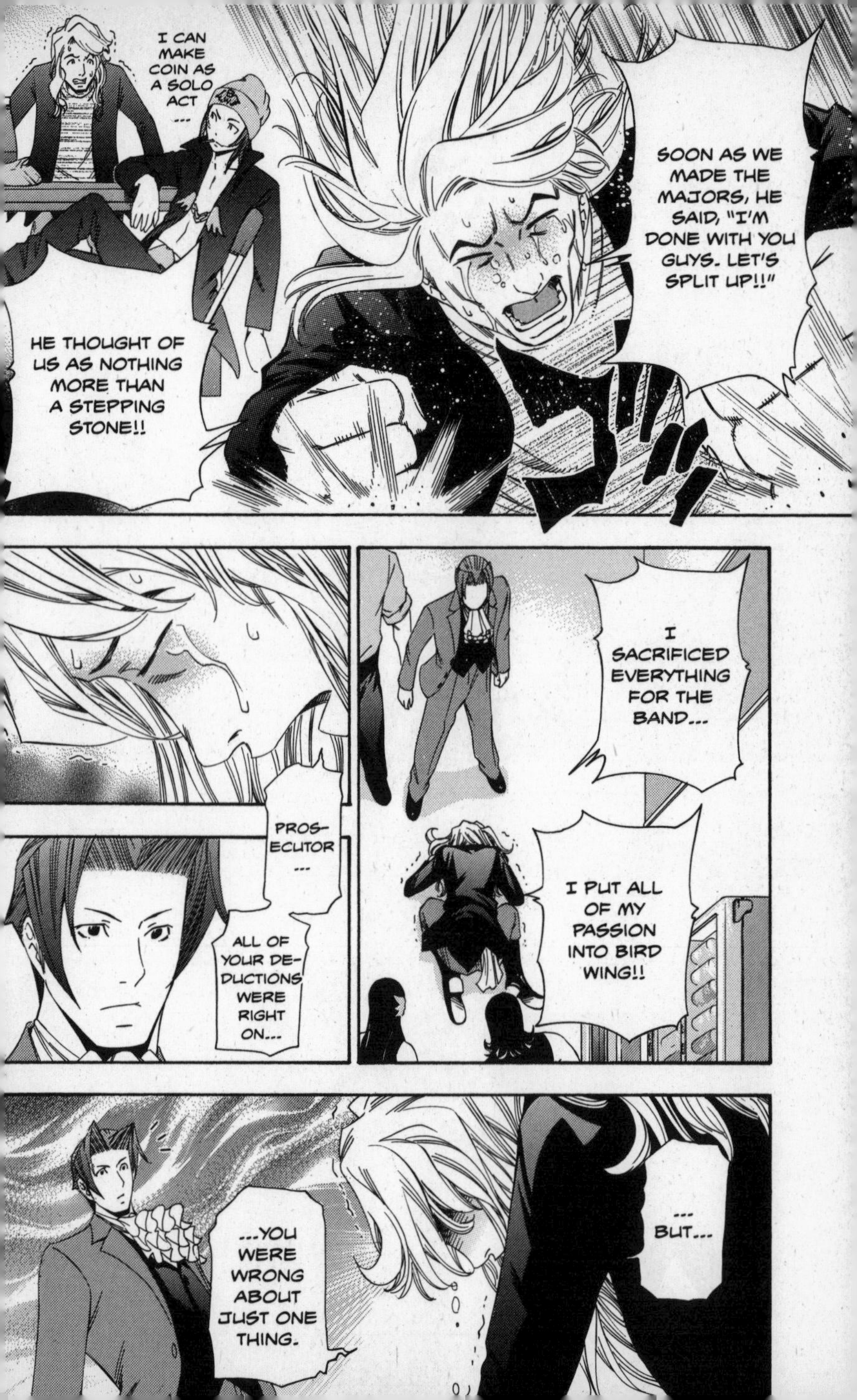
SOON AS WE MADE THE MAJORS, HE SAID, "I'M DONE WITH YOU GUYS. LET'S SPLIT UP!!"
I CAN MAKE COIN AS A SOLO ACT ...
HE THOUGHT OF US AS NOTHING MORE THAN A STEPPING STONE!!
I SACRIFICED EVERYTHING FOR THE BAND...
I PUT ALL OF MY PASSION INTO BIRD WING!!
PROS-ECUTOR ...
ALL OF YOUR DE-DUCTIONS WERE RIGHT ON...
... BUT...
...YOU WERE WRONG ABOUT JUST ONE THING.

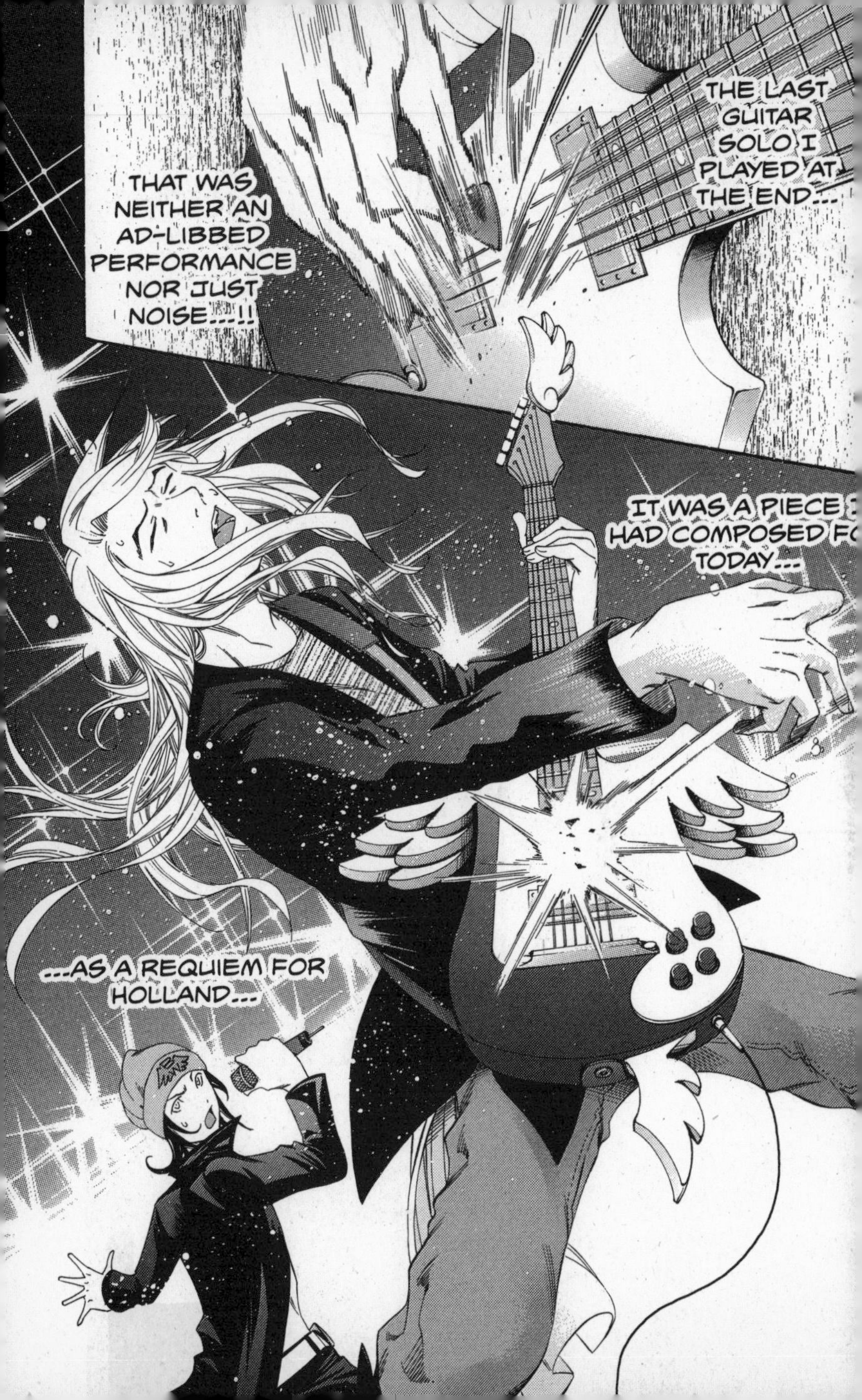
THE LAST GUITAR SOLO I PLAYED AT THE END...
THAT WAS NEITHER AN AD-LIBBED PERFORMANCE NOR JUST NOISE...!!
IT WAS A PIECE I HAD COMPOSED FO TODAY...
...AS A REQUIEM FOR HOLLAND...

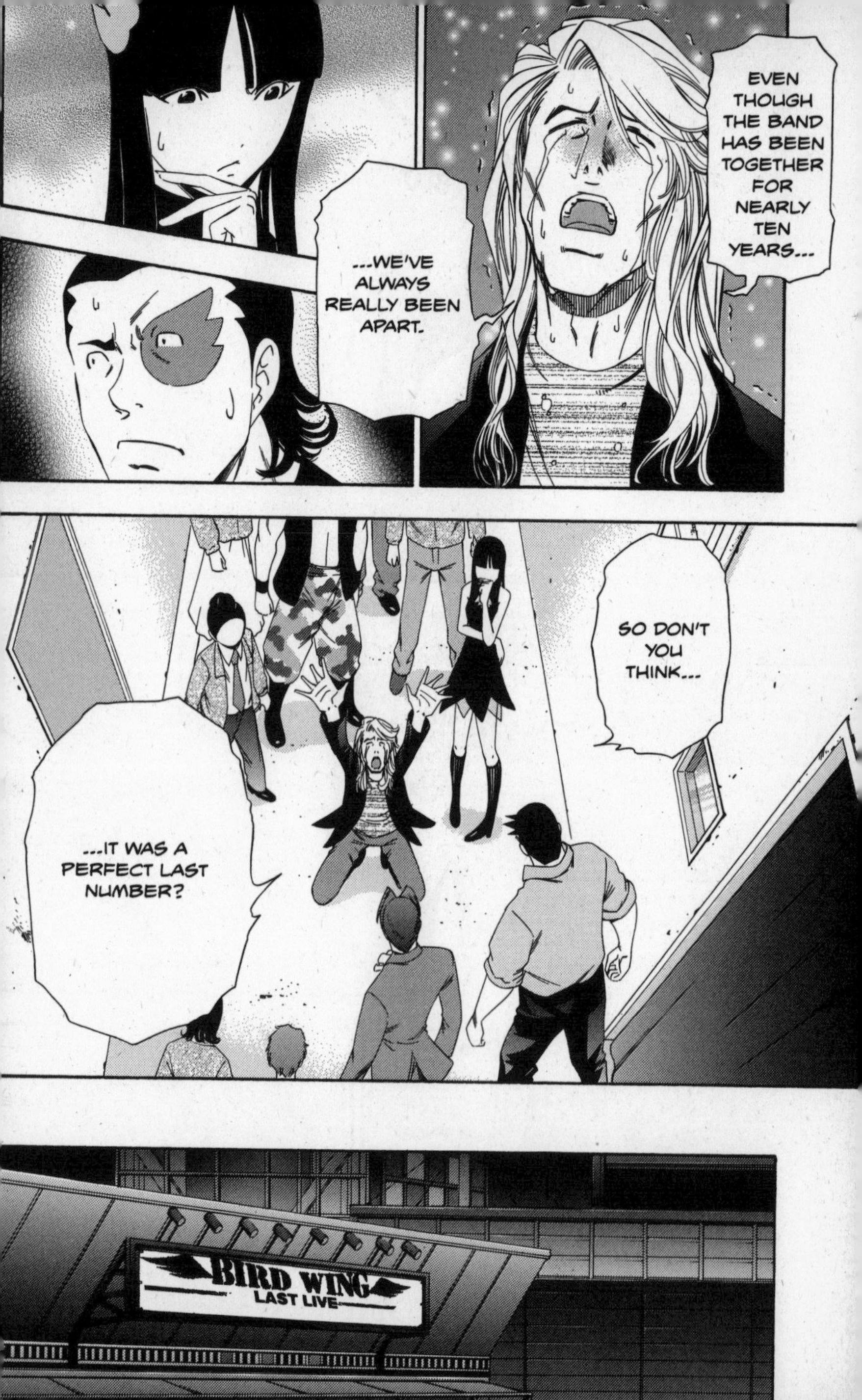
EVEN THOUGH THE BAND HAS BEEN TOGETHER FOR NEARLY TEN YEARS...
...WE'VE ALWAYS REALLY BEEN APART.
SO DON'T YOU THINK...
...IT WAS A PERFECT LAST NUMBER?
BIRD WING
LAST LIVE

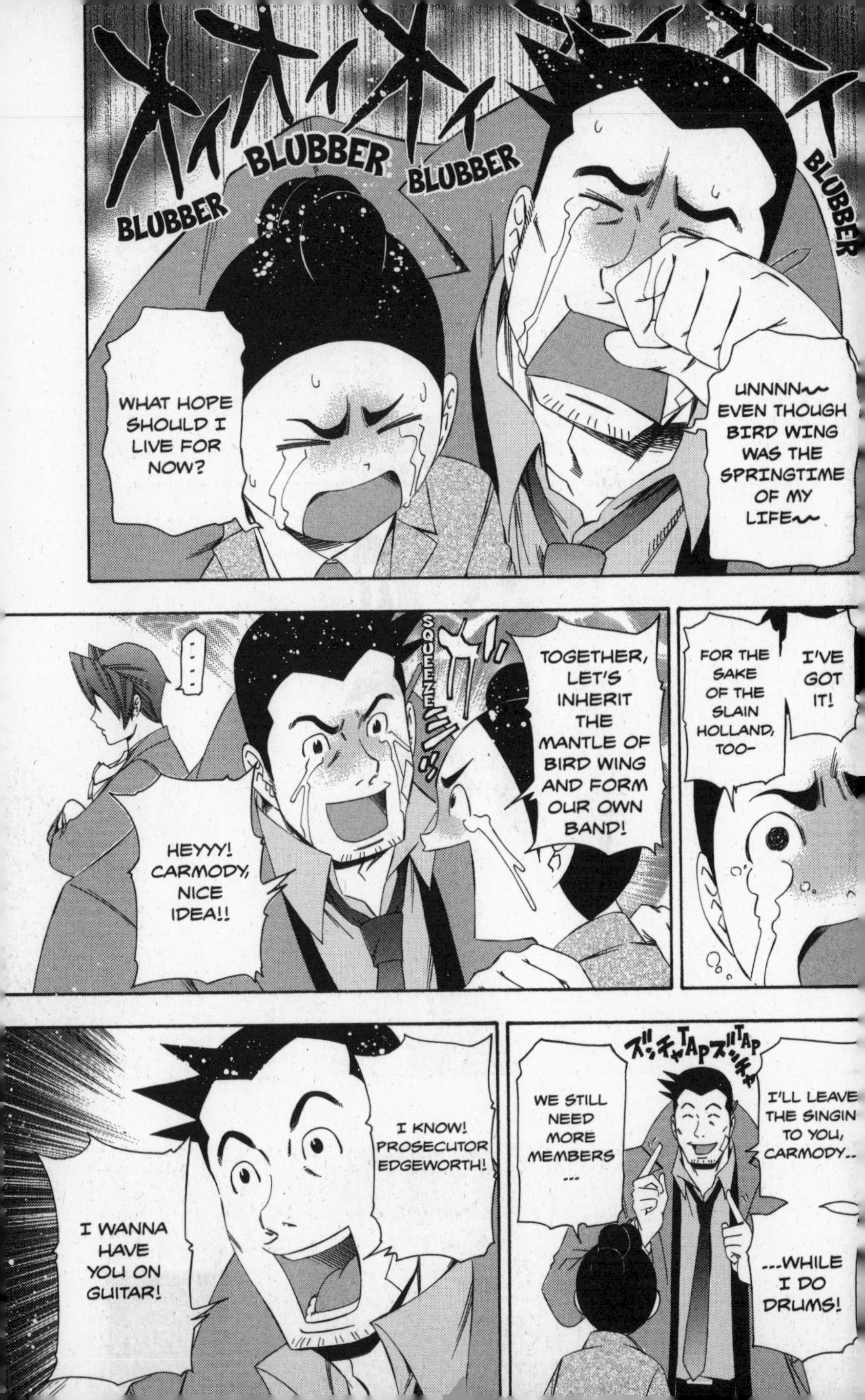
BLUBBER
BLUBBER
BLUBBER
BLUBBER
UNNNN~~ EVEN THOUGH BIRD WING WAS THE SPRINGTIME OF MY LIFE~~
WHAT HOPE SHOULD I LIVE FOR NOW?
I'VE GOT IT!
FOR THE SAKE OF THE SLAIN HOLLAND, TOO-
TOGETHER, LET'S INHERIT THE MANTLE OF BIRD WING AND FORM OUR OWN BAND!
SQUEEZE
HEYYY! CARMODY, NICE IDEA!!
....
TAP TAP
I'LL LEAVE THE SINGIN TO YOU, CARMODY..
WE STILL NEED MORE MEMBERS ...
...WHILE I DO DRUMS!
I KNOW! PROSECUTOR EDGEWORTH!
I WANNA HAVE YOU ON GUITAR!

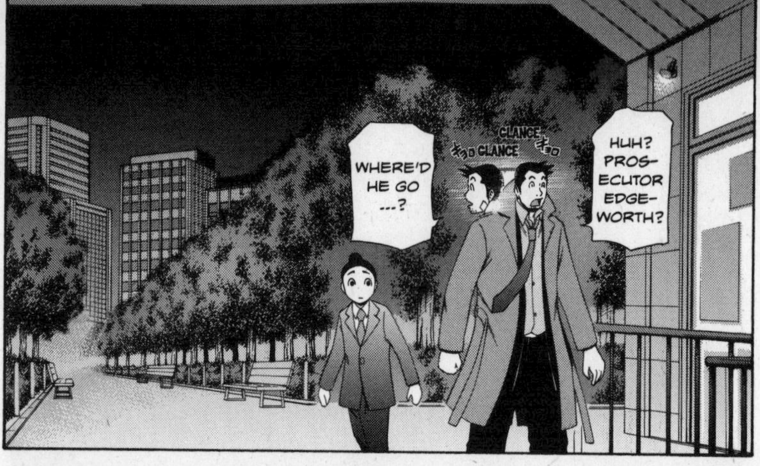
HUH? PROS-ECUTOR EDGE-WORTH?
キョロ GLANCE キョロ GLANCE
WHERE'D HE GO ...?
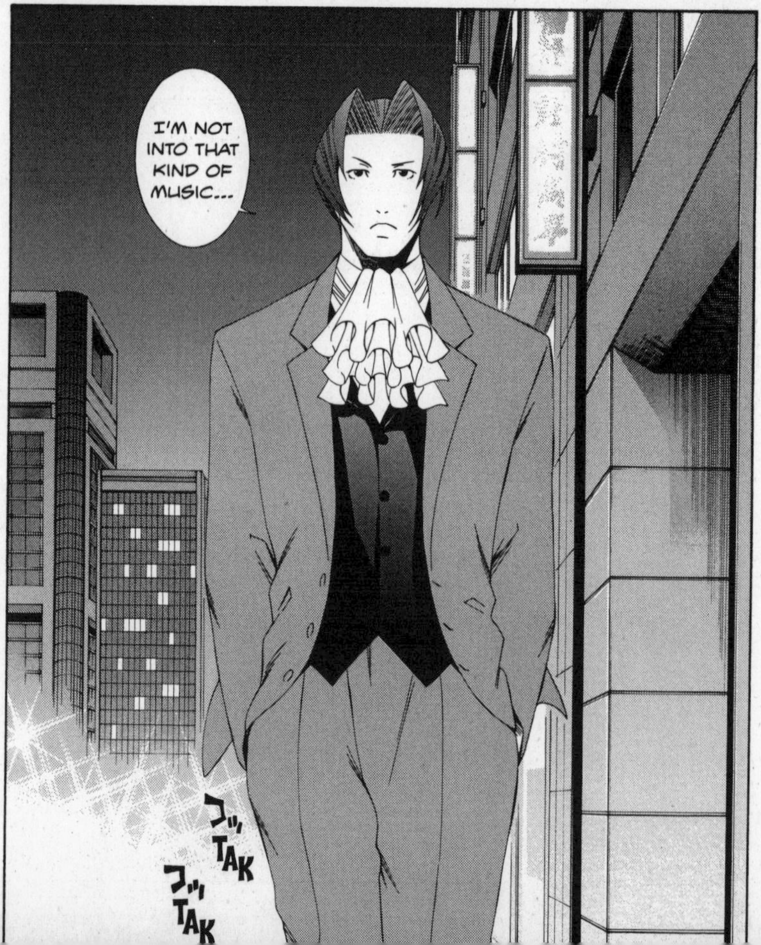
I'M NOT INTO THAT KIND OF MUSIC...
コッ TAK
コッ TAK

Ace Attorney Miles Edgewort

INVESTIGATIONS™

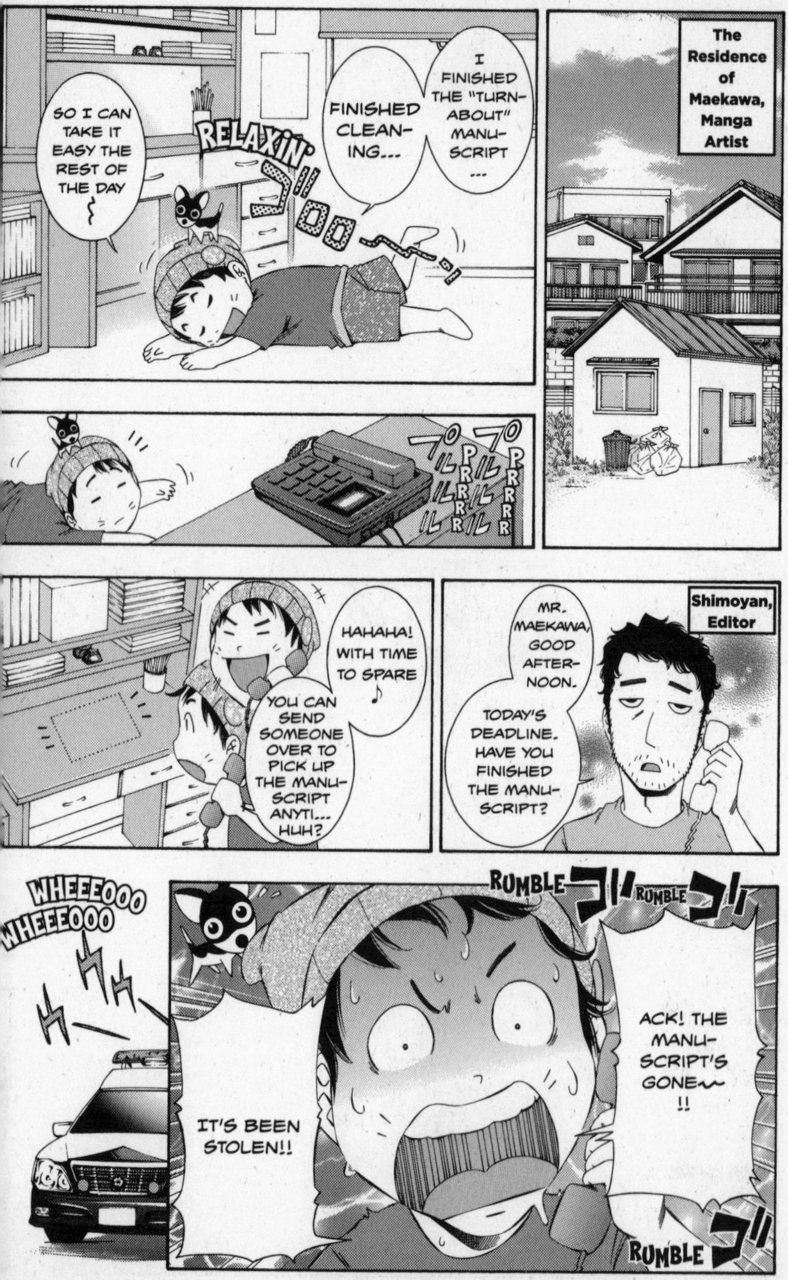

The Residence of Maekawa, Manga Artist
I FINISHED THE "TURN-ABOUT" MANU-SCRIPT ...
FINISHED CLEAN-ING...
RELAXIN'
SO I CAN TAKE IT EASY THE REST OF THE DAY
PRRRR PRRRR
Shimoyan, Editor
MR. MAEKAWA, GOOD AFTER-NOON.
TODAY'S DEADLINE. HAVE YOU FINISHED THE MANU-SCRIPT?
HAHAHA! WITH TIME TO SPARE ♪
YOU CAN SEND SOMEONE OVER TO PICK UP THE MANU-SCRIPT ANYTI... HUH?
RUMBLE RUMBLE
ACK! THE MANU-SCRIPT'S GONE~ !!
IT'S BEEN STOLEN!!
RUMBLE
WHEEEOOO WHEEEOOO

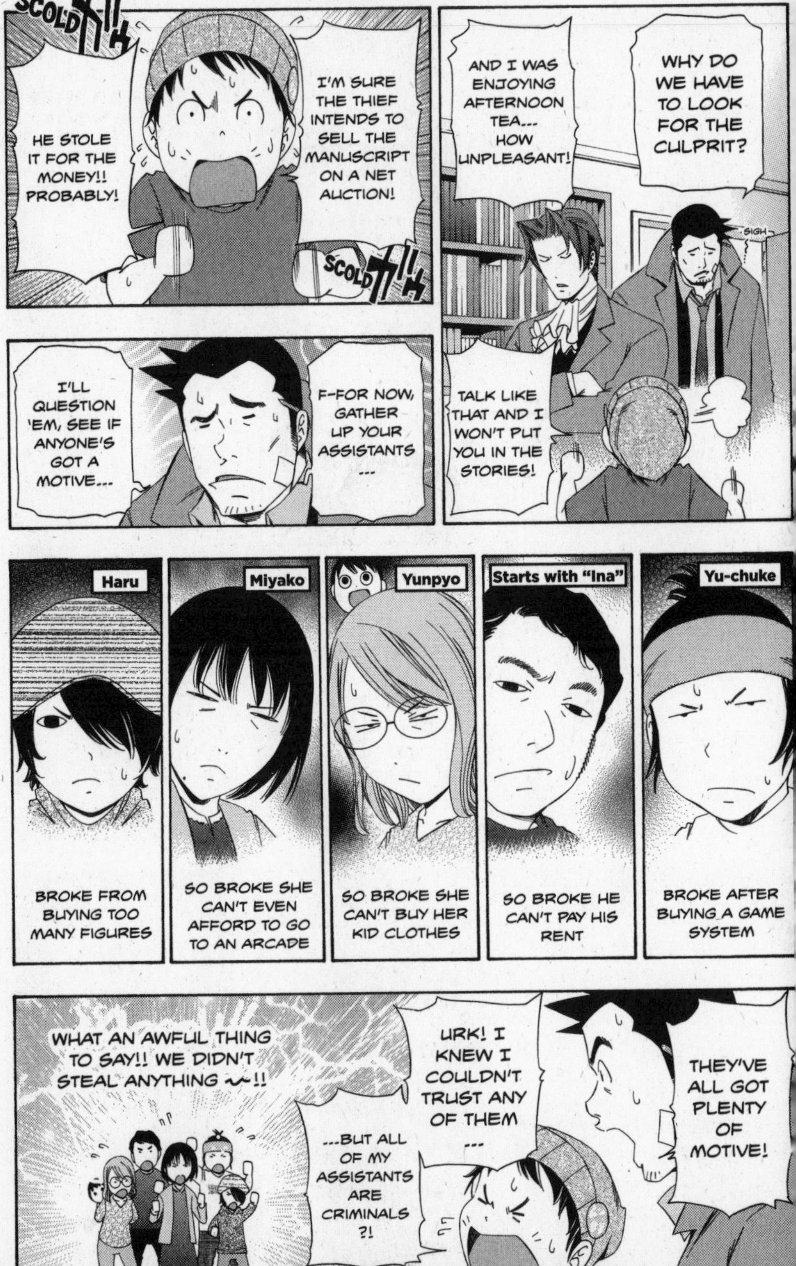
WHY DO WE HAVE TO LOOK FOR THE CULPRIT?
AND I WAS ENJOYING AFTERNOON TEA... HOW UNPLEASANT!
SIGH
TALK LIKE THAT AND I WON'T PUT YOU IN THE STORIES!
SCOLD
I'M SURE THE THIEF INTENDS TO SELL THE MANUSCRIPT ON A NET AUCTION!
HE STOLE IT FOR THE MONEY!! PROBABLY!
SCOLD
F-FOR NOW, GATHER UP YOUR ASSISTANTS ...
I'LL QUESTION 'EM, SEE IF ANYONE'S GOT A MOTIVE...
Yu-chuke
BROKE AFTER BUYING A GAME SYSTEM
Starts with "Ina"
SO BROKE HE CAN'T PAY HIS RENT
Yunpyo
SO BROKE SHE CAN'T BUY HER KID CLOTHES
Miyako
SO BROKE SHE CAN'T EVEN AFFORD TO GO TO AN ARCADE
Haru
BROKE FROM BUYING TOO MANY FIGURES
THEY'VE ALL GOT PLENTY OF MOTIVE!
URK! I KNEW I COULDN'T TRUST ANY OF THEM ...
...BUT ALL OF MY ASSISTANTS ARE CRIMINALS ?!
WHAT AN AWFUL THING TO SAY!! WE DIDN'T STEAL ANYTHING ~~!!

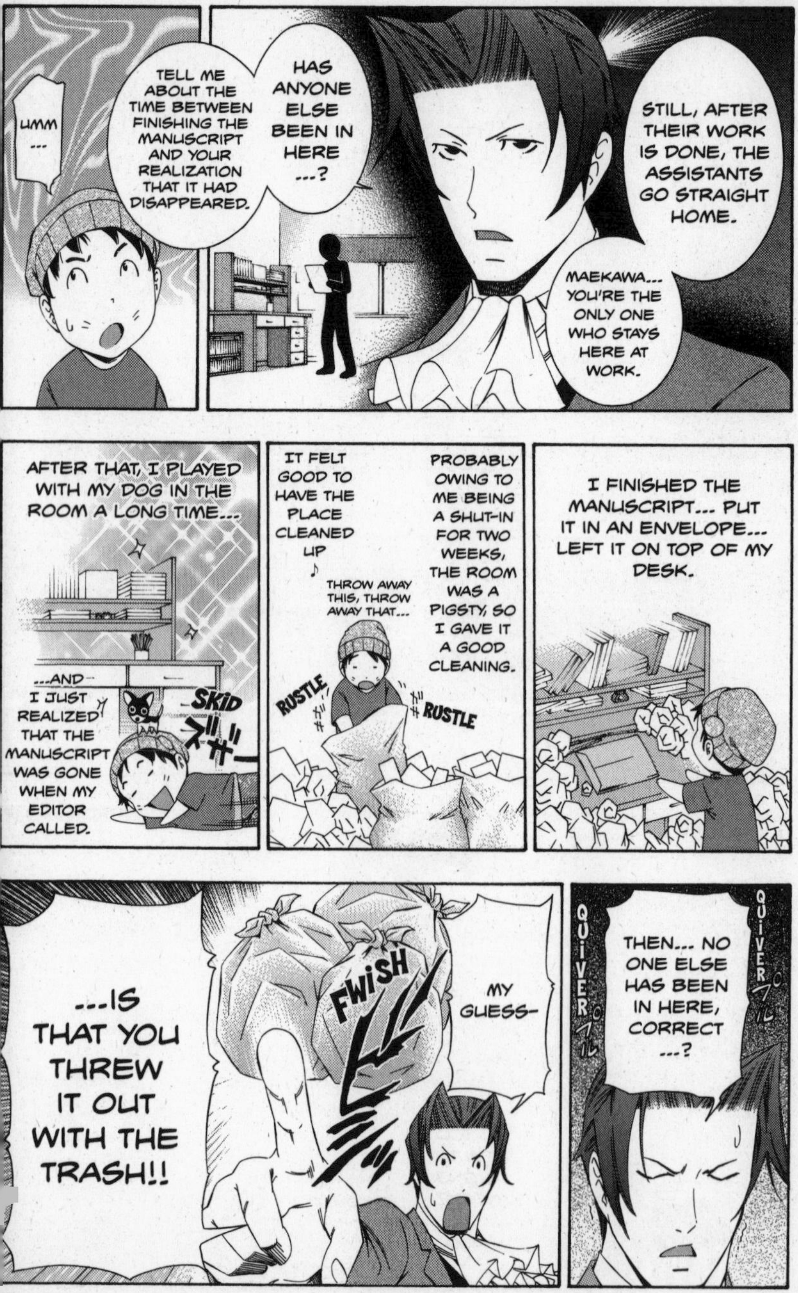
STILL, AFTER THEIR WORK IS DONE, THE ASSISTANTS GO STRAIGHT HOME.
MAEKAWA... YOU'RE THE ONLY ONE WHO STAYS HERE AT WORK.
HAS ANYONE ELSE BEEN IN HERE ...?
TELL ME ABOUT THE TIME BETWEEN FINISHING THE MANUSCRIPT AND YOUR REALIZATION THAT IT HAD DISAPPEARED.
UMM ...
I FINISHED THE MANUSCRIPT... PUT IT IN AN ENVELOPE... LEFT IT ON TOP OF MY DESK.
PROBABLY OWING TO ME BEING A SHUT-IN FOR TWO WEEKS, THE ROOM WAS A PIGSTY, SO I GAVE IT A GOOD CLEANING.
IT FELT GOOD TO HAVE THE PLACE CLEANED UP ♪
THROW AWAY THIS, THROW AWAY THAT...
RUSTLE
RUSTLE
AFTER THAT, I PLAYED WITH MY DOG IN THE ROOM A LONG TIME...
SKID
...AND I JUST REALIZED THAT THE MANUSCRIPT WAS GONE WHEN MY EDITOR CALLED.
QUIVER
QUIVER
THEN... NO ONE ELSE HAS BEEN IN HERE, CORRECT ...?
MY GUESS-
FWISH
...IS THAT YOU THREW IT OUT WITH THE TRASH!!

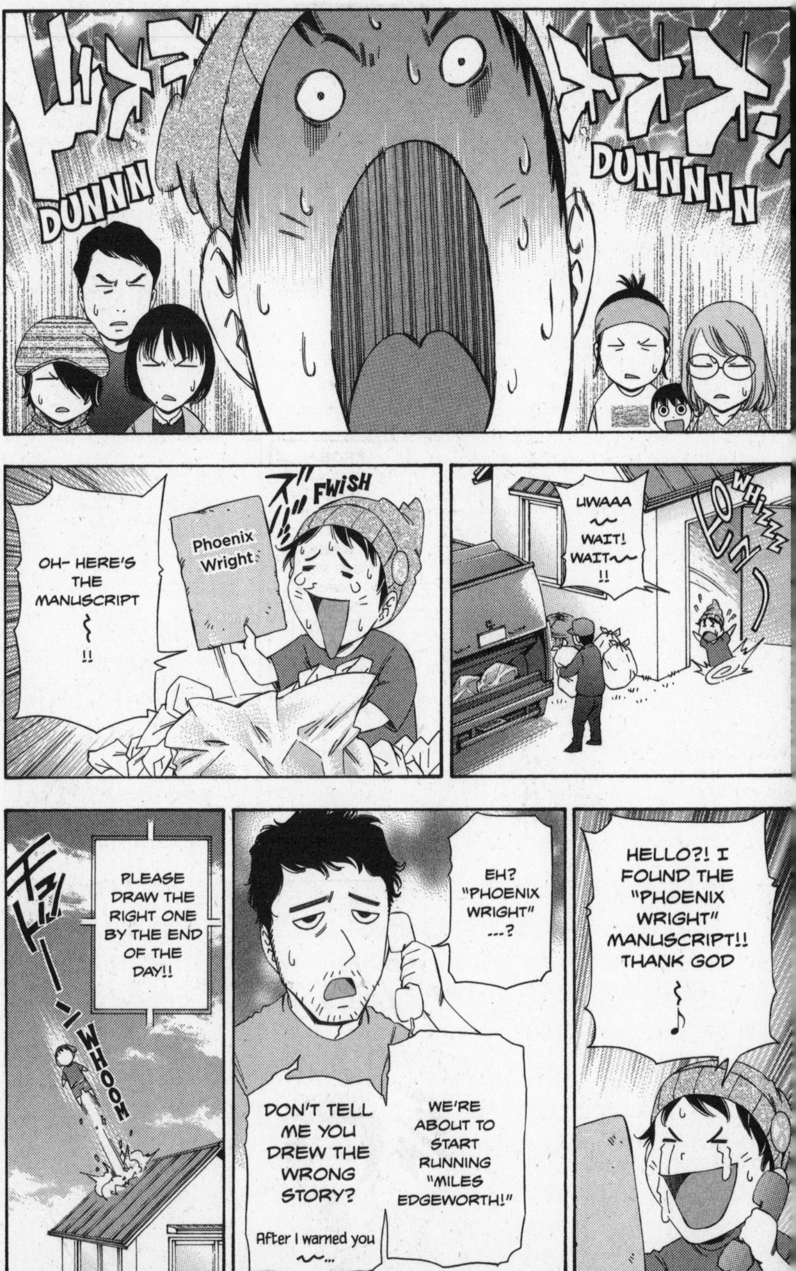
DUNNNNNN
DUNNN
UWAAA ~ WAIT! WAIT~~ !!
WHIZZZ
FWISH
Phoenix Wright
OH- HERE'S THE MANUSCRIPT ~ !!
HELLO?! I FOUND THE "PHOENIX WRIGHT" MANUSCRIPT!! THANK GOD ~ ♪
EH? "PHOENIX WRIGHT" ---?
WE'RE ABOUT TO START RUNNING "MILES EDGEWORTH!"
DON'T TELL ME YOU DREW THE WRONG STORY?
After I warned you ~...
PLEASE DRAW THE RIGHT ONE BY THE END OF THE DAY!!
WHOOM

TRANSLATION NOTES

Japanese is a tricky language for most Western-ers, and translation is often more art than science. For your edification and reading pleasure, here are notes on some of the places where we could have gone in a different direction with our translation of the work, or where a Japanese cultural reference is used.

Names, page 15
[15.3]
Though in the original Japanese, all of the char-acters have normal Japanese names, including the main characters, they've been Westernized here. Of course, Miles and Dick have already gone through the process, but I'm happy to get the chance to think up names for these new charac-ters. I just wish I could've come up with a name for the murderer in this story...

Gender-bender, page 48
[48.2]
Since pronouns aren't used in Japanese as nearly as much as we use them in English, it's easier to conceal a "gender-switch" trick like this. So as a translator, I had to go through mental gymnastics to make sure all of the dialogue was gender-neutral up until the reveal... or at least up until the murderer calls the witch a "woman". I did slip in the "her", as in "her underpants", but figured I could get away with it at that point.

Writing postcards, page 62

[62.3]

It's common in Japan to send postcards for a chance to win prizes advertised on TV shows and in magazines.

Doji, page 95

[95.5]

"Doji" means a blunderer or to commit a blunder. Although this guy's original Japanese name is "Douji", it's similar enough that the detective calls him the not-complimentary "Doji" by mistake. And of course, the joke is that the guy is a blunderer after all. Even though the joke is much more of a strained one in English, I gave it a shot. I mean, what other name is closer to "clumsy" or "blunderer"?

The right to remain silent, page 97

[97.4]

While there is no Fifth Amendment in Japan, people there do have the right against self-incrimination.

Bento, page 102

[102.3]

Bento is a Japanese boxed lunch usually consisting of a portion of white rice along with two or three side dishes. They're sold in convenience stores, at train stations, **bento** specialty shops or just made at home. Rather than having catered meals, behind-the-scenes staff in the entertainment industry often order **bento** for cast and crew, though naturally, these are of a higher quality than convenience store **bento**.

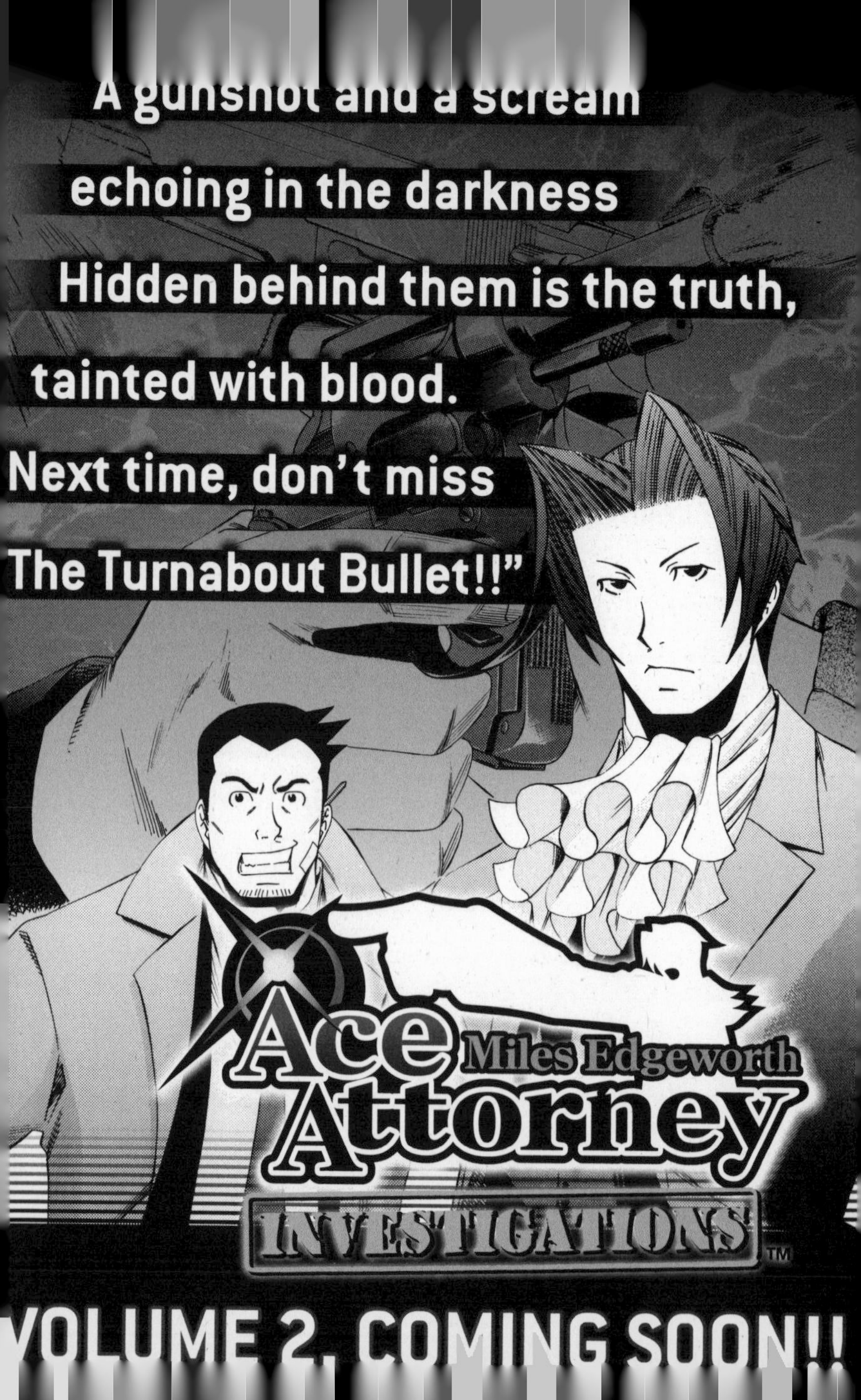

A gunshot and a scream
echoing in the darkness
Hidden behind them is the truth,
tainted with blood.
Next time, don't miss
The Turnabout Bullet!!"
Ace Attorney Miles Edgeworth
INVESTIGATIONS™
VOLUME 2, COMING SOON!!

Preview of *Miles Edgeworth: Ace Attorney Investigations™*, Volume 2

We're pleased to present you a preview from *Miles Edgeworth: Ace Attorney Investigations™*, Volume 2. Please check our website (www.kodanshacomics.com) to see when this volume will be available.

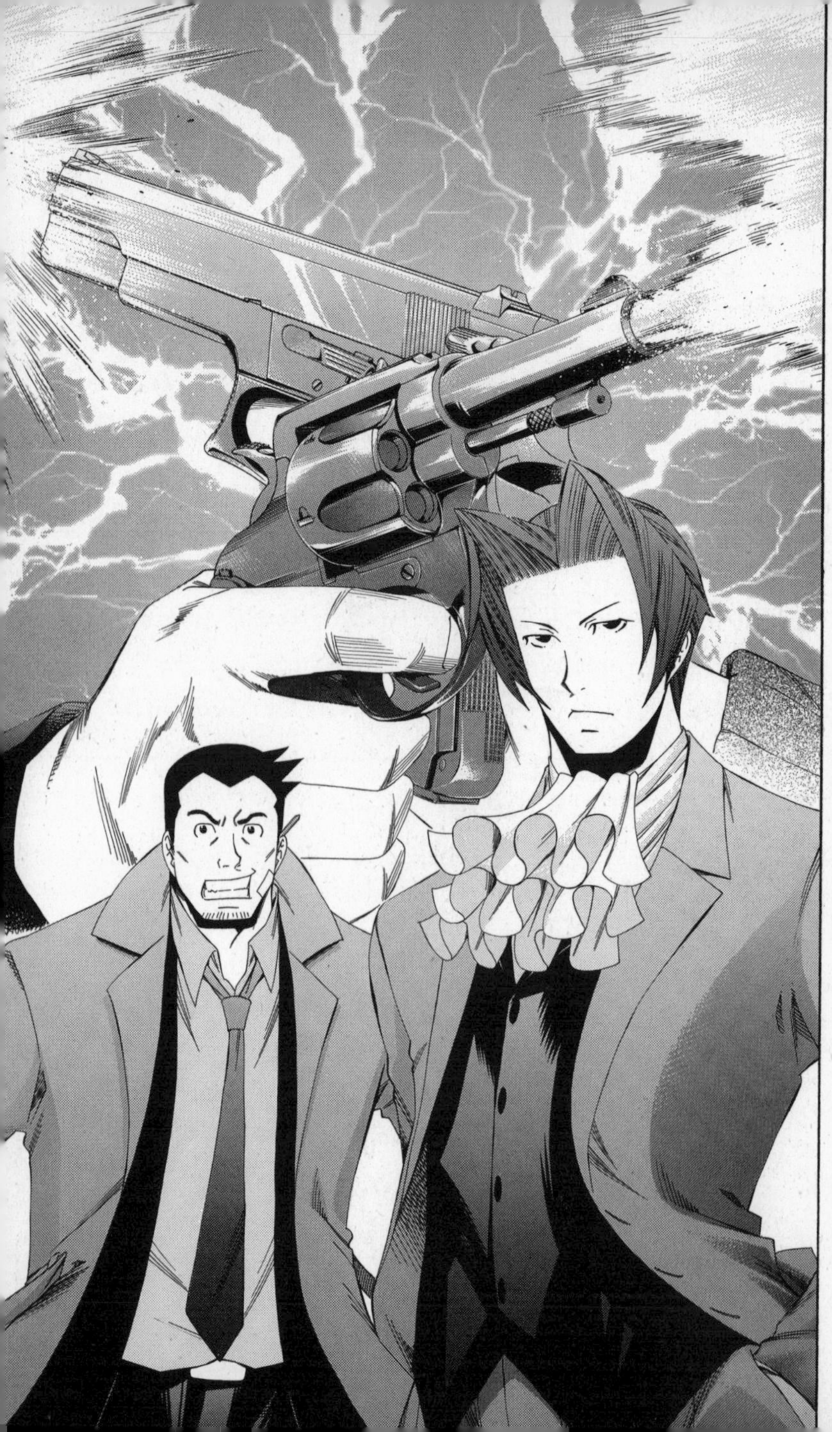

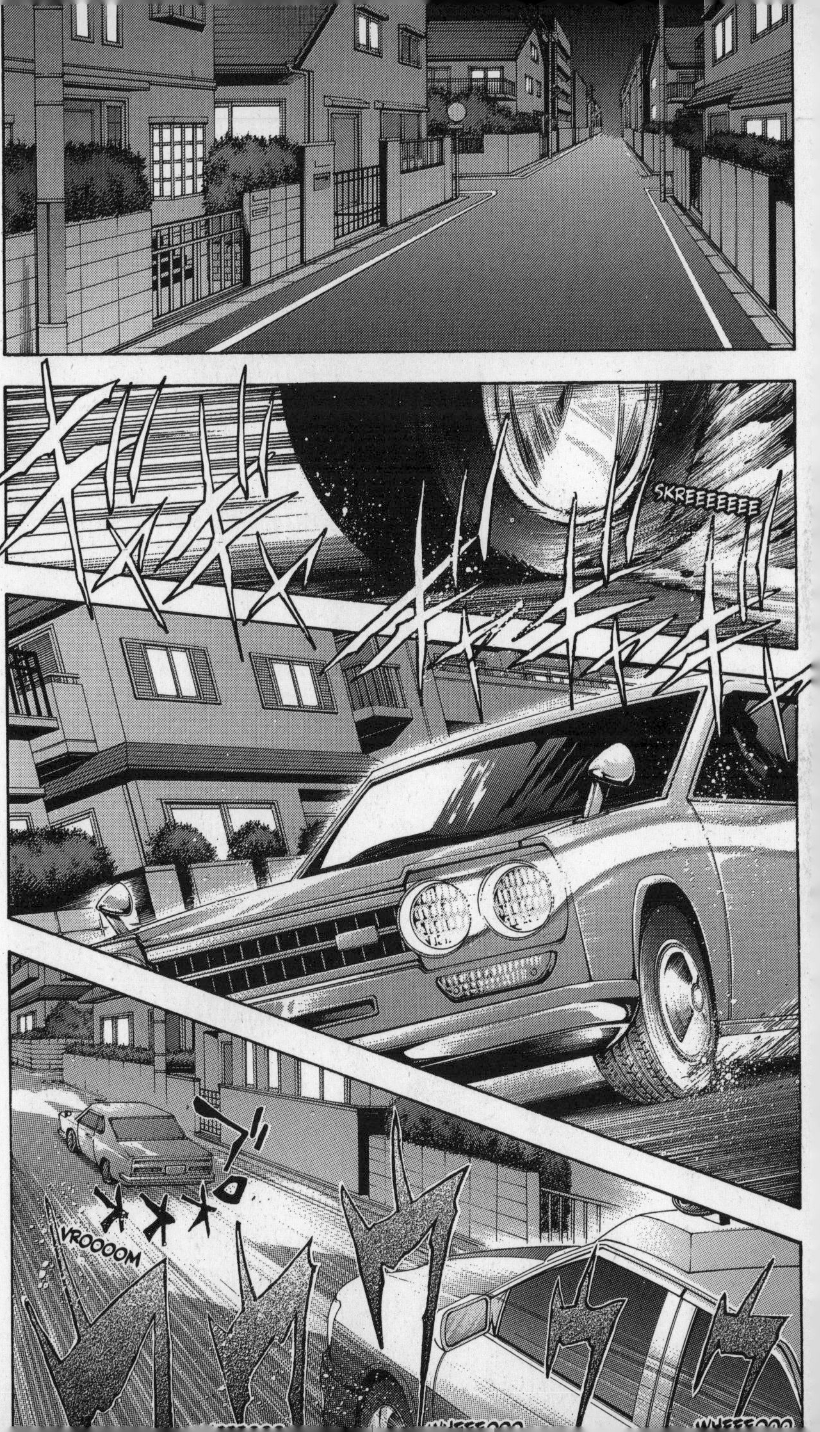
SKREEEEEEE
VROOOOM

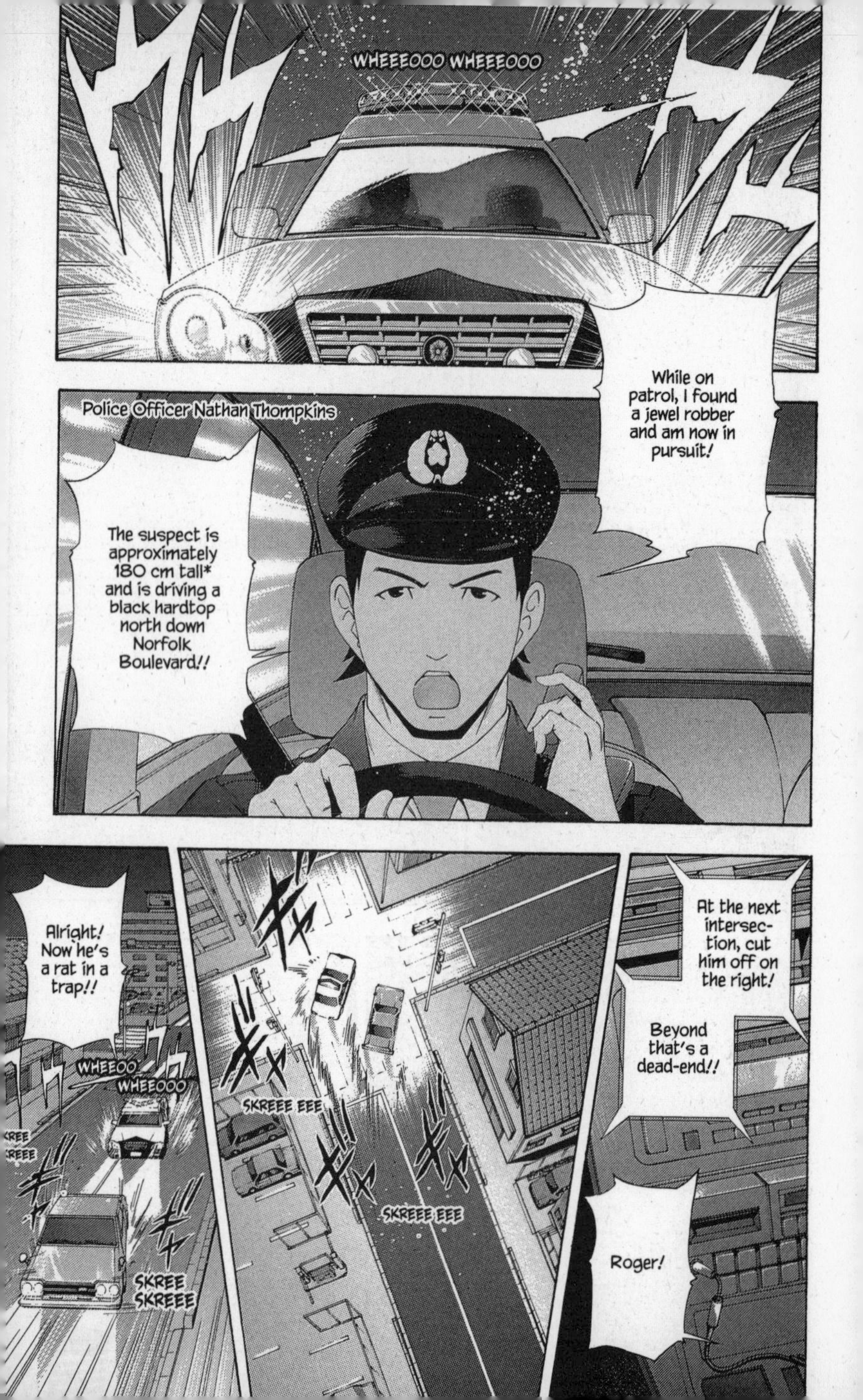
WHEEEOOO WHEEEOOO
While on patrol, I found a jewel robber and am now in pursuit!
Police Officer Nathan Thompkins
The suspect is approximately 180 cm tall* and is driving a black hardtop north down Norfolk Boulevard!!
At the next intersec-tion, cut him off on the right!
Beyond that's a dead-end!!
Roger!
SKREEE EEE
SKREEE EEE
Alright! Now he's a rat in a trap!!
WHEEOO WHEEOOO
SKREE SKREEE

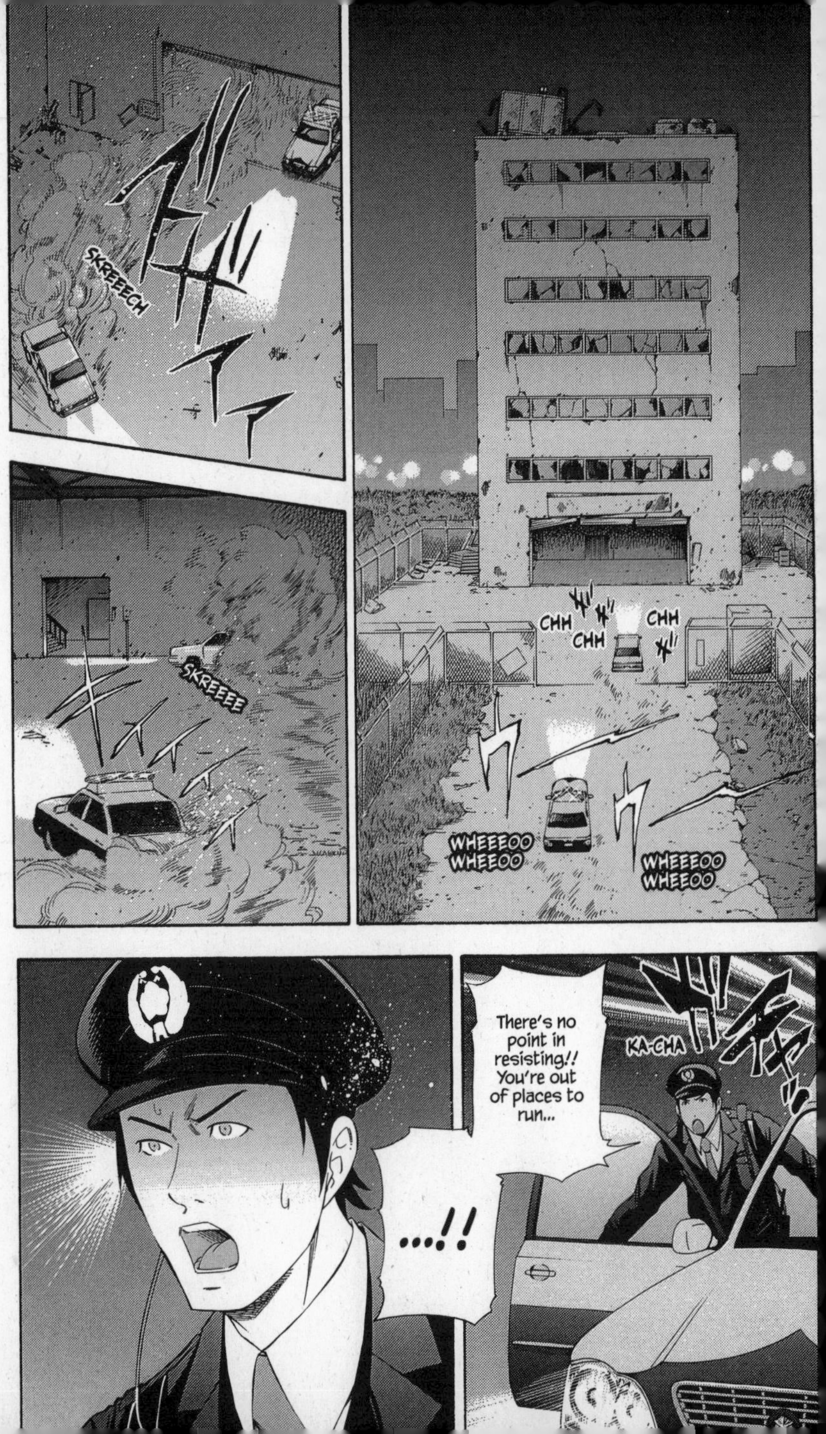
CHH
CHH
CHH
WHEEEOO WHEEOO
WHEEEOO WHEEOO
SKREEECH
SKREEEE
There's no point in resisting!! You're out of places to run...
KA-CHA
...!!

HRR HRRR

SHOVE

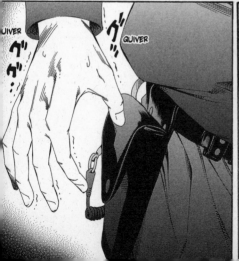

QUIVER

QUIVER

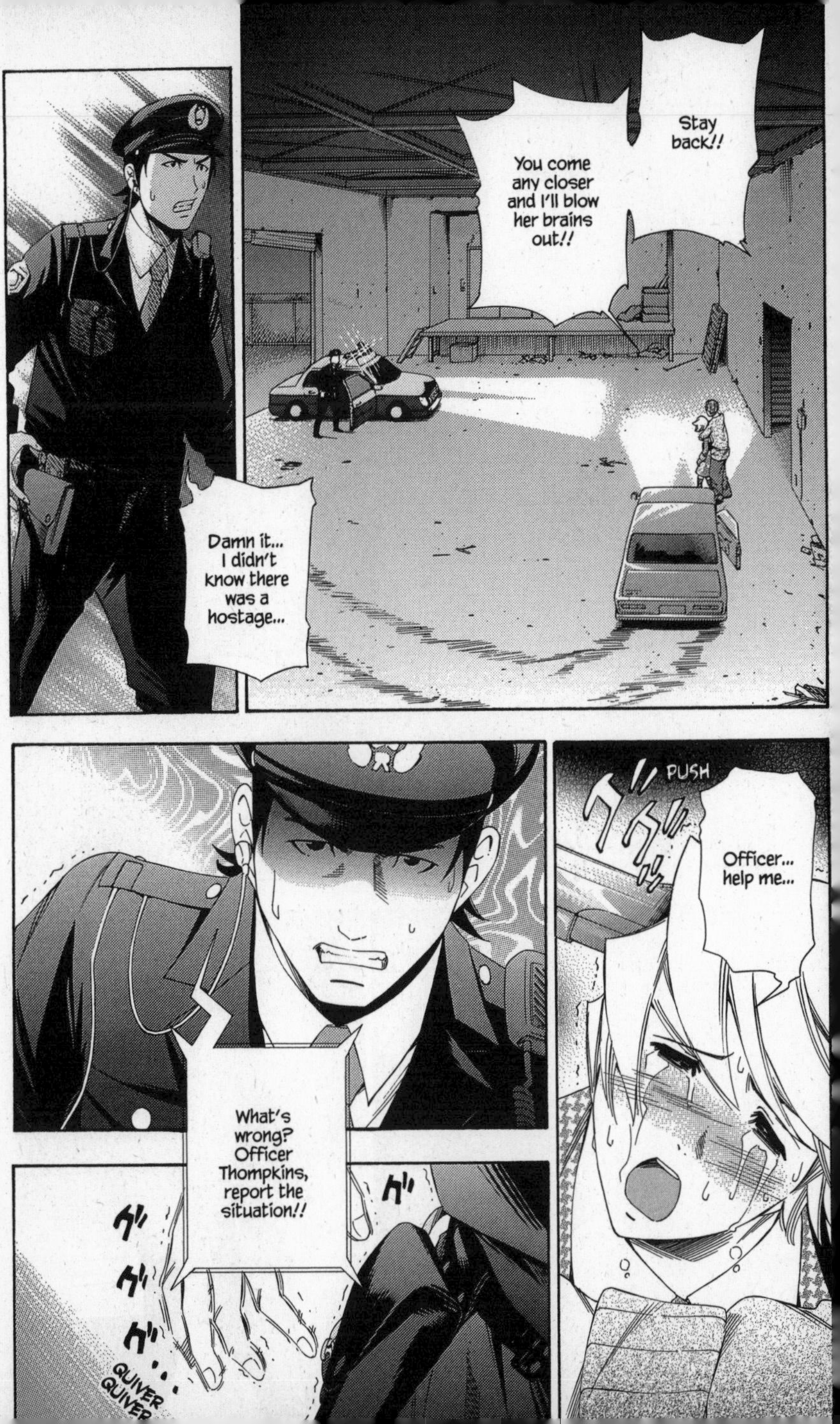
Stay back!!
You come any closer and I'll blow her brains out!!
Damn it... I didn't know there was a hostage...
PUSH
Officer... help me...
What's wrong? Officer Thompkins, report the situation!!
QUIVER QUIVER

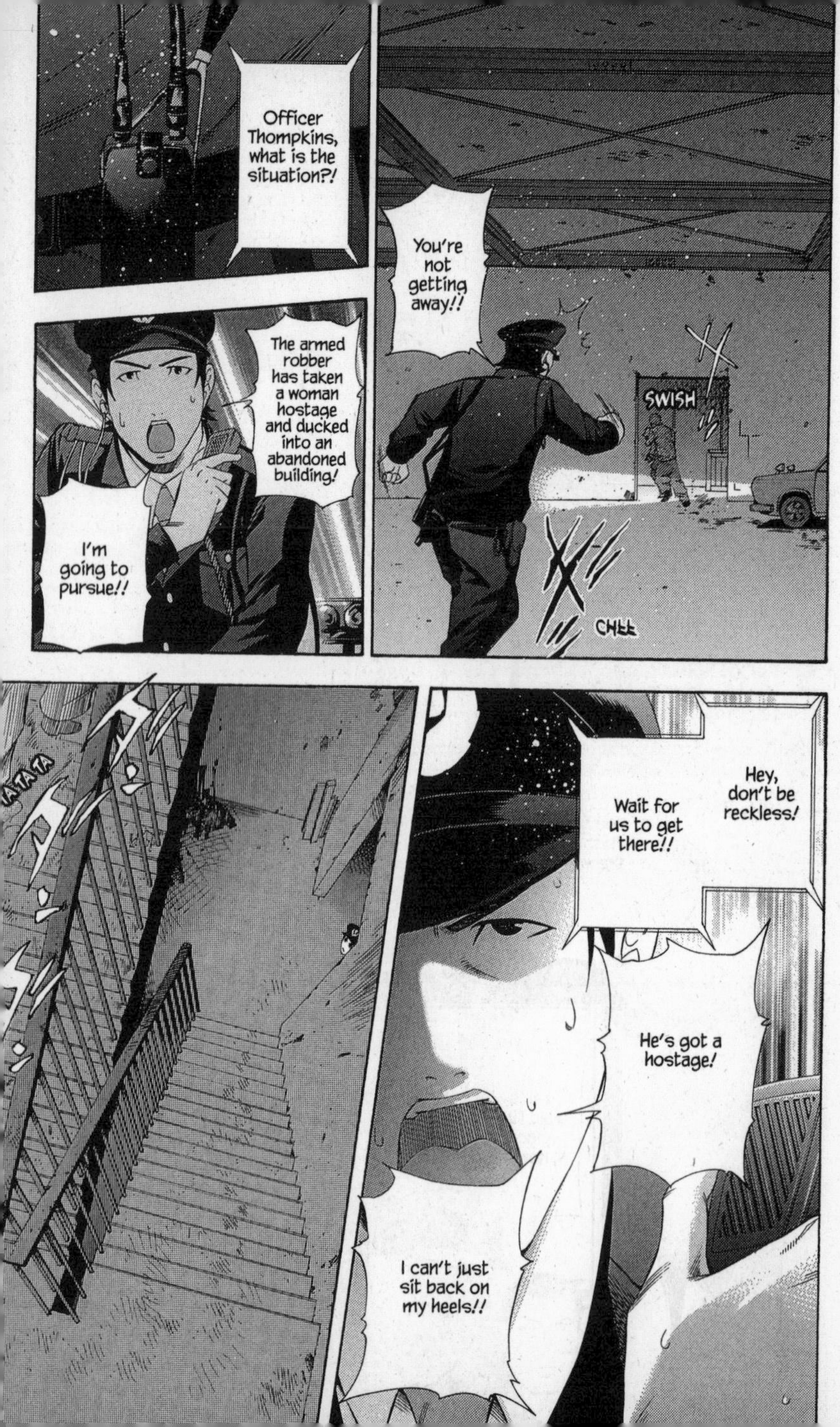
You're not getting away!!
SWISH
CHFF
Officer Thompkins, what is the situation?!
The armed robber has taken a woman hostage and ducked into an abandoned building!
I'm going to pursue!!
Hey, don't be reckless!
Wait for us to get there!!
He's got a hostage!
I can't just sit back on my heels!!

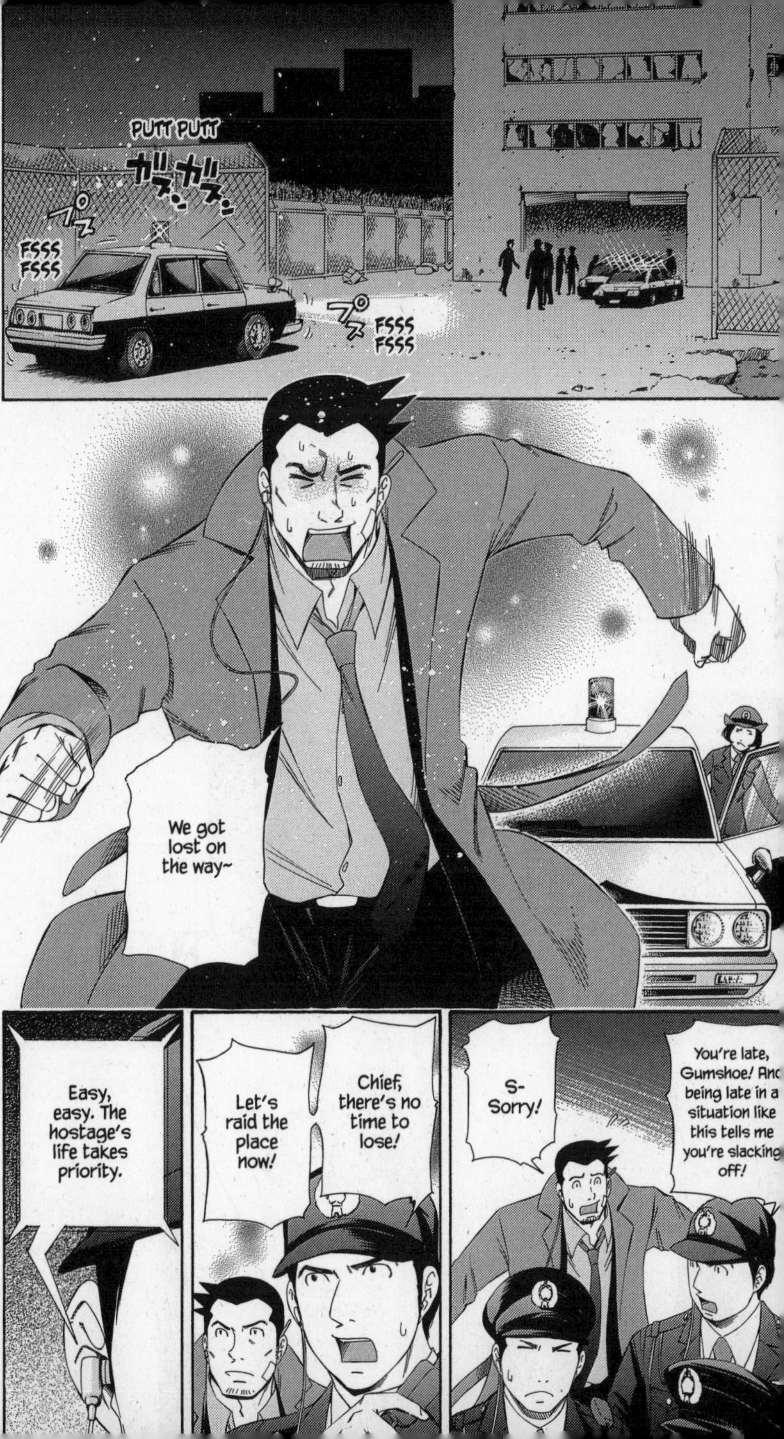
PUTT PUTT
FSSS FSSS
FSSS FSSS
We got lost on the way~
You're late, Gumshoe! Anc being late in a situation like this tells me you're slacking off!
S- Sorry!
Chief, there's no time to lose!
Let's raid the place now!
Easy, easy. The hostage's life takes priority.

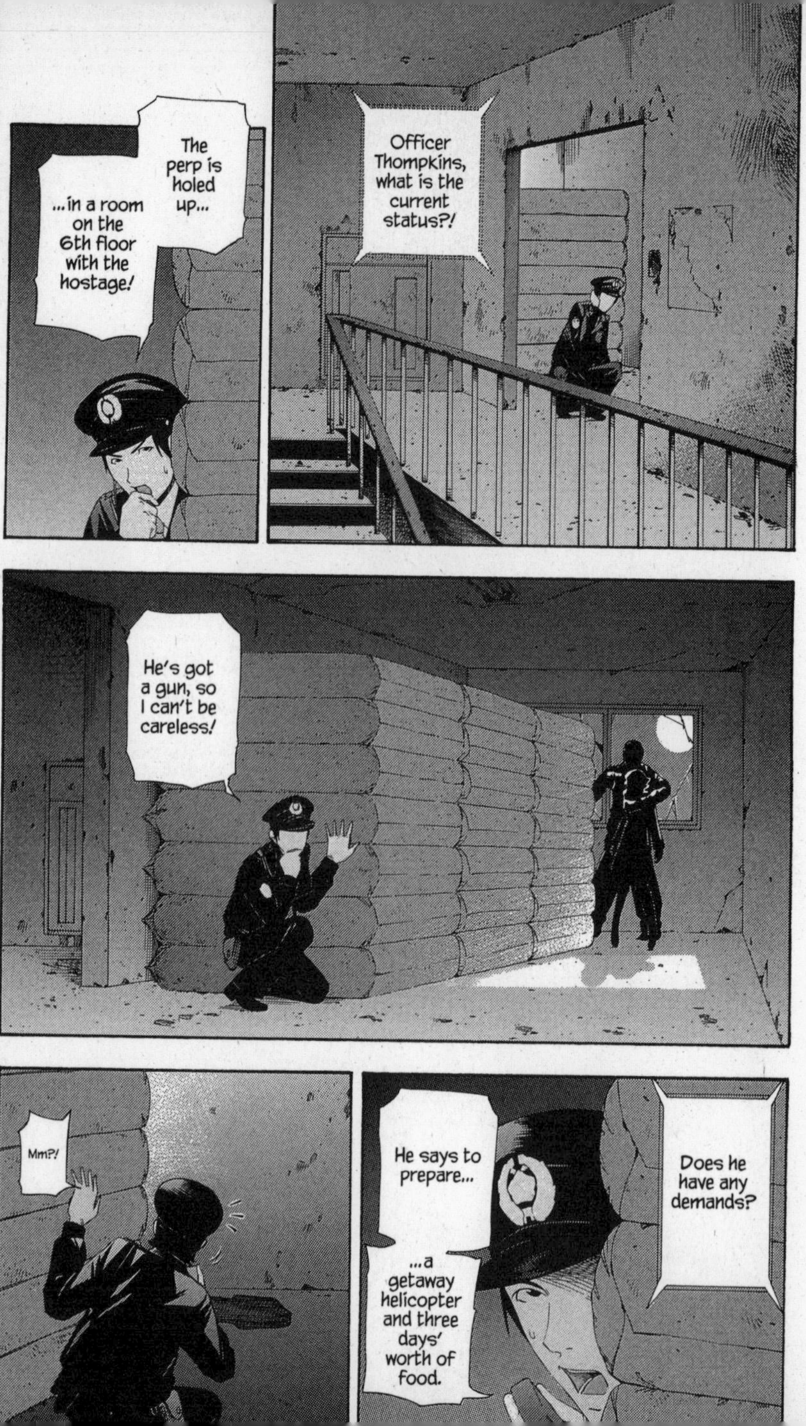
Officer Thompkins, what is the current status?!
The perp is holed up...
...in a room on the 6th floor with the hostage!
He's got a gun, so I can't be careless!
Does he have any demands?
He says to prepare...
...a getaway helicopter and three days' worth of food.
Mm?!

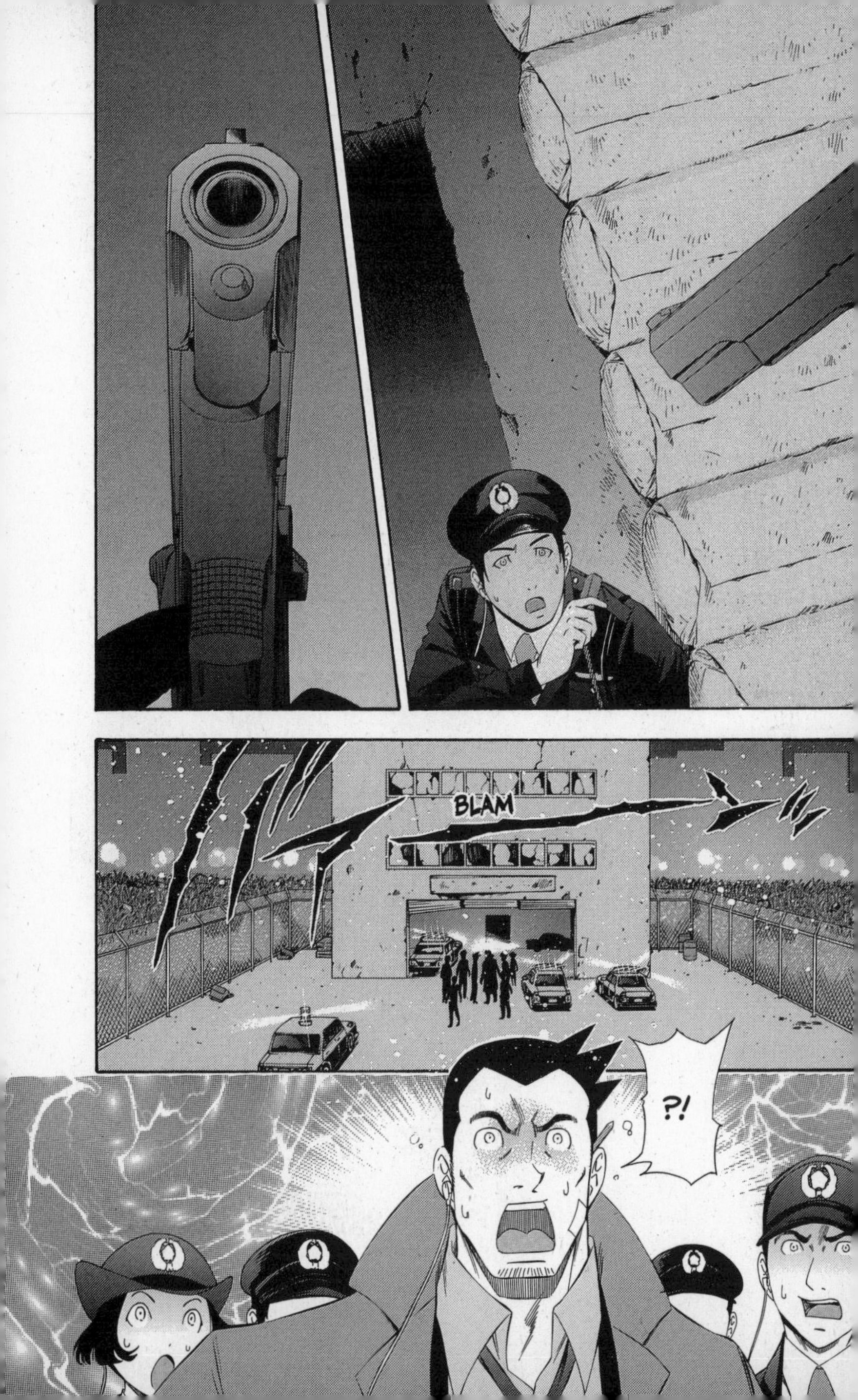
BLAM
?!

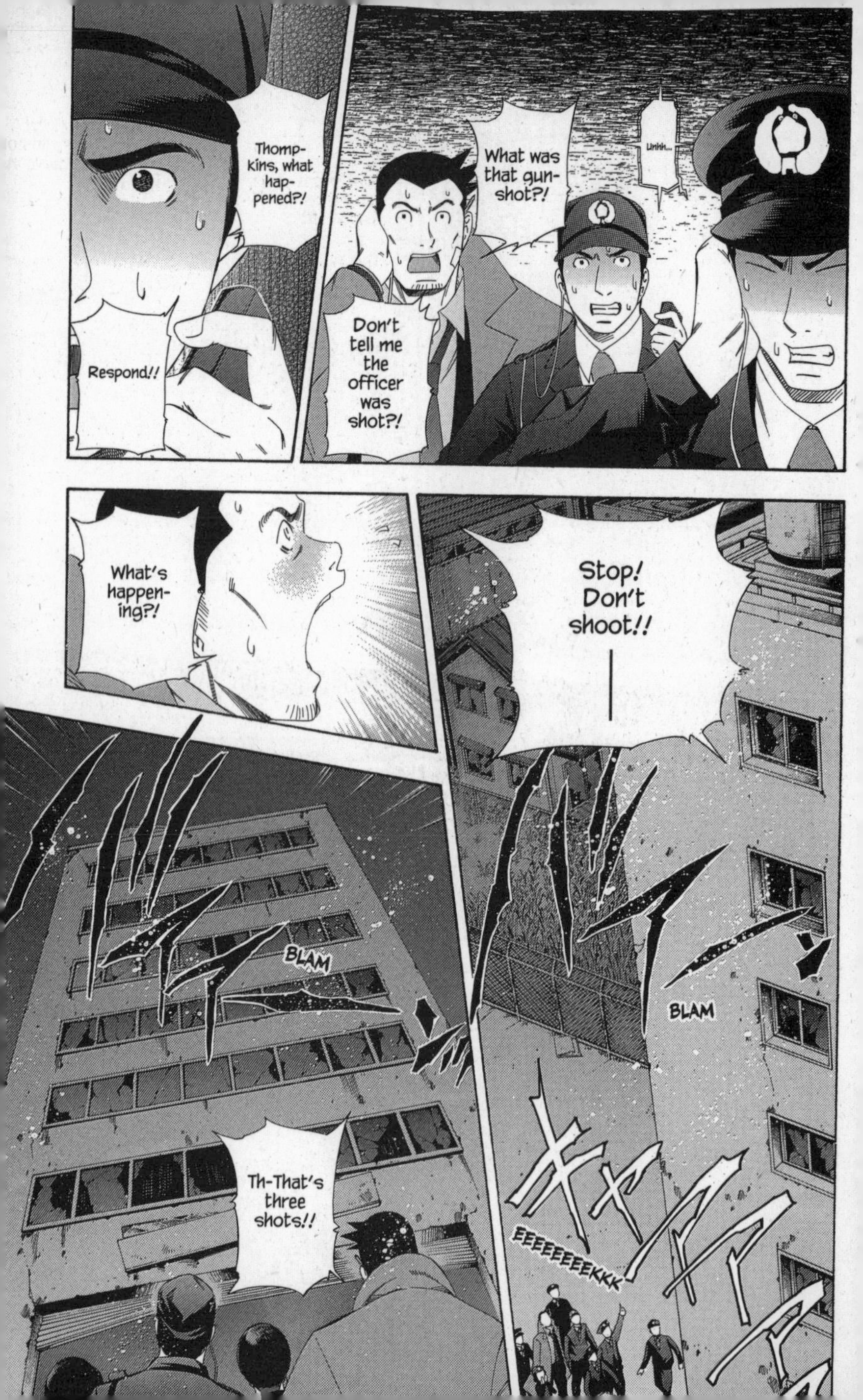

Unnh...
What was that gunshot?!
Don't tell me the officer was shot?!
Thompkins, what happened?!
Respond!!
Stop! Don't shoot!!
BLAM
EEEEEEEEKKK
What's happening?!
BLAM
Th-That's three shots!!

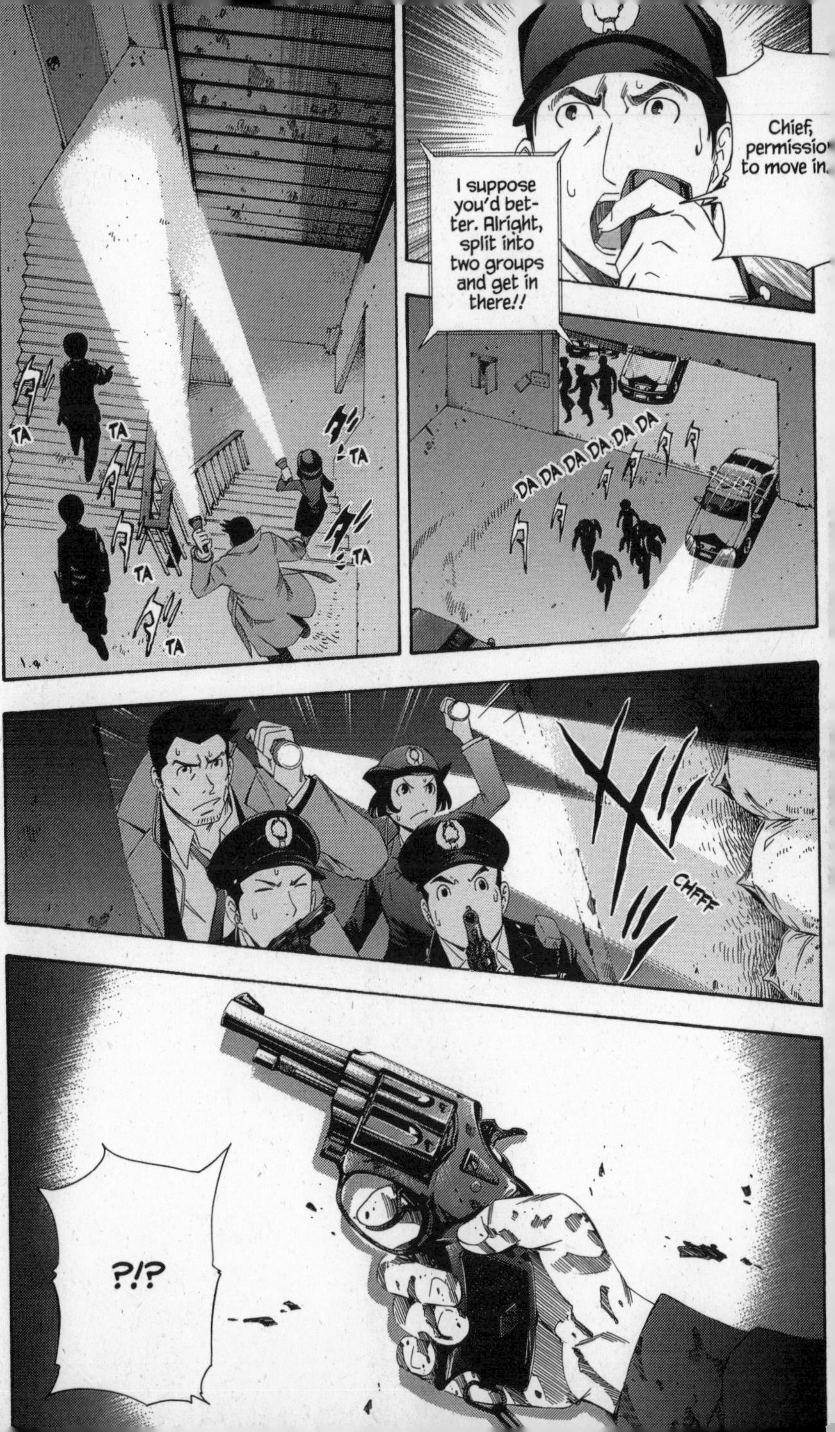
Chief, permissio to move in.
I suppose you'd bet-ter. Alright, split into two groups and get in there!!
DA DA DA DA DA DA
TA TA TA TA TA TA
CHFFF
?!?

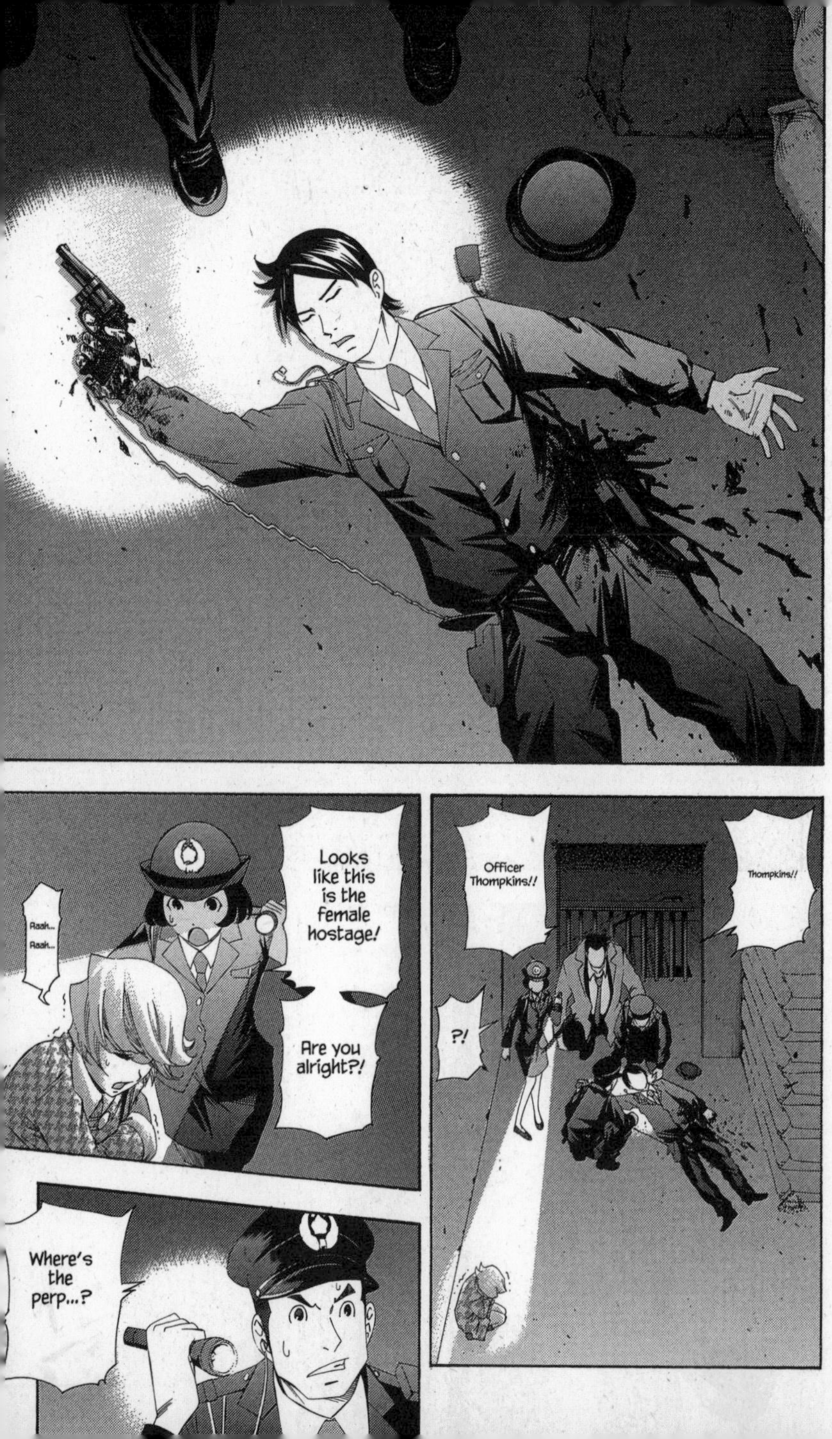
Thompkins!!
Officer Thompkins!!
?!
Looks like this is the female hostage!
Are you alright?!
Raah.. Raah..
Where's the perp...?

The perp died instantly from a shot to the fore-head...

That's some impressive aim...

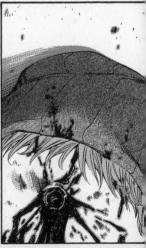